KU-024-008

CONTENTS

014171499

This is a comprehensive account [of the government and society in] thirteenth-century England, desig[ned as a handbook for students of the] period.

Three episodes stand out: the revolt of the barons against King John in 1215, the protest against the mis[rule of Henry] III which began in 1258 and the resistance to the demands [of the crown] on the resources of the land which c[ulminated ... .ng pla..s] these political events in the [... ... ...] nge, in .rder to provide a round[ed a]ccount of the century. The introduction demonstrates the constitutional in[fl]uence given by past historians, and by the political opponents of the [Cr]own [... the fr]aming of the [...] Magna Carta and [... ...] statute law. The central chapters desc[ribe the ... ...ture] of peasants, townsmen and professio[nal men, ... knights clergy and lay] mag[istr]ates. The book is completed by a [narrative which ... the ...] ews of the century in terms of royal ambition[s to dominate] Britain and to play a leading role in Europe, but more prof[o]undly as the [struggle] to reconcile royal power and the aspirations of the d[iff]erent [social groups i]n an ordered English state.

THE UNIVERSITY OF LIVERPOOL
SYDNEY JONES LIBRARY

... .n or renew, on or before the last da[te ...] ... late returned items. Books may [...] ... use of another reader. Un[...] ... ecall, books may b[...]

U.J.L. MAR 200[2]

5 S.
06 MAR

S.I.L.

U.J.L.
SEP 2002

S.
07 MA

University of Liverpool
Withdrawn from stock

...nditions of borrowing, see Library Regula[tions]

012511842

Cambridge Medieval Textbooks

ENGLAND IN THE THIRTEENTH CENTURY

Cambridge Medieval Textbooks

This is a series of specially commissioned textbooks for teachers and students, designed to complement the monograph series 'Cambridge Studies in Medieval Life and Thought' by providing introductions to a range of topics in medieval history. The series combines both chronological and thematic approaches, and will deal equally with British and European topics. All volumes in the series will be published in hard covers and in paperback.

Already published

Germany in the High Middle Ages *c.* 1050–1200
HORST FUHRMANN
Translated by Timothy Reuter

The Hundred Years War: England and France at War *c.* 1300–1450
CHRISTOPHER ALLMAND

Standards of Living in the Later Middle Ages: Social Change in England, *c.* 1200–1420
CHRISTOPHER DYER

Magic in the Middle Ages
RICHARD KIECKHEFER

The Struggle for Power in Medieval Italy: Structures of Political Rule
GIOVANNI TABACCO
Translated by Rosalind Brown Jensen

The Papacy 1073–1198: Continuity and Innovation
I. S. ROBINSON

Medieval Wales
DAVID WALKER

England in the Reign of Edward III
SCOTT WAUGH

The Norman Kingdom of Sicily
DONALD MATTHEW

Political Thought in Europe, 1250–1450
ANTONY BLACK

England in the Thirteenth Century
ALAN HARDING

Other titles are in preparation

ENGLAND IN THE THIRTEENTH CENTURY

ALAN HARDING

Professor of Medieval History, University of Liverpool

LIVERPOOL UNIVERSITY LIBRARY

FIAT LVX

CAMBRIDGE
UNIVERSITY PRESS

Published by the Press Syndicate of the University of Cambridge
The Pitt Building, Trumpington Street, Cambridge CB2 1RP
40 West 20th Street, New York, NY 10011-4211, USA
10 Stamford Road, Oakleigh, Victoria 3166, Australia

© Cambridge University Press 1993

First published 1993

Printed in Great Britain at the University Press, Cambridge

A catalogue record for this book is available from the British Library

Library of Congress cataloguing in publication data
Harding, Alan.
England in the thirteenth century/Alan Harding.
p.   cm. – (Cambridge medieval textbooks)
Includes bibliographical references and index.
ISBN 0 521 30274 9
1. Great Britain – History – 13th century.   2. England –
Civilization – Medieval period, 1066–1485.   I. Title.   II. Series.
DA225.H37   1993
942.03′4–dc20   92-30603 CIP
ISBN 0 521 30274 9 hardback
ISBN 0 521 31612 X paperback

PREFACE AND ACKNOWLEDGEMENTS

A century is an arbitrary stretch of time, which becomes history only as the processes taking place within it are understood. The most obvious processes are political, so that the first way chroniclers divided up the century was into the reigns of kings. For a long time history was about the way rulers exercised power in society, by open violence, but also by guile and the use of a growing apparatus of administration. As the records generated by administration were opened up, other types of interaction between the members of a community were discovered, such as the relations between lord and peasant in a manorial economy, and between employers and workers in the towns; or rather, it was gradually realized that these relationships could change over time, in patterns which might be fitted to the political themes. Social history reaches maturity when it can trace the growth of the framework of institutions, and of the culture which gives them significance. From at least the Tudor period the thirteenth century has been given crucial importance in English history as the period when Parliament and statute law emerged. At the same time it was perceived that the origins of Parliament needed to be traced to changing relationships within feudal society. On similar assumptions this book begins with an account of the uncovering of the sources for the history of England in the thirteenth century and the new interpretations that it provoked, and comes to the politics last, after tracing the social changes which lay behind them.

I would like to thank the University of Liverpool for the two terms' leave of absence which allowed me to complete this book.

ABBREVIATIONS

BBC   *British Borough Charters, 1042–1216*, ed. A. Ballard
(Cambridge: CUP, 1913); *British Borough Charters,
1216–1307*, ed. A. Ballard and James Tait (Cambridge:
CUP, 1923)

BIHR   *Bulletin of the Institute of Historical Research*

CH   *The Constitutional History of England* [to 1485], William
Stubbs, 3 vols. (Oxford: Clarendon Press, 1874–8);
5th edn of vol. I (1891); 4th edn of vol. II (1896); 5th
edn of vol. III (1896)

CM   *Chronica Maiora* [from the creation to 1259], Matthew
Paris, ed. H. R. Luard, 7 vols. (Rolls Series, London,
1872–83)

CRR   *Curia Regis Rolls*, in progress, 17 vols. to 1243
(London: HMSO, 1923–91)

CUP   Cambridge University Press

EcHR   *Economic History Review*

EHD, III   *English Historical Documents*, vol. III: *1189–1327*, ed.
Harry Rothwell (London: Eyre and Spottiswoode,
1975)

EHR   *English Historical Revew*

HEL   *The History of English Law before the Time of Edward I*,
F. Pollock and F. W. Maitland, 2nd edn, 2 vols.
(Cambridge: CUP, 1898)

HLE   *King Henry III and the Lord Edward*, F. M. Powicke
(Oxford: Clarendon Press, 1947)

HW   *Historical Writing in England*, vol. I: *c. 550 to c. 1307*, and vol. II: *c. 1307 to the Early Sixteenth Century*, Antonia Gransden (London: Routledge and Kegan Paul, 1974, 1982)

OUP   Oxford University Press

RP   *Rotuli Parliamentorum* ['Rolls of Parliament', 1278–1503], 6 vols. [no place or date given, but printed according to an order of the House of Lords in 1767; Index vol. 1832]

TRHS   *Transactions of the Royal Historical Society*

UP   University Press

CHRONOLOGICAL TABLE

1199–1216   KING JOHN

1204	Loss of Normandy
1208	England placed under interdict because of John's refusal to accept Stephen Langton as archbishop of Canterbury
1213	John makes peace with the Church
1214	Defeat of Bouvines ends John's hope of recovering French possessions
1215	Magna Carta granted, but John's reign ends in civil war and invasion by the French

1216–72   HENRY III

1217	William the Marshal, Ranulf of Chester and Peter des Roches rout the French and the rebels at the 'Fair of Lincoln'
1225	Reissue of the Charter
1227	Henry declares himself of full age
1230	Breton expedition
1232	Fall of Hubert de Burgh; Peter des Roches and Peter des Rivaux in ascendant
1234	Murder of Richard the Marshal; dismissal of des Rivaux
1236	Henry's marriage to Eleanor of Provence; the Statute of Merton
1238	Simon de Montfort, earl of Leicester, marries the king's sister; baronial protests

Bracton's *On the Laws and Customs of England* being
compiled around this time

1242   Failure of expedition to Poitou

1244   First baronial 'plan of reform'

1248–52   Simon de Montfort as lieutenant in Gascony

1254   Two knights elected by each shire court to agree an aid
for Gascon expedition; Edward endowed with Chester,
Bristol, Ireland and Gascony, and marries Eleanor of
Castile

1258   Henry forced by threat of interdict if he fails to meet his
undertakings regarding Sicily to make peace with
France and to agree to the barons' demands for reform;
the Provisions of Oxford

1259   The Provisions of Westminster; Treaty of Paris

1260–3   The king regains initiative; Simon de Montfort assumes
leadership of the barons

1264   The battle of Lewes

1265   Simon de Montfort's parliament; battle of Evesham

1266   The Dictum of Kenilworth and the 'Disinherited'

1267   The Statute of Marlborough re-enacts many of the
Provisions of Westminster

1270–4   Edward absent on crusade

1272–1307 EDWARD I

1275   The Statute of Westminister I

1278   Statute of Gloucester

1279   Statute of Mortmain

1282–4   Conquest and settlement of Wales

1283–5   Statutes of Acton Burnell, Merchants, Westminster II
and Winchester

1286   The writ *Circumspecte agatis* and demarcation of royal
and ecclesiastical jurisdictions

1289   Edward returns from Gascony; hearing of complaints
against judges and officials

1290   Statutes of Quia Emptores and Quo Warranto

1290–2   Problem of the Scottish succession; the 'Great Cause'
and Edward's decision in favour of John Balliol as king
of Scots

1294   War between Edward and Philip IV of France

1295   The 'model' parliament; alliance between Scotland and
France

I

INTRODUCTION: SOURCES AND INTERPRETATIONS

·

The interpretation of the past is a dialogue between the available evidence and historians who write from their own situation and understanding of society. This is equally true of the contemporary chroniclers and of historians working six hundred and more years after the period they study. The real subject of this first chapter is the changing ways in which thirteenth-century England was important to later generations.

THE CONTEMPORARY CHRONICLERS

The foundations of our image of thirteenth-century England were laid by forty or so contemporaries: some of them the anonymous authors of sets of annals, who continued year by year lists of outstanding events which they took over from previous annalists; at the other extreme, Matthew Paris, a major figure both as chronicler and artist, about whose personality and prejudices we know more than for almost anyone of the period. Thirteenth-century chroniclers of course continued to be churchmen, with the exception of a few London merchants who began to take an interest in compiling the annals of their city. As clerics they were peculiar in almost all being 'religious', however, that is monks or friars living by particular sets of rules as members of sometimes very rich communities – a marked change from the situation in the later twelfth century, when the 'secular' clergy who staffed the fast-growing royal administration had produced notable historians such as Richard FitzNeal and Roger of Howden. But the monastic chroniclers, like the seculars, showed a deep interest in the processes of royal government, and like them included official documents in their works. They also possessed a view of European politics which was coloured by their membership of international orders under pressure from a 'centralizing' papal government. The monastic chroniclers join a cosmopolitan vision with local preoccupations in a way which shows up brilliantly the widening scope of thirteenth-century royal and papal administration.[1]

Annals like these in the chronicle of Ralph of Coggeshall, the abbot of a Cistercian monastery in Essex from 1207 to 1218, are typical:

In the year 1211, the emperor Otto and the king of England [John] were excommunicated . . . John count of Brienne was crowned king of Jerusalem at Tyre.

In the year 1212, the son of the king of Scots was made a knight at London . . . Frederick king of Sicily was elected Roman emperor. The King extorted charters from all the clergy of England, witnessing falsely that they had granted of their own free will what he had taken from them by force.

The annals of Dunstable, which span almost the entire century with a commentary more detailed than the usual annalist's 'unadulterated record of events', were begun in 1210 by the prior, a former canon of Merton who served the king on a diplomatic mission to France, preached the crusade for Pope Innocent III, attended the Fourth Lateran Council and studied in the Paris schools on the way back. The particular value of the Dunstable annals, however, is their use of the rolls of the royal chancery, the exchequer and the judicial eyres (circuits of judges) to show the effect of national politics on the economy of an ecclesiastical lordship, right up to the war-burdened last decade of the century.[2]

The community of the great Benedictine abbey of St Albans – it claimed to be the premier abbey of the land – was more conscious than any of its rights against king and pope, and it was ideally placed one day's journey on the road from London to the north to

---

[1] Gransden, *HW*, 1.220–6, 344, 373; Richard Vaughan, *Matthew Paris* (Cambridge: CUP, 1958; reissued with supplementary bibliography, 1979); FitzNeal was bishop of London, treasurer of England and author of a lost history as well as the famous *Dialogue of the Exchequer*.

[2] Gransden, *HW*, 1.322–45, 424–5; *Radulphi de Coggeshall Chronicon Anglicanum*, ed. Joseph Stevenson (Rolls Series, London, 1975), pp. 164–5; *Annales Monastici*, 5 vols., ed. H. R. Luard (Rolls Series, London 1864–9), III.69–74, 387, 390.

observe the affairs of the kingdom. At St Albans, Roger of Wendover, of whom not much more is known than that he died in 1236, and Matthew Paris, a monk there from 1217, developed the methods and themes of the annalists into the most impressive of all thirteenth-century works of history. In his *Greater Chronicle* Matthew revised and continued Roger's *Flowers of History* (a title which already indicates a more literary and moralizing work than an annalist's bare record); adding new documents to those the older man had used, and between 1236 and his own death in 1259 writing up entirely out of his own collection of material a record unparalleled in scope. In Matthew's time at St Albans, King Henry III visited the abbey on at least nine occasions for periods of up to a week. There also came Queen Eleanor, Richard of Cornwall (the king's brother), the papal legate Otto, an Armenian archbishop (who told the monks about the Wandering Jew), Archbishop Boniface of Canterbury, a deputation of MAs from Oxford looking for the king and royal administrators who used the abbey as a stopping-place on their official journeys. Matthew himself never held office even in his own monastery, but he attended the feast of St Edward at Westminster in 1247, and in 1248 he was sent by the pope to recall the monastery of St Benet Holm in Norway to the observance of St Benedict's rule: the monks there already knew him because of his help in negotiating about their debts with London money-lenders – something he had done at the request of King Haakon.[3]

In his annal for 1250, Matthew Paris summed up the wonders of the previous fifty years – unequalled, he claimed, in any of the twenty-four preceding half-centuries since Christ. First in his list of wonderful events stands the appearance of the Mongols and their devastating conquests in the East. The triumphs and miseries of the crusades, which Matthew could have learnt about at first hand from Richard of Cornwall, and from English survivors of the calamity which overcame King Louis on crusade in Egypt in the last terrible year of 1250, provide a central theme. But the story of that dramatic half-century closes not with the disaster on the Nile, but with the death in Apulia of the Emperor Frederick II,

[3] D. Knowles, *The Religious Orders in England*, vol. 1 (Cambridge: CUP, 1948), pp. 18, 294–5; Gransden, *HW*, 1.360; Vaughan, *Matthew Paris*, pp. 12–17, 21ff, 31–4; for the St Benet Holm episode, see Paris, *CM*, v. 42ff; see D. Hay, *Annalists and Historians* (London: Methuen, 1977), pp. 66–71, for a comparison of the works of the St Albans school with the quasi-official *Grandes Chroniques de France*, which stemmed from the abbey of Saint-Denis.

'stupor mundi', the wonder of the world, after a generation of struggle against a hostile papacy. Matthew's real subject, developed to a counterpoint of signs in the sky, earthquakes and floods, is the worldly politics of the Roman church. These events were not at all remote from English concerns. Frederick was the brother-in-law of King Henry and Earl Richard, and the latter stayed with the emperor in Italy for several months on the way back from his own crusade in 1241. Richard was himself to be offered first the empire and then the crown of Sicily by a pope who worked, says the chronicler, on his 'unquenchable thirst for power and worldly dignity'. Richard declined, but King Henry got embroiled in the Sicilian venture, and the expense of it brought on the great political crisis of his reign. In 1257, moreover, Richard would accept the German crown when the electors chose him as their king and emperor-designate. It is interesting to see which English happenings rank with the struggles of empire and papacy. From John's reign there is the seven-year papal interdict, the surrender to the papacy and the civil war between king and barons – but no Great Charter. 'John Lackland' fulfils the prophecy that he would die holding none of his lands in peace: but Prince Louis, the barons' choice to replace him, is made to return home ingloriously – he too had injured St Albans. The Lateran Council forbids the use of ordeals by water and hot iron (compelling the use of juries to try criminals). Henry III tries twice to wrest back the property across the Channel, above all Normandy, of which his father had been deprived 'by judgement of the twelve peers of France', ostensibly for the murder of his nephew, Prince Arthur; and twice Henry returns 'inglorious, bankrupt and confounded'. Wales, on the other hand, bows to English laws when death takes away Prince Llywelyn and his two sons; and recalcitrant Gascony is subdued by Simon de Montfort, earl of Leicester. Westminster Abbey is rebuilt and endowed with a richly ornamented gold reliquary to contain St Edward's bones. An inadequate archbishop (Boniface of Savoy, uncle of Henry's wife) is intruded by the king into the see of Canterbury, and goes about exploiting his whole province, following the example of the visitations of the bishop of Lincoln (the great Bishop Grosseteste). King Henry and many of his nobles vow to go on crusade; and the abbot of Bury St Edmunds also wears the cross, setting a bad example to monks of worldly preoccupations and incurring general derision.[4]

---

[4] Paris, *CM*, III.8–9, 488–9, IV.435–56, V.79, 101, 191–6, 346–7, 361, 457, 627; cf. J. J. Saunders, 'Matthew Paris and the Mongols', in *Essays in Medieval History*

All of Matthew's talents as artist as well as writer went into the making of the *Chronica Maiora*. The margins are illuminated by pictorial symbols: heraldic shields (for Matthew was a pioneer of heraldry, too) reversed to mark the deaths of their bearers; two kings embracing, alongside the account of the peace made between Henry III and Louis of France in 1217. Others are full-scale battle-scenes, such as the one Matthew drew from his imagination underneath his narrative of the siege of Damietta; even illustrations of natural history, like the picture which is presumably drawn from life of the elephant given to King Henry by Louis IX and housed in the Tower – the first of these beasts, he thinks, ever seen this side of the Alps. More essential to a history are the itineraries and maps. The three manuscript volumes of the *Chronica Maiora* are equipped with a copy of an itinerary from London to Apulia, a map of Palestine and a map of England and Scotland, in that order. The itinerary is basically a list of towns in French, with the word 'Jurnee' (*journee*, 'a day's travel') and perhaps an indication of direction written vertically between them, running *up* the left and then the right of two columns on the page. Each town is repre-sented by a sketch of one or two of its architectural features, as Matthew imagined them – a castle wall and a church spire for instance. So, the itinerary starts from 'the city of London, which is the capital (*chef*) of England', and proceeds to Dover via Rochester and Canterbury, 'chief of the churches of England'. On the way it passes the Benedictine abbey of Faversham, the abbot of which, Matthew indignantly relates in the chronicle, lent horses to one of the king's dreadful half-brothers, Guy of Lusignan, who was returning destitute and on foot from St Louis's crusade, and never got them back. Across the sea it heads from Wissant 'eastward' (but in fact more nearly south) to Montreuil, Beauvais and Paris. The itinerary must have been based on information from travellers and makes general sense, for on average it covers a manageable thirty-five miles a day. The maps of England and Scotland are obviously drawn from more copious information, but they too are built round an itinerary, which is conceived as running due north from Dover to Newcastle, through Canterbury, London, St Albans, Northampton, Leicester, Doncaster, Boroughbridge and Durham, and therefore distort the south-east of the country. More

Presented to Bertie Wilkinson, ed. T. A. Sandquist and M. R. Powicke (Toronto: University of Toronto Press, 1969), pp. 116–32; N. Denholm-Young, *Richard of Cornwall* (Oxford: Blackwell, 1947), pp. 81–2.

than 250 places are named, including St Albans's chief cells from Wallingford north to Tynemouth. The purpose of Matthew's cartography is to make the movements of the chief figures in his history easier to follow.[5]

In his provision of maps and illustrations, Matthew Paris was an originator: the use of documents to illuminate the political issues of his time he simply carried to a higher level. Yet this was where he made his greatest contribution to historiography. He amassed so much material that he decided, apparently in 1247, to relegate many of the documents to an appendix rather than to copy them into the main text. The reader is often referred to this 'book of additions' (*Liber Additamentorum*), which became a separate entity when the chronicle was continued beyond its intended end in 1250. Anyone who desires, for instance, to see the transcript of a famous letter sent to the pope by the barons or 'community of England' in the summer of 1258, explaining why they had imposed a council of reform upon the king, is told he will find it *in libro additamentorum* 'against this sign' (a drawing of a chalice). Material earlier than 1247 was added to the collection and given marginal references in the chronicle. The collection of documents shows Matthew Paris the recorder of contemporary political events in the last years of his life, when he thought his main work of history-writing was complete. The historian who created a lasting image of his century appears in the interpretation of documents and events which had already receded some way into the past. Building on Roger of Wendover's misunderstandings, Matthew ran together King John's Magna Carta and King Henry's reissues of 1217 and 1225 (different in important respects) in such a way as to create the myth of an unending struggle for the liberties of 1215 against an irreconcilable government. He instilled his own prejudices and moral fervour into Wendover's account, and made 'the barons of 1215 fight his battles for him' against pope and king simultaneously. The confirmation in 1225 of liberties which had never been respected was mere royal deceitfulness to Matthew; and no less of a sham was the further reissue of 'King John's charter' in 1253 (of which the *Liber Additamentorum* contains the only surviving text), because Henry knew he could always bribe the pope to absolve him from his oath. The second great political crisis of the century which began in 1258 has to be pressed into the same mould, and the

---

[5] Paris, *CM*, II. 521, III.30, 48, V. 204–5, 489; Vaughan, *Matthew Paris*, pp. 209, 212–14, 227–8, 237–49, 252–3, 256, and plates VI, VII, XII, XIII.

parliament of Oxford is represented as demanding that the king faithfully hold to the charter which his father had made and Henry himself had many times sworn to observe.[6]

We have to go to the annals of the abbey of Burton on Trent for the text of the Provisions of the Oxford parliament, which show us not just another demand that the king keep faith with the promises of 1215 but a quite original scheme for supervising royal administration. The Burton chronicle was the work of an archivist with access to the diocesan records of Lincoln and Lichfield. The Norwich chronicle, an independent source for much of the time from 1264, and between 1291 and 1298 the work of a monk named Bartholomew Cotton, also makes use of a document collection. Cotton begins paragraph after paragraph: 'In the same year the king sent word to each of his sheriffs . . .'. He notes the vital requirement in the summons of four knights from each county in 1294 that they should have power to bind their county to do what the council ordained; namely, to levy a tax according to instructions which Cotton gives in French – presumably quoting from those actually handed to the knights (to work to sworn assessments by hundred juries and the reeve and four men of each township). He is especially valuable on the third major political crisis of the century, caused in 1297 by the strains of war with the Scots and the French. Cotton shows a real concern for authenticity. He describes the condition of papal letters and notes the lack of a date on the letter of submission of John Balliol (the king of Scots) to King Edward.[7]

By the end of the century there was a record-consciousness shown most strikingly by the king's manipulation of documents for his political advantage. In 1291, Edward went to Norham in the marches to adjudicate the succession to the Scottish crown, 'and summoned monks from some of the churches in England to come there with their chronicles' to support his claim to the overlordship of Scotland. He had already asked for information by

---

[6] The *Additamenta* are in vol. VI of Luard's edition: see Paris, *CM*, V.717, for the reference to the letter, which is at VI.400–5; Paris, *CM*, II.620, 645–7, III.92, V.449, 696, VI. 249–50; J. C. Holt, 'The St. Albans Chroniclers and Magna Carta', *TRHS*, 5th ser., 14 (1964), pp. 78–82; *idem, Magna Carta* (Cambridge: CUP, 1965), pp. 289ff.

[7] The Annales Monasterii de Burton, 1004–1263 are in *Annales Monastici*, ed. Luard, vol. I (pp. 446–53 for the Provisions of Oxford); cf. R. F. Treharne, *The Baronial Plan of Reform, 1258–1263* (reprinted with additional material, Manchester: Manchester UP, 1971), pp. 82ff; Gransden, *HW*, I.408–11 (on the Burton annals), 444–8 (on Cotton); extracts from Cotton are translated in *EHD*, III.209–20.

letter from at least twenty-five lesser monasteries, and what he got from Carlisle cathedral priory included a treaty of peace made by Alexander II of Scotland with Henry III in 1244 – a charter probably found in a copy of Matthew Paris's chronicle in the cathedral library. The chroniclers not only preserved documents for the king; they made the documents usable by placing them in context, as part of a coherent story. Edward ordered that the letter from the competitors for the Scottish crown submitting to his arbitration should be written into the chronicles, 'so that these events are remembered forever'. Alongside the myth of the community's defence of its liberties against the king there was being created a myth of sovereign authority exercised on the community's behalf. It was elaborated at rich southern monasteries like Worcester, and above all Westminster, which Edward endowed in 1297 with the Scottish regalia and coronation stone. It was also developed, in a more aggressive and popular form, at northern monasteries such as Guisborough and Bridlington which were close to the action (Guisborough, though a Bruce foundation, was to suffer a good deal from Scottish raids).[8]

For the second half of the century, the 'constitutionalist' and 'monarchist' myths which are tangled up in Matthew Paris's huge work are combined more methodically in the chronicle of another ancient Benedictine house, that of Bury St Edmunds. Its author displays the same breadth of interest and very much the same concerns as Matthew, but with a conciseness which gives more impetus to the political narrative. The accurate recording of eclipses and a positive obsession with taxes suggest that the chronicle was the work of the sacrist, responsible for the abbey's time-keeping as well as its fabric and finances. But domestic concerns are still interrupted by reports of international affairs: for instance, embassies to the West from the Tartar khan, raising heady prospects of a great alliance against Islam – until in 1291 'the city of Acre, with everything in it, was captured and razed to the ground by the infidel Sultan of Cairo'. Bury St Edmunds was visited by the court hardly less often than St Albans, and its chronicler was able to give a particularly informed and balanced account of the crisis of the 1290s, compounded of military triumphs and frustration in Scot-

---

[8] *The Chronicle of Bury St Edmunds, 1212–1301*, ed. and tr. Antonia Gransden (London: Nelson, 1964), pp. 98, 103; *Edward I and the Throne of Scotland, 1290–1296: An Edition of the Record Sources for the Great Cause*, ed. E. L. G. Stones and G. G. Simpson, 2 vols. (Oxford OUP for the University of Glasgow, 1978), I.137–62; Gransden, *HW*, I.442, 451, 455ff.

land, Wales and France, and at home the strains of a war economy which brought the king into political conflict with the barons and clergy. The description of Edward's achievements in 1296 contains a note of pride in king and country as well as in Bury's eminence.

> Thus the king of England . . . obtained absolute power over England, Scotland and Wales, the former kingdom of Britain long torn and divided. Such a victory by any person of royal rank, achieved so swiftly in such a short time and in so great an emergency, could hardly be recalled. In Wales he captured one prince and subdued another. In Scotland, as has been said, he triumphed nobly: the king of England put all Scotland under his English laws and ordained that it should be watched over and governed by his officials. When he had successfully accomplished this he left with his army for England and directed his journey to Bury St Edmunds. There he ordered his parliament to be held with the chief men and magnates of the realm.

On the political issues of the last decade of the century the Bury chronicler tries to be fair to both sides. He emphasizes that the king asked the parliament for an aid 'to help his country'. But indignation creeps into the narrative as the king turns viciously against archbishop and clergy because of their loyalty to 'the Eternal King', and obedience to 'the chief shepherd of the universal Church' who had forbidden them to pay anything to the secular power. The clerks who made peace with their royal master 'acted with the weakness of women'. The chronicler also points out Edward's storing up of resentment against the lay barons who resisted his demands, and his deceitfulness in the face of demands for the confirmation and observance of Magna Carta.[9]

Bury's is one of a number of chronicles which carry the political story to a climax in the 1290s and then fall away in the new century as stalemate is reached at home and in Scotland. The jubilee year of 1300 is the last which it treats in any detail. Much time is spent on the king's visit to enlist St Edmund's aid in his Scottish campaigns by the inducement of confirmations of the monks' privileges against the encroachments of his own justices. Even more is taken up in recounting an ancient miracle of the patron saint, whose 'brimming cup' saved a certain lord and his wife when they were tempted by the devil to seek martyrs' crowns by slaughtering each other; in gratitude, the couple gave the abbey the manor of Warkton. The purpose of the monastic chronicle

---

[9] Gransden, *HW*, I. 397–400; *The Chronicle of Bury St Edmunds*, ed. and tr. Gransden, pp. 23–4, 97, 103, 133–41, 151–4.

remained the setting of a community's privileged position in a moral context, but this proved a stimulus to a rich political history of the dealings of royal government with the lords of the land.[10]

This perspective was the dominant one in the thirteenth century, but there were others. History-writing could not escape the influence of romance, the vernacular poetry about King Arthur and his court which was producing some of the great works of European literature. It appears most clearly in *L'Histoire de Guillaume le Marechal*, a biography in Anglo-Norman of a real-life knight errant whose marriage to an heiress brought him the earldom of Pembroke, and whose loyalty to King Richard and King John gave him a central political role culminating in the regency of England after John's death. Writing for the Marshal's family a few years after William's own death in 1219, the unknown poet gives a perspective which is valuable just because of his distaste for the new-style politics.

I must pass rapidly over the war that broke out between the king [John] and his barons, because there were too many circumstances that are not creditable to relate . . . The barons . . . made it known that if they did not obtain their liberties they would withdraw from his service and do him all the harm they could . . . But note well that the Marshal took no part whatever in this movement. He grieved for the excesses into which those on both sides had allowed themselves to be drawn, and had no share in the agreement concluded between the barons and the citizens of London . . . The Londoners brought in Louis, who for a long time was master of the country. He captured Farnham, Winchester, Porchester and Southampton. There the ribalds of France drank very many tuns [of wine]. They were boasting foolishly that England was theirs and that the English, having no right to the land, could only evacuate it. These boasts had no effect. Later I saw eaten by dogs a hundred of them whom the English slew between Winchester and Romsey. That was how they kept the land.

Though there is a good deal of heroic speech-making ('Hear ye, true and loyal knights . . . beware that there is amongst you no coward!'), and the Marshal is given the elaborate death-bed scene of an elder statesman, the poet paints a generally realistic picture which brings out other important factors (personal loyalty, honour and prowess) in addition to the royal ambition and corporate privilege emphasized by the monastic chroniclers.[11]

---

[10] Gransden, *HW*, I.443; *The Chronicle of Bury St Edmunds*, ed. and tr. Gransden pp. 156–61, and cf. pp. 134, 136, for earlier examples of the king's regard for the abbey's privileges.

[11] Gransden, *HW*, I.325, 345–55; *EHD*, III.81, 87.

A century on, an Augustian canon of Bridlington, Peter Langtoft, composed a verse chronicle in Yorkshire French which shows
how a romance style could breath new life into the story of
Plantagenet imperialism. The chivalry of a European-wide order
of knights could be adapted to support a growing national feeling,
which was already present in the references to the French in the
Marshal's biography. But it is the war 'against the stinking Scot'
which gives his whole story coherence. Merlin had prophesied
that one realm should be made of two different kingdoms.
Edward's unwillingness to share his conquests with his knights, as
King Arthur would have done, provoked the earls' refusal to
accompany him to France. 'The commonalty of Scotland hears
the news and rejoices.' In the new century, William Wallace
'and all his puny line' at last receive the reward of traitors and
thieves: only for Robert Bruce, leaning upon the altar of the
church of the Friars Minors in Dumfries, to slay 'the Badenagh
[John Comyn of Badenoch, another competitor for the Scottish
throne] through felony of heart,/Because he would not agree with
him,/To raise war against King Edward', and to have himself
made king of Scots at Scone. Edward, 'of chivalry, after King
Arthur, the flower of Christendom', dies at Burgh by Sands, near
Carlisle, in 1307, forcing himself back to Scotland, leaving the
young Edward to attempt to fulfil the vow to destroy 'King
Robin'.[12]

Midway between the history of William the Marshal and Langtoft's work, Robert of Gloucester combined, in his chronicle of
events from Brutus, the legendary founder of Britain, to the
Barons' War, 'the accuracy of detail, characteristic of monastic
chronicles, with the dramatic power typical of Romance literature'.
And because he wrote, uniquely, in English verse, he makes 'the
good knights of England' whom he delights in listing in a battle or
at a tournament appear to be English patriots. To the baronial
leaders, even to the French-born Simon de Montfort, whose
brother had been constable of France, he gives a tinge of English
statesmanship. The final tragedy of the Barons' War is represented
as the outcome of the jealousy of Gilbert de Clare, earl of
Gloucester, the other main baronial leader, and Simon's sons.
Prince Edward, captured along with his father at the battle of
Lewes in 1264, was allowed to escape and join forces with his

[12] Gransden, *HW*, 1.476–86; *EHD*, III.230, 249, 254, 259–60, 264–5.

friends in the Welsh marches, and at Evesham on 4 August 1265 they caught and killed Earl Simon and released the king. Also killed were Simon's son Henry,

> that so gentle knight was
> & Sir Hugh the Despenser the noble justice,
> & Sir Piers de Montfort that strong were & wise,
> Sir William de Verous & Sir Ralph Basset also . . .
> & many a good body were slain there in that field
> & amongst all else it was most pitifully done
> that Sir Simon the old man dismembered was so . . .
> & his head they smote off & to Wigmore it sent
> To Dame Maud the Mortimer they sent it most foully . . .

Meanwhile, darkness covered the earth, as at the Crucifixion,

> this saw Robert
> That first this book made & was very soreafeard.

The chronicler goes on to trace the complexities of the political settlement, but the tale does not quite end with peace restored and Edward's assumption of the cross. The final scene is at mass in the Italian city of Viterbo, where in 1271 Guy de Montfort slew Edward's cousin Henry of Almain, detached from the crusade on an errand of reconciliation.[13]

A different perspective again is provided by the town chroniclers. Like monasteries, towns were privileged corporations, though at the beginning of the century London alone seems to have stood above the abbey of Bury St Edmunds in wealth as measured by the royal exchequer. Pride in the towns' political liberties rather than in their commercial success gives the first urban histories their special tone. Economic development is nevertheless in the background, for it was the spring of a social differentiation which compelled the town oligarchies to exercise their power more vigorously over the craftsmen and proletariat. 'The Chronicles of the Mayors and Sheriffs of London', part of the *Liber de Antiquis Legibus* (*Book of Ancient Laws*) which remains amongst the city's records, stretch from 1188 to the coronation of Edward I in 1274, but are a full history only for the period after 1258, during which they were compiled. The author was probably a layman, Arnold FitzThedmar, alderman of the Bridge ward: his

---

[13] *The Metrical Chronicle of Robert of Gloucester*, ed. W. A. Wright (Rolls Series, London, 1887), pp. 732–8, 752–3, 764–6, 770, 775–6; Gransden, *HW*, 1.437; Treharne, *The Baronial Plan of Reform*, p. 439.

biography, which relates that his maternal grandparents came to England as pilgrims to the shrine of St Thomas Becket, and that his father was a native of Bremen, is included with the chronicles in the manuscript. The year of the chronicles is not the calendar or the regnal year, but the year of office of the two sheriffs who are named at the start of the annal, running from Michaelmas to Michaelmas. The chronicler is certainly interested in commercial matters, such as the enforcement of the assize of weights and measures, the burning of the nets of Thames fisherman, who fished with too tight a mesh, and the trade war with Flanders. They usually appear, however, in the context of the city's relations with the king, sometimes friendly but often strained. Ceremonial welcomes and feasts for the king in London are naturally recorded. But in 1258 we hear that a roll of accusations against the mayor and his associates was mysteriously left in the king's wardrobe, which turned Henry's friendship to anger. In his account of the investigation of the charges that the procedure for tallaging the city had been perverted to exempt the rich and oppress the poor, the chronicler is on the side of the oligarchy and against the people gathered in the folk-moot, for they are ready to sacrifice the liberties of the city in order to see their betters humiliated. The mob, including serfs and others not Londoners at all, howl 'nay, nay, nay' when the king's sly minister asks if the accused are to be allowed to escape by compurgation (simply swearing their innocence).[14]

The year of 1258 also saw 'that mad Parliament at Oxford', the Provisions of which the mayor and aldermen are shown accepting under duress. The chronicler depicts the London of this time as even more than usually at the centre of affairs, for on one day came 'the king of Almain [Richard of Cornwall], returning from the parts beyond sea' and on the next 'the king of Scotland came, with his queen'. But he also conveys a new sense of political and social danger. When the barons extend their influence over London, 'the commons of the city', 'the little people' (*minutus populus*), 'the fools of the vulgar classes' (*fatui de vulgo*), rule the roost. The barons win

---

[14] See *The Great Roll of the Pipe for the Third Year of the Reign of King Henry III, Michaelmas 1219*, ed. B. E. Harris (Pipe Roll Society, NS vol. 42, London, 1976), pp. 37 (farm of Norwich £108), 42 (farm of abbey of Bury, £500), 73 (farm of London and Middlesex, £300); Gransden, *HW*, 1.509–11; *EHD*, III.159; *De Antiquis Legibus Liber: Cronica Maiorum et Vicecomitum Londoniarum*, ed. Thomas Stapleton (Camden Society, vol. 34, London, 1846), pp. 29–37, 41, 43, 115–16, 126–7, 135, 139–42, 144–5, 159–61.

the people of the city with empty promises of liberties, and a
populist mayor plays up to the craft gilds, encouraging them to
make new statutes for themselves which are in fact 'abominations'
that damage every merchant coming to English markets and so the
whole body of the realm. The chronicler is worried by the new
alliances being made with and among the common people, and
gropes for a terminology for this 'class' dimension of politics
which he is one of the first to discern. The alderman and magnates
are thrust aside as the commons form conventicles, hundreds and
thousands binding themselves together by oath, ostensibly to keep
the peace but in fact to plunder the Jews and the money-lenders
from Cahors. In the early part of 1264, the Londoners join with
the burgesses of the Cinque Ports 'and almost the whole middle
class of England' (*fere omnis communa mediocris populi regni Anglie*)
to reject the judgement of King Louis in the dispute between king
and barons, since they had not been party to the arbitration.
Appointing themselves a constable and marshal, they march out to
destroy the king of Almain's manor of Isleworth. 'And this was
the beginning of woes, and the source of that deadly war, through
which so many manors were committed to the flames, so many
men, rich and poor were plundered, and so many thousands of
persons lost their lives.' The stormy darkness accompanying
Simon de Montfort's death is observed in London too, and soon
comes the report of the sending of the Earl's head to the Lady of
Wigmore, with his testicles dangling each side of his nose. Then it
is discovered that before Evesham forty of the leading citizens,
including FitzThedmar, had been singled out for murder because
of their loyalty to the king – an example of wickedness which the
chronicler thinks should be recorded for posterity as carefully as
good deeds. Simon's followers are now purged; 'parliaments',
'congregations' and 'conventicles' are proscribed, and the nobility
are forbidden the city without the king's special permission. The
theme of struggle between the aldermen and the lower orders
roused by demagogic mayors becomes obsessive. The social differentiation of London and the turbulence of the Barons' War
combined in the *Chronicles of the Mayors and Sheriffs of London* to
introduce a new note to history-writing.[15]

Outside London, civic perspectives on events were often provided by the friars. As members of vigorous new international

---

[15] *Cronica Maiorum*, ed. Stapleton, pp. 37–40, 45, 55–6, 61, 75–6, 86, 99, 114, 119,
129–30, 143, 148, 152, 156, 161–2, 164, 168–70; *EHD*, III.161–2, 168–70, 173.

organizations with a missionary purpose which took St Francis to Egypt and later Franciscans to the Mongol court and on to China, friar-historians possessed a wide vision. The friars lacked the estates, privileges and institutional supports of the monks, whom they regarded with a measure of the same hostility felt by towns-men towards monastic landlords. Towns and the business of towns were the friars' natural environment. Leading positions in the universities and the ecclesiastical hierarchy quickly fell to them; kings as well as popes used them to conduct inquisitions, such as Louis IX's great inquiries into the abuses of his servants in 1247. In his *Annals of Six Reigns* (from Stephen to Edward I), an Oxford friar, the Dominican Nicholas Trevet, has much to say about foreign events, especially when Dominicans are involved. Mention of the death of Thomas Aquinas on the way to the Council of Lyons in 1274 is the opportunity for a complete listing of that friar's works; and the loss of the Holy Land in 1291 occasions the remark that the patriarch who drowned when the Christians were driven into the sea was 'of the order of Preachers'. At home London events are well reported. But Trevet's real theme is the achievement of the Angevin kings. He makes the interesting remark that the responsibility of historians to honour their princes, exemplified by the French, has been neglected in England since John's reign. Of Edward's reign he gives a particularly rounded account, and though he was writing more than a decade later, he closes the book with the great king's death. A conspicuous element in Trevet's history of English kingship is parliamentary legislation: the statutes which he says 'are called of Marlborough' (1267), 'the first statutes of Westminster' (1275), 'of Gloucester' (1278), 'of Acton Burnell' (named from the place in Shropshire where a parliament was held in 1283), 'Westminster the second' (1285) and 'Westminster the third' (1290).[16]

The return via urban and mendicant chronicles to a more sympathetic history of royal government is apparent in the work of Thomas Wykes, a friend of Dominican scholars who lived in London and Oxford before entering the Augustinian abbey of Osney in 1282 at the age of sixty. This chronicler too is appalled by the sworn conspiracies which sprang up 'in almost every city and borough' under the encouragement of the earl of Leicester –

---

[16] Gransden, *HW*, I. 495–7; *Nicholai Triveti Annales*, ed. T. Hog (English Historical Society, London, 1845), pp. 1–2, 274, 279, 287, 293, 299, 309, 312, 316, 318; Gransden, *HW*, I. 501–7.

the groups of ribalds who proclaimed themselves 'the bachelors' and terrorized the leading citizens with their daring acts of violence. The law was enfeebled as in the biblical realm 'where the king is a boy, and the princes feast in the morning'. The rioters who plunder Richard of Cornwall's property meet no punishment but God's – four of them are killed by a falling beam in a chapel they are wrecking. Wykes is equally concerned by the economic disruption, such as the soaring price of corn and other commodities caused by the 'pirates' of the Cinque Ports. His revulsion at the cruelty of de Montfort's men towards the London Jews is sincere, but it is the economic wrong-headedness of the government's Jewish policy which most worries him, down to the final expulsion of 1290. As the strong story line of the Barons' War and its aftermath runs out, it is replaced by the theme of parliaments, taxation and statute-making. Wykes is our source for the holding of a number of the parliaments of the 1260s. He describes the translation of the bones of Edward the Confessor to a splendid new shrine in Westminster Abbey in 1269, and tells how immediately afterwards the nobles began to deal with the business of the king and the kingdom as they had been accustomed to do 'in the parliamentary way' (*parliamentationis genere*). On this occasion, we are told, Henry's astuteness and cupidity extorted a tax of a twentieth of the goods of the laity, which aroused the resentment of a populace willing enough to laugh at the taxing of the clergy. But it is the statutes which once again take first place in the account of the parliaments of King Edward.[17]

FROM THE FOURTEENTH TO THE EIGHTEENTH CENTURIES:
THE PLACE OF THE THIRTEENTH CENTURY IN ENGLISH
CONSTITUTIONAL HISTORY

The thirteenth-century chroniclers were fine 'contemporary historians' who vividly conveyed the impact of government pressure on monastic communities, the growing national assertiveness and the political tensions of town life. They were first and foremost reporters, not interpreters, and included any documentary evidence which came their way simply as a matter of course. The history-writing of the later medieval period was a moralizing history in

---

[17] *Chronicon Thomae Wykes*, in *Annales Monastici*, ed. Luard, IV. 111ff; Gransden, *HW*, 1.436–70; for a list of parliaments at this period, see *Handbook of British Chronology*, 3rd edn, ed. E. B. Fryde, D. E. Greenway, S. Porter and I. Roy (Royal Historical Society, London, 1986), pp. 542–4.

which the supposed manner of King John's death was given more prominence than the making of the Great Charter. Early in the fourteenth century Walter of Guisborough, a chronicler who specialized in moral tales, gave a new twist to an old story that John had been poisoned at the Cistercian abbey of Swineshead because of his lust for the abbot's beautiful sister: according to Guisborough some of the king's servants joined the plot, outraged by his words at supper. Taking a loaf, John asked what it cost and on being told 'a halfpenny' swore that it was the very abundance of the land which made the barons and people revolt against him: if he kept life and health for a year, he would make such a loaf cost sixpence. We know that at least once John had legislated on the price of bread, but Walter of Guisborough was clearly not writing administrative history. He was embellishing legend to give John's tyranny a wider significance than a dispute over baronial rights, and thus to make the events of the reign more intelligible.[18]

By the second half of the fourteenth century prose chronicles were being composed in English. Patriotic, chivalric and colloquial, the *Brut* (so-called because its starting-point was not the Creation but the arrival of the legendary hero thought to have given Britain its name) was popular among the knightly class. Among townsmen a similar vogue was enjoyed by the London chronicles. This whole historiographical tradition was passed on to the Tudors by the *New Chronicles of England and France* of Robert Fabyan, an alderman and sheriff of the city who died in 1513. Late medieval histories devoted more space to John's reign than its length justified, though the granting of Magna Carta is barely mentioned. The history of the reign that was worked out in the later middle ages comprised: the loss of Normandy to the king of France (who made war 'by exciting of the pope', Fabyan learns from 'some authors'); John's resistance to Innocent III's appointment of Langton to the see of Canterbury and the consequent imposition of an interdict on England (about the effectiveness of which Fabyan cites contrary opinions); the king's ruthless treatment of the Cistercians; and his eventual submission, acceptance of Langton and resignation of England to be received back from the pope as a fief of the Church. John's 'dissension with his lords' fits

[18] Paris, *CM*, II.480–1, 667–8; *Wykes*, p. 59; *The Chronicle of Walter of Guisborough*, ed. Harry Rothwell, Camden Series, vol. 89 (Royal Historical Society, London, 1957), pp. 154–6; Gransden, *HW*, I.472–3; H. G. Richardson and G. O. Sayles, *Law and Legislation from Aethelberht to Magna Carta* (Edinburgh: Edinburgh UP, 1966), pp. 148–9.

into this pattern of relations with the pope and the French. The barons were roused by the displeasure the king bore them for their failure to support him against Pope Innocent, as well as his refusal to hold to 'the laws of Saint Edward'. He broke the peace made at Runnymede and brought in foreign mercenaries, so the barons called in aid Prince Louis of France.[19]

The length of Henry III's reign made it difficult for the chroniclers to maintain the strong story line of John's. The *Brut* describes the lords and 'the common people' helping to drive out Prince Louis, in return for the confirmation of 'the franchises granted at Runnymede' and a charter 'which yet be-eth holden throughout England'. The saintly Archibishop Edmund marries Henry to Eleanor of Provence and stands with an harmonious family group, 'a sweet sight', at the new queen's coronation. Then there is a demand for additions to the charters which the barons and 'all the commons of England' purchase for a thousand marks of silver. Suddenly we are at Oxford in Henry's forty-third year (1258), at the ordaining of a law for the amendment of the realm. The king is forced to swear along with the lords to 'hold that statute evermore; and who that it brake should be dead.' War comes when Earl Richard persuades Henry to seek papal absolution from his oath, and Lewes, Evesham, the revolts of the disinherited, the departure of a crusade led by the Lord Edward and Henry's death follow swiftly. According to the *Brut*, Henry's reign is a story of developing tension between kingly power and popular freedoms. Simon de Montfort is identified as the 'wolf of a strange land' prophesied by Merlin, who brought 'strong war' to a land long at peace – and yet Simon's death 'was great harm to the commons of England, that so good a man was shent [destroyed] for truth, and died in charity, and for the common profit of the same folk'.[20]

Produced in the middle of the Hundred Years War, the English *Brut* found more meat in the reign of the warlike Edward I, 'the worthiest knight of the world . . . for God's grace was in him, for he had the victory of his enemies'. The complexities of domestic politics and administration appear only in the descriptions of the king's punishment of coin-clippers, banning of grants of land into

[19] Gransden, *HW*, II.73, 220–2, 227, 245; *The Brut or Chronicles of England*, ed. F. W. D. Brie (Early English Text Society, vol. 131, London, 1906), p. 170; *The New Chronicles of England and France by Robert Fabyan*, ed. Henry Ellis (London: J. Rivington, 1811), p. 322; May McKisack, *Medieval History in the Tudor Age* (Oxford: Clarendon Press, 1971), p. 95.
[20] *The Brut*, ed. Brie, p. 178.

'the dead hand' (*mortmain*) of the Church, disciplining of his justices and clerks for the abuses he discovered on his return from Gascony in 1289 and expulsion of the Jews from England in the following year 'for their usury and misbelief'. The picture is of a masterful king who keeps the clergy in their place, imposes his lordship and a better law on the Welsh and after 1290 is preoccupied with doing the same to the Scots and defeating their new-found French allies. There is no trace in the *Brut* of the king's great dispute with the barons and community in 1297, though that arose from Edward's war taxation.[21]

Polydore Vergil's *Anglica Historia*, completed in 1513, introduced humanist history-writing to England. The rudiments of an argument about the thirteenth-century history of England were established by a critical use of sources combined with a readiness to put words into the mouths (and ideas into the heads) of historical characters. The construction of a reasoned account of thirteenth-century politics from the increasingly available chronicle material was helped by the printing also of statute collections, and of the laws 'collected in a little book which is called Magna Carta'. Polydore is able to set the Charter in the context of an unending fight for the good old law. What the barons demanded from John in 1215 was the long-promised restoration of 'the ancient laws and institutes of England', as represented by 'the laws of Edward the Confessor'. Again at Oxford in 1258 it is 'the liberty and laws so often promised' which Henry is compelled to swear to. Original to Polydore, and of great interest, is the identification of the crisis of 1297 as the climax of the struggle, when 'the English obtained from their prince this ultimate liberty, which they preserve with stubborness': the right not to have taxes imposed on them without consultation.[22]

Humanist history made the political experience of the past available to new generations and at the same time opened up that experience to be newly interpreted. The first aspect of thirteenth-century politics to come vividly alive for the Tudors was actually

---

[21] *Ibid*, pp. 179, 181–5, 188, 192, 195–6.

[22] Denys Hay, *Polydore Vergil: Renaissance Historian and Man of Letters* (Oxford: Clarendon Press, 1952), pp. 19, 88–9, 106ff, 138–9, 143, 190–1; F. J. Levy, *Tudor Historical Thought* (San Marino: Huntington Library and Art Gallery, 1967), pp. 33–7, 45, 53–68, 170–3, 178; Thomas Langley, *An Abridgement of the Notable Worke of Polidore Vergil* (London, 1546), fol. 20v; Polydore Vergil, *Anglica Historia* (Basle, 1534), pp. 266, 269, 281–2, 287, 296, 314, 320, 340, 343; Faith Thompson, *Magna Carta: Its Role in the Making of the English Constitution* (Minneapolis: University of Minnesota Press, 1948), p. 159.

the tension between King and Church. Protestant reformers were intent on showing how the Church had departed from its primitive ideals in search of political power, and thus encroached on the realm of the State. Passages in medieval chronicles which depicted churchmen resisting rightful kings on papal authority were eagerly seized upon. The morality play, *King Johan*, written between 1538 and 1560 by John Bale, combined vigorous abuse of the papacy with political moralizing put into the mouths of characters like 'Imperial Majesty', 'Sedition' (always clerical), 'Commonalty', 'Usurped Power' ('also the Pope'), 'Private Wealth' and 'Civil Order'; but also with shrewd criticism of the way previous historians had treated real figures such as Stephen Langton, the legate Pandulph and King John himself. Nobility complains:

> You priests are the cause that Chronicles doth defame
> So many princes and men of notable name
> For you take upon you to write them evermore;
> And therefore King John is like to rue it sore
> When you write his time, for vexing of the clergy.

Clergy are told by Nobility that they have no legitimate complaint about taxation: 'He that defendeth you ought to have part of your goods.' Magna Carta as an achievement for the people of England by barons under clerical leadership could have no part in Bale's drama.[23]

In the hands of a reformer with a message to drive home but also with a good historical perspective, the morality play was a very effective instrument for separating out the political forces at work in the rein of King John. Bale showed that real history-writing involves argument between the present and the past, without which the simple record of the chronicles remained opaque. By 1600 history plays had become a major literary genre, but only two more were concerned with the thirteenth century. As a supreme example of the tragedy of state, the reign of King John was an obvious subject for Shakespeare – in fact his only historical subject before the emergence of Lancaster and York. The true dramatist is not interested in the political issues in themselves,

---

[23] John Bale, *King Johan*, in *Four Morality Plays*, ed. P. Happe (Harmondsworth: Penguin English Library, 1979), pp. 341–2, 363–4, 371, 379, 383, 403, 410–11; Polydore himself omitted his story of John's severity to the University of Oxford from his second edition of 1546, because opinion was by then so firmly on the king's side: Hay, *Polydore Vergil*, p. 123; Levy, *Tudor Historical Thought*, pp. 36, 42, 64ff, 88–97, 100–1, 110–11.

however (again, Magna Carta gets no mention), so much as in the strains they impose on human relationships. At the heart of Shakespeare's play are the consequences for John of the suspicious death of Prince Arthur in his custody, and, through them all, the unswerving devotion to his sovereign of the Bastard Faulconbridge, King Richard's son, and his simple anti-French patriotism. In *King Edward the First* George Peele relates (with a dramatist's disregard of chronology) the destruction of the last Welsh prince, the birth of Edward of Caernarvon and the humiliation of John Balliol, king of Scots. But its climax is the last sickness of Queen Eleanor amid these triumphs; her delirious talk of long-past infidelities with Edmund Crouchback and a French priest; her death and that of her daughter Joan, now branded a bastard; and the distraught Edward's raising of Charing Cross in their memory.[24]

The poets and dramatists did make a special contribution to the vision of the past by imagining the impact of public events on private lives, but they hardly became historians in the process. Bale had been able to show history as argument in that way, because all that was available to him to argue with was the one-dimensional narrative of the chronicles, and historians were now becoming dissatisfied with such limited material. The humanists learnt that narrative was not the only way to present the past. Coins and monuments and the language of documents also had tales to tell. Polydore's own observation of the palace of the Savoy gives point to his description of Henry III's Savoyard in-laws; his knowledge of the coronation stone taken from Scone and 'even now preserved at Westminster' illuminates his account of Edward I's dealings with the Scots. Associated with this interest in material evidence was the discovery of anachronism. Through its concrete remains, life in the past was seen to be different. Recognizing the unique difference of a particular past time became the greatest of historical skills – applying to it terms appropriate to another time or to the present was the historian's special sin. The triumph of humanist historiography was Lorenzo Valla's demonstration in 1440 that 'the Donation of Constantine', the document (immensely influential in the middle ages) by which the first Christian emperor purported to confer on the pope the government of the West, must by reason of its language be a late fabrication. Valla's tract was

[24] George Peele, *King Edward the First* (Oxford: OUP, Malone Society Reprints, 1911).

rendered into English in 1534, and his critical methods were used by reformers attempting to discredit King John's supposed deed of gift of England to the papacy.[25]

Both gentry and peasantry wanted to hear tales of the deeds of local heroes in an historical landscape. It was the gentry, however, who were able to have their past documented for them by a newly professional group of antiquaries, and their place in English society confirmed by a new sort of historical literature. The equivalent in English of the Italian humanist's description of his city's wealth and architectural splendours was the itinerary which described the topography, buildings and great families of the English counties. Between 1535 and 1543 John Leland made a 'Laborious Journey and Search' to rescue the chronicles in the doomed monastic libraries. Out of his discoveries he proposed to write a book called 'British Antiquity [De Antiquitate Britannica], or else Civil History', which he significantly intended 'to divide into so many books as there be shires in England, and shires and great dominions in Wales', each one containing 'the beginnings, increases and memorable acts of the chief towns and castles of the province allotted to it'; and to compile a 'British Nobility', which would trace the lineages of the 'lords, captains and rulers of this realm' from Roman times. In his *Itineraries*, this first of a self-conscious race of 'antiquaries' developed the fifteenth-century William Worcester's somewhat haphazard descriptions into a virtual gazetteer of a large part of England and its ruling families. Simon de Montfort appears in it in the guise of the founder of the Greyfriars of Leicester; 'Richard King of Romans and Earl of Cornwall' as patron and rebuilder of the town and castle of Wallingford 'sore defaced by the Danes' wars'; the Bigod earls of Norfolk, thirteenth-century marshals of England, as founders of Cartmel Priory and a hospital in York, and as lords of Settrington in Yorkshire, a place which they disputed with the Aumale lords of Holderness. Towns were also authorities demanding description: so we are given, for instance, the geographical extent of the 'franchises and liberties of York'.[26]

[25] Levy, *Tudor Historical Thought*, pp. ix, 39, 84, 230–6, 243–4; Hay, *Polydore Vergil*, p. 90; Stuart Piggott, 'Antiquarian Thought', in *English Historical Scholarship in the Sixteenth and Seventeenth Centuries*, ed. Levi Fox (Oxford: OUP for the Dugdale Society, 1956), pp. 93–103.

[26] Keith Thomas, *The Perception of the Past in Early Modern England* (Creighton Trust Lecture, University of London,. 1983), pp. 7, 10–11; McKisack, *Medieval History in the Tudor Age*, pp. 173–4; D. R. Woolf, 'History, Folklore and Oral

In his *Perambulation of Kent*, the forerunner of all county histories, published in 1570, William Lambard brought together geography, archaeology, history and law to describe 'the Estate [or State] of Kent'. This 'chorography' 'created a usable past' for the county authorities by tracing the growth and structure of local administration. After the *Perambulation* Lambard put his best history into treatises such as *Eirenarcha*, a book of instructions for JPs, which recognized the thirteenth-century origins of the office. The most celebrated antiquary of all was William Camden, headmaster of Westminster school, whose *Britain, or a Chorographical Description of the Most Flourishing Kingdoms, England, Scotland, and Ireland, and the Islands Adjoining, out of the Depth of Antiquity* went through four editions within eight years of its publication in 1586. But only the last section of Camden's *Britannia*, an expert account of the 'Law Courts of England', ecclesiastical, temporal and 'one mixed of both' – that is, Parliament – reaches forward to the thirteenth century. (Even then, it is only the *name* of Parliament, 'of no great antiquity, and the same borrowed out of France', which Camden would have regarded as so recent.) The way Camden altered the image of the middle ages was by applying to them the categories of the classical history and political theory which were his main concern. He takes advantage of the mentions of both the earls of Leicester (under Leicestershire) and the battle of Evesham (under Worcestershire) to denounce 'our Catiline, Simon Montfort', who tried 'under the pretence of restoring the commonwealth and maintaining liberty' to turn a monarchical state into an oligarchy, 'raised a most dangerous war, [and] spoiled shamefully a great part of England'. In contrast, Bishop Grosseteste is praised as a man incredible in his time for the knowledge of literature and the learned tongues, 'a terrible reprover of the Pope', and 'a mallet of the Romanists'.[27]

Tradition in Early Modern England', *Past and Present*, 120 (1988), p. 37; William Worcester, *Itineraries*, ed. J. H. Harvey (Oxford: Clarendon Press, 1969), pp. 55, 113, 209, 213, 215; for Worcester, see also Gransden, *HW*, II.328–41; *The Itinerary of John Leland in or about the Years 1535–1543*, ed. Lucy Toulmin Smith (London: George Bell and Sons, 1907), pp. xxxvii–xliii, 15, 55–6, 58, 78, 119; Levy, *Tudor Historical Thought*, pp. 126–8.

27 Levy, *Tudor Historical Thought*, pp. 138–41; William Lombard, *Eirenarcha: Or of The Office of Justices of Peace 1581/2*, facsimile with introduction by P. R. Glazebrook (London: Professional Books, 1972); *Britain or a Chorographical Description of the Most Flourishing Kingdoms, England, Scotland and Ireland, and the Islands Adjoining, out of the Depth of Antiquity . . . Written First by William Camden*, tr. Philemon Holland (London, 1610), pp. 153, 177–82, 523–4, 540, 577–8; for

For John Stow, who published his *Survey of London* in 1598, the thirteenth century was the time when King John provided for the repair of London Bridge; King Henry (as he 'found recorded') had 6,000 poor people fed at Westminster on the Feast of the Circumcision 1236; and a great lead conduit was built in the reign of King Edward to supply fresh water to the city. Stow avowedly followed in the footsteps of Leland, Lambard and those others who had provided 'such special descriptions of each place' as would 'make up a whole body of the English chorography'. But Stow's introduction provides 'in generality' a view of the workings of the realm's best-documented community which is new in its social and economic emphasis. London is described with its 'walls, gates, ditches, and fresh waters, the bridges, towers and castles, the schools of learning and house of law, the orders and customs, sports and pastimes, watchings and martial exercises, and lastly the honour and worthiness of the citizens'. With its burgeoning population, London was 'a mighty instrument to bring any great desire to effect, if it may be known to a man's devotion'. The Crown had many times been compelled to seize the city's liberties because of the threat of disorder, and when Simon de Montfort was defeated 'London felt it most tragical'. Stow has to insist, however, that London was the instrument, 'never the author' of rebellion.[28]

It was when records were enlisted on both sides in a great political argument, and the establishment of facts about the past shown to be relevant to contemporary issues, that a full-scale model of English history took shape, and that thirteenth-century developments were given a worthy place within it. The political argument was of course that between King and Parliament which culminated in the Civil War; its historical dimension the antiquity of the landed aristocracy, of the law in which the rights and power of the aristocracy were enshrined, and of the parliament in which the ruling class were represented. The antiquaries (many of them heralds) served the family pride of country squires and city merchants, but also the sense of county and civic community

---

Camden, see Levy, *Tudor Historical Thought*, pp. 129–30, 148–55, and F. Smith Fussner, *The Historical Revolution: English Historical Writing and Thought 1580–1640* (New York: Columbia UP, 1962), pp. 230–52.

[28] John Stow, *A Survey of London* (London, 1598; modern reprint in Everyman's Library with introduction by H. B. Wheatley, n.d.), pp. xxiii, 17, 23, 44, 56–8, 83, 107, 250–2, 482, 490–2, 498; Levy, *Tudor Historical Thought*, p. 163; Fussner, *The Historical Revolution*, pp. 219–20, 226–9.

which had grown quickly in the later middle ages. They wrote essentially for the rulers of county and city, and fostered new sensitivities: to the roles of the gentry as justices and members of parliament; to the importance of institutions and administration in the growth of society. The storm raised by Arthur Hall in 1581 shows how antiquarianism could lead to serious historical investigation in the case of Parliament. Merely cantankerous Hall may usually have been, but on this issue he appears to have grasped that the reputation of the body to which he proudly belonged could only be enhanced by a true understanding of its history, which involved sacrificing the antiquaries' idea of its origin in the Anglo-Saxon Witenagemot. Applying exactly the right question to information supplied him by Lambard – when did king, lords and commons become associated in a law-making procedure? – he insisted that Parliament came into existence only about 1250.[29]

The uncovering of the massive store of record material, and more specialized research into it, were the essential basis of a new problem-solving type of historical discourse, the inspiration of which was to a considerable extent political. The scrutiny of the chronicles rescued from monastic libraries widened into an exploitation of every possible source of information about the past. A concern on the part of the government for the orderly preservation of contemporary records in a 'State Paper Office' was extending to the medieval records, and an interest in the history of central government was developing alongside the chorography of the shires. Lambard is found in the last year of his life expounding to the queen the 'records of estate' contained in the 'rolls, bundles, membranes, and parcels in her Majesty's Tower of London', and the meaning of 'ordinationes, parliamenta, cartae, litterae'. Arthur Agarde's work among exchequer records equipped him to address the Society of Antiquaries on the meaning of terms of land measurement. In his researches he discovered feet of fines and plea

---

[29] Fussner, *The Historical Revolution*, pp. 214–20; J. G. A. Pocock, *The Ancient Constitution and the Feudal Law: A Study of English Historical Thought in the Seventeenth Century. A Reissue with a Retrospect* (Cambridge: CUP, 1987), pp. 36–7, 43–5, 47–9, 124–5, 261–2; *English Historical Scholarship in the Sixteenth and Seventeenth Centuries*, ed. Fox, pp. 35, 78, 100–2, 110–11, 124; J. R. Maddicott, 'The County Community and the Making of Public Opinion in Fourteenth Century England', *TRHS*, 5th ser., 18 (1978); Levy, *Tudor Historical Thought*, pp. 119, 136–7, 140–1, 159–60; Camden, *Britain*, tr. Holland, p. 177; G. R. Elton, 'Arthur Hall, Lord Burghley and the Antiquity of Parliament', in *History and Imagination: Essays in Honour of H. R. Trevor-Roper*, ed. H. Lloyd-Jones, V. Pearl and B. Worden (London: Duckworth, 1981), pp. 88–103.

rolls of the time of Richard I, John and Henry III in chests in the old chapter house of Westminster Abbey, and calendared *quo warranto* and other pleadings of the reign of Edward I which he found 'in a little room adjoining the Court of Receipt' at Westminster; and he made a bag of such Parliament Rolls as he could find, especially of Edward I's time. John Holland of the Inner Temple illuminated the history of trial by battle from a deed of the forty-second year of Henry III, which he gave to the Lord Chief Justice; and contributed to the discussion of the meaning of 'sterling' the idea that the word derived from the town where Edward I, on an incursion into Scotland, first caused such coins to be minted. Although continuous public records had got under way a little before 1200, their exploration brought the thirteenth century, when their wealth becomes obvious, into the centre of historical debate.[30]

The tendency of protagonists of the antiquity of Parliament and the rights of the Commons within it to claim that the fundamental laws of England were in principle immemorial provoked defenders of the king's prerogative to assemble the documentary evidence for their actual historical origins. Sir Edward Coke knew more of the legal records than any man, and that the stream of statutes which began in the thirteenth century was one of the great repositories of English law. But his purpose and approach were the reverse of historical ones. His achievement, which was to collect together in his *Reports* and *Institutes of the Laws of England* a body of precedents which made the law a force of enormous power in the English constitution, depended on an identification of 'the law of his own day with the law of the earliest records' and 'the doctrine that the latter contained what had been law since time out of mind before the Conquest'. Magna Carta (still King Henry's of 1225) takes its place at the head of Coke's exposition of statute law, which comprises the second of the four parts of his *Institutes*. It is held to have been 'for the most part declaratory of the principal grounds of the fundamental laws of England', for which the reader is also referred to 'our ancient [in fact thirteenth-century] authors, Bracton, Britton . . . Fleta, and many records, never before published in print'. Chapter 39 of the Charter (29 in Henry III's and Coke's version), the one which forbade a free man's condem-

[30] Levy, *Tudor Historical Thought*, pp. 120, 126–8, 154, 164–5; Fussner, *The Historical Revolution*, pp. 69–106, 220–3; McKisack, *Medieval History in the Tudor Age*, pp. 81, 114, 167–8; R. B. Wernham, 'The Public Records in the Sixteenth and Seventeenth Centuries', in *English Historical Scholarship*, ed. Fox, pp. 11–30.

nation 'except by the lawful judgement of his peers or by the law of the land', was already being invoked by Puritans against the summary procedures of the Court of High Commission. Under James I, the Commons used this and another chapter freeing merchants from 'evil tolls' against royal grants of monopoly, forced loans and the imposition of new forms of taxation.[31]

Coke's 'myth of the confirmations' – really, the doctrine that the whole line of statutes which began in the thirteenth century simply reaffirmed the immemorial principles of English law already clear before the Norman Conquest – was the chief weapon of Parliament in its confrontation with the monarchy from the 1620s onwards. The privileges of Parliament were held to be of ancient right, not royal grant. The presentation of the Charter and the first statutes as embodying an ancient and 'fundamental' law may have assisted the claims of 'the High Court of Parliament', but in fact it diminished the historical role of parliaments in statute-making. The point about an immemorial law was that historical kings could not be shown to have made it – but nor could historical parliaments. Since the chief contents of this immemorial law which even courts and judges were held to have amended only in minor ways were the rights and obligations of the landed aristocracy, which therefore must also be immemorially ancient, the argument widened out to embrace the history of English society. A new type of scholar became equipped to prove that the aristocracy had in fact a definite moment of creation at the hands of William the Conqueror, and that both common law and Parliament were part of the aristocracy's subsequent evolution. Unfortunately for Coke and the other parliamentarians who based their resistance to the Crown on the prescriptive rights of the landed aristocracy, jurists in France and Scotland, and belatedly in England itself, had been learning that the laws of their countries had developed continuously, under influences of which royal power was a major ingre-

---

[31] For the possession of collections of statutes by the leading antiquaries of the later sixteenth century, see J.–Ph. Genet, 'Droit et histoire en Angleterre', *Annales de Bretagne et des Pays de l'Ouest*, 87 (1980); Pocock, *The Ancient Constitution*, p. 45; Sir Edward Coke, *The Second Part of the Institutes of the Laws of England, Containing the Exposition of Many Ancient and Other Statutes* (London, 1797), third of the unnumbered pages of the Proeme; cf. Holt, *Magna Carta*, pp. 2–10, for Coke's reinstatement of the Charter as a political document; Sir Herbert Butterfield, *Magna Carta in the Historiography of the Sixteenth and Seventeenth Centuries* (Stenton Lecture, University of Reading, 1969), p. 15; P. Styles, 'Politics and Historical Research in the Early Seventeenth Century', in *English Historical Scholarship*, ed. Fox, pp. 58–9; Thompson, *Magna Carta, pp. 186–7.*

dient. In his *Jus Feudale*, published in the year of the Union of the Crowns (1603) and dedicated to King James VI & I, the Paris-educated Scot Sir Thomas Craig instructed his fellow Britons that feudal landholding was brought to England and then to Scotland after 1066. Craig was able to show that feudal law was Frankish custom, adapted by the Normans to their needs and imposed on England by the Conqueror. Rather more speculatively, he fitted Parliament into this picture as 'an ingenious device' used by subsequent rulers to *evade* the demands of the English people for the restoration of their pre-Conquest laws. In Parliament, the king created a body 'to whose deliberations all amendments upon existing laws and institutions, as well as proposals for new legislation, were referred', but whose summoning he reserved to himself, along with 'the sole power of giving effect to its measures by royal assent'; a body consequently enjoying 'complete freedom of discussion of public affairs, but without the king's consent . . . impotent to accomplish anything'. It was at least a plausible picture of the way English institutions were evolving in the thirteenth century, for it explained the relationship of king and community in the making of statutes, which Craig recognized to be the 'most important constituent of the Law of England'.[32]

The crux of the feudal argument was the appearance of the Commons in Parliament and the king's part in this momentous event. Sir Henry Spelman, the legal scholar who imported to England the comparative method and philological skill of the French humanists in order to work out the nature and origins of feudal tenure, showed that from the Norman settlement to the thirteenth century the basic political relationship in England was that between the king as lord paramount and the barons who were his immediate tenants and vassals. It was the tenants-in-chief who represented the under-tenants and the rest of the population in the great councils of the king. The royalist charter-scholar, Sir William Dugdale, vastly extended knowledge of the medieval baronage and emphasized the importance of the king's summoning of individual nobles in the fashioning of Parliament. How, then, had the Commons entered the picture? It must have been as feudal society

---

[32] Pocock, *The Ancient Constitution*, caps. 1–4, pp. 44–5, 234, 289; Thompson, *Magna Carta*, pp. 9–10, 302, 336–9; cf. Holt, *Magna Carta*, p. 9, for the anticipation of Coke's interpretation in fourteenth-century statutes; Styles, 'Politics and Historical Research', pp. 57–61; Sir Thomas Craig of Riccarton, *Jus Feudale*, tr. J. A. Clyde, 2 vols. (Edinburgh: Hodge, 1934), I.84, 88–90, 96, 103.

began to decay, and the king turned to the knights of the shire and the burgesses as makeweights to baronial power. Once again the crucial changes were found to have manifested themselves in the thirteenth-century records, though they were the products of a very gradual social alteration.[33]

The achievements and limitations of royalist historiography were summed up by Robert Brady's *Introduction to the Old English History*, published in 1684. Brady's exposure of anachronisms, misunderstandings, 'partial citations' and plain falsifications of the record, which made the *Introduction* so original, was actually impelled by a passionate hatred of those who sought to 'batter and bomb the Government', and 'disturb the peace and quiet of the Nation'. He accused them of doing this by advocating utopian forms of government which had never existed and were totally impractical; or by alleging that the people were the 'Origin of all Power and Government' and possessed of fundamental rights and privileges to be found 'in Records, and Histories, in Charters, and other Monuments of Antiquity'. When William Petyt claimed in his *Antient Right of the Commons* that the knights and burgesses 'hath ever been' an essential constituent part of Parliament, did he mean, Brady demanded, from eternity, or ever since Adam, or since the Britains, the Romans or the Saxons inhabited the Island? All this was negative, if very effective. The positive achievement of the *Introduction* was to show when and how the Commons did come to be represented directly. Ordinary free tenants were never included amongst the *Barones Regni* with whom the king took counsel (Matthew Paris's account made it clear that there would not have been time to get representatives to Runnymede in 1215), nor were they part of the *Magna Concilia* or *Colloquia* which began to be called parliaments 'about the middle of Henry III's reign'. Brady was unoriginal in affirming that 'the Commons of England Represented by Knights, Citizens and Burgesses in Parliament, were not introduced nor were one of the three Estates in Parliament before the 49th [year] of Henry III': but he was the first to see that such a momentous precedent had to be given a full political context. The explanation of Simon de Montfort's famous sum-

---

[33] Pocock, *The Ancient Constitution*, pp. 99–123, 149, 169, 171–3, 178–9, 183–5, 212–13, 242; William Blackstone, *Commentaries on the Laws of England*, 4 vols. (Oxford: Clarendon Press, 1765–9; facsimile, University of Chicago, 1979), IV.418–20; Levy, *Tudor Historical Thought*, p. 166; Butterfield, *Magna Carta*, pp. 19–21.

mons of knights and burgesses to a parliament at Hilary 1265 must be sought in the course of a struggle reaching back at least as far as the Oxford parliament of 1258, and in the gathering storm-clouds in the marches and the north. 'Without the History of this Nick of Time, this Writ is not fully understood.'[34]

The great tradition of antiquarian scholarship did not slacken, but it was removed from the mainstream of politics by the Glorious Revolution of 1688, which swept Brady away along with his royal patron and gave Parliament the victory. The works of Dugdale which made possible 'the scientific study of English social history in the Middle Ages', the *Monasticon* (1655–73) and the *Baronage* (1675–6), were continued in collections and studies of medieval deeds by the group of men who revived the Society of Antiquaries in 1707, most notably Thomas Madox's *Formulare Anglicanum*, published in 1702. Thomas Rymer's *Foedera*, a collection in fifteen volumes of all the treaties made by the Crown of England and of many domestic public documents (1702–13), and Madox's *History and Antiquities of the Exchequer* (1711) gave administrative history a firm scientific basis and remain indispensable to this day. There was a new specialization on the part of these men, a concentration of intellectual energy on selected themes, but also a determination *not* to use the 'Ancient Records and Memoirs of this Kingdom', as their predecessors had done, 'to frame hypotheses concerning the Ancient State of Things from either Modern or Present Appearances'. Attempts to make convocation out as a clerical parliament and to carry its history back beyond its true thirteenth-century origins provoked a proper study of the synods of the medieval Church, culminating in the monumental *Concilia* published by David Wilkins in 1737.[35]

Notoriously the triumphant Whigs acquired their own interpretation of history, but it was one that had to live amid the strong currents of political, economic and social theory which stemmed from the eighteenth-century Enlightenment. Their historical vision was the exact antithesis of Coke's unchanging immemorialism. Because it was teleological (written towards a conclusion decided in advance), it has been stigmatized as the archetype of bad history. But it was at least history, a picture of development, and one

---

[34] Robert Brady, *Introduction to the Old English History* (London, 1684), pp. 3–4, 37–9, 86, 122, 130–43; Pocock, *The Ancient Constitution*, pp. 190, 256.

[35] David C. Douglas, *English Scholars* (London: Eyre and Spottiswoode, 1939), pp. 26, 249–84, 291–314, 349; R. J. Smith, *The Gothic Bequest: Medieval Institutions in British Thought, 1688–1863* (Cambridge: CUP, 1987), pp. 28–38.

capable of weaving together the perceptions of Spelman, Dugdale, Brady and Madox about the crucial changes in English aristocracy and government on the one side, and on the other the more theoretical accounts of social evolution presented by such works as Montesquieu's *Spirit of the Laws* (1748), Adam Ferguson's *Essay on the History of Civil Society* (1767) and Adam Smith's *Inquiry into the Nature and Causes of the Wealth of Nations* (1776).[36]

In the *History of England* published by the great philosopher David Hume between 1754 and 1761, the debate over the emergence of Parliament within feudal society broadened into an analysis of the mechanisms of constitutional change. Hume had discussed social morality and the origins of property, justice and government in his *Treatise of Human Nature* and *Enquiry Concerning Human Understanding*, in which he already showed dissatisfaction with the concept of 'the natural' in human affairs, and a preoccupation with the notion of causality or 'necessary connexion'. We simply 'learn by experience the frequent conjunction of objects'. 'Anything like *connexion* between them' is beyond our comprehension. In politics as in the rest of life 'new principles of conduct and behaviour' could not be derived from contemplation of the course of nature: 'the experienced train of events' was the true 'standard by which we regulate our conduct', and we judge the veracity of the historian by our own experience of mankind. Hume managed to incorporate into a clear and engrossing narrative the whole range of sources made available by the antiquaries, which were opened to him on his appointment in 1752 as librarian of the Faculty of Advocates.[37]

In the medieval volumes of his *History*, the last to be written, Hume recognized that there was a kind of system in feudal governments which 'was preferable to the universal licence which had everywhere preceded it'. The true seeds of advance in medieval

---

[36] H. T. Dickinson, 'The Eighteenth Century Debate on the "Glorious Revolution"', *History*, 61 (1976); Smith, *The Gothic Bequest*, pp. 6–7; Peter Gay, *The Enlightenment: An Interpretation*, 2 vols. (London: Weidenfeld and Nicolson, 1966–70); Peter Stein, *Legal Evolution* (Cambridge: CUP, 1980), pp. 19, 33, 111–12, 117–18.

[37] *A Treatise of Human Nature*, ed. Selby-Bigge (Oxford: Clarendon Press, 1888), pp. 474–5, 493, 534, 541; *Enquiry Concerning Human Understanding*, in *Hume: Theory of Knowledge*, ed. D. C. Yalden-Thomson (Edinburgh: Nelson, 1951), pp. 71, 75, 78, 92, 147; 'The Life of David Hume, Esq. Written by Himself', prefixed to his *The History of England*, new edn, 8 vols. (London, 1812), i.vii, x–xiv; Duncan Forbes, *Hume's Philosophical Politics* (Cambridge: CUP, 1975), pp. 308–10.

England lay, however, in the accidental discovery of Justinian's law-books about the year 1100. The study of law and 'civil employments and occupations' soon became honourable among the English gentry, whose island situation released them from the need to be constantly in arms. So Hume makes the growth of the common law one of the main themes of thirteenth-century history. He had read his Coke and Hale, and followed them in emphasizing Edward's legislative achievement, though he judges it an imprudent statute that allowed the barons to entail their estates and build up great blocks of family lands. It was characteristic of Hume and his age that he combined enthusiasm for the laws of the king with an uncomprehending prejudice against revealed religion and its laws. Edward's merits included his activity 'in restraining the usurpations of the church', and an absence of superstition, 'the vice chiefly of weak minds' (apart, that is, from an 'ardour for Crusades', which was in any case really a 'passion for glory'). Though 'a friend to law and justice', the English Justinian could not be called 'an enemy to arbitrary power', which was evident in his violence towards the Jews as well as the clergy, and in his unleashing of 'the new and illegal commission of Trailbaston'. Moreover, his treatment of the Welsh and the Scots, and his transactions with the papacy, displayed 'that neglect, almost total, of truth and justice which sovereign states discover in their transactions with each other, an evil universal and inveterate', and a source of misery to the human race. Nevertheless, 'the advantage was so visible in uniting the whole island under one head, that those who give great indulgence to reasons of state in the measures of Princes, will not be apt to regard this part of his conduct with much severity'. The ambiguities in Hume's attitude to Edward stem from his perception that social processes and the interplay of institutions are more the stuff of history than the actions, heroic or wicked, of great individuals. The ultimate proof of Edward's greatness was his possession of the art of managing the barons, which John and Henry had conspicuously lacked. And that art consisted in exploiting trends which were European-wide – not only the growth of law and techniques of government, but also the increase of 'the lower and more industrious orders of the state' with whom the king could ally himself against the baronage. John was certainly vicious, though he never sought the protection of the emperor of Morocco by offering to become a Mahommedan. The significance of Magna Carta was not, however, that it tried to impose 'seemingly exorbitant' checks upon the king, but that it mitigated 'the rigours of the feudal law'; and not just for the barons, since they needed 'the concurrence of the people' and were forced to pass on some of their new-won liberties to the 'inferior ranks of men'.[38]

For Hume, the historian's business was to trace the building up of institutions by political invention and communal experience. The heart of his argument is a long appendix analysing 'The Feudal Government and Manners', which comes between the reigns of John and Henry III, and sets the observations of Spelman, Dugdale and Madox within Montesquieu's wider and more sociological vision. The 'feudal system' is seen to have provided the king with essential revenues, but by the end of the thirteenth century to have become an inadequate support for government in either peace or war. Older institutions which had become embedded in feudalism proved of more lasting worth, above all the uniquely English county courts. Even

the greatest Barons were obliged to attend the sheriffs in these courts, and to assist them in the administration of justice. By these means they received frequent and sensible admonitions of their dependence on the King or supreme magistrate: They formed a kind of community with their fellow Barons and freeholders: They were often drawn from their individual and independent state, peculiar to the feudal system; and were made members of a political body: And, perhaps, this institution of county courts in England has had greater effects on the government than has yet been distinctly pointed out by historians, or traced by antiquaries.

If the idea of a feudal constitution appealed naturally to an eighteenth-century parliament of landowners, it was derived from a thirteenth-century feudalism which Hume recognized as moving quickly away from its original purpose.[39]

In this perspective, Henry III's reign assumed new significance. To Hume the apparently 'frivolous events' of Henry III's fifty-six years cried out for the application of 'general theorems' which would enable the scientific historian 'to comprehend, in a few propositions, a great number of inferences and conclusions'. One of these propositions was that feudal rigours then began to be dissolved by the passion of avarice, and 'the common rights of mankind, the only rights that are entirely indefeasible', asserted themselves in the liberties, political and commercial, obtained by

[38] Hume, *History of England*, II.43, 85–9, 98, 141–2, 220, 222–3, 229–30, 234, 236, 273, 296–308, 319–23, III.305–6.
[39] *Ibid.*, II.122 (footnote), 130–2, 265; Smith, *The Gothic Bequest*, p. 50.

townsmen. Under Henry progress was still halting. The king himself is castigated for 'want of economy'; and emphasis is placed on the complaints, expressed in great councils 'which began to be called parliaments', that his exactions drove away foreign merchants and stifled commerce with all nations. The judgement on de Montfort is similarly negative, and Hume regards the passions Simon provoked, and his popular canonization, with the puzzled consternation of an enlightened philosopher who was disturbed by the party strife of his own time. It was by 'hypocritical pretensions of sanctity' that the earl 'gained the favour of the zealots and clergy', by a 'seeming concern for public good [that] he acquired the affections of the public'. The populace of the cities and 'all the disorderly ruffians of England' he roused by simply offering hopes of plunder. He and the baronial party were in reality out to advance their own power. He cannot be praised for appointing conservators of the peace, the lineal ancestors of justices of the peace – this 'new kind of magistracy, endowed with new and arbitrary powers', were the agents of Simon's tyranny. It was impossible even to give him credit for originating the House of Commons by his summons of that famous parliament of 1265, for great institutions were not suddenly invented. 'Leicester's policy, if we must ascribe to him so great a blessing, only forwarded by some years an institution, for which the general state of things had already prepared the nation.'[40]

Only as feudalism and 'the old Gothic fabric' decayed, knights settled down as landed gentry and representatives of their shires in parliament, and borough representatives were joined with them, did commerce start to flourish. There could be little progress as long as merchants from Brabant were liable to be ambushed in Berkshire by members of the king's own household, as happened in 1249; or Simon de Montfort was prepared to justify piracy in the Channel by his allies from the Cinque Ports with the boast that 'the kingdom could well enough subsist within itself, and needed no intercourse with foreigners'; or interest rates climbed to 50%. As for agriculture, Hume takes the great variations in corn prices allowed for in the assize of bread of 35 Henry III (which were still lower than some chroniclers recorded) as clear proof of bad tillage. He calculates that the average price of corn was half 'the middling price' in his own time, but of cattle 'near ten times lower', which accords with the rule that 'in all uncivilized nations, cattle, which

[40] Hume, *History of England*, II.94, 155, 167, 178, 181, 185, 193–4, 198, 215–16.

propagate of themselves, bear always a lower price than corn, which requires more art and stock to render it plentiful'. Hume investigated no further the purely social and economic factors (such as a taste for luxury) which Adam Smith and other Scots were placing at the centre of the civilizing process. Society was formed by the institutions of government and law, rather than by economics. A landmark in the growth of the arts no less than of liberty was the definitive arrival of borough representatives in what Hume anticipated Stubbs in regarding as the model parliament of 1295.[41]

Ultimately institutions were much more important in history than great men, who too often frustrated progress. Edward resisted to the end the campaign for the Charters, and damaged commerce by his expulsion of the Jews, though this unintentionally turned Englishmen into usurers ('as it is impossible for a nation to subsist without lenders of money'). He made laws for the protection of merchants from overseas; but he also enforced the barbaric rule that made 'one answerable for the debts, and even the crimes, of another that came from the same country'; and he showed his ignorance of commerce by forbidding the export of coin. Even in the areas of government and law, Edward's measures had unintended results: the repression of associations for robbery and violence simply turned men to 'formal combinations to support each other in law-suits'. Hume is contemptuous of his own 'rude and unpolished nation' in the middle ages. The famous words of Sir Thomas Kirkpatrick to Robert Bruce when the latter was unsure if he had killed the Red Comyn, 'I'll mak siccar', has to be translated into the Augustan 'I will secure him.' It was doubtful, thought Hume, if Scotland possessed any history worth Edward's while to destroy. But England could maintain its territorial conquests no more successfully than any other European country at that time, except when they were over a primitive society like the Welsh, still fixed in pastoralism.[42]

Hume's blend of narrative and reflection on its political meaning has remained one of the most characteristic styles of British

[41] *Ibid.*, II.224–5, 227–8, 266, 272–8, 290, 566–8, III. 301–6; for the attack on the Brabantine merchants, see M. T. Clanchy, 'Did Henry III Have a Policy?', *History*, 53 (1968), pp. 203–11; *David Hume's Political Essays* ed. Charles W. Hendel, (New York: Liberal Arts Press, 1953), xv,pp. 123ff; Adam Smith, *Wealth of Nations*, introduced by E. R. A. Seligman, 2 vols. (London: Everyman's Library, 1910), I.362; Forbes, *Hume's Philosophical Politics*, p. 226.

[42] Hume, *History of England*, II.236–7, 245, 249, 282–3, 290, 298, 316–17, 320, 324–5.

history-writing. This history is confident of progress, not because there are laws of social improvement, but because it believes that human passions for truth and freedom continually reassert themselves. If it cannot integrate the forces of order and of spontaneity, it at least holds them in balance: on the one hand, the grand design of an Edward I, and on the other 'the undesigned development of the material which the design attempted to mould' (that is, the nation). In this perspective, the historian's concern is with the mechanisms of constitutional change. The first effect on English historians of the frightening turbulence across the Channel was to heighten their sense of England's long-term constitutional achievement. The spirit of the nation asserted so vengefully in France in the years after 1789 could be traced in England also, but there it had worked itself out more benevolently through long centuries. Henry Hallam saw the framing of Magna Carta as England's first 'national' event which had brought all free men together in an 'almost sacramental' communion.[43]

The epic *Constitutional History of England* published by William Stubbs between 1873 and 1878, one of the great books of the nineteenth century, aimed to be more than a particularly detailed account in the Humean mode of the 'expansion of the machinery' of the constitution: it was to trace constitutional development as the expression of 'the spirit of liberty'. In his inaugural lecture as Professor of Modern History at Oxford in 1867, Stubbs had insisted that Ancient History studied a dead world, but Modern History (in which he included the medieval period) was the examination of 'the living, working, thinking, growing world of today'. There was a continuity of life and development' which joined the present to the early medieval times when the 'principle of nationalities' was established, and further back to the foundation of the Church, which 'brought into the world and proclaimed and made possible . . . the principle of freedom'. The whole period from 1155 to 1215 is treated in the last two chapters of volume I of the *Constitutional History* as a time of 'the growing together of the local machinery' of Anglo-Saxon society with 'the administrative organisation' imposed by the Angevin kings; a 'continuous growing together and new development, which distinguishes the process of organic life from that of mere mechanic contrivance', culminating in a national unity of blood, language and law. The century which began with Magna Carta was 'an age of growth' of

[43] Stubbs, *CH*, II.304, 306, III. 632, 638.

another kind, 'of luxuriant, even premature development, the end of which was to strengthen and likewise to define the several constituent parts of the organic whole'. It is announced as a time of 'luxuriant invention' in architecture and science as in politics and society, and is covered in the first two chapters of the second volume (chapters 14 and 15 of the whole), which are entitled 'The Struggle for the Charters' and 'The System of Estates, and the Constitution under Edward I'. The power of Stubbs's work derives from this sense that at the heart of English history, of any national history, lies the shaping of institutions (the 'machinery') in the melting-pot of political conflict but under the pressure of longer-lasting social ideals. The spirit of liberty showed itself better in the institutions of the whole people than in the politics of the great.[44]

Chapter 14 of the *Constitutional History* traces the political struggle through the reigns of Henry and Edward in a fairly conventional way, and may be judged an advance on Hume's account mainly in the greater detail and precision made possible by the historical enterprise of the intervening hundred years. The long-held concern of Parliament for the national records which had lain scattered for centuries between Westminster, the Tower of London and the lawyers' quarter of the City, had born fruit in the printing of the *Rolls of Parliament* from 1278 to 1503 in accordance with an order of the House of Lords of 1767 (six volumes appeared by 1783 and an index volume in 1832); in the appointment of the first Record Commission in 1800; and in the creation of the Public Record Office by an act of 1838. By the expiry of their term in 1848 the Record Commissioners had published, just in relation to the thirteenth century, the *Statutes of the Realm*; a new edition of Rymer's *Foedera*; transcripts of the chancery rolls of charters and letters patent to 1216, and of letters close to 1227; abstracts of cases in the king's central courts (*Placitorum Abbreviatio*); extracts from the Fine Rolls of Henry III (recording payments due to the king); the records of countrywide surveys of the 1270s into the king's landed rights and the abuses of local officials (the 'Hundred Rolls'); baronial justifications of their franchises, pleaded before the king's justices in eyre (*Placita de Quo Warranto*); the valuation of ecclesiastical benefices made *c.* 1291 in preparation for a crusading tax (the *Taxatio Ecclesiastica*); and a vast collection of *Parliamentary Writs and*

[44] Stubbs, *CH*, I. 1, 585, 681, II.1–2; *idem*, *Seventeen Lectures on the Study of Medieval and Modern History* (Oxford: Clarendon Press, 1886), pp. 2, 13–15, 19, 22–3; J. W. Burrow, *A Liberal Descent. Victorian Historians and the English Past* (Cambridge: CUP, 1981), pp. 145–7.

Writs of Military Summons, edited by Sir Francis Palgrave, who was to become in 1851 the first Deputy Keeper of Public Records under the formal custodian, the master of the rolls (the senior chancery judge). It was a master of the rolls who launched in 1857, while the Record Office was still rising on the site of the Rolls Chapel in Chancery Lane, the printing of a series of *Chronicles and Memorials of Great Britain and Ireland during the Middle Ages*, to run in parallel with the publication of the government records by the Record Office staff. For the thirteenth century the scholars of 'the Rolls Series', Stubbs among them, quickly produced a volume of London customs, the five priceless volumes of monastic annals, collections of the letters of Henry III and of Robert Grosseteste and the chronicles of Bartholomew Cotton and Peter Langtoft. The publication of the records of government had a special meaning for Stubbs's generation, which saw the burgeoning of government ministries and the belated creation of a professional civil service, the Record Office's own staff among its ranks. Administrative history was becoming the new Whig history, its end the modern state rather than the parliamentary constitution. In his inaugural lecture, Stubbs looked forward optimistically to a time, which could 'not be far off', when 'all the records of the medieval world will be in print'. His own *Select Charters*, published in 1870, was to start generations of undergraduates on their historical studies with their feet planted amongst administrative documents.[45]

Chapter 15 of the *Constitutional History* is remarkable in three respects: for the extent to which it is written from original sources (chronicles, Palgrave's *Parliamentary Writs*, Patent and Close Rolls), with hardly a reference to a secondary authority; for the comparative method Stubbs employs in the interpretation of the *administrative* evidence; and (the real originality of his work) for the way he uses the evidence to root Parliament firmly in the *social* structure. 'The idea of a constitution in which each class of society should, so soon as it was fitted for the trust, be admitted to a share of power and control, and in which national action should be determined by

---

[45] Stubbs, *CH*, ii.96–105, 111ff, 165; *A Bibliography of English History to 1485*, ed. Edgar B. Graves (Oxford: Clarendon Press, 1975), pp. 111–18; *British National Archives*, Government Publications Sectional Lists, No. 24 (London HMSO, frequently revised); David Knowles, *Great Historical Enterprises* (Edinburgh: Nelson, 1963), cap. 4: 'The Rolls Series'; Philippa Levine, 'History in the Archives: The Public Record and its Staff', *EHR*, 101 (1986), pp. 20–41; Stubbs, *Seventeen Lectures*, pp. 11–12; T. F. Tout, *Chapters in the Administrative History of Medieval England*, 6 vols. (Manchester: Manchester UP, 1920–33), i.2–3.

the balance maintained between the forces thus combined, never perhaps presented itself to the mind of any medieval politician.' But there was a general tendency in medieval Europe towards the creation of 'national assemblies composed of properly arranged and organized Estates', a tendency impelled on the one hand by the rise of a third estate of townsmen demanding recognition, and on the other by the wish of the king to mobilize 'the energy of the united people in some great emergency'. In England the culmination of the tendency was not, for Stubbs, Simon de Montfort's isolated political expedient of 1265 but the 'model parliament' of November 1295, in which Edward added representatives of 'the whole body of beneficed clergy, as an estate of the realm possessing taxable property and class interests', to the lords (who already included prelates), and the knights and burgesses. The consummation of 1295 explained how the entire nation was able to assert itself against the king in that crisis of 1297 which historians back to Polydore Vergil had seen as the political climax of Edward's reign.[46]

The bulk of chapter 15 is taken up with showing how nationwide estates could form in the context of strong local institutions. Hume had pointed to the crucial role of the county court, which Stubbs now sees as the first 'really exhaustive assembly' of the several orders of society, and as such comparable to the provincial estates of France. The estate of the clergy was given coherence by its convocations and synods, the estate of the baronage by summonses to great councils and for military service. But the claim of the nation as a whole to make representations to the king in return for the payment of taxes was expressed by the county community, and it was in the county court that the boundaries of the political community were set. The third estate of the commons was defined there in a way peculiar to England. Because the English aristocracy was not a caste, the writs which ordered the sheriffs to return knights to represent the shires could have the effect of joining the lesser landowners to the burgesses who were returned for the towns by the same procedure, and detached them from the barons who received individual summonses to Parliament. More than an

---

[46] Stubbs, *CH*, I.iii, 35, 198, II. 166–7, 204, 233 (a reference to Brady), 235–6, 266–7, 304–8, 312; *idem, Select Charters and Other Illustrations of English Constitutional History from the Earliest Times to the Reign of Edward the First*, 9th edn, revised H. W. C. Davis (Oxford: Clarendon Press, 1913), pp. xv–xvi; Burrow, *A Liberal Descent*, pp. 106–7, 119, 124–5, 134–5, 139, 141, 144–5; and *idem, Evolution and Society* (Cambridge: CUP, 1966), p. 141.

administrative procedure was needed to forge the local notables into the commons in Parliament, however: it was provided by their generations of co-operation in the ancient local assemblies, from long before the king employed them in 'the execution of the remedial measures which form so large a part of the political history of the [thirteenth] century'. Stubbs makes the local communities embodied in the Commons achieve political influence too quickly, but his picture is generally convincing because he keeps a balance between social forces and political expedients. He knows that Parliament was just one element of the developing machinery for the exercise of royal power, along with keepers of the peace, justices of assize and gaol delivery, commissions to array troops, contracts with captains and the syphoning of money from the exchequer to the wardrobe to finance military campaigns; and that it was overshadowed by the king's small permanent council. Political improvisation produced the confusion of 'great councils' and 'parliaments': a term not restricted to representative assemblies. In reality the Commons were a marginal appendage of the Lords – and the largest section of the community, the peasants and artisans, were not represented at all. One whole estate remained outside the parliamentary constitution altogether, their lives regulated by customs applied in the manorial courts, customs 'rarely touched by statute'.[47]

THE TRIUMPH OF ADMINISTRATIVE AND SOCIAL HISTORY

The *Constitutional History* is the last epic narrative of English history. After Stubbs, the Whig history to which he had given a new twist 'broke into tributaries'. Political, administrative, legal, economic, cultural and intellectual history have developed as separate specialisms, and few historians have dared to claim expertise in more than one or two of them. Their chronologies are quite different, political history finding its characteristic expression in a fast-moving story of events, social history in a more anthropological and synchronic description of complex, intermittent and above all gradual processes of change. The weaving together of the more and more specialized disciplines of political and social history has become increasingly hard, but the tension between political innovation and social continuity is a permanent stimulus to historiography because it is a fact of life. The communities' resistance

[47] *CH*, II.166–318.

to a centralized state showed itself in the second half of the
nineteenth century in the gathering pace with which county
historical societies were founded and local records printed. Particularly striking is the flow of editions of manorial records.[48]

An edition of a roll of criminal cases heard in 1221 in his native
county of Gloucestershire was the first book published (at his own
expense) by F. W. Maitland. Then a practising but not very
successful lawyer, Maitland was apparently encouraged in his early
explorations of the Public Record Office in 1884 by his friend Paul
Vinogradoff, a Russian scholar who had come to London in pursuit
of his researches on medieval land tenure. Over the next two
decades, back at Cambridge as Reader and then Downing Professor
of the Laws of England, he made himself the virtual patron saint
of English historians by a series of breath-taking raids on the public
records. His method was to fasten on a particular record or law-
book – Domesday Book; a plea-roll; a Year Book of reports of
legal arguments; Bracton's great treatise *On the Laws and Customs
of England*, along with a large thirteenth-century collection of cases
which was believed to be 'Bracton's Note Book'; or the records of
the Lenten Parliament of 1305 – and analyse its make-up to reveal
the political and social circumstances of its origin. In the introductions to *Select Pleas in Manorial and Other Seignorial Courts in the
Reigns of Henry III and Edward I* (1889) and to *Memoranda de
Parliamento* (the records of the 1305 parliament published as a final
flourish of the Rolls Series in 1893), in *Domesday Book and Beyond*
(1897), in *Township and Borough* and in *Roman Canon Law in the
Church of England* (both 1898), he injected a new excitement into
historical research and established the monograph on a particular
issue as a normal way of presenting it.[49]

[48] Burrow, *A Liberal Descent*, p. 294; John Sturrock, *Structuralism* (London: Paladin,
1986), pp. 57–68 (on the different chronologies); the publications of record
societies, central and local are listed by E.L.C. Mullins in *Texts and Calendars*,
vol. I: *–1956*, and vol. II: *1957–1982* (Royal Historical Society Guides and
Handbooks, no. 7, London 1958, and no. 12, London, 1983); *Bibliography of
English History to 1485*, ed. Graves, pp. 666–91.
[49] G. R. Elton, *F. W. Maitland* (London: Weidenfeld and Nicolson, 1985); S. F. C.
Milsom, 'F. W. Maitland', *Proceedings of the British Academy*, 66 (1982 for 1980),
pp. 265–81; *Selected Historical Essays of F. W. Maitland*, intr. Helen M. Cam
(Cambridge: CUP, 1957); F. M. Powicke, *Modern Historians and the Study of
History* (London: Odhams Press, 1955), p. 10; F. W. Maitland, *Roman Canon
Law in the Church of England* (London, 1898), p. 52; *idem*, 'William Stubbs,
Bishop of Oxford', in *The Collected Papers of Frederic William Maitland*, ed. H. A. L.
Fisher, 3 vols. (Cambridge: CUP, 1911), III.495–511: reprinted in *Selected*

The argument of the introduction to *Memoranda de Parliamento* that the essence of a parliament was the king's council receiving petitions, not the attendance of representatives, has been taken as a fundamental attack on the conclusions of Stubbs. Yet Maitland expressed the greatest admiration for the way the *Constitutional History* combined the narrative power of the great historian with an understanding of institutions worthy of a lawyer. In the writing of his most extended work, *The History of English Law before the Time of Edward I* (published in 1895 with Sir Frederick Pollock as nominal co-author), he avowedly tried to follow Stubbs's 'highly original plan, which by alternating "analytical" and "annalistic" chapters weaves a web so stout that it would do credit to the roaring loom of time'. Though it risked putting off both those who wanted a story of events and those who looked for 'a natural history of the body politic and its organs', it may 'be suggested that in the present state of our knowledge concerning men and their environment both methods must be used'. Maitland was in truth Stubbs's heir in his concern with the common life of men and their environment, on which the politics of the rulers were an excrescence. 'He wished to know and understand the people of all ranks in medieval England', says G. R. Elton, 'and therefore wrote history that cannot be confined in such artificial categories as legal, or constitutional, or indeed social.' But it was his legal training that gave him the imaginative insight into the patterns of existence of people in the past which comes from the analysis of particular cases and the efforts of judges and juries to sort out the issues. The most vivid passages of *The History of English Law* are descriptions, often couched in the present tense, of what Maitland sees happening in the roll he has in front of him; how, for instance, the justices question the hundred jurors about the deeds of suspected felons, or a villein comes into the court of the manor and claims land as his by hereditary right.[50]

Maitland was sensitive to the charge that an account of the past without a core of political narrative was not history at all. He

Historical Essays, intr. Cam; *Letters of F. W. Maitland*, ed. C. H. S. Fifoot (Selden Society, supp. series, vol. 1, London, 1965), pp. 86, 143–4, 195, 225–8; H. E. Bell, *Maitland: A Critical Assessment* (London: Black, 1965), pp. 121–3; James Campbell, *Stubbs and the English State* (Stenton Lecture, University of Reading, 1989), p. 12.

[50] Elton, *F. W. Maitland*, pp. 30, 98; *Letters*, ed. Fifoot, p. 195; F. Pollock and F. W. Maitland, *The History of English Law before the Time of Edward I*, 2nd edn, 2 vols. (Cambridge: CUP, 1898), I.xxiii–xxv, 376–9, II.646–7; cf. *ibid.* II.358–9 for stories of intestacy, and II.498 for a description of the physical penalties for thieving.

professed to being incapable of telling a story in the way that Stubbs had done, and at the same time insisted a little too much that historians could 'not write about the growth of parliament without writing about the law of land tenure', or about 'the liberty of the subject' except 'in a discourse on civil and criminal procedure'. The 'annalistic' chapters of *The History of English Law* are certainly the least inspiring, because they do no more than sketch the institutional context of legal growth in terms of courts and procedures. The claims for the importance of what happened between 1154 and 1272 which Maitland sets out in a peroration to the *History* appear both conventional and almost embarrassingly inflated. 'It was a critical moment in English legal history and therefore in the innermost history of our land and of our race'; 'a perilous moment' when old indigenous customs were brought into contact with the new science of Roman law, and English law might have succumbed to 'misunderstood and alien institutions' or alternatively refused to learn from them. It was 'the parting of the ways of the two most vigorous systems of law that the modern world has seen, the French and the English', which was not a disagreement 'about what may seem the weightier matters of jurisprudence . . . but about "mere matters of procedure", as some would call them': whether trial should be by jury, or by the judges' interrogation of witnesses. It was

for the good of the whole world that one race stood apart from its neighbours, turned away its eyes at an early time from the fascinating pages of the *Corpus Iuris*, and, more Roman than the Romanist, made the great experiment of a new formulary system [that is, of legal actions each begun by a writ appropriate to the dispute] . . . These few men who gathered at Westminster round Pateshull and Raleigh and Bracton [judges in Henry III's reign] were penning writs that would run in the name of kingless commonwealths on the other shore of the Atlantic Ocean; they were making right and wrong for us and for our children.

Straining to provide a story, Maitland exaggerated the precocious development of English law and the importance of procedures within it; and ignored the similarities of legal innovation in England and in France, such as the common development of actions by bill (rather than by writ). Modern research has shown him too preoccupied with the development of concepts of property in the king's courts, and neglectful of their real origins in the relationships of feudal lord and tenant. This is an example of his excessive belief in the continuous production of the law by the judges, which entailed a playing-down of statute law (and had a part in his choosing to end the *History* on the eve of Edward I's legislation). Finally he was guilty, it is said, of teleology: of an unhistorical telling of the story backwards from a known result, the state of English law in the late thirteenth century, which (like Stubbs) he regarded as a sort of consummation.[51]

This final criticism is largely rebutted by Maitland's explanation that he could go no further than the works of the great antiquaries down to Madox, and the publications in his own century of the Record Commissioners, the Rolls Series and learned societies such as 'the Camden or the Surtees, the Pipe Roll or the Selden' would safely take him; there was no going beyond 1272 till the scandalous neglect of the Year Books was remedied. Insofar as the criticism has substance, it is because teleology is difficult to avoid in tracing the formation of social patterns, especially when it is done from sources (like the manor-court rolls) which became available only at the end of the period under review. Maitland's contribution to history-writing stemmed from his genius, acknowledged to far outweigh his faults, in reading from the plea-rolls the ways of life of the different groups in English society, and especially of the local communities of township and borough. The chief story in Maitland's work is the emergence of the 'moral personalities' of these groups, as it was reflected by their activity in the courts. Telling it involved a full understanding of the economic arrange-ments of the medieval village, and of the field system of his beloved Cambridge; and though he deferred to Ashley, Cun-ningham and Vinogradoff on agricultural matters it was Maitland who did most to bring the village alive as a social unit. His priorities are shown by the fact that one of his earliest enterprises as the first literary director of the Selden Society, founded in 1887 to advance the knowledge of the history of English law, was an edition of thirteenth-century pleas in the courts of the manors of the abbots of Bec, Ramsey and Battle, and of the abbess of Romsey. At the other end of the spectrum, in the *Memoranda de Parliamento* he does not so much demolish Stubbs's view of the importance of social estates in constitutional development, as show another way in which Parliament was a response to social evolution in its role as the final court of appeal for petitioners, who were local communities as often as they were individuals.[52]

---

[51] Pollock and Maitland, *HEL*, I.xxxiv–xxxvi, 224, II. 672–4; Milsom, 'F. W. Maitland', pp. 275ff; Elton, *F. W. Maitland*, pp. 32, 45, 50–3, 60.

[52] Pollock and Maitland, HEL, I.xxxv, 362–4, II. 672; F. W. Maitland, *Township and Borough* (Cambridge: CUP, 1898), pp. 106ff; *Select Pleas in Manorial and Other*

While Maitland extended the social dimension in Stubbs's constitutional history by his legal history, Cunningham, Ashley and Thorold Rogers were doing the same under the banner of economic history. William Cunningham, who graduated with Maitland at the top of the Moral Science tripos in 1872, lectured at Harvard and at Cambridge and ended his career as archdeacon of Ely, came near to writing epic history in the Stubbsian manner, at least in aspiration. His *Growth of English Industry and Commerce* (first edition 1882) exhibits the national strain in this early economic history. The subject is conceived as the tracing of the State's promotion of its interests by economic policy, a theme which replaced the growth of the constitution in relevance, as late nineteenth-century Britain faced an increasingly competitive world. It was a practical study aimed at maximizing national wealth. Cunningham's account of thirteenth-century England is still divided, according to the constitutional historian's scheme, between sections on 'Feudalism' and on 'Representation and Legislation', the change-over coming in 1272. But in 'Feudalism' it is the growth of royal administration, particularly in relation to towns and foreign trade, that provides the main thread. There are also the most coherent descriptions so far of the municipal and manorial economies, which are valuable for their accounts of the sources but appear formal and abstract beside Maitland's lively examples. Typically, Cunningham emphasizes the value of the Hundred Rolls, the findings of a royal inquiry of 1274–5, as evidence of the growth of the economy since Domesday and especially of the wool trade. Manorial and borough courts are held to inform us chiefly about standards of fair dealing and about the ambiguous attitude to foreigners, whose trade was welcomed but competition resented. The beginnings of 'national economic organization' did not come until the reign of Edward I, from which time 'the local institutions were gradually superseded by the more effective work of Parliament', and royal legislation regulated trade and protected foreign merchants.[53]

In other hands political economy was losing its adjective and

---

Seignorial Courts, vol. 1, ed. F. W. Maitland (Selden Society, vol. 2, London, 1889), pp. lxviii, lxxi–lxxii; see the introduction to the *Memoranda de Parliamento*, ed. F. W. Maitland (Rolls Series, London, 1893), most easily accessible in *Selected Historical Essays*, intr. Cam, pp. 83–4.

[53] S. Collini and D. N. Winch, *That Noble Science of Politics* (Cambridge: CUP, 1983), pp. 247–75; W. Cunningham, *The Growth of English Industry and Commerce during the Early and Middle Ages*, vol. 1, 5th edn (Cambridge: CUP, 1910), pp. xvi–xvii, 175–82, 232–3, 237, 247–9, 261, 378–80.

being seen as a social rather than a political science. Before Cunningham, or Stubbs and Maitland, did their main work, the original figure of J. E. Thorold Rogers had started to gather the evidence for a true economic history of the English people from the thirteenth century onward. A friendship with the much older Richard Cobden, whose sister married one of Rogers's brothers, helped to turn this Oxford curate and classics don into a radical politician with an interest in the economic conditions of the working class. From 1858 till his death in 1890 he was Professor of Statistics and Economic Science at King's College, London, and for five years in the 1860s also Professor of Political Economy at Oxford, losing that chair because of his politics. Having resigned his orders, from 1880 to 1886 he sat as a member of parliament for Southwark and Bermondsey. He wrote student textbooks on political and 'social economy', but his great work was *A History of Agriculture and Prices in England from 1259 to 1793*, published in seven volumes between 1866 and 1902, the conclusions of which were drawn out in *Six Centuries of Work and Wages: The History of English Labour* (1884) and *The Economic Interpretation of History* (1888). For Rogers, the solution of current social mischiefs was to be found in history, not in the theories of political economy. Economic history could not avoid partisan comparisons of the present with the past, yet it stood behind all other sorts of history, and was indeed irrefutable in its attention to facts, in contrast to the 'doubtful meaning' of constitutional and legal history.[54]

A History of Agriculture and Prices begins in 1259 because Rogers found continuous information from that year (chiefly in the muniment-rooms of Merton and other Oxford colleges): 'it would seem that landowners began about that time to keep regular accounts'. A price series beginning so 'accidentally' and planned to be carried on for centuries was unlikely to support a view of thirteenth-century institutions as any sort of consummation. Something of the tone of Stubbs and Maitland nevertheless appears in the importance Rogers gives to the village community, and in his contention that 'during this long reign of Henry III the mass of the English people passed from the condition of serfs, perhaps even of slaves, into that of freemen'. Such fundamental but insensible changes were revealed only 'by comparing states of society at

[54] Collini and Winch, *That Noble Science of Politics*, pp. 264, 269–74; J. E. Thorold Rogers, *The Economic Interpretation of History* (London: Fisher Unwin, 1888), pp. vi–vii, ix–xiii, 1–2, 4–5, 12; J. E. Thorold Rogers, *Six Centuries of Work and Wages*, 8th edn (London: Swan Sonnenschein, 1906), p. 301.

different epochs': in this case by setting the evidence of the late thirteenth-century manor-court rolls against that collected by Madox 'as to the state of the poorer classes in the days of John'. Though the 'moral and material progress of society almost always escapes the attention of the contemporaneous historian', the differences between Roger of Howden's and Matthew Paris's criticisms of government were also revealing: the change from a general bewailing of oppression to 'indignant comment on unwise administration' was itself proof of the 'the material progress which marked Henry's government', and of a radical change in the general condition of the people'. For economists the significant events of Edward's reign were the legislation to permit the tying up of landed estates by entail (though the social effects of that did not work through until the fifteenth century), and impositions which confirmed that wool was the source of England's strength among nations.[55]

Of the two great themes pursued by nineteenth-century historians, the emergence of the English system of government and the evolution of agrarian society in England, it was the first which most obviously continued to draw sustenance from thirteenth-century history. But there has been a marked shift of interest from constitutional to administrative history, no doubt influenced by the enormous growth of central government in response to the emergencies of the twentieth century. In his *Chapters in the Administrative History of Medieval England*, published in six volumes between 1920 and 1923, T. F. Tout mined the records of central administration in the thirteenth and fourteenth centuries to get behind the surface events of politics in a quite different way from economic history, exposing the realities of bureaucratic rivalry and routine. Great councils and parliaments were always 'occasional and intermittent': administrative machinery operated continuously. The political pattern set in thirteenth-century England Tout presented as a struggle for control of the administrative machinery. As exchequer and chancery went 'out of court', other offices of the royal household remained to give immediate expression to the king's will, and to provide 'a counterpoise to public ministers inspired with aristocratic ideals'. A duplicate team of 'ministers of the household were set up over against the ministers of the state'.

[55] J. E. Thorold Rogers, *A History of Agriculture and Prices in England from 1259 to 1793*, 7 vols. (Oxford: Clarendon Press, 1866–1902), I.1–7; *idem, Economic Interpretation*, pp. 3, 8–9, 13, 16 and cap. 2; *idem, Six Centuries*, pp. 183–7, 218, cap. 6.

Personal favourites of the king were hated not for their unworthiness, but 'because they were the official heads of an organised court system, which, in practice, could make ineffective the action of public ministers and national parliaments controlled by the baronage'.[56]

The 'court system' had two pillars: the privy seal, the importance of which Tout learnt from the treatise of a French scholar published in 1908, and the royal wardrobe, its rise to dominance very much his own discovery. Both the wardrobe, as the place where the money paid into the king's chamber was stored and disbursed, and from which military operations and other great royal ventures came to be financed, and the privy seal, needed to give force to the wardrobe's instructions now that the great seal was at a distance with chancery and exchequer, emerged into the light of day in John's reign. Their potential for creating political conflict appeared for the first time in 1231–2, when Henry III, newly of age, made his Poitevin kinsman, Peter des Rivaux, treasurer of the chamber and wardrobe, and deposed the justiciar, Hubert de Burgh (ending the justiciarship as the highest administrative office). Tout makes des Rivaux's appointment, and his dismissal under baronial hostility in 1234, almost more significant then the upheaval of 1258, when the barons permanently eliminated the alien element from the wardrobe but took no serious measures to alter the machine they had got into their hands or stem the development which had continued since 1234. In response to the demands of Edward I's campaigning the wardrobe split into specialized branches, and though still following the court it acquired permanent bases or treasuries at Westminster and the Tower of London. 'Besides its domestic aspect' it was developing 'as a complementary or supplementary department of state'. The privy seal was likewise being used more and more 'as a state seal . . . employed in numberless cases that had no direct relation to the household or the king's private affairs'. Towards the end of the reign a new 'secret seal' was therefore required to expedite household business. According to Tout's story, the barons awoke to the dangers of the wardrobe system when it was almost past its peak. At the end of the century they began to complain about the use made of the privy seal, and it became 'a constitutional

---

[56] Tout, *Chapters in the Administrative History of Medieval England*, 1.4–5, 20–1, 178–9, II.146.

principle' with them 'to uphold the traditional position of the exchequer and chancery'.[57]

Tout's attempt to identify the state in administrative terms, as the offices of government which had moved out of the king's household into the sphere of 'public accountability', was valuable if only because it provoked subsequent historians to argue the case that no one thought in such terms until long after the thirteenth century. Instead of departmental rivalry they have seen only kings trying to use whichever group of their servants was best at extracting money from a naturally resentful baronage. Any constitutional evolution they still located in parliament and the law-courts, though here too the king's administrative interest was seen as predominating. In other areas the constitutional or at least institutional approach was still being fruitfully applied: to the history of medieval towns in Charles Gross's *Gild Merchant*, published back in 1890, and his Selden Society volumes of *Cases concerning the Law Merchant*, completed by Hubert Hall (1908–32); in Mary Bateson's *Borough Customs* (1904–6); in *British Borough Charters* by Adolphus Ballard and James Tait, Tout's colleague at Manchester (1913–23); and in Tait's *Medieval English Borough* (1936). W. A. Morris applied it to *The Medieval English Sheriff to 1300* (1927); and Helen Cam to local institutions generally, in studies such as *The Hundred and the Hundred Rolls* (1930).[58]

If there has been an archetype of the administrative historian, it was H. G. Richardson, an exception to the growing academic monopoly of history-writing, since he followed a civil service career, becoming a principal in the Board of Agriculture and Fisheries, secretary of the Foot and Mouth Disease Research Committee and finally Secretary of the Tithe Redemption Commission. The centre of his interest could perhaps be described as the business transactions and environment of professional men, from the parish clergy of the thirteenth and fourteenth centuries who were the subject of his first essay of 1912, to the Jews whose money financed the market in land and supplied the coffers of the Angevin kings through a special exchequer, on whom he published a book in 1960. In between, Richardson produced an edition of the Memoranda Roll for the first year of King John (a valuable

---

[57] *Ibid.*, I.5, 23–5, 151–69, 200, 214–32, 242–3, 312, II.60, 66, 76–8, 131–45, 153–7, 227–31.

[58] S. B. Chrimes, *An Introduction to the Administrative History of Mediaeval England*, 3rd edn (Oxford: Blackwell, 1966), pp. 94–5; *Bibliography of English History to 1485*, ed. Graves.

introduction to the record of the exchequer's day to day workings); and articles on commissions of sewers (i.e. land drainage as a function of local government), the exchequer year, the training of clerks in business methods in medieval Oxford, the forgery of deeds, the marriage and coronation of John's queen, Isabella of Angouleme, the careers of some of John's civil servants and the operation of mercantile law in the London of Edward I. Histories of usury in canon law and on the administrative history of London from the eleventh to the fourteenth centuries were among projects worked on for decades but never brought to completion. In 1926 a new seam was opened up, when Richardson obtained two months' leave from his civil service duties to go and work in the Archives Nationales on the records of the Parlement of Paris. From this came a paper to the Royal Historical Society treating 'the origins of Parliament' in England in a comparative way, and a meeting in the Public Record Office with G. O. Sayles, a lecturer at Glasgow University, which developed into a forty-year collaboration on parliamentary history.[59]

Unlike Camden, Richardson believed that the French and English parliaments shared more than a name. On both sides of the Channel the name of parliament (originally signifying just a 'parley') was appropriated by new bodies with a mixture of political, administrative and judicial functions – but it was the last which required the regularity of meeting which turned intermittent occasions into permanent institutions. In its beginning the English parliament was what the French parliament remained until its abolition on the eve of the Revolution: a high court receiving petitions for justice. The proof was in the Provisions of Oxford, the subject of a joint paper by Richardson and Sayles in 1933, where a stipulation that there should be three parliaments a year at fixed times stood beside a mechanism for laying complaints against royal and baronial officials. Sayles had arrived at a similar view of parliament to Richardson's through his study of the court of king's bench. (He was to edit for the Selden Society seven volumes of 'select cases' from king's bench, rich in material on the whole administration of justice, the first three of which, covering the reign of Edward I, appeared between 1936 and 1939.) Parliament, the argument ran, was needed essentially as a court of final resort

---

[59] G. O. Sayles, 'Henry Gerald Richardson, 1884–1974', *Proceedings of the British Academy*, 61 (1975), pp. 497–521; details of writings in *Bibliography of English History to 1485*, ed. Graves.

above the two main central courts of king's bench and common pleas which existed in parallel from Henry III's majority, and it grew out of 'afforced' meetings of king's bench. In this perspective, a parliament was not defined by the presence of representatives, but by the provision of machinery at parliament time for the answering of petitions for justice. It was only 'from the standpoint of the modern age that the feeble beginnings of popular representation have any importance in parliamentary history', for the Commons neither presented nor discussed the petitions (which were addressed to the king and his council), at least in the thirteenth century.[60]

In articles under the joint authorship of Richardson and Sayles, and in Sayles's *King's Parliament of England*, published the year after Richardson's death in 1974, R. F. Treharne and J. G. Edwards came under attack for dissenting from these views. Treharne had published in 1932 the fullest account of the baronial reform movement of 1258 to 1263, and in subsequent papers continued to explore broad political and constitutional problems. For the Montfortians, he argued, the parliament evisaged in the Provisions of Oxford was an institution for bringing the Crown's rapidly growing executive power under the law: but in the event a permanent check on the king's government (*gubernaculum*) simply proved unacceptable to thirteenth-century opinion. Parliament remained an occasion, which it was inappropriate to credit with 'functions' either political or judicial. From his early paper of 1925 on 'The Personnel of the Commons in Parliament under Edward I and Edward II', Edwards showed an interest in the representatives of the shires and boroughs, the reason for whose summoning to appear 'with full powers' he elucidated in a fundamental article of 1934. (It was, he believed, so that they could commit the communities for whom they stood attorney to the payment of taxes agreed upon with king and lords.) In 1954 and 1955, Edwards went on the offensive, arguing against Richardson and Sayles that

---

[60] H. G. Richardson, 'The Origins of Parliament', the version printed in *Essays in Medieval History, Selected from the Transactions of the Royal Historical Society*, ed. R. W. Southern (London: Macmillan, 1968), pp. 159, 163, 166–7, 174–5, 177; H. G. Richardson and G. O. Sayles, 'The Provisions of Oxford', *Bulletin of the John Rylands Library*, 7 (1933), pp. 291–321; G. O. Sayles, *The Functions of the Medieval Parliament of England* (London: Hambledon, 1988), pp. 7–14, 28; *idem*, *The King's Parliament of England* (London: Arnold, 1975), pp. 63, 83ff; for the crucial role of the Council, see J. F. Baldwin, *The King's Council in England during the Middle Ages* (Oxford: Clarendon Press, 1913), and *Select Cases before the King's Council*, ed. I. S. Leadam and J. F. Baldwin (Selden Society, vol. 35, London, 1918).

neither justice nor any other type of business could be regarded as the 'essence' of parliament, which was valuable to the king precisely because of its omnicompetence. Furthermore, many parliamentary petitions asked for 'justice' only in a general sense that embraced such obviously political demands as redress for the abuses of the king's ministers in their official capacities. Richardson and Sayles relied too much on *Fleta*'s inclusion of the king's 'council in his parliaments' amongst the courts listed in what was after all a legal treatise; and they had illegitimately transferred Maitland's 'essence' of parliament from the physical *sessions* of the council to the judicial *functions* which they assumed to have been the council's most important business.[61]

In response Richardson and Sayles invoked 'the incomparable Maitland' to counterbalance the authority of Stubbs which they discerned behind Edwards's work. Their particular target was Stubbs's description of the parliament of 1295 as 'a perfect representation of the three estates . . . and a parliament constituted on the model of which every succeeding assembly bearing that name was formed'. They designed *The Governance of Mediaeval England from the Conquest to Magna Carta* (1963) as a general attack on the Stubbsian enterprise, devoting its entire first chapter to anatomizing 'Stubbs: Man and Historian'. The bishop, they maintained, had not done the necessary research in the record evidence: he had merely selected texts to bolster up foregone conclusions. But his chief offence was teleology and the anachronism which went with it. In the words of the French scholar, Charles Petit-Dutaillis,

[61] H. G. Richardson and G. O. Sayles, *Parliaments and Great Councils in Medieval England*, reprinted from the *Law Quarterly Review*, 76 (1961), pp. 33, 36, 47–8; Sayles, *The King's Parliament*, p. 63; R. F. Treharne, 'The Nature of Parliament in the Reign of Henry III', *EHR*, 74 (1959), reprinted in *Historical Studies of the English Parliament*, ed. E. B. Fryde and E. Miller, 2 vols. (Cambridge: CUP, 1970), I. 73, 81, 88–9; idem, 'The Constitutional Problem in Thirteenth-Century England', in *Essays in Medieval History Presented to Bertie Wilkinson*, ed. Sandquist and Powicke, pp. 55, 62, 70, 76; *idem*, 'Knights in the Period of Baronial Reform and Rebellion, 1258–65', *BIHR*, 21 (1948); J. G. Edwards, 'The Plena Potestas of English Parliamentary Representatives', in *Oxford Essays in Medieval History Presented to H. E. Salter* (Oxford: Clarendon Press, 1934), reprinted with 'The Personnel of the Commons', in *Historical Studies of the English Parliament*, ed. Fryde and Miller, I.136–67; cf. Sayles, *Functions*, p. 55, for a denial of the importance of *plena potestas*; J. G. Edwards, '"Justice" in Early English Parliaments', *BIHR*, 27 (1954), reprinted in *Historical Studies of the English Parliament*, ed. Fryde and Miller, I, at pp. 282, 287; *idem, Historians and the Medieval English Parliament*, David Murray lecture, no. 22, 1955 (University of Glasgow, 1960); three volumes of Richardson's and Sayles's edition of *Fleta* have so far appeared (Selden Society, vols. 72, 89, 99, London, 1953–83).

Stubbs 'projected into the past the image of the constitutional monarchy which he saw working under his own eyes and to which he attributed the greatness of his country'. It was the 'idea of a constitution' that, for Richardson and Sayles, falsified Stubbs's approach to parliament 'as to the whole mechanism of government'. He was unable to regard Henry II, John, Edward I and Edward II as men of their day; 'he saw them rather as figures appropriate to the parts he allotted to them in his imaginary drama of the constitution'. There is a moral fervour of its own in the way Richardson and Sayles dismiss as an absurdity the holding out of English parliamentary experience as a model for new nations in the twentieth century. Parliament was 'a device of royal administration', a product of 'use and wont' requiring its English environment if it was to work with even partial efficiency. The vehemence of *Governance* stemmed from a conviction that Stubbs had never seriously tried to discover how any part of medieval government actually worked. He 'had no experience of administration and seemingly no intuitive perception of administrative processes'. His lack of feeling for government was shown already by his denigration of King John for (sensibly) standing up to the blackmail of the papal Interdict; and by his exaltation of Archibishop Stephen Langton, a barren academic 'without administrative or political training' to the improbable role of architect of Magna Carta.[62]

The controversy about the early history of parliament distinguishes the administrative perspective from the older constitutional history. The administrative view can be as blinkered as the constitutional one, so that (for instance) Edward I is admired for an administrative ruthlessness which from another point of view appears the source of his political misjudgements of the 1290s. Yet much of the work of Richardson and Sayles shows the two approaches converging to produce a richer account of political practice. In 1931 the king's ministers, clerks and judges who did the work of the medieval parliament came under their scrutiny; and in 1934, the generation of statute law, typically as it was manifested in exchequer and chancery records. Their Selden Society volume, *Select Cases of Procedure without Writ under Henry*

[62] Sayles, *The King's Parliament*, pp. 6, 11, 13; Richardson and Sayles, *Parliament and Great Councils in Medieval England*, p. 32; *idem* and *idem*, *The Governance of Mediaeval England from the Conquest to Magna Carta* (Edinburgh: Edinburgh UP, 1963), pp. vi–vii, 2–3, 5, 6, 9, 14, 16, 17, 265, 337–8, 354; for the other side of the argument, Stubbs, *Select Charters*, p. 478; Edwards, 'Plena Potestas', p. 146; James Campbell, *Stubbs and the English State*, pp. 10, 13.

III (1941), was a landmark in legal historiography, for it revealed the beginnings of the more direct procedures by oral 'plaint' and then by written 'bill' which transformed the system of royal justice in the later middle ages. This volume, along with an edition in 1935 of material which had escaped the printed *Rotuli Parliamentorum* and the texts in Sayles's *Functions of the Medieval Parliament* of England (which brought to a conclusion in 1988 a project thought up sixty-four years earlier) also proved their contention that Parliament had begun as part of the judicial apparatus. At the same time, however, Richardson and Sayles were really demonstrating the truth of Edwards's argument that obtaining justice was essentially a political process, for the petitioning they described was the first means of communication between the people at large and the government.[63]

One result of the work of the administrative historians and the editors of official records has been to reinforce the idea of Edward I's administrative imperialism, and the conception of British history as basically the history of the English state – a conception which is only now being subjected to intensive criticism. In the most detailed accounts of the period yet provided, *Henry III and the Lord Edward* (1947) and *The Thirteenth Century* (1953), F. M. Powicke was able to do better justice to the '"British" century *par excellence*' of the middle ages (the phrase belongs to R. R. Davies), by tracing more layers of culture, those of the aristocracy and clergy as well as officialdom, out beyond England, and showing their European dimensions. A letter written to his mentor Tout in 1904, while he was engaged in his first serious research, an account of Furness Abbey for the *Victoria County History* of Lancashire, suggests Powicke's idea of the historian's task: the recovery of 'the forgotten interests of ordinary political history' would be the product of the familiarity he was acquiring with 'ecclesiastical and manorial and local terminology'. But to yield a newly convincing political narrative he was to discover that the administrative developments needed to be woven together with the vagaries of great personalities and European-wide intellectual movements. His first book, first published in 1913, drew out the permanent effects

---

[63] H. G. Richardson and G. O. Sayles, 'The King's Ministers in Parliament, 1272–1307', *EHR*, 46 (1931); *The Early Statutes* (reprinted from the Law Quarterly Review, 50 (1934)); *Select Cases of Procedure without Writ under Henry III*, ed. H. G. Richardson and G. O. Sayles (Selden Society, vol. 6, London, 1941); *Rotuli Parliamentorum Anglie Hactenus Inediti, 1279–1373* (Camden Society, 3rd ser., 51, 1935); Sayles, *Functions*, p. ix.

of John's loss of Normandy to Philip Augustus on government and politics in both England and France. Amongst the most important of these were the concepts of nationality and (conversely) of what it meant to be an alien, which arose when lords had to choose whether to stay with their English or their Norman (now French) estates. Feudal politics and administration are the substance of *The Loss of Normandy*, but at the end Powicke embraces the suggestion of Gerald of Wales that Philip's success owed much to the chivalry, art and intellectual brilliance of France. In his next book, *Stephen Langton* (1928), he sought to bring his subject 'into relation with the common man in England and with the intellectual life of Europe, to break down the barriers which prevent us from considering as a whole, in the light of the influences that played upon them, the men and affairs of politics and religion'. The 'clear, sensible, penetrating, but not original mind' which Langton employed in the service of the Church at the most critical period in its medieval history, and of the movement for sound government in the secular realm of England, was one sharpened in the schools of Paris: on questions about the extent of papal power; about the duty of the Church to aid kings in a just and urgent cause, even though the secular power had no right to demand taxes from the clergy; and about the distinction between a commonwealth, ruled by common counsel, and a monarchy (like England) where subjects could expect the king only to observe natural law and judicial custom. Powicke saw the reconstruction of the English Church after the wounds of John's reign as part of the work set in train for the whole western Church by the Fourth Lateran Council of 1215, the decrees of which summed up a generation not only of papal legislation but 'of ceaseless discussion by theologians, of whom Langton had been one, on the sacraments, the details of ecclesiastical discipline, monastic administration, the duties of prelates and officials, current heresies and moral questions'.[64]

A conviction that otherwise English government and politics could not be fully understood spurred Powicke to open up lines of

---

[64] *The British Isles 1100–1500: Comparisons, Contrasts and Connections*, ed. R. R. Davies (Edinburgh: John Donald, 1988), pp. 1–2; J. G. A. Pocock, 'British History. A Plea for a New Subject', *Journal of Modern History*, 47 (1975); R. W. Southern on Powicke in *The Dictionary of National Biography 1961–1970*, ed. E. T. Williams and C. S. Nicholls (Oxford: OUP, 1981), pp. 856–8; F. M. Powicke, *The Loss of Normandy*, 2nd edn (Manchester: Manchester UP, 1961), pp. 286–303, 306–7; *idem, Stephen Langton* (Oxford: Clarendon Press, 1928), pp. vii, 95, 121–2, 142, 151, 157, 160–1.

research into intellectual history, and in 1936 to produce along with A. B. Emden a new edition of Hastings Rashdall's *Universities of Europe in the Middle Ages*, first published in 1895. In the introduction to volume I, he dubbed the 'intense intellectual life' of the schools 'a process of incessant wisdom and folly' which provided a window into medieval society. In the introduction to volume III on the English universities, Emden pointed out the extent to which masters from Paris and Oxford took over English bishoprics in the reign of Henry III, claiming the archbishopric of Canterbury in 1234 with the election of Edmund Rich. As Powicke argued in later papers, the University of Oxford was never a place of learning for its own sake, but 'a national institution, a home of institutional compromises between the secular and ecclesiastical authorities', and 'a reservoir upon which the royal court could draw for its servants'. English politics were stimulated throughout the thirteenth century by the intervention of strong-minded churchmen, Grosseteste rather than Langton their archetype: men who carried the thought-system of the universities, itself renewed by Aristotelian philosophy and the learning of the Friars, into diocesan administration and the defence of ecclesiastical rights against royal (and, if need be, papal) government. The work Powicke promoted on 'the Grosseteste problem', the enigma of the intellectual and idealist who was also a hard and uncompromising ruler of his diocese, sharing some of the faults as well as the qualities of his friend, Simon de Montfort, has certainly confirmed the importance in thirteenth-century government of a background of international scholastic training. But the real reason why Powicke stressed the part of ideas was because he understood that a political society such as England had become by the thirteenth century depended on a widespread grasp of abstract concepts like 'common utility' and 'necessity': their expression in the international language of clerics must not be allowed to mask the fact that the capacity to think in these terms was essential equipment of the lay administrators of particular communities.[65]

[65] H. Rashdall, *The Universities of Europe in the Middle Ages*, ed. F. M. Powicke and A. B. Emden, 3 vols. (Oxford: Clarendon Press, 1936), I.xxxvii, xl–xli, III. xix–xx; Powicke, *Stephen Langton*, p. 161; *idem*, *Ways of Medieval Life and Thought: Essays and Addresses* (London: Odhams Press, 1950), pp. 134–42, 146–7, 178, 198–204, 223–5; *idem*, 'Robert Grosseteste', *Bulletin of the John Rylands Library*, 35 (1952–3), pp. 498–507; *idem*, *HLE*, pp. 287–8; W. A. Pantin, 'Grosseteste's Relations with the Papacy and the Crown', in *Robert Grosseteste, Scholar and Bishop*, ed. D. A. Callus, with an Introduction by Sir Maurice Powicke (Oxford: Clarendon Press, 1955), p. 205; R. W. Southern, *Robert*

'The Interplay of Experience and Ideas in the Formation of Medieval Political Societies' was the subject of many of Powicke's articles. The first of his presidential addresses to the Royal Historical Society (1934–6) was devoted to 'Some Problems in the History of the Medieval University', the third to 'Reflections on the Medieval State'. The State was defined as 'a condition only possible to intelligent beings who possess a faculty which we call the power of choice', and its emergence was made dependent on the self-awareness and breadth of experience of 'responsible laymen'. This was a European development within which Englishmen showed 'an unusual kind of competence'. Powicke insisted that the State was 'more than a complex of institutions'; and he is wrongly charged with writing 'high-flown constitutional history'. It was rather an 'organized public life . . . the relations between men which enabled them to discuss, plead and act together in councils, law courts, armies and business' – men 'with the capacity to be influenced in their normal daily life by abstractions', who recognized the value of custom but also the need for authority to enforce change in the laws. Before the beginning of statutes, the plea-rolls of John's reign already showed the making of positive law and the defining of social relations by judges who were 'suddenly called on to deal with problems of prescription and agency and the like'. Significant historical work had to deal in abstract ideas like 'the community of the realm', Powicke believed, but they should be ideas which the people in the histories had employed themselves. In his Oxford inaugural lecture of 1929 he both affirmed the value of history for the historian and his own generation, and insisted that the theories and values arrived at must be dictated exclusively by the material handed on from the past, which came in the form of texts. It was for this reason that textual criticism, and the tracing of the ways different sorts of texts bore upon each other, were central to an historian's work. As he argued in the *Economic History Review* for 1946, past events could not be completely explained by economic statistics any more than in terms of political purposes. Mankind had been rightly 'reluctant to distinguish between its social impulses', and had 'sought to transcend material considerations, not only as an ideal or in times of conscious conflict, but day by day, in the adoption of ways of life'. Only in modern times had 'our conceptions of economic forces'

Grosseteste: The Growth of an English Mind in Medieval Europe (Oxford: Clarendon Press, 1986), pp. 5, 246–7, 289.

come to determine nearly all our political actions. Economics had taken the place once held by religion, but 'its emphasis on the particular interests of persons and groups tends to incoherence'. It was a significant factor only when it was transcended by wider political and social purposes. The strength of English parliamentary government, 'the most stable form of government in the world' so far, lay 'in its capacity to deal with our economic life as part of the community'.[66]

Henry III and the Lord Edward is most successful when it is describing the culture of the western European governing class as it was manifested in the politics of the kingdom of England. It does not give a rounded picture of 'the Community of the Realm in the Thirteenth Century', despite the attention given to the reconciliation of a divided country in the chaotic years after Evesham; when (so it is asserted on the basis of a case from *Select Cases of Procedure without Writ*) even the peasants of Peatling Magna were capable of grasping the concept of the *communitas regni*; and when secular taxes, resumed after a long interruption, were described by the king himself as granted by a 'commune' (*communa*) of all the freemen and burgesses of England. In 1965 K. B. McFarlane demolished Powicke's 'feeble attempt to extenuate' Edward's treatment of the earls for his own or his family's material advantage, and showed how little community there was even among the group around the king. The most original part of this work of Powicke's is the penultimate chapter, 'The Conflict of Laws', which analyses the conquest of Wales as the assimilation of one aristocratic culture to another in terms of land-tenure and social habits. In the preface, Powicke had claimed the book as 'a study in social history, not in the sense in which the term is generally used, but in the sense of social life, relations, and forces in political action'; for in separation, he believed, social life lost its interest and political movements their meaning. He recognized, however, that 'description of social ties and institutions as such' was now expected, and promised to give it in his forthcoming volume of the Oxford History of England, which appeared in 1953. Insofar as *The Thirteenth Century: 1216–1307* fulfils the

---

[66] Powicke, *Ways of Medieval Life and Thought*, pp. 4, 5, 122, 126–9, 132, 134, 136–44; the disparaging remark is from P. R. Coss, 'Bastard Feudalism Revised', *Past and Present*, 125 (1989), p. 36; Powicke's inaugural lecture is printed in his *Modern Historians and the Study of History* (London: Odhams Press, 1955): see especially pp. 170, 173–8, and in the same volume, pp. 185–7, 189, 194–8, 200, 212, 226–30, 235–6, 241, 243, 247–8.

promise of a more social history, it does so by a greater use of purely administrative history, which can reach down through the layers of English society to the same extent that it is unable to make lateral connections between England and her neighbours. So much of royal administration was concerned with the judicial investigation of the king's rights in the localities, and their diminution on the one hand by the liberties claimed by the barons and on the other by the abuses of the king's own officials. When the Crown was constrained to recognize baronial rights, it insisted that the barons should concede similar rights to their tenants. 'The periods of sustained administrative activity' such as 1234–40, 1258–60 and 1274–90 were also 'periods of legislative activity', as inquiries brought to light grievances which only statutes could answer – by giving protection, for instance, to the ordinary gentry and to village communities against the unreasonable demands of seignorial courts and bailiffs.[67]

A vast amount of information on social life had become available to Powicke in studies of the administration of justice: in the volumes of cases before the justices in eyre, edited by Lady Stenton and others; in Helen Cam's studies of the lengthening list of questions the itinerant justices were required to ask about the administration of the shires, and of the great inquiry set on foot in 1274 which produced the 'Hundred Rolls'; in the petitions of aggrieved individuals and corporations the development of which was traced by Richardson and Sayles (and would be taken back further by J. C. Holt); in the volumes of cases which reached the central courts in the time of John and Henry III (the *Curia Regis Rolls*); in Sayles's volumes on king's bench under Edward I; and in the work, much of it also published by the Selden Society, on borough courts and customs, the application of the law merchant and the court of the exchequer. T. F. T. Plucknett showed Powicke how much concern for the accountability of bailiffs of manors and liberties, both to their employers and to the community at large, and for the interests of the merchant class, was at the heart of Edwardian legislation. The work on parliament, taxation and representation shed light on the social roles of the county gentry and leading burgesses; and studies of the legislation and territorial

[67] Powicke, *HLE*, pp. 509–10, 513, 565, 659, 668, 683; K. B. McFarlane, 'Had Edward I a Policy towards the Earls?', *History*, 50 (1965), pp. 148–50, 155, 158–9; F. M. Powicke, *The Thirteenth Century: 1216–1307* (Oxford: Clarendon Press, 1953; 2nd edn, 1961; issued in paperback, 1991), pp. 38–9, 67–8, 143–4, 324, 365, 367, 540 etc.

administration of the Church (in which the name of C. R. Cheney is prominent) revealed something of the moral life of local communities, such as family relationships, concern for reputation and communal responsibility for the support of the parish church.[68]

But Powicke showed little interest in groups below the aristocracy for their own sakes, and villeins make no appearance in his books. By contrast A. L. Poole, the author of the previous volume of the Oxford History of England, interspersed analyses of 'government and society', 'rural conditions', 'learning, literature and art' and 'justice and finance' between chapters of political narrative. In 1944, seven years before the publication of *Domesday Book to Magna Carta*, Poole had given the Ford lectures on *Obligations of Society in the Twelfth and Thirteenth Centuries*. The first lecture (on 'the classification of society') began with an acknowledgement of the material recently made available from the plea-rolls of the central courts and from exchequer accounts; and subsequent lectures described 'peasants', 'knights' and 'sergeants' in terms of their differences of legal and economic status, particularly as they were reflected in the levels of 'amercement' (or fines) imposed by the courts, and in the case of free tenants also in the amounts of money exacted as 'feudal incidents'. What was lost by Poole's technique was the coherence and forward thrust of Powicke's political narrative, for it is difficult to describe the total life of a social group and also take full account of how it changes. There is not just the technical problem of making a coherent picture from a variety of evidence scattered over time and place. It also has to be asked whether there is a single history to be written

---

[68] *A Centenary Guide to the Publications of the Selden Society* (Selden Society, London, 1987); between 1926 and 1967, Lady Stenton edited for the Selden Society *Pleas before the King or his Justices, 1198–1212* and eyre rolls from the first quarter of the century for Lincolnshire, Northamptonshire, Worcestershire, Yorkshire, Gloucestershire, Warwickshire and Staffordshire; H. M. Cam, *Studies in the Hundred Rolls*, Oxford Studies in Social and Legal History, VI (Oxford: Clarendon Press, 1921); *idem*, *The Hundred and the Hundred Rolls* (London: Methuen, 1930); Richardson and Sayles (eds.), *Select Cases of Procedure without Writ*; Holt, *Magna Carta*, caps. 3, 4; *CRR*; T. F. T. Plucknett, *The Legislation of Edward I* (Oxford: Clarendon Press, 1949); on representation and taxation: H. M. Cam's studies, collected in *Liberties and Communities in Medieval England* (Cambridge: CUP, 1933), and *Law-Finders and Law-Makers in Medieval England* (London: Merlin Press, 1962); S. K. Mitchell, *Taxation in Medieval England*, ed. S. Painter (New Haven: Yale UP, 1951); B. Wilkinson, *Studies in the Constitutional History of the Thirteenth and Fourteenth Centuries* (Manchester: Manchester UP, 1937); *idem*, *The Constitutional History of Medieval England, 1216–1399*, 3 vols. (London: Longmans, 1948–58); C. R. Cheney, *Medieval Tests and Studies* (Oxford: Clarendon Press, 1973).

of a society varying regionally in its state of development and changing at different rates in its cultural and political dimensions. H. S. Bennett's pioneering attempt in 1937 to describe *Life on the English Manor* between 1150 and 1400 uses a great range of sources, from cartularies and manor-court rolls to wills and the records of bishops' and archdeacons' visitations, but the coherence achieved is static and literary rather then historical. The aim is to provide a well-documented version of Langland's 'faire felde ful of folke' as an imaginary peasant might have seen it on a June day in 1320.[69]

In *English Villagers of the Thirteenth Century*, published in 1941, George Homans again sought to describe a 'state of affairs as a whole'; by 'as a whole', this professor of sociology at Harvard meaning as many as possible of the aspects of the peasantry as a social order. He recognized that the picture he painted could not be complete, partly because the evidence was fragmentary, 'and partly because different generations of scholars see with different eyes: the men of the present day cannot tell what the future will find they have overlooked'. He also knew that he had been forced to consider the thirteenth-century English village 'as if it were unchanging, or rather as if it were the social order of an island in Melanesia, which an anthropologist can describe only as it exists at the time he lives there'. Yet he had not even enjoyed the anthropologist's advantage of being able to talk to his villagers: they took for granted so much we want to know about them, which therefore made no impression on the custumals and court rolls Maitland had been right to see as 'the foremost medieval sources of what is called social history'. The work of Bennett and Homans was nevertheless valuable in tying village culture firmly to mutual dependence on the land: Homans's the more valuable as it is less impressionistic and displays its author's professional ability to place in a theoretical framework the peasants' husbandry skills, family relationships and inheritance patterns, routines of manorial co-operation, folk ceremonies and religious feasts. Homans's most valuable insight, since confirmed by the work of Maurice Beresford and W. G. Hoskins, was that 'the study of landscapes is a good beginning for the study of the societies of men, because men must live on and off the land as the first condition of their survival': an insight which led him to confine his study to the social order of one particular

---

[69] A. L. Poole, *Obligations of Society in the Twelfth and Thirteenth Centuries* (Oxford: Clarendon Press, 1946); *idem, From Domesday Book to Magna Carta* (Oxford: Clarendon Press, 1951; 2nd edn, 1955). 254; H. S. Bennett, *Life on the English Manor* (Cambridge: CUP, 1937), pp. 3–4.

landscape, the 'champion' or open-field country of the Midlands and south. An element of change was brought into the picture of rural society, and English history linked to Europe's in a quite different way than through crusading, the politics of Church and Empire or emergent national conflicts, by a great expansion of economic history based on the study of land use. For western Europe the thirteenth century has come to be seen as the time when 'the frontier closed' – when no more land could be brought into cultivation from the forest and the waste, and rural society was forced to adapt in other ways to continued population growth and commercial development.[70]

In the tradition of Vinogradoff, whose *Villainage in England* had appeared in 1892, but now from an economic rather than a legal standpoint, two Russians have made the seminal twentieth-century contributions to the history of the thirteenth-century English peasantry. One came to England in 1919 and died Sir Michael Postan, the other, E. A. Kosminsky, remained in Soviet Russia, but both were inevitably influenced by the agrarian concerns of modern Russia and by Marxism, at least in the questions they asked. As student and lecturer at the London School of Economics, Postan moved amongst social and political scientists: Hugh Gaitskell was a friend there, and the Director of the School was William Beveridge (later author of the *Report*), who worked in Thorold Rogers's vein on *Prices and Wages in England from the Twelfth to the Nineteenth Century*. Postan was encouraged by R. H. Tawney to apply his cosmopolitan grasp of the literature, theoretical as well as historical, to modern as well as medieval economic development – which he had every opportunity of doing, as editor from 1934 of

---

[70] G. C. Homans, *English Villagers of the Thirteenth Century* (Cambridge, Mass.: Harvard UP, 1941), pp. 3–11, 12, 109–20, 410; A Macfarlane, *The Origins of English Individualism: The Family, Property and Social Transition* (Oxford: Blackwell, 1978), pp. 136–8; for a recent attempt to describe peasant society, see B. A. Hanawalt, *The Ties that Bound* (Oxford: OUP, 1986); see also G. C. Homans, 'Men and Land in the Middle Ages', *Speculum*, (1936); *idem*, 'The Explanation of English Regional Differences', *Past and Present*, 42 (1969); M. W. Beresford, *The Lost Villages of England* (London: Lutterworth Press, 1954); W. G. Hoskins, *The Making of the English Landscape* (London: Hodder and Stoughton, 1955); M. W. Beresford and J. K. S. St Joseph, *Medieval England: An Aerial Survey*, 2nd edn. (Cambridge: CUP, 1979); *The Medieval English Landscape*, ed. L. Cantor (London: Croom Helm, 1982) – p. 53 n. 3 for references to the open-field controversy; D. C. North and R. P. Thomas, *The Rise of the Western World* (Cambridge: CUP, 1973), pp. 46–7; for the Russian interest in English agrarian history, see P. Gatrell, 'Studies of Medieval English Society in a Russian Context', *Past and Present*, 96 (1982).

the *Economic History Review*, Professor of Economic History at
Cambridge from 1938, and over the years editor of three medieval
and two modern volumes of the *Cambridge Economic History of
Europe*. A paper to the Royal Historical Society in 1937 on 'The
Chronology of Labour Services' established the theme of his work
on medieval agrarian history. Lords exacted labour from their
villeins to cultivate the land they kept 'in demesne' and produce
crops for their own consumption or for sale. Postan argued from
estate surveys that a twelfth-century trend to the leasing out of
demesne and the commutation of labour services to money rents,
especially on peripheral manors, was halted and partly reversed in
the thirteenth century – the reason being a conjuncture of technical
improvements, capital investment and rising productivity, which
made it advantageous for landlords to expand their demesne
farming again. But the Malthusian crisis was already being prepared underneath the thirteenth-century boom. The chapter Postan
wrote for the second (1966) edition of the *Cambridge Economic
History of Europe*, volume I, was a magisterial statement of his
findings. The basic fact of the thirteenth-century economy was
that the people were becoming too numerous for the land. The
determination of landlords to keep the best lands for themselves,
and the reluctance of villeins to grow more for the lord's benefit,
were but two examples of the widening conflicts of interest within
rural society. Though he did not believe that economic evidence
showed the long-term improvement in the condition of the peasantry as a whole which legal historians purported to find, Postan
did recognize that there were considerable differences of wealth
amongst the peasants themselves. The 'village rich' could purchase
substantial quantities of land, not only as 'a "factor of production",
i.e. the means towards higher output and income, but also [as] a
"good" worth possessing for its own sake, and enjoyed as a
measure of social status, a foundation of family fortunes, and a
fulfilment and extension of the owner's personality'. (In 1960,
Postan had published along with C. N. L. Brooke a collection of
villein charters in a Peterborough Abbey manuscript, which
showed numerous land transactions between even 'unfree' peasants
by the second half of the thirteenth century.) A group comparable
to the Russian kulaks certainly existed in England, employing
labourers and deriving income from rents and money-lending.[71]

[71] Graves (ed.), *Bibliography of English History to 1485*, pp. 694–5; E. Miller's
obituary of Postan, in *Proceedings of the British Academy*, 69 (1983), pp. 543–57;

Kosminsky's book of 1935 on 'the English Village in the Thirteenth Century' was translated out of Russian under the somewhat colourless title of *Studies in the Agrarian History of England in the Thirteenth Century* only in 1956 (though its subject-matter had been known from early articles in the *Economic History Review*). Kosminsky was interested in the structure of manors especially on small estates (as opposed to the big ecclesiastical ones which had received so much attention); in 'the divisions among the English peasantry (in particular with regard to the size of their holdings)'; and in 'the various ways in which the labour force on the thirteenth-century manor was exploited'. His analysis of 'the agrarian structure of medieval England', largely from the 'Hundred Rolls' of 1275 and 1279 (a source in print and available in Russia) and according to Marxist–Leninist concepts of 'the feudal mode of production', yielded important insights. The focus on the less-regimented small estates showed up the disparities between peasant holdings and the precarious living standards of the villein mass, but also that the peasants did hold the majority of the land, owing money rents more often than labour services. The chief criticism levelled at this work by Postan was that the Marxist structural analysis drove out historical perspective. Kosminsky acknowledged the criticism, but claimed that his analysis rather than Postan's revealed the true motive forces of change: not demographic crisis, but the appearance of 'more capitalistic forms of economic life' represented by the production of commodities for the market and an intensifying struggle for the profits (in terms of rent) between the peasants and their lords, the latter backed by the state and the common law. Robert Brenner sharpened the debate in 1974 by arguing that differences in economic development between late medieval and early modern England and France were determined by differing class relationships, which were cultural as much as economic in origin. The disabilities of the English peasantry were not primarily economic, as Postan insisted, but were rooted in their legal condition (detailed in the thirteenth century by Bracton and enforced through both royal and seignorial courts), which prevented their obtaining secure property rights

M. M. Postan, 'The Chronology of Labour Services', *TRHS*, 4th ser., 20 (1937), pp. 169–93; and in *Cambridge Economic History of Europe*, vol. I. *Agrarian Life of the Middle Ages*, 2nd edn, ed. M. M. Postan (Cambridge: CUP, 1971), pp. vi, 548–632; *Carte Nativorum: A Peterborough Abbey Cartulary*, ed. C. N. L. Brooke and M. M. Postan, (Northamptonshire Record Society, vol. 20, Northampton, 1960).

and allowed landlords to transfer the land to capitalist tenant farmers.[72]

The 'Brenner debate' is evidence of an attempt to marry economic and legal chronology with social analysis to produce a more penetrating social history: one which may also suggest some of the underlying motivations of politics. The unit in which the cultures of lords and peasants were joined, whether in conflict or co-operation, was the lordship; and the fortunes of a number of the great ecclesiastical lordships – the archbishop of Canterbury's, the bishop of Worcester's, and those of Peterborough and Westminster Abbeys – and of the social groups within them have now been traced by economic historians. Towns like the bishop of Worcester's Stratford-on-Avon have been given their place in the rural economy, as the places where commodities were marketed, textiles manufactured and the services of smiths and carpenters concentrated: the very greatest landlords might be 'remarkably insensitive to market forces', but at least higher rents could be extracted from urban tenants. At many levels of landed society, amongst the lesser landlords perhaps more than the peasants, the forces of disturbance and change were provided by the land market. By the thirteenth century the integrity of the fees of the knights who came with the Conqueror had been sacrificed to the necessities of maintaining family status and making provision for daughters and younger sons. In financial transactions the small landowners such as the knightly tenants of Peterborough Abbey were easy prey to the Jews and city merchants to whom they mortgaged their lands for ready cash, and to the great abbeys and lay magnates eager to buy up the pledged estates to round off their own when the debts could not be paid. The foundation of new towns up to the middle of the thirteenth century, the growth of old cities such as London and York, and the widening of overseas trade can all be linked to the intensifying exploitation of the land. In the towns also social differentiation increased and provoked a turbulent politics which

---

[72] E. A. Kosminsky, *Studies in the Agrarian History of England in the Thirteenth Century*, tr. R. Kisch, ed. R. H. Hilton (Oxford: Blackwell, 1956), pp. v–vi, ix–x, 324–8, 338; E. Miller and J. Hatcher, *Medieval England – Rural Society and Economic Change 1086–1348* (London: Longmans, 1978), pp. 123, 143 147–8, 234–5; R. H. Hilton, *The English Peasantry in the Later Middle Ages* (Oxford: Clarendon Press, 1975), cap. 10: 'Rent and Capital Formation in Feudal Society'; *The Brenner Debate: Agrarian Class Structure and Economic Development in Pre-Industrial Europe*, ed. T. H. Aston and C. H. E. Philpin (Cambridge: CUP, 1985), pp. 4–5, 7–8, 13, 17, 25–6, 38, 79, 107; Postan in *Cambridge Economic History*, I.611.

was often turned outwards against foreign merchants, or, as at Bury St Edmunds, the monastic lord. Edward I's relentless taxing of wool exports and his fostering of foreign trade by statutes providing for a speedier recovery of debts are examples of the way kings were having to develop commercial policies. The reverse of Powicke's dictum may be the truer: economic interests give coherence to political and social purposes in history, as much as derive coherence from them.[73]

A concept which has been offered to link the economic, social and political events of the thirteenth century is that of 'feudal crisis'. Its roots obviously lie in that old preoccupation of historians – the origin and decline of military feudalism. Sidney Painter's *Studies in the History of English Feudal Barony*, published in 1943, was a landmark in the incorporation of fluctuating economic resources into the story. Simon de Montfort appears in this book as a franchise holder, a recipient of extensive revenues from the

---

[73] R. H. Hilton, 'A Crisis of Feudalism', in *The Brenner Debate*, ed. Aston and Philpin, p. 124; Knowles, *Religious Orders*, I, for the economies of religious houses; F. R. H. du Boulay, *The Lordship of Canterbury* (London: Nelson, 1966); E. King, *Peterborough Abbey 1086–1310* (Cambridge: CUP, 1973); Barbara Harvey, *Westminster Abbey and its Estates in the Middle Ages* (Oxford: Clarendon Press, 1977), p. 331; C. Dyer, *Lords and Peasants in a Changing Society: The Estates of the Bishopric of Worcester, 680–1540* (Cambridge, CUP, 1980), pp. 59–61, 107–8, 110–11; R. H. Hilton, *A Medieval Society: The West Midlands at the End of the Thirteenth Century* (London: Weidenfeld and Nicolson, 1966), cap. 7; *idem The English Peasantry*, cap. 5, on the small town in agrarian society; on the fortunes of the knights and the land market, see Postan in *Cambridge Economic History*, I.593–5; King, *Peterborough Abbey*, pp. 53–4; *idem* 'Large and Small Landowners in Thirteenth Century England', *Past and Present*, 47 (1970); H. G. Richardson, *The English Jewry under Angevin Kings* (London : Methuen, (1960), cap. 5; M. W. Beresford, *New Towns of the Middle Ages* (London: Lutterworth Press, 1967); P. Spufford, *Money and its Use in Medieval Europe* (Cambridge: CUP, 1987), pp. 250–1; Miller and Hatcher, *Rural Society and Economic Change*, pp. 79ff; Knowles, *The Religious Orders in England*, I.67–71, for the monastic wool trade; for a recent critical view of trading relations, R. H. Britnell, 'England and Northern Italy in the Early Fourteenth Century: The Economic Contrasts', *TRHS*, 5th ser., 39 (1989), pp. 176ff; R. S. Gottfried, *Bury St Edmunds and the Urban Crisis: 1290–1539* (Princeton: Princeton UP, 1982), esp. cap. 6; J. Tait, *The Medieval English Borough* (Manchester: Manchester UP, 1936); G. A. Williams, *Medieval London: From Commune to Capital* (London: Athlone Press, 1963); Susan Reynolds, *An Introduction to the History of English Medieval Towns* (Oxford: Clarendon Press, 1977); for towns and trade generally, see *Cambridge Economic History of Europe*, vol. II: *Trade and Industry in the Middle Ages*, ed. M. M. Postan and E. E. Rich (Cambridge: CUP, 1952), and vol. III: *Economic Organisation and Policies in the Middle Ages*, ed. M. M. Postan, E. E. Rich and E. Miller (Cambridge: CUP, 1963); pp. 306–16 of the latter for E. Miller on governments and trade.

borough of Leicester – and as the man who sold 'his noble wood of Leicester' for about £1,000 when he needed money for a crusade. In 1961, J. C. Holt's study of *The Northerners* pointed to the economic straits of the barons who rebelled against King John. If the knights became an independent force in politics by the time of the Barons' War it was because of their economic grievances as much as their social power – grievances against the demands of both king and magnates, who were impelled by their own pressing needs. The proponents of 'feudal crisis' bring in the concept of a 'structural contradiction between large-scale feudal landownership and the smallholding peasant unit of production', which intensified as 'increasing numbers of peasant families were forced into the sub-class of smallholders without adequate subsistence'. The struggle waged by the peasants 'against the landlords who tried to exact from them more of their surplus produce' was just one result of trends which were also responsible for the increasing demands of the king on the landowners, and for the turbulence of the towns where the produce was marketed.[74]

Contemporary chroniclers noted all these things: later historians are concerned to trace the logic which connects them. That is the reason for building up a history of thirteenth-century England from accounts of the development of the different social groups.

[74] S. Painter, *Studies in the History of the English Feudal Barony* (Baltimore: Johns Hopkins Univ. Stud. 61, 1943), pp. 118, 166; J. C. Holt, *The Northerners* (Oxford: Clarendon Press, 1961), pp. 18, 33–4, 49, 57–8; J. R. Maddicott, 'Magna Carta and the Local Community 1215–1259', *Past and Present*, 102 (1984); Postan in *Cambridge Economic History*, II. 595; R. H. Hilton in *The Brenner Debate*, ed. Aston and Philpin, pp. 6, 8–9, 121, 127–8, 131–2; Guy Bois, in *ibid*, p. 113; R. H. Hilton, 'Peasant Movements in England before 1381', *EcHR*, 2nd ser., 2 (1949).

2

THE PEASANTS AND THE LAND

The economic trends which were changing society at all levels at the beginning of the thirteenth century were population growth, agricultural boom and the linked phenomenon of inflation. England was in the middle of 'a massive increase in both population and the acreage of agricultural land'. Perhaps 2 million people at the time of the Domesday inquest in 1086 would have risen to possibly 5 or 6 million on the eve of the Black Death in 1347. The increase was most marked in areas of reclamation from woodland and from the East Anglian fens, and in the northern and western uplands where it started from a low base, but every county saw a doubling of its inhabitants and Yorkshire probably a tenfold increase. More agricultural labourers produced more crops to meet the swelling demand, and the crops were traded more widely in a growing number of markets; but another result of a sharp rise in a population living from the soil was a land-hunger the consequences of which became apparent as the thirteenth century advanced.[1]

There was also from the 1160s to the early fourteenth century something like a quadrupling of prices. In the long term it was caused partly by the inability of agricultural production to keep up with the growth of the population it had to feed, and partly by the development of a market economy in which money circulated at an accelerating rate in pursuit of a widening range of goods. Much

[1] E. Miller and J. Hatcher, *Medieval England – Rural Society and Economic Change 1086–1348* (London: Longmans, 1978), pp. 29–32, 45.

of the price rise was, however, concentrated in a severe burst of inflation around the year 1200. This may have been caused by a flooding-in of continental silver in payment for massively increased wool exports to Flanders. But exports are unlikely to have been so important within the agricultural economy, and more plausible reasons are the accidents of bad weather and poor harvests and a breaking-down of the price restraints imposed by custom and by the purveyors who bought supplies for the king. The social and political consequences of this fairly sudden inflation are more certain. Fixed payments were slashed in value, forcing landlords to turn to short-term letting which permitted frequent adjustments of rent and the recovery of lost ground by the imposition of high entry fines. Or, more radically, they took land back into demesne, to get the direct benefit of the rising prices by producing for the market. Much evidence about the effects of inflation on the peasant mass of the population is available in the series of plea-rolls which had just begun to be kept by the king's justices; and though manor-court rolls do not survive in significant quantity until the second half of the century, manorial surveys and custumals setting out tenants' rents and services become more plentiful after 1200 with the spread of demesne farming, and manorial accounts also begin in the early part of the century. The legal evidence in particular enables the historian of rural society to steer between a static impressionism on the one hand and on the other a mere illusion of change produced by the first-time recording of what may have been old-established patterns of behaviour. The new processes of the common law allowed for real developments in social norms, which were expressed in rich detail in a great mass of plea-roll cases.[2]

VILLEINS

One significant change in rural society which was taking place at the beginning of the thirteenth century was the definition of

---

[2] *Ibid.*, pp. 67–9; P. D. A. Harvey, 'The English Inflation of 1180–1220', reprinted from *Past and Present*, 61 (1973), in *Peasants, Knights and Heretics*, ed. R. H. Hilton (Cambridge: CUP, 1976); *idem*, 'The Pipe Rolls and the Adoption of Demesne Farming in England', *EcHR*, 27 (1974); P. Spufford, *Money and its Use in Medieval Europe* (Cambridge: CUP, 1987), pp. 243–5; S. Painter, *The Reign of King John* (Baltimore: Johns Hopkins Press, 1949), pp. 130–6; P. D. A. Harvey, *Manorial Records* (British Records Association, Archives and the User, no. 5, London, 1984).

villeinage itself. Impelled by monetary inflation as much as by the need for labour – there were plenty of landless labourers who could be hired to work the expanded demesnes – many landlords turned the now unprofitable rents owed by the customary tenants back into labour services. The villein was seen as part of the equipment of the lord's home farm, a chattel to be bought and sold along with the land, and sometimes, indeed, apart from it. From soon after the Norman Conquest kings had instructed sheriffs to aid lords in recovering villagers (*villanos*) who had absconded from their manors. On the other side, the newly articulated common law of Henry II's reign had provided a means by which the fugitive peasant, brought into the sheriff's court by this writ of *de nativo habendo*, could claim his liberty from the lord's constraints. A definition of serfdom was found in the economic imperatives of the time: when the peasant brought his claim to freedom before the king's justices in eyre by a writ of *de libertate probanda*, a relatively heavy and open-ended obligation to work his lord's land, originally just a matter of custom and practice, was used to mark the villein off from the free man – taken indeed as the sign of a condition into which the serf or *nativus* was born. As a matter of birth, unfreedom could also be proved by 'suit of kin' – an ancient technique used in many societies, which paraded the peasant's relatives, his *sequela* or 'brood', to acknowledge their common status. A third mark of servility was the payment recorded in manor-court rolls, which become available from the middle of the thirteenth century, of the tax on the marriage of villein women called *merchet*. One explanation of merchet is that it was intended to compensate the landlord for the loss of further generations of labourers when a female serf married and took her breeding capacity outside the manor. Lords had no power to prevent villein marriages which the developing law of the Church recognized as valid, but they would ensure they did not lose by such marriages. For a similar reason another payment called *legerwite* was taken from villein women who were convicted in the church courts of extra-marital sex (usually when it was made undeniable by pregnancy) and escaped the penance imposed by archdeacon or rural dean by a payment out of what the lords claimed was their money.[3]

[3] R. H. Hilton, 'Freedom and Villeinage in England', *Past and Present*, 31 (1965); *Royal Writs in England from the Conquest to Glanvill*, ed. R. C. van Caenegem (Selden Society, vol. 77, London, 1959), pp. 336–44; P. R. Hyams, 'The Action of Naifty in the Early Common Law', *Law Quarterly Revue*, 90 (1974); *idem*, 'The Proof of Villein Status in the Common Law', *EHR*, 89 (1974); *idem, Kings, Lords*

The treatment of a large proportion of the villagers as a distinct race of serfs who could be bought and sold along with their plots of land and made to pay their lords in order to get married was an undoubted humiliation. Later on, actions of defamation could be brought for calling someone a villein, a name implying rustic simplicity as well as servility. But the real sources of the struggles between lords and peasants were not directly moral but economic, and centred on the unpaid labour the villein had to provide on the lord's demesne and the conditions of his tenure of the plot of land he lived from. Agricultural profits were increasing, but many peasants were kept at a level of bare subsistence as the surplus was transferred to the lord by a mixture of labour rent and money rent. A certain amount of work for the lord might be required of peasants who were counted free: the characteristic of the villeins' services was precisely their uncertainty, so that they did not know in the evening what they would have to do in the morning; and similarly, the lands villeins held of their lords, they held 'only from day to day at will of their lords and by no certain service'. The uncertainty was in what would be required at a specific time, for manorial extents were careful to set out the quantity of work that was owed on the lord's demesne – two or three days a week where services were heaviest, rising to four or five during the busy summer months, with extra 'boon days' when the tenant must bring along his farm-hands to plough or gather the crops – and they also defined a day's work as (say) gathering three bundles of thorn or carrying four cart-loads of corn.[4]

and Peasants in Medieval England: The Common Law of Villeinage in the Twelfth and Thirteenth Centuries (Oxford: Clarendon Press, 1980); for the tests of status, *Bracton on the Laws and Customs of England*, tr. S. E. Thorne, 4 vols. (Cambridge, Mass.: Harvard UP, 1968–77), III.108–9; J. Scammell, 'Freedom and Marriage in Medieval England', *EcHR*, 27 (1974); E. Searle, 'Merchet in Medieval England', *Past and Present*, 82 (1979); P. A. Brand, P. R. Hyams, R. Faith, E. Searle, [debate on] 'Seigneurial Control of Women's Marriage', *Past and Present*, 99 (1983); T. North, 'Legerwite in the Thirteenth and Fourteenth Centuries', *Past and Present*, 111 (1986); examples in *Select Pleas in Manorial and Other Seignorial Courts*, vol. I, ed. F. W. Maitland (Selden Society, vol. 2, London, 1889), pp. 12, 92–4, and pp. 102–3 for extent of labour services; *CRR*, IX.337, for an accusation that a lord had sacked the appellant's house by night and burnt down his barn, because he had married off his daughter without permission.

4 *Select Cases of Defamation to 1600*, ed. R. H. Helmholz (Selden Society, vol. 101, London, 1985), nos. 66, 81, 83, 89; *The Mirror of Justices*, ed. W. J. Whittaker (Selden Society, vol. 7, London, 1895), p. 79; Pollock and Maitland, *HEL*, I.365–74; *Agrarian History of England and Wales*, vol. II: 1042–1350, ed. H. E. Hallam (Cambridge: CUP, 1988), pp. 678–95; *Select Pleas in Manorial Courts*, ed. Maitland, p. 95.

But the increasing demands which thirteenth-century circumstances tempted landlords to make on their tenants were those
which yielded the quickest return in money. From the moment in
1218 that they entered the new house provided for them by Peter
des Roches, the Premonstratensian canons of Halesowen in Worcestershire turned the screw. In the course of the century they
forced up the annual rent a peasant paid for a yardland of 25–30
acres (a standard villein holding) from 3s. 4d. to 6s. 8d. and the
entry fine on taking it from 6s. 8d. to 13s. 4d. The methods used
are indicated by the judgement the villagers obtained against the
abbot before the justices in eyre at Shrewsbury in 1256, for
imprisoning them at will, distraining their goods and preventing
them from pleading in the county court for the return of those
goods. As manorial lord and as grantee of the public jurisdiction
of the hundred court, the abbot could mulct the villagers in his
own court on all sorts of charges. In 1270, a man was fined 12d.
there for letting his dog worry sheep, another 6s. 8d. for erecting
a fence without permission; a man and woman were together fined
4s. in 1280 for ploughing the abbot's demesne badly, and others
were punished for fishing within the lord's enclosure; and in 1282
Peter of Hales was to make amends for depriving the abbot of four
days ploughing at the spring sowings, valued at 16d. The fine of
£10 imposed on the men of Halesowen in 1276 for collective
offences including refusal to elect a reeve was as much as fifteen to
twenty times the price of an ox. The villagers spent their time
evading by guile or force their customary obligations like grinding
their corn (for a fee) at the abbot's mill and the inevitable distraint
when their default was discovered. When they resorted to force
against the lord's bailiffs, and rescued their impounded beasts, the
abbot replied with greater force, at the same time getting the
bishop or rural dean to excommunicate the rebellious tenants, and
the king's justices to adjudge them 'villeins for ever'. The struggles
at Halesowen are paralleled on the manors of the abbeys of Ramsey
and St Albans, and no doubt, though they are not similarly
recorded, on those of many lay lords.[5]

[5] Zvi Razi, *Life, Marriage and Death in a Medieval Parish: Economy, Society and
Demography in Halesowen 1279–1400* (Cambridge: CUP, 1980), p. 9; *idem*, 'The
Struggles between the Abbots of Halesowen and their Tenants in the Thirteenth
and Fourteenth Centuries', in *Social Relations and Ideas: Essays in Honour of R. H.
Hilton*, ed. T. H. Aston *et al.* (Cambridge: CUP, 1983), pp. 156ff, 161–3; *The
Roll of the Shropshire Eyre of 1256*, ed. A. Harding (Selden Society, vol. 96,
London, 1980), pp. 236–7; *Agrarian History*, II, ed. Hallam, pp. 845–6.

The peasants were not always worsted in the battle, however. Though the abbot of Halesowen won at law in 1285, his successors seem to have found it prudent to rest on their gains, and even lessen their demands until new circumstances were created around 1350 by the Black Death. The one steady development in thirteenth-century agrarian society was the incorporation of the peasantry into a common culture of rights and obligations. Groups of villagers learnt to petition the king and complain in the king's courts about their landlords, whose legal powers were less absolute than they seemed, since the right to excercise them in a particular case could always be contested at law. From the king downwards, lords relied on the distraint or seizure of tenants' chattels to make them answer in courts for their rents and services and comply with the judgements given there. (A sort of distraint of the king's own possessions, to be exercised by twenty-five great barons, was prescribed as a way of making John comply with Magna Carta.) The common law offered assistance to the lord 'not powerful enough to constrain his tenant in respect of his services or customs', but it also insisted that the tenants be 'dealt with justly in accordance with the judgement and reasonable custom of the lord's court'. The lord was not permitted at common law to sell the distresses to clear the tenants' liabilities, or even to milk the cows he seized, because the sole purpose of the distraint was to compel the tenant to answer for his default. But much violence continued to be generated by distraint at all levels, so that Simon de Montfort could describe the process as 'the beginning of all wars'.[6]

The Statute of Westminster I did indeed envisage military operations on the part of the sheriff and his posse when the distresses were driven within castle walls and the lord refused to return ('replevy') them when the tenant gave satisfaction. This was important to free peasant farmers, but it was no help to the villeins

---

[6] Razi, 'The Struggles between the Abbots of Halesowen and their Tenants', pp. 157–9; J. C. Holt, *Magna Carta* (Cambridge: CUP, 1965), pp. 239–40; *The Treatise on the Laws and Customs of the Realm of England Commonly Called Glanvill*, ed. G. D. G. Hall (London: Nelson, 1965), pp. 112, 142–3; Pollock and Maitland, *HEL*, I.353, II.577; S. F. C. Milsom, *Historical Foundations of the Common Law*, 2nd edn (London: Butterworths, 1981), pp. 104–5, 142–3; *Early Registers of Writs*, ed. E. de Haas and G. D. G. Hall (Selden Society, vol. 87, London, 1970), pp. 162ff; T. F. T. Plucknett, *The Legislation of Edward I* (Oxford: Clarendon Press, 1949); *Court Rolls of the Manor of Wakefield*, vol. I (1274–97), ed. W. P. Baildon (Yorkshire Archaeological Society Record Series, vol. 29, Leeds, 1901), p. 150 (a pitched battle between Earl Warenne's and the earl of Lincoln's men, arising from distraint).

whose chattels, along with their persons, were reckoned to be their lords' from the start: to individuals like Nicholas son of Bernolf, who appealed Thomas de Lascelles in 1218 for putting him in the stocks as he was trying to replevy his plough beasts, turning his family out of their house and killing his son, but was returned to custody when he was found to have been Thomas's *nativus* and reeve, who 'could not render account of his receipts'; or to the group of villeins who were forced to acknowledge before the justices in eyre in Berkshire in 1248 that they held their tenements in Berrington in villeinage of the prior of Lanthony, and had illegally 'come with iron forks and other arms' to rescue beasts distrained from them because of their withdrawal of 'tallage, merchet, and sumpter and carriage [services] once a year at Lanthony'; or to the villeins of the abbot of Burton, who had 27 boars, 40 oxen, 50 cows, 506 sheep and 77 pigs seized from them as distresses in 1280. Nevertheless, lords who held on 'against gage and pledge' to the chattels of tenants whose villein status they were unable to prove found themselves having to pay damages or might even be imprisoned themselves. A resolute peasant family could win a series of cases against a distraining landlord.[7]

Property in labour was in any case of secondary importance to the control of land. It was treated as actionable 'waste' for the temporary holder of an estate to free villeins living on it, but manumission seems in fact to have been sought infrequently. Peasants, bond and free, were tied to manors essentially because in them lay the strips of arable by which they lived and to which they were as fiercely attached as any gentry to their estates. The livelihood of the villein was put in jeopardy less by the law's definition of his status than by his exclusion from the benefit of Henry II's new legal procedures for the protection of land tenure. It was simply beyond the resources and ambition of royal justice to give protection to the holdings of many below the feudal aristocracy (those specified as 'free tenements' in the petty assizes), and the bulk of the peasantry were of necessity left as 'tenants at will' of their lords. Access to the king's court to plead an action of

---

[7] Plucknett, *Legislation of Edward I*, pp. 57–63; H. M. Cam, *The Hundred and the Hundred Rolls* (London: Methuen, 1930), pp. 82–5, 156; *Rolls of the Justices in Eyre for Yorkshire 1218–19*, ed. D. M. Stenton (Selden Society, vol. 56, London, 1937), no. 1024; *Roll and Writ File of the Berkshire Eyre of 1248*, ed. M. T. Clanchy (Selden Society, vol. 90, London 1973), nos. 7, 221, 235, 295, 818, a229; *CCR*, XI, no. 2141, XVI, no. 122; *Select Cases in the Court of King's Bench*, ed. G. O. Sayles, 7 vols. (Selden Society, London, 1936–71), III, no. 61.

'novel disseisin' (to recover one's land from someone who had recently seized it) or of 'mort d'ancestor' (to claim land occupied by another tenant as one's right by inheritance) became the effective mark of the free tenant, and other tests like certainty of service, or freedom to go where one chose, were used mainly in support of this all-important distinction.[8]

Two factors had long since combined with the villein family's natural attachment to its holding to make villein tenure far more important than servile status. One was the frequency of marriages between bond and free; the other, the pressure on land which made free men willing to hold tenements by villein services provided they had some security of tenure. In Michaelmas term 1296, John son of Robert de Estgate brought an assize of novel disseisin in king's bench against William de Mortimer, who objected that John was his villein. The jurors told what must have been a common story. Bartholomew Hauteyn, John's grandfather, was a freeman who begot Robert of Estgate with one of the Mortimers' bond women. Robert (who would have taken his status from his father) 'afterwards increased in goods and by his trading improved himself so much' that he acquired by charters from the Mortimer family the tenements which were now in dispute. Robert often stayed on the Mortimer manor of Barnham, where his mother lived, and gave the lord 'head-penny', but he paid no other servile dues. It was after his death that William de Mortimer drove John, Robert's son by a free woman, out of his tenements. The judgement of the court was therefore that the land should be restored to John and William pay 24s. in damages.[9]

---

[8] *CRR*, I.126, VII.294, for the tests of whether the tenant can go where he chooses, and whether assizes have ever been taken concerning the land; for the withholding of actions of novel disseisin, mort d'ancestor, trespass and dower from villeins: *Civil Pleas of the Wiltshire Eyre 1249*, ed. M. T. Clanchy (Wiltshire Record Society, vol. 26, Devizes, 1971), nos. 27, 320, 327, 339, 406, 418, 552; *Cases in King's Bench*, ed. Sayles, III, nos. 26, 61; *Pleas before the King or his Justices*, ed. D. M. Stenton, III (Selden Society, vol. 83, London, 1966), nos. 853, 959; *Rolls of the Justices in Eyre for Lincolnshire 1218–9 and Worcestershire 1221*, ed. D. M. Stenton (Selden Society, vol. 53, London, 1934), nos 215, 279; *Rolls of the Justices in Eyre for Gloucestershire, Warwickshire, and Shropshire (1221–2)*, ed. D. M. Stenton (Selden Society, vol. 59, London, 1940), nos. 295, 1458; *Bracton's Note Book*, ed. F. W. Maitland, 3 vols. (London, 1987), nos. 281 (where the justices are confused by the combination of certain services and merchet), 475, 1005.

[9] *Cases in King's Bench*. ed. Sayles, III, no. 26 (extracted in *EHD*, III, no. 199(b); *CRR*, IV. 195–6, for proof of freedom by production of free men on father's side against bond men on mother's; *Gloucestershire Eyre*, ed. Stenton, no. 615, for the rule that a woman who marries a villein cannot share in inherited land.

Already by the second quarter of the thirteenth century, mixed marriages and the attraction of good land, even if it must be held by villein services, had confused Glanvill's picture of villeinage. As a status, it increasingly eluded proof by suit of kin, a primitive technique evolved for an age of peasant endogamy which had passed. (Merchet may in fact have originated as a vain attempt to check marriage beyond the confines of the manor.) Bracton was more concerned to understand villeinage as a tenure and how it should be protected in law. In his discussion of novel disseisin he wrestles long with the problem, drawing on cases decided before his eyes by a great generation of judges, and developing a theory which Maitland was to call 'the relativity of serfage'. According to Bracton, though a man 'is the villein of one and holds of him in villeinage, with the permission of his lord he may hold freely and thus be the free man of the other'. Without a remedy against his manorial lord, a villein could certainly bring an action for disseisin of a free tenement granted by someone else. But did the receipt of free tenements make him enough of a free man to assert (by actions of mort d'ancestor) the right to inherit them, or was a villein's heir always his lord? And what legal protection did the free man have for his villein lands, which might be the source of his livelihood? In his discussion of the case of John of Montacute and Martin of Bestenovere, which came before Martin of Pateshull on eyre in Sussex in 1219, Bracton gets to the point of saying that a free man holding 'in villeinage by villein customs . . . must not be ejected against his will, provided he is willing to do the customs belonging to the villeinage, because they are done by reason of the villeinage and not by reason of the person'. However, the issue was Martin of Bestenovere's status, not his tenure, and a case of 1245 shows four sons of a free man who were married to bond women hestitating to protest their freedom lest they lose their tenements.[10]

THE MANOR

The best guarantee of a peasant family's security of tenure proved to be not the common law but the customary law of manorial communities. Villeins were denied writs to bring such cases into

---

[10] *Bracton on the Laws and Customs of England*, tr. Thorne, III. 98–114, esp. pp. 101, 107; Hyams, *King, Lords and Peasants*, pp. 56–9, 82ff, 112, 119; *idem*, 'Proof of Villein Status', pp. 730, 740, 748; Pollock and Maitland, *HEL*, I. 415; *Bracton's Note Book*, ed. Maitland, nos. 70, 88, 1103; *Lincolnshire and Worcestershire Eyre*, ed. Stenton, no. 228.

the common law courts, but the development of manorial courts to the point of conducting properly recorded proceedings (in a few instances by the mid-thirteenth century) can be seen as a further step in the extension of legal rights to the whole landed community begun by Henry II's assizes. The villagers on royal manors pioneered the assertion of rights for the peasantry which may fairly be regarded as 'public' or 'civic' because they were obtained from a landlord who was also the king, exercised in manorial courts which were also royal courts, and invoked the authority of public records. In 1224, the defendants to a suit for land in the Berkshire manor of Bray objected that it was villein land in the lord king's demesne, and the case was therefore dismissed; but the plaintiffs were told that they should 'seek a writ of right according to the custom of the manor if they so wished'. This is the first clear reference to 'the little writ of right close' which was directed by the king to his bailiffs rather than to his sheriff, and ordered them to do right in the manor court to a plaintiff 'deforced' of his land.[11]

The manorial privileges of the king's villeins must have developed in step with Angevin government, and by the early thirteenth century they were already attracting the envy of the villeins of other lords. The most remarkable part of the story is the rising tide of claims from villeins on what they maintained had once been royal demesne that they should enjoy the same privileges – claims which supplied the impetus for the assertion of peasant rights, all the way to the great revolt of 1381. Villeins on what came by the 1240s to be called 'ancient demesne' of the Crown saw themselves as a distinct class with rights which were indelible. Soon they would seek proof that they did indeed inhabit former royal land in 'the first public record': Domesday Book. Some Surrey men complained to the baronial justiciar in 1258 that Peter of Savoy, the queen's uncle, had increased their rent on the manor of Witley, given to him five years earlier, by £18 7s. 6d. a year over what they had paid when it was in the king's hands. The case was adjourned to the Candlemas parliament of 1259, at which Peter claimed that the manor had been in the king's hands only temporarily, as land forfeited by a Norman lord who adhered to the king of France after 1204; and since he was able to show 'from the book called Domesday' that Witley and its '37 villeins and three cottars' had not belonged to the king in 1086, the complainants were

---

[11] R. S. Hoyt, *The Royal Demesne in English Constitutional History* (Ithaca: Cornell UP, 1950), pp. 108, 192; *Early Registers of Writs*, ed. de Haas and Hall, p. 37.

deemed to have no action 'as sokemen of ancient demesne'. Met by the outrage of their lords and, as in a case of 1275 between the men of King's Ripton and the abbot of Ramsey, by a detailed list of the services that had in fact been extracted from them over the years, the peasants who took the defence of what they conceived to be their customary rights to the king's courts and on to parliament were usually defeated. Yet they came back time and again with assertions of their freedoms under the Crown even back to 'the time of King Cnout', and in the next century would collect funds ('common purses') to pay for their appeals to Domesday Book, so that in the run-up to the revolt of 1381 a frightened gentry presented petitions in parliament against what they saw as a 'great rumour' or conspiracy of the peasantry.[12]

The repository of the village community's sense of its rights was the manor court, which belonged to the peasants who transacted the essential business of their lives there, as much as it did to the lord. The customary law of the peasantry was the sum of the practices worked out in the manor court. Of primary importance were customs about the inheritance and conveyance of land. The manor court existed in the first place to regulate the villein's holding, which indeed it defined as the separate entity later to be called copyhold (tenure certified by the copy of an extract from the manor-court roll). It is significant of the economic importance of peasant tenures that the manor court came to the fore at the same time that the honour court, which supervised the holdings of the lord's feudal tenants (and to which overlords required suit from the manorial lords themselves) began to fade away. Ancient demesne status was desirable above all because the tenure and transmission of the lands of those who enjoyed it had come to be regulated by a customary law of which the suitors of the manor court were the guardians. On the royal manor of Havering the customary tenants performed standard work services for their 120-acre holdings, but their lands were freely passed on both by private charter and by public surrender in the manorial court for regrant by the lord's steward to kinsfolk or purchasers. On the manor of King's Ripton, by then in the hands of the abbot of Ramsey, there was a separate court 'of ancient demesne' in which the peasants

---

[12] *Bracton on the Laws and Customs of England*, tr. Thorne, II. 37, III.108, 132, 295; Pollock and Maitland, *HEL*, I.385ff; Hoyt, *The Royal Demesne*, p. 175–8, 192–8, 210–11; M. K. McIntosh, 'The Privileged Villeins of the English Ancient Demesne', *Viator*, 7 (1976), pp. 315–17, 321; Cam, *Hundred and the Hundred Rolls*, pp. 195, 249; and see next footnote.

employed a formula that was to have a great future in the conveyancing of estates at all levels; vendors surrendered land 'to the use of' purchasers, to whom the abbot's steward automatically regranted it on the payment of a set fine. Land was also passed 'by hereditary descent according to the custom of the manor' to 'heirs by blood'.[13]

Customs for the defence, inheritance and conveyance of peasant land also figure in the records of manors outside ancient demesne, but only as one element in a variety of proceedings. That court rolls became more common in the 1270s seems to have been because a new facility in record-keeping answered a need to register all the rights and obligations of communities long bound together in the working of the open fields. A manor was probably recognized by its possession of a court. At first this might assemble at irregular intervals, when the lord had a purpose for it: it would be convened by a new lord to take homage from the free tenants and fealty from the villeins, and could be summoned to meet at the house of a bond man, to forestall his attempt to sell his land as though he was free. Eventually, 'from three weeks to three weeks' became established as a norm. In court, the first duty of the steward and reeve was to defend the lord's franchise, but the tenants themselves 'presented' the customs of the manor and reported 'whether there be any voidance in the tenement of free or bond and what the lord shall have there by way of heriot or otherwise'. Within the village community distinctions between bond men and free men seem increasingly unimportant, if the proceedings in the court of Merton College's Oxfordshire manor of Cuxham are typical. At a session of the court, held on the feast of the Translation of St Thomas the Martyr (7 July) 1301, John at the Green, the one freeholder in the village, is recorded as doing fealty and giving 7s. relief to his lord on entering his father's tenement 'by charter'; and the lord is credited with a cow worth 6s. received by way of heriot on the death of a leading villein,

---

[13] Pollock and Maitland, *HEL*, I. 388; *Early Registers of Writs*, ed. de Haas and Hall, pp. li–lii, writs: CC41–3, R54–6; *CRR*, XVI, nos. 117k, 149b, 1822; *Select Cases of Procedure without Writ under Henry III*, ed. H. G. Richardson and G. O. Sayles (Selden Society, vol. 60, London, 1941), no. 76; *Select Pleas in Manorial Courts*, ed. Maitland, pp. 99ff; R. H. Hilton, 'A Thirteenth-Century Poem on Some Disputed Villein Services', *EHR*, 66 (1941); *idem*, 'Peasant Movements in England before 1381', *EcHR*, 2nd ser., 2 (1949), reprinted in *Essays in Economic History*, ed. E. M. Carus-Wilson, vol. 1 (London: Arnold, 1954), pp. 80–4; R. Faith, 'The "Great Rumour" of 1377 and Peasant Ideology', in *The English Rising of 1381*, ed. R. H. Hilton and T. H. Aston (Cambridge: CUP, 1984); *RP*, III.21–2.

Robert Waldridge, whose widow Alice did fealty and found pledges that she would 'pay the lord his rightful dues and maintain the said tenement in as good a state as she received it, or better'.[14]

Twelve other cases were dealt with at the Cuxham court in 1301. Richard Cook, a cottager who held by the service of maintaining two lamps in the church, was ordered to be distrained to answer for taking in a strange woman; John Quatermain, to come and do fealty; and Roger Walsh, the lord's villein (who was separately amerced 3d. for non-appearance), to answer for slandering the bailiffs. Walter Prat pledged to pay an amercement of 6d. for trespassing by night in the lord's corn; Gilbert Aumoner and Robert Oldman, to pay amercements of 3d. each for digging up the green in front of the lord's door and spoiling his pasture (for which offence Simon Gardiner's amercement was respited); and Hugh Gifford, an amercement of two pullets for trespassing in the corn. William Heycroft and John at the Green reached a compromise over a complaint of trespass. At the end two inquests (*inquisiciones*) are recorded. Concerning the taking away and concealment of the lord's rights, and injuries to the lord in township or fields, 'the whole village' finds that Adam, the tenant of the prior of Wallingford's mill, has a quickset hedge growing on the lord's land; and further that the reeve could have managed the lord's affairs better with respect to manuring. Finally, William Heycroft and Robert Oldman, the tenant of the lord's mill, ask for jury trial, which upholds William's complaint that Robert levied a toll of a bushel of corn from him: so the corn is to be returned and Robert amerced. Not counting the heriot, the lord gets 9s. 2d. and two pullets out of the proceedings, which involved the one free tenant, five of the thirteen villein tenants and two of the eleven cottagers in the village.[15]

---

[14] Pollock and Maitland, *HEL*, 1.369–70; *Select Pleas in Manorial Courts*, ed. Maitland, pp. xlii–xlvii, 17, 20–1, 34, 40–2, 104ff, 112, 120–2, 124–6; *The Stoneleigh Leger Book*, ed. R. H. Hilton (Dugdale Society, vol. 24, Warwick, 1960), pp. 40, 44–5, 102, 108–10; *Court Rolls of the Wiltshire Manors of Adam de Stratton*, ed. R. B. Pugh (Wiltshire Record Society, vol. 24 Devizes, 1970), nos. 4, 30, 71, 197 etc.; *Court Rolls of the Manor of Wakefield*, vols. I (1274–97), and II (1297–1309), ed. W. P. Baildon (Yorkshire Archaeological Society Record Series, vols. 29, 36, Leeds, 1901, 1906), 1.118; II.xxii, 81–2, 100; *Manorial Records of Cuxham, Oxfordshire, c. 1200–1359*, ed. P. D. A. Harvey (London: HMSO, 1976), pp. 42ff, 79ff, 620–2; P. D. A. Harvey, *A Medieval Oxfordshire Village: Cuxham, 1240 to 1400* (Oxford: Clarendon Press, 1965), pp. 115ff, 122; *The Court Baron*, ed. F. W. Maitland and W. P. Baildon (Selden Society, vol. 4, London, 1890), p. 102.
[15] Harvey, *A Medieval Oxfordshire Village*, p. 122.

Elsewhere a village might be divided between two or more manorial lords, or a manor might embrace a number of separate hamlets, but at Cuxham the bounds of the manor coincided with those of the parish and the village, so that its court rolls give a picture of a complete economic and social unit in its everyday workings. The by-laws enforced in manor courts were often made by assemblies of the whole village (especially where all the land was let to the peasants) and reflect the ways in which people made a living from the land in the various parts of the country. In the normal husbandry of the midlands and south, crops and fallow were rotated over two or more open fields, through which the lord's and the tenants' lands were distributed as arable strips, and pasture and waste were used in common. The villagers chose haywards and woodwards to see that resources were shared among them fairly and used to the community's best advantage. In the summer the animals had to be kept out of the growing corn, 'and ordinances of autumn' were needed to regulate the harvesting and the subsequent (necessarily co-ordinated) turning-out of the cattle to graze on the stubble. (The manuring of the soil was an essential function of cattle in this agriculture, and in any case too little permanent pasture was retained for them.) At harvest, the farmers were determined that there should be no abuse of the age-old right of the poor of the village to glean the spilled ears: at Welwyn Rectory Manor in Hertfordshire in 1287, 'It is ordered by a judgement of the whole court that men and women who are able to reap be distrained not to glean after the fashion of paupers and that those who harbour them be punished, and whatever the gleaners have gathered be seized.' There was suspicion of any nocturnal activity in the fields, and at Newton Longville, Bucks., in 1290, concern about the gathering of other people's peas and beans, crops which may have been recently introduced to the village.[16]

At Cockerham, a manor belonging to the Austin canons of Leicester but far away on the Lancashire coast, the preoccupations revealed by the customs written down at a court held by Brother William Geryn, the monastery's cellarer, in 1326 were different.

---

[16] *Ibid.*, p. 9; W. O. Ault, 'Village Assemblies in Medieval England', in *Album Helen Maud Cam*, Studies Presented to the International Commission for the History of Representative and Parliamentary Institutions, no. 23, (Louvain: Louvain UP, 1960); *idem*, *Open-Field Farming in Medieval England* (London: Allen and Unwin, 1972), pp. 81–7; *Agrarian History*, II, ed. Hallam, pp. 274, 373, 377, for the necessity of agreement on rotation and grazing in open fields.

There is mention of keeping animals out of the corn, and of reaping, but the most cherished resource was peat, of which the peasants were not to 'dig more turves than they can conveniently and sufficiently use for burning', and not to sell to strangers without the lord's permission, the reason being that it was the fuel for the salt cotes where seawater was evaporated off to produce salt. No tenant was to take peat from outside his holding; or 'of his own authority . . . to alter the boundaries of any sands or turf which has been assigned in ancient times'; or 'destroy in any manner the ancient and appointed way on our moss which in English is called Morethweyte or dig turves thereon'; or 'in his digging for turves . . . encroach upon the ancient boundaries assigned to the salt marsh'. Farming for meat was more important in the north and meat required salt for its preservation. At Cockerham, tenants were not to demand from the lord a higher price for their meat than they could get in the market from outsiders. There, extra grazing was provided not by hill pastures but by the sea marsh, the tenants of which were obliged to 'maintain the sea dikes each of them at his own place'. Mixed farming on compact smallholdings (the Cockerham 'crimbles') needed hardly less communal regulation than the arable farming of the south.[17]

The economic imperatives reflected in by-laws and court proceedings merge into social concerns, represented at Cockerham by the setting of a penalty of 40d. for the ale-wife who sold a gallon of ale at a dearer price than a silver halfpenny when the price of a quarter of oats did not exceed 2s. 6d.; of the same amount for anyone calling a neighbour a thief, and 12d. for calling a woman a whore; and of the seizure of a tenant's land if he took part with a stranger or relative in a dispute with his neighbour or impleaded him in a court other than the lord's. Manorial custom often gave a villein's widow much more than the one third of her husband's holding to support her in her widowhood which she would have received by the common law right of 'free bench'. Partible inheritance, where it survived as a way of providing for all the sons of a peasant family, depended on the authority of the manor court. But 60 out of 102 transfers of holdings recorded in early Wakefield court rolls were from father to one son only, and at least

[17] *Two Custumals of the Manor of Cockerham*, ed. R. S. France (Lancashire and Cheshire Antiquarian Society Transactions, vol. 64, Manchester, 1954), pp. 42–7; *Agrarian History*, II, ed. Hallam, pp. 399, 401, 408, 595, for the agriculture of the north, and for salt-making in Lincolnshire.

in the north the primogeniture of the aristocracy seems to have become the norm amongst the peasantry, too. When William son of Soigny of Holmfirth wanted to endow both his sons he had to divide his lands between them in his lifetime, first securing the elder's agreement. On William's death, the steward of Wakefield consequently gave the seisin of a bovate to one brother with the white end of his rod and of a bovate to the other with the black end. But this was a special arrangement which had to be spelled out in the Wakefield manor court in 1275 on behalf of the younger son's heir.[18]

The social importance of the seignorial court increased if the landlord possessed the powers and responsibilities conferred by the franchise of 'view of frankpledge'. This gave him within his own lands the peace-keeping jurisdiction normally exercised by the sheriff in his twice-yearly 'tourn' of the hundred courts, which was another component of the developing Angevin system of justice though one utilizing the ancient subunit of the hundred called a 'tithing'. (The tithing was notionally a group of ten men but was more likely all the inhabitants of a distinct settlement, who were bound to stand pledge in court for their members.) By the later thirteenth century lords are found holding their own tourns, later known as 'courts leet', and using juries of the chief pledges of tithings to regulate local society in ways that would still have relevance centuries later in the early years of the industrial revolution. The leet would be held at the same time as a manor court and the two jurisdictions would fuse together, except where the manor and its lord owed suit to the court of an overlord with view of frankpledge, as Merton College's Cuxham did to the court leet of Richard of Cornwall as lord of the honour of Wallingford. The proceedings of the 'tourns' in Earl Warenne's manor of Wakefield with its subordinate townships like Halifax are recorded from 1275, just as the Hundred Rolls inquiry was investigating such claims to public authority by the great lords of the land. The

---

[18] *Two Custumals*, ed. France, pp. 42–3, 47; R. H. Hilton, *A Medieval Society: The West Midlands at the end of the Thirteenth Century* (London: Weidenfeld and Nicolson, 1966), pp. 74–5, 150ff; *idem, The English Peasantry in the Later Middle Ages* (Oxford: Clarendon Press, 1975), p. 99; G. C. Homans, *English Villagers of the Thirteenth Century* (Cambridge, Mass.: Harvard UP, 1941), p. 181; *Royal Justice and the Medieval English Countryside: The Huntingdonshire Eyre of 1286*, ed. A. R. and E. B. DeWindt (Toronto: Pontifical Institute of Mediaeval Studies, 1981), no. 67, for the custom of free bench at St Neots; *The Court Baron*, ed. Maitland and Baildon, p. 147; *Agrarian History*, II, ed. Hallam, pp. 696–7; *Wakefield Court Rolls* ed. Baildon, I.40–1, II.xxii.

inquiry heard that the bailiffs of the earls of Lincoln and Warenne held tourns on their Yorkshire manors, amercing those who did not come and arresting those indicted by juries, and that the earls exercised other powers, in Warenne's case it was believed for about forty years past. Warenne's reported outburst in 1279, when the magnates were summoned before the justices in eyre to show warrant for their territorial rights, that their forefathers had won them by the sword as the Conqueror's 'partners and helpers', does not diminish the suspicion that leet jurisdiction was assumed by landlords as their rightful share in what were in fact relatively new forms of government. In the counties of the north and west where the institution of frankpledge had never taken root, magnates appointed their own 'serjeants of the peace' to maintain law and order.[19]

The court leet, like the manor court, acted for the community as much as for the lord, and free men and bond men sat together on the juries which presented defaults (perhaps the failure of an abbot or other dignitary to put in an appearance), described offences and assessed the consequent amercements. The court's staple diet consisted of presentments of assaults ranging from blood-shedding to 'villain words'; of the obstruction of highways and watercourses; of breaches of Henry III's assizes forbidding the harbouring of strangers and fixing the price of ale; and of the raising of the hue and cry – the community's means of stopping a fight, but often used maliciously. Like the hundred juries who presented crown pleas before the justices in eyre, leet juries had a series of articles of inquiry to answer, no less than fifty-five at Stoneleigh, such as: 'Concerning housebreakers who are awake at night and sleep by day, and who frequent the tavern, and about whom nobody knows how they get a living, for they do no work.' The Wakefield rolls give a rich picture of life in the townships. Amongst the twenty to thirty items at an average court session, licences may be purchased to dig for coal, all manner of debts sued for, a woman amerced for chattering in court, essoins submitted for non-appearance (and a

---

[19] *Select Pleas in Manorial Courts*, ed. Maitland, pp. xxixff; Cam, *Hundred and the Hundred Rolls*, pp. 124–8, 185–7, 205–13; *The Court Leet Records of the Manor of Manchester 1552–1686, 1731–1846*, ed. J. P. Earwaker (Manchester City Council, Manchester, 1884–90); Harvey, *A Medieval Oxfordshire Village*, p. 147; *Wakefield Court Rolls*, ed. Baildon, i.x, 33, 172, 233 etc.; *Shropshire Eyre*, ed. Harding, pp. xvii–xviii; Judith M. Bennett, *Women in the Medieval English Countryside* (Oxford: OUP, 1987), pp. 160–8.

plaintiff non-suited for being seen in court after essoining) and cases sent to jury trial or wager of law. In 1274 there was much deliberation before Adam Strekayse was cleared of a forest offence after being stopped with a broken and bloody arrow in his possession (had he killed game?); in 1285 Sara the widow of Henry son of Robert of Hartshead was sent to wage her law accused of destroying a horse by striking it with a hatchet on the right hind leg; in the 1290s persons were charged with returning from the Scottish war without licence; and Nicholas of Wiston was said in 1298 to have 'received many times a strange harpist (*extraneum cytheristam*)', who was believed to have been afterwards beheaded (Nicholas was ordered to surrender the harp, which had been left with him).[20]

Though many lords could summarily execute thieves caught on their lands with the loot, seignorial courts were debarred from hearing crown pleas like homicide, robbery and rape. It was to the king's justices that juries of liberties reported on these cases along with other matters raised by the articles of the eyre. (So it was that the men of Hales were able to bring to light the abuses of their own lord.) It is necessary to go to the eyre rolls for evidence of the ways thirteenth-century peasants met their deaths: drowned crossing rivers; caught up in mill-wheels; falling from trees, horses and ladders; run over by carts and animals; or killed by unknown malefactors, in brawls outside ale-houses or accidentally at play. Before the justices who sat at Shrewsbury for a month early in 1256 (the previous eyre in the county had been in 1248), 183 homicides and 61 deaths by misadventure were presented. Of the numerous suspected killers and thieves, only 19 suffered hanging and 23 abjured the realm: but townships were amerced 111 times for not following the hue and cry, 67 times for burying bodies before the coroners could inspect them and 52 times for failing to arrest criminals. On 30 occasions juries were amerced for making defective presentments, or falsely valuing deodands (the instruments, such as carts and horses, of accidental killing) or the chattels of outlawed or executed felons.[21]

[20] *The Court Baron*. ed. Maitland and Baildon, pp. 27–30, 97ff; *Manorial Records of Cuxham*, ed. Harvey, pp. 46–7; *Court Rolls of the Wiltshire Manors of Adam de Stratton*, ed. Pugh, pp. 4–8; Hilton, *A Medieval Society*, pp. 150ff, 230; *Wakefield Court Rolls*, ed. Baildon, I. xii–xiii, 18–21, 73, 145, 206, 253, 257, 282; II. xi, xiv, 44–5, 92.
[21] *Shropshire Eyre*, ed. Harding, pp. xvi–xviii, nos. 541, 643–9, 656–72, 728.

THE PARISH

Clerics figure prominently in both the civil litigation and the criminal activity recorded in the rolls. A man convicted of felony in the king's court would often claim benefit of clergy and be handed over to the bishop's officer for punishment. (Bishops kept prisons for criminous clerks because the Church did not impose blood-punishments.) More interesting than the clergy's criminality is the impact on local society of their special skills and function. A session of the Wakefield tourn at Halifax in 1277 was told that the vicar of Halifax had been consulted about how to recover some deeds given for safe-keeping to a woman who now refused to return them; but his advice that a daughter be used to 'get them from her mother by some artifice' did not work. The vicar appears again in the next item in the roll, accused of levying

a new custom on the whole parish; for whereas they were accustomed to give one calf as a tithe on seven calves, he now makes the whole parish give [one] of six, and they may nowise count till they come to ten . . . and the Parson . . . deals in the same way with lambs; they can get no remedy except through the Earl's bailiffs.

The rector of a parish – the man with the *right* to the tithes, who often had someone else to stand in for him as vicar – might equally complain in the court leet that he had suffered from the ill-tithing of the lord's goods.[22]

Tithing, that is the taking of a tenth of everything of which 'God gives the increase' to support the parish clergy in the cure of souls, was only one of the ways in which the Church as an institution bore heavily on the village community. (Of course, bishops and abbots were also private landlords, and in that role also frequently of a demanding sort.) From the same root in the administration of the hundred as the court leet there had developed the jurisdiction of the archdeacon. Before the Conquest, secular and ecclesiastical causes were dealt with together in the king's courts, but the reforming papacy had worked to disentangle them, to a large extent so as to enforce its ideal of clerical celibacy. In particular the swarms of chaplains – clergy employed by the parsons to assist them in their parishes, or by lords to serve in their

[22] *Berkshire Eyre*, ed. Clanchy, no. 999; *Shropshire Eyre*, ed. Harding, nos. 566, 673, 749, 791, 794, 857 etc.; *Wakefield Court Rolls*, ed. Baildon, I. 173; *The Court Baron*, ed. Maitland and Baildon, p. 105.

private chapels – needed to be controlled. At the end of Edward I's reign, the Wakefield leet heard how 'Alice wife of John Kyde of Wakefield was abducted by night by the servant of Nicholas, the parish chaplain of Wakefield, on the chaplain's horse and by his command, and with the woman's consent'; Alice afterwards returned to her husband, and no doubt the story was told in the court leet because she had gone off with money from her husband's purse, gold rings, a gown, a new hood from her husband's pack and other valuable things (all of which suggests that John was a trader rather than an ordinary peasant). The moral aspects of the case were reserved to the church court, though the representation of the villagers there by a panel of parishioners must have made it seem very like the view of frankpledge – except that the jurisdiction of the archdeacon on his tour of the rural deaneries was far more peremptory and oppressive than those of the lord's steward. Clerks and laymen equally came under his stern discipline, and in 1281 Archbishop Pecham was disturbed that simple priests were being made to look fools at the rural chapter in front of the laity.[23]

A parson might cite his parishioners in the chapter for habitually working on Sundays, and the rural dean excommunicate whoever had burnt down an abbot's hedges, but by the time of the first surviving records at the very end of the thirteenth century, the ruridecanal court spent most of its effort correcting the laity in matters of sexual morality. At chapters held in churches in Droitwich deanery in the diocese of Worcester on four days between mid-May and mid-July 1300 ('and there will be another when needed') 107 persons from fifteen parishes were cited: one for wife beating, ten for adultery, all the rest for fornication, quite often repeated with the same partner. Some were excommunicated for contumacy, and others who denied the sin were required to swear their innocence with up to nine oath-helpers; but most confessed – if they were pregnant like Margery of the Churchyard, who fornicated with William servant of the rector of Northfield, they could hardly do otherwise – and were 'whipped in the usual way', once to three times through the market place. Of course, this was the punishment for a rector's servant, a nurse, a drover, a weaver, a shepherd and an ironmonger, not for their betters, whose sexual

[23] J. Scammell, 'The Rural Chapter in England from the Eleventh to the Fourteenth Century', *EHR*, 86 (1971); *Wakefield Court Rolls*, ed. Baildon, II. 93; C. Dyer, *Lords and Peasants in a Changing Society: The Estates of the Bishopric of Worcester, 680–1540* (Cambridge, CUP, 1980), pp. 363–4.

misdemeanours would be dealt with more respectably in the bishop's courts.[24]

The other surviving record of this period, from the archdeaconry of Sudbury in the diocese of Norwich, shows a more regular court handling a wider range of social problems. The rector of Gedding is cited for non-residence (he was consorting with Magga, the stepdaughter of Sir Adam Fitzhugh), and for neglecting to give alms to the poor of his parish; and other clerks and chaplains are charged with not submitting citations and not attending to services. Lay people are accused of disturbing divine service by talking in church, of associating with an excommunicated woman and of sheltering an adulterous couple and a woman pregnant by a clerk. An argument about a gold brooch is brought before the court as arising from breach of faith, a concept which made churchmen the arbiters in types of dispute which secular courts had not yet learnt to handle. The great majority of sexual offences are for contravention of the Church's marriage law, not simple fornication. Two men are cited for maltreating their wives and one is charged with not fulfilling his undertaking to maintain his daughter. Adultery cases are outnumbered by eight citations for the contraction of marriages in secret. Marriages were made by the parties' expression of consent followed by consummation, and secrecy did not invalidate them. But repeated diocesan statutes in the thirteenth century tried to ensure that the contract was not entered into in taverns and other 'suspect places', was in due form of words and properly witnessed and took place only after the threefold calling of bans in church; for otherwise the prevention of bigamous and incestuous marriages, and of the social ills caused by unstable marital relationships, would be an impossible task for ecclesiastical judges.[25]

Many aspects of village life besides marriage relationships were affected by the flood of diocesan legislation released by the Fourth Lateran Council of 1215, though the rights and discipline of the clergy are its main preoccupation. The leadership provided by the parish priest remains impossible to assess. Parochial clergy can

---

[24] The Droitwich proceedings are printed in *EHD*, III.724–9; for commentary, Hilton, *A Medieval Society*, pp. 261ff.

[25] A Gransden, 'Some Late Thirteenth-Century Records of an Ecclesiastical Court in the Archdeaconry of Sudbury', *BIHR*, 32 (1959); *Councils and Synods, with Other Documents relating to the English Church*, vol. II: A.D. 1205–1313, ed. F. M. Powicke and C. R. Cheney (Oxford: Clarendon Press, 1964), pp. 996–9; R. H. Helmholz, *Marriage Litigation in Medieval England* (Cambridge: CUP, 1974), esp. pp. 172ff.

rarely be identified, since the tithes of the parish had very often been appropriated by monasteries, and the portion which bishops required to be assigned to the vicars and chaplains with the actual cure of souls was insufficient to attract the educated and ambitious men whose careers are known. The presumption is that they were often indistinguishable from the peasants they served and along with whom they must have worked in the fields for six days of the week. What diocesan statutes tell us is that villeins sometimes illegally sought ordination in order to gain their freedom, and that clerical concubinage was a large problem (it is known also that the actual inheritance of benefices lingered on in the Welsh marches). Archdeacons were ordered to inquire into the literacy of those with the rule of parishes (who were to be past the first year of their priesthood), and in the bishopric of Exeter to see that every incumbent possessed and used a written summary of the faith. The people were to be taught about the dangers of clandestine marriages, pregnant women about their needs at childbirth and mothers and nurses about the risk of suffocating babies they took to bed with them. Nothing was ever to be charged for spiritual ministrations. The sick were to have the sacrament of the lord's body carried to them with all reverence, the priest singing penitential psalms as he came and went and the people kneeling, their hands joined in prayer, as he passed. Rectors should reside in parishes, devoting their resources to the ends they were given for, providing hospitality, performing works of charity and relieving the poor. The latter were to have tithes remitted to them and receive a share of the income taken as a punishment from incontinent and negligent clergy.[26]

The demands of the clergy for tithes and offerings must have been felt by the villagers to outweigh by far the benefits they conferred. The extent of the burden of tithes is indicated by the detailed regulations, distinguishing between 'praedial tithes' to be paid in the parish where the crops grew and the personal tithes (levied on the profits of labour) to be paid where the sacrament was received; and pronouncing on issues such as the tithing of sheep which slept in one parish and were driven into another for grazing and shearing. Particularly controversial and difficult must have been the collection of the 'small tithes' of such things as lambs

[26] *Councils and Synods*, ii, ed. Powicke and Cheney, pp. 24–5, 35, 60, 180, 186, 204–5, 228, 461–2, 640, 1017–18, 1031–3; Julia Barrow, 'Hereford Bishops and Married Clergy, c. 1130–1240', *Historical Research*, 60 (1987).

and chickens which were allotted to the vicar when the great tithes of the main crops went to an absent rector, and the country clergy also relied for their living on the offerings required of parishioners at Christmas, Easter and their church's dedication festival, and on mortuary dues – commonly the dead farmer's best beast. All this the parishioners had to bear along with the expense of the visitations of the archdeacon and his retinue, and the penances and excommunications imposed at them for infringements of clerical rights.[27]

Yet the demands of the clergy encouraged lay people in a sense of their own rights and responsibilities. The parish church was the centre of communal life, and Sunday mass was the occasion for proclamations about all sorts of secular matters, for instance illicit woodcutting. The repeated prohibitions by king as well as bishop of secular activities in church buildings and churchyards are evidence of the people's obstinate claim to them for the holding of markets, fairs and courts, and to accommodate recreations of all sorts (particularly at festivals) – play-acting, bear-baiting, wrestling-matches, ball-games, all manner of allegedly 'dirty team-games which encouraged lewd behaviour'. Churches were the obvious locations for the 'lovedays' to which so many legal disputes were remitted for arbitration. The comprehensive Exeter diocesan statutes of 1287 found it necessary both to order the demolition of secular buildings erected in churchyards and to forbid the felling of trees planted in them as wind-breaks.[28]

By this time the villagers' interest in the affairs of their church was receiving more positive encouragement from the insistence of English bishops that the landholders of the parish should contribute, in proportion to the size of their tenements, to the upkeep of the church and the provision of the increasingly costly church ornaments. Groups of parishioners negotiated with rector and archdeacon about the size of their contribution, though by *c.* 1240 it was an established 'custom of the English church' that the nave and churchyard were entirely the laity's responsibility (so that the

---

[27] *Councils and Synods*, II, ed. Powicke and Cheney, pp. 315, 491, 1010–11, 1036–40, 1050–7, 1389; C. R. Cheney, *From Becket to Langton: English Church Government 1170–1213* (Manchester: Manchester UP, 1956), pp. 161–2.

[28] Emma Mason, 'The Role of the English Parishioner, 1100–1500', *Journal of Ecclesiastical History*, 27 (1976), p. 27; cap. 6 of the Statute of Winchester (1285), *EHD*, III.462; Pollock and Maitland, *HEL*, I.613–14; *Councils and Synods*, II, ed. Powicke and Cheney, pp. 35–6, 195, 202–4, 432 (44), 601, 1003–10, 1035, 1039; *Wakefield Court Rolls*, ed. Baildon, I.5, 134, 148, II.xxv, xxvi.

chancel, left to the parson, was often neglected). Parishioners also negotiated the terms on which chapels and graveyards were provided for settlements remote from the parish church – the hamlets which significantly were most prone to become 'deserted villages' in a time of economic depression. Those who paid naturally wanted to supervise the work, and soon felt the need to accumulate permanent funds from legacies, and from church rates such as the majority of the inhabitants of Wiverton in Nottinghamshire agreed to pay in 1298. By 1261 lay wardens (*custodes, procuratores parochie*) had begun to be chosen to administer and account to the parishioners for these special funds to maintain the fabric of the church buildings: usually endowments of land and rents which had to be entrusted to laymen because royal legislation prevented their placing in the 'dead hand' of the Church.[29]

A parish fund for general purposes, dispensed by permanent churchwardens, was still to come, but it was brought nearer by the requirements first set down by the provincial Council of Oxford in 1222 for the provision of church ornaments and service books, of which inventories were to be presented to the archdeacons for inspection, and by repeated injunctions to relieve the poor. The latter were to be attended to by the stewards or *economi* of rectors who did not reside nor have vicars; 'church-reeve' is another term which looks forward to the churchwarden. The untrustworthiness of poor vicars and the prevalence of thefts from churches caused the laity to demand a greater share in the custody of church furnishings (much of which, like the candles and the bell-ropes, they regularly provided) than the clergy were willing to concede. The Exeter statutes deplored arguments between rectors and their parishioners, who set up alms-boxes in churches on their own authority, and actually preached that all alms should be collected there in future and offerings withheld from the priests. Such presumption and conspiracy were to be heavily punished and the boxes removed.[30]

Probably it was in the more urbanized parishes that the laity were getting above themselves to the extent of diverting offerings

[29] Mason, 'Role of the English Parishioner', pp. 23–7; C. Drew, *Early Parochial Organisation in England: The Origins of the Office of Churchwarden*, St Anthony's Hall Publications, no. 7 (York: Borthwick Institute of Historical Research, 1954), pp. 6, 8–10, 13–15, 21; Dyer, *Lords and Peasants in a Changing Society*, pp. 262, 363; *Councils and Synods*, ed. Powicke and Cheney, pp. 408–9, 1002–5.

[30] Drew, *Early Parochial Organisation*. pp. 9, 15ff; *Councils and Synods*, II ed. Powicke and Cheney, pp. 907 (c. 11), 1005–8.

to the purposes they decided, celebrating unofficial feastdays and venerating unauthenticated relics, and battling physically to get their churches' banners before the others in the annual procession to the cathedral church. But everywhere in England, as throughout western Europe, there were by the end of the thirteenth century real 'communities', sometimes called 'of the vill' and occasionally 'of the parish', which were compounded of the material organization of the manor and the moral authority of the Church. After the Reformation this social institution would be taken over by the State to administer a comprehensive poor law by means of church-wardens and (originally manorial) constables – as the 'civil parish' thus becoming the basis of public welfare provision and true local government in both England and America. The growth of the communal action given prominence by a whole line of historians from Stubbs to Cam does seem to have been one of the two most significant trends in thirteenth-century peasant society. The objection that perhaps ancient collectivities were simply being registered for the first time in court records is answered by the fact that these records were of new institutions which were providing the local communities with the framework necessary for their working. Newly developed techniques of royal, baronial and ecclesiastical administration gave the local community its structure: through the duties they laid upon the village to give answers through the reeve and four men to the articles of the eyre and the great series of special inquiries; through the requirement (by ordinances of 1233, 1242 and 1285) that local people keep watches and have constables; and through the use of village juries and groups of parishioners to present offences in the leet and rural chapter.[31]

THE PEASANT LAND MARKET, AND DIFFERENTIATION WITHIN PEASANT SOCIETY

The other significant trend in rural society was economic differentiation amongst the peasantry. Distinctions between free and unfree

[31] *Councils and Synods*, II, ed. Powicke and Cheney, pp. 205, 1021, 1044; Drew, *Early Parochial Organisation*, pp. 5, 22–4; C. Platt, *The Parish Churches of Medieval England* (London: Secker and Warburg, 1981), cap. 5: 'The Community of the Parish'; Pollock and Maitland, *HEL*, 1.560–1; Susan Reynolds, *Kingdoms and Communities in Western Europe, 900–1300* (Oxford: Clarendon Press, 1984), pp. 148–54; Helen Cam, *Law-Finders and Law-Makers in Medieval England* (London: Merlin Press, 1962), cap. 4: 'The Community of the Vill'; *Select Pleas in Manorial Courts*, ed. Maitland, pp. lxvi–lxviii; Homans, *English Villagers*, p. 335.

came to mean little in the proceedings of the local courts, which sought to compensate villagers of whatever status for unpaid debts, malicious accusations and the slandering of neighbours as usurers and thieves. Nor, despite the Halesowen evidence, was the opposition of tenant and landlord the dominant feature of manor court and leet; by the end of the century the majority of fines imposed in these courts were a standard 3d. or 6d., and expressed community discipline rather than seignorial exploitation. That the fines had fallen to this low level was probably because the jurors who assessed them knew the peasants' poverty. This impoverishment points to the real origin of social divisions. An expanding mass of peasant cultivators struggled to survive on ludicrously small resources – and static resources, since the potency of the technological revolution which had produced the horse collar and the watermill was fading, and the possibilities of colonization in waste and woodland running out. Every parcel of land was at a premium. The most striking evidence of this was the appearance of a peasant land market, through which a few farmers with enterprise and capital were able to accumulate holdings and advance themselves while the majority declined.[32]

The exact mechanism and timing of the spread of the land market down from the magnates and knights to the small freeholders and villeins is still disputed. A necessary prelude was the transfer of emphasis from status to tenure evident in Bracton's treatment of villeinage. The holding which supported the peasant's labour began to be assigned a monetary value which could be realized. Probably the first parcels of land to be precisely measured and paid for were small 'assarts' carved from the waste and additional to the peasant's main holding. The intensity which the competition for the remaining waste had reached by 1236 is indicated by the fourth chapter of the Statute of Merton, framed in answer to the complaint of 'many magnates of England who [had] enfeoffed their knights and freeholders with small tenements in their large manors' and then found that they could not profit from the 'wastes, woods and pastures' because the new tenants claimed rights of common in them. By the terms of the statute, proof that there was sufficient pasture for the tenements and free access to it

---

[32] *Wakefield Court Rolls*, ed. Baildon, I, 1, 3, 15, 17, 281 etc.; *Royal Justice and the Medieval English Countryside*, ed. DeWindt and DeWindt, pp. 84ff, 108ff; A. N. May, 'An Index of Thirteenth-Century Peasant Impoverishment', *EcHR*, 26 (1973).

would be a good defence to actions of novel disseisin against manorial lords who enclosed pasture land.[33]

The growth of population exerted increasing pressure on patterns of tenure, particularly in East Anglia, where the custom of dividing family holdings between sons was most common. In the years 1282–4 the replacement rate on the Norfolk manor of Gressenhall was 1.6: that is, twenty-five male heirs succeeded sixteen deceased tenants. Once begun, fragmentation tended to accelerate. In 1302 amercements for failing to perform a day's harvest work were imposed in Gressenhall manor court on twelve tenants 'of the land that was Henry Gille's', which in 1293 had been taken over by his three sons. The 104 tenements in Norwich cathedral priory's manor of Martham around the year 1220 had been broken up by 1292 into over 900, averaging less than two and a quarter acres each and held by about 370 individuals; one had no less than 23 tenants. On the sandy and infertile soil of Sedgeford in north-west Norfolk the average holding of the 230 or so tenants *c.* 1280 needed to be larger and was about ten acres, but fifty of the actual tenements were less than three acres in size. Outside East Anglia, the same break-up of the old family tenements has been observed on manors belonging to the chapter of St Paul's Cathedral, London, at Caddington and Kensworth in Bedfordshire.[34]

The land market was stimulated by the tenurial fragmentation. Subdivision reduced the land in Martham to 2,100 fragments with an average size of just over one and a half roods, many of which would have fallen below subsistence level. Tenants with less than an acre each did better to sell or rent out their entire holdings, in dealings which must very often not have come to court to be

---

[33] *The Peasant Land Market in Medieval England*, ed. P. D. A. Harvey (Oxford: Clarendon Press, 1984), pp. 19–28; Andrew Jones, 'Caddington, Kensworth, and Dunstable in 1297', *EcHR*, 2nd ser., 32 (1979), p. 319; Jean Birrell, 'Common Rights in the Medieval Forest: Disputes and Conflicts in the Thirteenth Century', *Past and Present*, 117 (1987); *EHD*, III. 352.

[34] Cicely Howell, 'Peasant Inheritance Customs in the Midlands 1280–1700', in *Family and Inheritance: Rural Society in Western Europe 1200–1800*, ed. J. Goody, Joan Thirsk and E. P. Thompson (Cambridge: CUP, 1976), pp. 126, 135; *idem*, *Land, Family and Inheritance in Transition: Kibworth Harcourt 1280–1700* (Cambridge: CUP, 1983); cf. A. Macfarlane's criticisms in *The Origins of English Individualism: The Family, Property and Social Transition* (Oxford: Blackwell, 1978), pp. 109–11; *The Peasant Land Market*, ed. Harvey, pp. 7–28; Janet Williamson, 'Norfolk: Thirteenth Century', in *ibid*, pp. 39–50, 56–60, 64–68, 87–105; E. Miller, *The Abbey and Bishopric of Ely* (Cambridge: CUP, 1951), p. 132; Jones, 'Caddington, Kensworth, and Dunstable in 1297'.

recorded, though the earliest manor-court rolls show lords prepared, for payment, to allow their villeins to alienate their lands.
On the other hand the situation allowed a minority of farmers to
accumulate small parcels gradually into large holdings (perhaps
mortgaging the land they had already taken on lease), at a time
when the capital was not available to buy up and stock full-size
tenements. In the Isle of Ely the process was already well advanced
by 1251: at Doddington eight men had less than an acre each,
twenty-three from 1 to 10 acres, seven from 10 to 20 acres, three
from 20 to 50 acres, four from 50 to 100 acres, and one man over
100 acres. Two of the aproximately 230 tenants at Sedgeford in
Norfolk in 1279–82 held only cottages with no arable attached to
them, but several over 25 acres each and one 54 acres. By a series
of small purchases, possibly of the uneconomically small endowments of his neighbours' sons, the villein Martin Suvel was able to
provide for his own sons and also build up his 3-acre patrimony
into a holding of over 35 acres. By five separate charters, Albin of
Stanford, a freeholder and for a time the priory's steward in
Sedgeford, accumulated 27½ acres. The accumulation of fragments
of mixed villein and free land, held from landlords great and small,
created 'a class of thriving yeomen' who must have had a dominat-
ing position in the local community. At the other extreme was a
landless group, consisting of anonymous 'undersettles' who appear
in the record only because they owe some service on the demesne
at harvest time: some of them younger sons and daughters, some
'strangers coming from without to hire houses from divers persons
and hold nothing of the lord'.[35]

The peasant land market clearly served the ambitions of enter-
prising individuals, even though many of the large holdings did
not survive past the next generation, either because the necessary
investment was not sustained, or because there was a prejudice
against such accumulations and a belief that they ought to be
broken up amongst all the children. But only its adaptation to the
wider purposes of families and communities in a changing economic situation will explain the land market's vigour and the
crumbling of the standard tenements before it. In some places the
partible inheritance which helped to create the conditions for a
peasant land market seems itself not to have been an ancient custom

---

[35] P. R. Hyams, 'The Origins of a Peasant Land Market in England', *EcHR*, 2nd
ser., 33 (1970); *The Peasant Land Market*, ed. Harvey, pp. 23–7, 48; cf. Macfarlane, *Origins of English Individualism*, pp. 124–30.

but a new development in response to demographic pressure: as the family group became too large to function communally, and the possibility of acquiring extra land by assart ran out, coheirs who would earlier have worked their inheritance jointly began to seek specific allotments. These same brothers who decided to share out the family lands on their father's death might choose to pass their separate hearths on to their eldest sons (or their youngest, the older ones having been sent out with as much of an endowment as could be scraped together). As forms of inheritance, partition and primogeniture (or ultimogeniture) were just different ways of fulfilling a commitment to the family unit in different and fast-changing circumstances. Landlords with an interest in preserving the integrity of tenements and the attached services tended to put their weight behind inheritance by one son. It was the land market, however, that adjusted peasant tenures to economic reality, by allowing a trade in fragments of land which partible inheritance had made too small for subsistence.[36]

Inheritance customs should be seen as the adaptable instruments (rather than the age-old determinants) of village life. The provision for widows by customs of 'free bench' and for retired parents by maintenance agreements was another product of the definition of individual property rights which the rise of the land market entailed. Manor-court rolls often record an elderly couple or a widowed father or mother handing over the family holding to a son, or it could be to an unrelated purchaser, in return for food and drink, or a grain allowance if the parent did not wish to continue to share the hearth, and perhaps a tunic worth 2s. 6d. and 6d. a year for shoe repairs. These maintenance agreements are evidence of economic differentiation within the peasantry and of widespread impoverishment, but also that the needs of particularly vulnerable groups were receiving communal recognition. In a sample of seventy agreements from England south of the Trent between the mid-thirteenth century and the onset of the Black Death studied by Dr Dyer the quantities of corn provided 'according to the custom of the vill' or 'according to that which her status requires' ranged from nine quarters (seventy-two bushels) down to one bushel, the larger amounts in the twenty cases where full or half yardlands (around fifteen to thirty acres) were surrendered.

---

[36] *The Peasant Land Market*, ed. Harvey, pp. 75ff, 341, 350; Miller, *The Abbey and Bishopric of Ely*, pp. 89, 132–51; *The Court Baron*, ed. Maitland and Baildon, pp. 113, 146.

An example of the dozen or so best provided for is Margaret atte Green of Girton, Cambridgeshire, who in 1291 was granted two quarters of wheat and two quarters of barley annually – enough, Dyer calculates, to yield 2.3 lb of bread and 2.6 pints of ale a day and an intake of 3,000 calories, 'more than sufficient according to modern assumptions for the needs of an elderly sedentary woman'. In a period of land-hunger, those with land to trade could demand generous provision, though others beside the grantees might have to be maintained from the grants. Even just for themselves the thirty or more recipients of twelve to sixteen bushels of corn a year could only have got a daily ration of 2,000 calories from bread and puddings (none would have been left for brewing), which is sufficient to sustain only light work. The twenty-five with eight bushels or less would have starved without other earnings, which in the case of the more able-bodied might have come from their own small plots, but in that of the infirm from 'gleaning, begging and stealing'.[37]

These 'inadequately fed old people' probably represent 'only a part of a large pool of underemployed and undernourished small-holders and landless in the bottom ranks of rural society'. But there are many uncertainties about the condition of the rural mass of the English population and how it was changing, until the Black Death brutally inserted a new factor into the equation in the mid-fourteenth century. What was in the average farmer's diet? The evidence from the early fourteenth century suggests that perhaps a third of smallholders possessed no livestock at all; and the only animals the better-off kept entirely for meat were pigs. The average peasant with only ten to twenty sheep even in sheep-farming areas, could not have afforded to slaughter any of them for meat. Excavations at Wharram Percy in Yorkshire have shown that villagers twenty miles inland might include sea fish in their diet. Herrings were cheap and appeared in the feasts which lords

[37] *The Peasant Land Market*, ed. Harvey, pp. 18, 39, 42–3, 56, 58, 81, 350–5; Rosamond Faith, 'Peasant Families and Inheritance Customs in Medieval England', *Agricultural History Review*, 14 (1966), pp. 81ff; Homans, *English Villagers*, pp. 126–7; Dyer, *Lords and Peasants in a Changing Society*, pp. 86, 106, R. M. Smith, 'Families and their Land in an Area of Partible Inheritance: Redgrave, Suffolk, 1260–1320', in *Land, Kinship and Life-Cycle*, ed. R. M. Smith (Cambridge: CUP, 1984); Bennett, *Women in the Medieval English Countryside*, pp. 160–8; C. Dyer, 'English Diet in the Later Middle Ages', in *Social Relations and Ideas*, ed. Aston *et al.*, pp. 197–216; *idem*, *Standards of Living in the Later Middle Ages: Social Change in England c. 1200–1520* (Cambridge: CUP, 1989), pp. 151–5.

provided for their tenants when they performed their harvest 'boon-works'. The members of an average peasant household of five, with two cows, could have consumed no more than an ounce of dairy produce each a day. They might nevertheless have enjoyed a more varied diet than their lord, who would have disdained to eat cheese, or the peas and beans grown in the fields and the cabbages and onions from garden-plots. But this sustenance was always at the mercy of seasonal fluctuations and harvest failures – increasingly so for the majority who scraped it from dwindling tenements.[38]

What resources might villagers have had in cash to buy extra food and ale? How did a farmer find the money to keep his household in the brass pots and pans costing 2s. each, which most households seem to have possessed in the thirteenth century to cook their vegetables and puddings; or in bed-coverings with sheets at 3s. 4d., linen undergarments at 8d. each for all the family, woollen tunics at 3s. and leather shoes at 6d.; and also manage to have essential farming equipment such as a cart priced at 10s.? How was the building of a new homestead financed, at its most substantial a forty-five-foot longhouse with two barns, which the excavation of deserted village sites has shown were often timber-framed from the thirteenth century and provided with at least a stone base to the walls? For 10s. a landlord could run up a flimsy cottage for a smallholder, but wealthier peasants were buying materials and the services of skilled craftsmen in the market place, at a total cost of £2–£3 for a building of three bays.[39]

The range from the prosperity of the greater tenant farmers to the bare sufficiency of the lesser men may be represented by the tax assessment of the Suffolk village of Wattisfield in 1283. One of the jurors who made the assessment had livestock and grain worth £4 14s., another goods worth only 11s. 4½d., the latter sum equivalent to just a cow and half a dozen sheep, even if nothing is allowed for corn. Lower still were those with less than half a mark (6s. 8d.) in goods, who were not enumerated in 1283 because they

[38] Dyer, *Standards of Living*, pp. 110–17, 154–8, 160–87; *idem*, 'English Diet', pp. 206–8; M. M. Postan, 'Village Livestock in the Thirteenth Century', in his *Essays on Medieval Agriculture and General Problems of the Medieval Economy* (Cambridge: CUP, 1973), pp. 219, 233; *Shropshire Eyre*, ed. Harding, no. 513; D. A. Hinton, *Archaeology, Economy and Society: England from the Fifth to the Fifteenth Century* (London: Seaby, 1990), pp. 150, 163–4, 180.
[39] Postan, 'Village Livestock', p. 216; Dyer, *Standards of Living*, pp. 120, 176, 180–1.

were exempted from the tax; and almost completely out of sight at the bottom, clusters of sub-tenants with not much more than their cottages, and landless serfs whose most valuable possessions were not worth 6d.[40]

The smaller tenants may have had an income in addition to their agricultural production, for wages were an important factor in local economies. Brewing and baking were resorts of those with little land, though brewing at least was a sporadic and unreliable trade, largely of single women, which fell off in years of poor harvest as people made do with water. Or paid employment might be sought on the lord's demesne. For five weeks of harvest on two manors of the priory of Norwich where villein services were light, there were hired in 1296 twenty carters, four stackers and thirty-one reapers. Though the richer farmers might offer employment too, the lord often claimed priority in the recruitment of labour; and in competing for such work the better-off smallholders, possessing carts and equipment, had an advantage. As demesne cultivation intensified, landlords had also begun to employ *famuli* as full-time ploughmen, carters, harrowers and herdsmen; men with the benefit of annual contracts which they could invoke in the manor court, and an element of inflation-resistant payment in corn and milk, and accommodation in the lord's household. In 1300, something like half the adult males of Cuxham, a village of 150 people spread over 30 households, were wage-earners, nine of them *famuli* on the lord's demesne and fourteen cottagers employed more widely on a part-time basis. A more down-trodden group were the 'life-cycle servants', the children and unmarried daughters, liable to be exploited sexually as well as economically.[41]

A quite different class of wage-earners were the many rural artisans: the smiths, carpenters, weavers, potters, glass-makers, cart-wrights and fletchers. Best-paid were the building workers. The work of Thorold Rogers showed that a thatcher's wages, for instance, rose from 2d. to 3d. a day between 1261 and 1311 in cash terms, though inflation reduced their value in real terms. The most experienced masons employed on the building of Edward I's new monastery of Vale Royal in Cheshire in the summer of 1278 could earn as much as 3s. a week: a mason working on Exeter cathedral

---

[40] Dyer, *Standards of Living*, pp. 131–3.
[41] *The Peasant Land Market*, ed. Harvey, p. 99; Ault, *Open-Field Farming*, p. 29; Harvey, *A Medieval Oxfordshire Village*, pp. 75–86, 113–35; E. Clark, 'Medieval Labor Law and English Local Courts', *American Journal of Legal History*, 27 (1983), p. 335.

for forty-six weeks in 1299–1300 earned a total of £4 17s. 2½d. But there were enormous differentials in wages between these men and the unskilled worker who might gain a mere 1d. a day; most of the work was piece work, seasonal and intermittent; and the countryside was full of men prepared to walk considerable distances in search of it. The 30s. to £2 which the average labourer might earn in a year in 1278, and the 2s. to 5s. the *famulus* got in addition to his food ration, would have been sufficient to live on with barley at 3s. 9d. a quarter: when it rose to 5s. there would have been nothing left over for ale and clothes[42]

Regional differences complicated the tracing of differentiation in the ranks of the peasantry. The great divide was between the east and south of the country, and the west and north: between the fenland parts of Holland in Lincolnshire which stood first in wealth in 1334, assessed at £68 per thousand acres, and the hill country of the North and West Ridings of Yorkshire and the rough grazing of Lancashire, counties ranked thirty-sixth to thirty-eighth and assessed respectively at £7 0s., £6 10s. and £4 12s. per thousand acres. Only exceptionally were the flocks of the Cistercian monasteries and cattle farms like Earl Warenne's at Sowerby commercial enterprises to be compared with the southern grain factories. Within northern England, the border counties (excluded from the 1334 assessment) were by the end of the thirteenth century becoming a distinct sub-region, characterized by the widespread practice of transhumance – the movement of sheep and cattle between winter towns and summer shielings, sometimes organized by 'surnames' (e.g. the Charltons) in face of Scottish incursions. But even in the north the pressure was to extend the arable: virtually nowhere in England was exclusively pastoral farming pursued until the pressure of population was removed in the later middle ages. Of course, the crops that could be grown were different. Acid soils and a limited growing season dictated spring-sown grains, and in the north-west there was an almost complete reliance on oats (and a diet of oat-cakes and oatmeal puddings) instead of autumn-sown wheat, or rye or barley, which were the staple bread-corns in different parts of the south.[43]

[42] Dyer, *Standards of Living*, pp. 211–33.
[43] R. S. Schofield, 'The Geographical Distribution of Wealth in England, 1334–1649', *EcHR*, 2nd ser., 18 (1965), p. 504; E. Miller, 'Farming in Northern England during the Twelfth and Thirteenth Centuries', *Northern History*, 12 (1976); Postan, 'Village Livestock', pp. 225, 239–42; G. Elliott, 'Field Systems of Northwest England', in *Studies of Field Systems in the British Isles*, ed. A. R. H.

The use of the common fields was just being worked out in parts of the north, as land was brought into cultivation for the first time. It was hard to find the regular three-course rotation of crops (e.g. wheat, barley and a fallow year) which would have been encountered universally in the midlands. In some places there was a single field which grew oats for one half of every year, and for the other half lay fallow to be manured by the village livestock. When the fertility of the field was exhausted, the villagers could shift their arable elsewhere on the edge of the moor. In this natural cattle country, it was the wish to ensure that a proportion of both the lord's and the tenants' lands lay fallow all the year round and was available as common pasture that led to the establishment of a two- or occasionally three-field system. Within the arable the still developing and flexible field arrangements of the north-west made it easy to introduce new crops such as peas and beans, which were being gathered at Hale for the town of Liverpool in 1324.[44]

AGRARIAN CHANGE IN THE THIRTEENTH CENTURY

A recent achievement of economic historians has been to show that field systems throughout England, and not just in the north, were in a state of dynamic evolution in the thirteenth century. The controversy that remains is whether the population increase effectively created them. Dr Thirsk has argued that it was the partition of tenements that divided the fields of the village into myriads of separately held strips, which demanded common management if crops were to be rotated beneficially and the village livestock fed, for the depletion of the waste compelled the full use of the arable for pasture after cropping. On this view the open fields, in which neighbours had long co-operated and quite intensive rotations involving new crops had already been worked out, matured into true common fields, subject to regulation by the village community, only around the middle of the thirteenth century (just, one remembers, when manor-court rolls appear). A Norfolk study supports Dr Thirsk's theory of the way the arable strips might have evolved, but suggests that communal regulation would not have followed without the intervention of the landlord. Whether or not the lord's was the decisive influence, village communities

Baker and R. A. Butlin (Cambridge: CUP, 1973), pp. 57–67; J. McDonnell, 'the Role of Transhumance in Northern England', *Northern History*, 24 (1988).
[44] Miller, 'Farming', pp. 9–11; *Studies of Field Systems*, ed. Baker and Butlin, pp. 637–8.

did become capable of the extensive reorganization of their agricultural arrangements, such as a change from two fields to three or
four; and the reapportionment by lot of shares in the meadow and
sometimes of the arable strips themselves, so that everyone had an
equal chance of good land and poor. In eastern Norfolk development of the field system went as far as the elimination of fallowing:
to make more space for legumes in the rotation of crops and better
fertilization of the soil, livestock were fed in their stalls and manure
carted from the farmyard for ploughing into the arable.[45]

Here is an example of agricultural progress which lightens the
picture of a universal worsening of conditions, but the evidence
for that is strong. A comparison of the assessments for the taxes of
1291 and 1341 – the first a papally authorized tax on the clergy, the
second a parliamentary tax on the whole land but also a tithe of
corn, wool and lambs assessed by parishes – shows that much
arable had gone out of cultivation in the interval in counties as
diverse as the North Riding of Yorkshire, Shropshire, Sussex and
a group of counties to the north of London: Bedfordshire, Cambridgeshire and Buckinghamshire. In 1341 a reason for abandonment was sometimes given: 'because of the infertility of the soil',
'for lack of a plough team', or 'for lack of husbandry because the
tenants are poor'. Sometimes, as at Hound Tor on the edge of
Dartmoor, abandonment of a large farm can be dated archaeolog-
ically to the early fourteenth century though the specific reasons
for it remain obscure. But it is clear that in many places the limits
of the soil which could long sustain its fertility had been broken
through – at the same time as the tenements of a section of the
peasantry were shrinking below viability.[46]

---

[45] *Studies of Field Systems*, ed. Baker and Butlin, pp. 259, 261, 626–7, 631, 643–52;
Joan Thirsk, 'The Common Fields', and 'The Origin of the Common Fields',
Past and Present, 29 (1964), 33 (1966); J. Z. Titow, 'Medieval England and the
Open-Field System', *Past and Present*, 32 (1965); D. Sylvester, 'The Open Fields
of Cheshire', *Transactions of the Historic Society of Lancashire and Cheshire*, 108
(1956); M. W. Beresford and J. K. S. St Joseph, *Medieval England: An Aerial
Survey*, 2nd edn (Cambridge: CUP, 1979), pp. 23–4; B. M. S. Campbell,
'Population Change and the Genesis of Commonfields on a Norfolk Manor',
and 'Agricultural Progress in Medieval England: Some Evidence from Eastern
Norfolk ', *EcHR*, 2nd ser., 33 (1980), 36 (1983).

[46] A. R. H. Baker, 'Evidence in the "Nonarum Inquisitiones" of Contracting
Arable Lands in England during the early Fourteenth Century', *EcHR*, 2nd ser.,
19 (1966); Miller and Hatcher, *Rural Society and Economic Change*, pp. 54–63;
Dyer, *Standards of Living*, pp. 124–9; Hinton, *Archaeology, Economy and Society*,
pp. 149, 171–3; for possible explanations of 'The Low Yields of Corn in Medieval
England', see W. H. Long in *EcHR*, 2nd ser., 32 (1979); C. Dyer discusses the

For the landlords the demesne economy, which was still 'exuberantly profitable' in mid-century, ran out of steam. As yields stagnated and grain prices fluctuated, the bishop of Winchester's estate managers pared his demesne down from 13,000 acres in 1269 to below 10,000 acres in 1310, seeing that what could be got in rents for scarce land continued to move vigorously upwards: the profits from the Winchester estates, which had fluctuated between £3,050 and £5,350 in the years 1221–83, stabilized at £3,700–£3,800 in the decade preceding the Black Death. For the peasants working on the bishop's lands things went much worse. The secular rise in prices would have required them to work perhaps 25% harder at the end of the century than at the beginning – if the work was available. But prices did not rise smoothly: they fluctuated catastrophically in times of poor harvests, and people died. Matthew Paris describes vividly what happened in the bad years of 1257 and 1258, when the destruction of the harvest by incessant rain combined with a shortage of money (due Matthew alleges to the exactions of the pope and of Richard of Cornwall as king of Almain) to force the price of corn up to 10s. a quarter and then to 15s. and beyond. For lack of a modicum of corn, people sold their animals, reduced their households and left their lands uncultivated. The swollen and livid bodies of famine victims lay in the streets, and had to be buried in mass graves. England herself would have perished, according to Matthew, if corn had not been shipped in from Germany: but many could still not afford to buy it, and worthy and once prosperous people were reduced to begging, before fasting and the advocacy of St Alban and other saints brought better weather and the halving of prices. There were further bad years in 1270–2, and from the 1290s taxation (for Edward's wars) again exacerbated the effects of harvest failures. The payment on Winchester manors of the 'death duties levied on holdings of customary tenants' called 'heriots' shows a secular rise in adult mortality to a level higher than that in any other pre-industrial society so far examined. The climax was reached in 1315–18 in what 'seems to have been the worst famine in England and indeed in northern Europe in the last millennium', its social impact

progress of retraction, bringing out the complexity of the evidence, in *The Rural Settlements of Medieval England*, ed. M. Aston, D. Austin and C. Dyer (Oxford: Blackwell, 1989); Mark Bailey criticizes the whole concept of marginality in his *A Marginal Economy? East Anglian Breckland in the Later Middle Ages* (Cambridge: CUP, 1989).

demonstrated amongst other ways by the soaring of the crime rate to five times its normal level.[47]

What we cannot know is how much worse the situation might have been without the institutions of village life which were built up over the thirteenth century. The definition of villein status, with its rights as well as its obligations; the development of manor courts and leets and the inheritance customs and methods of land transfer applied within them; the appearance of informal systems for the exchange of labour and resources; the growth of the communal activity of the parish; and the continued adaptation of the field systems: these may be regarded as the crucial changes in the agrarian base of English society before the Black Death. Attempts have been made to fathom the solidarity of the medieval village by identifying those who stood pledge for their fellows when they contracted debts, or were summoned to answer in the local court for misdemeanours, or were bound over to good behaviour there. (If the obligations were not fulfilled, the pledges also suffered penalties.) It has been claimed that in the Huntingdon-shire village of Holywell-cum-Needingworth 77% of all known pledgings were extra-familial (most of the other 23% being pledg-ing by husbands for wives accused of brewing in breach of the assize of ale), and that this 'points to a definite spirit of co-operation in the village'. On the other side, much of the pledging has been identified as the exercise of patronage by a few wealthy villagers over smallholders, who were forced to use them just because of the lack of close ties among neighbours. An exhaustive study of 13,592 interactions (both pledgings and law-suits between vil-lagers) involving 575 people in the Suffolk village of Redgrave in the period 1259 to 1293 seems to confirm that smallholders and cottagers lacked the resources to engage in reciprocal pledging and for this reason were compelled to contract for pledges among the wealthy to whom they also hired themselves as servants. In Redgrave, pledging among kinsmen and near neighbours was an activity of the middling tenants, but this group also displayed a

---

[47] Miller and Hatcher, *Rural Society and Economic Change*, pp. 59, 64–9, 246; Dyer, *Standards of Living*, pp. 216, 138, 258–73; J. Z. Titow, *English Rural Society, 1200–1350* (London: Allen and Unwin, 1969), pp. 96–102; D. L. Farmer on prices and wages, in *Agrarian History*, II, ed. Hallam, esp. pp. 772–9; Paris, *CM*, v.660, 690, 701–2, 710–12, 728; M. M. Postan and J. Z. Titow, 'Heriots and Prices on Winchester Manors', *EcHR*, 2nd ser., 11 (1958–9); I. Kershaw, 'The Great Famine and Agrarian Crisis in England, 1315–22', *Past and Present*, 59 (1973); B. Hanawalt, 'Economic Influence on the Pattern of Crime in England, 1250–1350', *American Journal of Legal History*, 18 (1974).

high level of conflict over the tenure and use of land. It is impossible to tell whether personal relations between peasants were generally warm or increasingly calculating. Nor can we know what they were like between peasants and landlords, though here we can see a growing 'contractualism' in tenurial relationships, to which free tenants may have been more vulnerable than villeins with their stronger protection from custom against market forces. But in the end the institutional bonds developed between villagers brought together in a unity of economic purpose – a unity made vividly present by aerial photographs of now deserted villages set in their common fields – are more impressive than all the differences of power and wealth.[48]

[48] E. B. de Windt, *Land and People in Holywell-cum-Needingworth, 1252–1457* (Toronto: Pontifical Institute of Mediaeval Studies, 1972), p. 249; M. Pimsler, 'Solidarity in the Medieval Village? The Evidence of Personal Pledging at Elton, Huntingdonshire', *Journal of British Studies*, 17 (1978), pp. 8–11; R. M. Smith, 'Kin and Neighbors in a Thirteenth-Century Suffolk Community', *Journal of Family History*, 4 (1979), pp. 246–9; J. Hatcher, 'English Serfdom and Villeinage: Towards a Reassessment', *Past and Present*, 91 (1980), pp. 24–5, 39; Beresford and St Joseph, *Medieval England*, pp. 21–116.

3

TRADERS AND TOWNSMEN

MARKET TRADERS

The translation of communal life into politics is clearer in the towns, which were specialized communities for the promotion of trade, the practice of religion and the exercise of secular government. That trade in agricultural produce was the force behind urban growth is shown by the process of town foundation, which reaches its peak in the 1230s at about the same time as the agricultural boom and falls off steeply in the early fourteenth century. Behind the plantation of new towns, and following a similar time-scale, lay a general establishment of new markets throughout the countryside. Very often these must have crystallized a mass of informal trading of which we get glimpses in such incidents as a case of homicide in Liverpool heard in 1305 by the justices of trailbaston: this was found to have arisen from an argument between Robert Clark and William Brown as they travelled from Chester (perhaps by way of the Birkenhead ferry) – an argument about money, goods and chattels which William had received from Robert 'to trade with for their common profit' and for which he refused to account.[1]

---

[1] M. W. Beresford, *New Towns of the Middle Ages* (London: Lutterworth Press, 1967), pp. 308, 327ff; G. H. Tupling, 'Markets and Fairs in Medieval Lancashire', in *Historical Essays in Honour of James Tait*, ed. J. G. Edwards, V. H. Galbraith and E. F. Jacob (Manchester: Manchester UP, 1933), and in *Transactions of the Historic Society of Lancashire and Cheshire*, 49 (1933) and 51 (1936); R. H. Britnell, 'The Proliferation of Markets in England, 1200–1349', *EcHR*, 2nd ser., 34 (1981); Public Record Office: JUST 1/422.

The rural market, like villeinage, was a basic institution which demanded recognition in the laws of King and Church. Long before 1200 the holding of markets and the exaction of tolls from those who came to trade in them were valuable rights for which landlords would often obtain the security of royal charters. It was in John's reign, however, that it became necessary to devise ways of resolving the conflicts of interest created by the multiplication of grants. The launching by Pope Innocent III in 1201 of a campaign against the use of the churchyard for buying and selling after Sunday service, and the turning of it into 'a den of thieves', led to the widespread foundation of new markets on the second day of the week, especially in ecclesiastical lordships. Partly, no doubt, on account of the fees it collected for grants of legal privilege, and partly in order to support (or, if the fee was big enough, override) the Church's ban on Sunday trading, the Crown tightened its control of market foundations. A genuine concern for commerce and the consumer cannot be excluded, however; and those brought into the king's courts in increasing numbers charged with founding new markets to the harm of existing market rights could advance quite sophisticated economic arguments in their defence. The abbot of Pershore, summoned before the justices in eyre at Shrewsbury in 1256 to defend his setting-up of a Monday market at Hawkesbury (Gloucestershire) to the harm of Matthew de Bezil's Tuesday market at Sherston, answered that on the contrary it was 'to the convenience and advantage of Matthew's market', since merchants went on to sell on Tuesday what they bought on Monday, and trade was increased all round. But the jurors eventually found that Matthew had suffered damage to the amount of 4s., for the two markets were a mere three leagues apart: the abbot's men now did their buying and selling of corn, meat and other things at Hawkesbury, avoiding Sherston altogether; and further, the corn merchants who used to buy corn at Sherston to carry to Bristol now bought at Hawkesbury, because it was nearer.[2]

[2] R. H. Britnell, 'English Markets and Royal Administration before 1200', *EcHR*, 2nd ser., 31 (1978); *idem*, 'Proliferation of markets'; A. L. Poole, *From Domesday Book to Magna Carta* (Oxford: Clarendon Press, 1951; 2nd edn, 1955), p. 76; *The Chronicle of Jocelin of Brakelond*, ed. H. E. Butler (London: Nelson, 1949), pp. 132–4; *The Earliest Lincolnshire Assize Rolls*, A.D. 1202–9, ed. D. M. Stenton (Lincoln Record Society, vol. 22, Lincoln, 1926), p. xl; *Councils and Synods, with Other Documents relating to the English Church*, vol. II: A.D. 1205–1313, ed. F. M. Powicke and C. R. Cheney (Oxford: Clarendon Press, 1964). pp. 35, 174, 194, 297, 432 etc.; Statute of Winchester (1285), in *EHD*, III.462; for examples of royal

The customary carrying services of villein tenants which were used to provision the great lord's household (for example to bring wine from Winchelsea to Battle Abbey) were defined more precisely in order to get a regular supply of produce into local markets. A customary tenant might be obliged to do (say) forty journeys of ten leagues each in the year; or if he held from the monks of Ely, to carry the lord's corn for sale at King's Lynn, Cambridge, Norwich, Bury, Huntingdon, Ipswich and Hertford. Westminster Abbey required each of its virgaters at Stevenage to carry twenty quarters of oats or fifteen quarters of other grains a year; and St Augustine's Canterbury specified the quantities of sturgeon, salmon and lampreys to be carried by its tenants at Plumstead. Some lords demanded carrying services at weekends so as not to interfere with week-work on the land. Maintenance was expected if the tenant was required to be away overnight. Bracton defined a new market as harmful at law if it was held within two days of an existing market and within six and two-thirds miles of it, because a 'reasonable day's journey consists of twenty miles' and a 'day's journey is divided into three parts': the 'first part, in the morning, is given to those going to the market; the second to buying and selling, which ought to suffice for all except perhaps for those merchants who have stalls, who lay out and expose their wares for sale . . .'; the third part is left for those returning from the market to their homes' – before nightfall, because of the danger of ambush by robbers. At this very time, however, a faster circulation of goods through the markets was being made possible by a revolution in transport which, in the south-east of the country, saw the horse and cart vitually replace both the large but ponderous ox-cart and the light pack-horse.[3]

The great majority of thirteenth-century markets were purely local. They provided for burgeoning populations of agricultural

grants, *Calendar of Charter Rolls*, 1 (London: HMSO, 1903), pp. 2, 33, 216, 255, 252 etc.; for disputes over markets, *Introduction to the Curia Regis Rolls*, ed. C. T. Flower (Selden Society, vol. 62, London 1943), pp. 332–4; *CRR*, I.397, 449–50, VIII.267–8, XVI, nos. 247, 1531, 1579, 1689 etc.; *Rolls of the Justices in Eyre for Gloucestershire, Warwickshire, and Shropshire (1221–2)*, ed. D. M. Stenton (Selden Society, vol. 59, London, 1940), no. 1342; *The Roll of the Shropshire Eyre of 1256*, ed. A. Harding (Selden Society, vol. 96, London, 1980), no. 403.

[3] D. Postles, 'Customary Carrying Services', *Journal of Transport History*, 3rd ser., 5 (1984); *Bracton on the Laws and Customs of England*, tr. S. E. Thorne, 4 vols. (Cambridge, Mass.: Harvard UP, 1968–77), III. 198; J. Langdon, 'Horse Hauling: A Revolution in Vehicle Transport in Twelfth and Thirteenth-Century England?', *Past and Present*, 103 (1984).

workers paid in coin and craftsmen like weavers and fullers who did not grow their own food, and for the peasant farmers eager to sell their produce. The aggregate demand from agrarian communities for manufactures and services was many times that of towns, and greatest where population and agricultural output grew fastest, as in the newly colonized parts of Lincolnshire. In 1349 Norfolk possessed 121 markets, of which at least 62 had been granted in the thirteenth century, Lancashire a mere 40. The country market was so important in supplying the necessities of life that when the eyre was in session markets round about were suspended so that provisions could be concentrated on the eyre town with its hundreds of extra mouths to feed. Similarly, markets in the Welsh border counties were stopped during Henry III's campaigns into Wales in 1228 and 1231, and in the counties neighbouring Portsmouth while Henry prepared to embark for France in 1242, so that the army could be supplied.[4]

Rural markets linked into a wider trade, for example operating as collecting-points for the corn supplied to larger towns: the markets of Henley-on-Thames and King's Lynn fulfilled this role for London, and Hawkesbury for Bristol. In return for the produce, middlemen brought back the cash the villagers needed to pay rents and buy commodities like salt, ironware, earthenware, pitch and tar. Stoney Stratford, founded on Watling Street at the boundary between two parishes, and the new coastal markets of Portsmouth and Hull clearly hoped to exploit a midde-distance trade. But increasingly purchasing for the lords' demesnes was done in more specialized urban markets or a few great fairs. Some merchants bypassed the markets altogether and bought wool by individual contracts with landlords not only for the wool from the demesne flocks but also for much of the peasant farmers' production, which the landlords undertook to collect.[5]

---

[4] Britnell, 'Proliferation of Markets', pp. 210, 215–21; and 'Production for the Market on a Small Fourteenth-Century Estate', *EcHR*, 2nd ser., 19 (1966); E. Miller and J. Hatcher, *Medieval Society – Rural Society and Economic Change 1086–1348* (London: Longmans, 1978), pp. 69, 76–7; L. F. Salzman, *English Trade in the Middle Ages* (Oxford: Clarendon Press, 1931), pp. 134–5; A. Everitt, 'The Marketing of Agricultural Produce', in *Agrarian History of England and Wales*, vol. IV: *1500–1640*, ed. J. Thirsk (Cambridge: CUP, 1967), pp. 468–9, 474–5.

[5] Britnell, 'Proliferation of Markets', pp. 213–17; N.S.B. Gras, *The Evolution of the English Corn Market* (Cambridge, Mass.: Harvard UP, 1915), pp. 48–9, 62–3; Eileen Power, *The Wool Trade in English Medieval History* (Oxford: OUP, 1941), pp. 42–7; Beresford, *New Towns of the Middle Ages*, pp. 398, 447–9, 511–12; I. Kershaw, *Bolton Priory: The Economy of a Northern Monastery 1286–1325* (Oxford:

The right to hold one or more fairs in the year was often included in the grant of a market, and like a market a fair may have existed for a long time before a royal grant confirmed it. The abbot of Abingdon, summoned to the king's court in 1212 to show why he held a fair at Shillingford to the harm of a fair which the earl of Aumale possessed by royal grant at Wantage, maintained through his attorney that what we had was not a fair but 'an assembly called a wake (*vigilia*)', and that his predecessors had held it since the Conquest. A wake was a gathering of people from neighbouring villages to celebrate the patronal festival of the parish church with a mass, sports and, inevitably, buying and selling from which lords were usually quick to profit. So they would seek royal confirmation of the fair – or an extension of it, as the bishop of Hereford purchased in 1241 a grant extending the traditional three days of his fair at the feast of St Ethelbert to six.[6]

The major fairs, such as those of St Giles at Winchester, Northampton, St Ives in Huntingdonshire, and Stamford and St Botolph's at Boston in Lincolnshire, provide the best measure of the extent of commercial activity in thirteenth-century England. These fairs were small fry by continental standards. Nevertheless a citizen of Lincoln is found at St Botolph's fair in 1287 negotiating the sale of the wool-crop of the abbey of Welbeck for ten years ahead to merchants of Douai. Merchants from France, Germany, Italy and Spain, and all the mercantile communities of England, came to the fair of St Ives, and pipes of red wine imported through Boston were sold there. The excellent records of the St Ives fair court show Henry Curteis of Leicester suing merchants of Rouen in 1287 for £8, the price of woolfells purchased from him and his partner, which should have been paid in installments, half at Northampton fair and half at Winchester fair (Henry produces a sealed letter obligatory to prove it); and Sir William of Hereford, citizen of London, claiming from Ralph of Lyons in 1293 the residue of £42 3s. owed for a consignment of wool, of which the first installment had been paid at Boston, but not the second due at the fair of St Edward at Westminster. In a dispute between Englishmen, John Beeston of Nottingham complains in 1275 that

---

Clarendon Press, 1973), pp. 89–91; *Walter of Henley and Other Treatises on Estate Management and Accounting*, ed. D. Oschinsky (Oxford: Clarendon Press, 1971), p. 399.

[6] *CRR*, VI. 296–7; *Introduction to the Curia Regis Rolls*, ed. Flower, p. 333; G. C. Homans, *English Villagers of the Thirteenth Century* (Cambridge, Mass.: Harvard UP, 1941), pp. 299, 373–4; *Calendar of Charter Rolls*, I. 225, 252, 259.

Gilbert Chesterton of Stamford caused him loss of trade to the value of £10 by unjustly attaching seven sacks of wool, wrongly believing him to be 'of the commonalty of Nottingham' and 'peer and parcener' of two other Nottingham merchants who owed Gilbert money.[7]

Overseas merchants appear to be selling rather than buying cloth at St Ives, though we know from continental evidence that English cloths, 'northamptons' and 'stamforts' in particular, were going to French, north Italian, Spanish and probably German markets, if in declining quantities after the middle of the century. It was 'cloth from parts beyond the sea to the value of £33' which Richard of Welborne, citizen and draper of Norwich, allegedly bought from Richard Hoppman of Lynn at Stamford fair, giving his writing obligatory that he would pay £20 on Ascension Day at St Ives and the rest at Lynn on the following feast of the Holy Trinity; when he failed to pay he was distrained by twenty pieces of cloth to answer in the St Ives court and make good his denial that the writing was his. It will also have been overseas cloth that Londoners sold either in London or at St Ives and sued for the price of in the St Ives court. But in 1300 a royal clerk was to go to the fair to purchase 1,000 yards of English cloth, 8,000 yards of canvas and ten dozen towels for the king's great wardrobe. The English cloth industry was spreading out from a few large towns into the countryside as the watermill was adapted for the mechanical fulling of cloth. At St Ives the regular appointment of alnagers to measure cloth; the use of pieces of 'good burel cloth' to pay for horses; and the distraint of a defendant by two pieces of serge appraised by a jury of merchants at ten marks: all this suggests that cloth was the staple commodity of inland trade. Robert Grosseteste advised the countess of Lincoln to buy her robes at St Ives, where quite a lot of the trading seems in fact to have been street-trading in which small quantities of wool, hides and cloth changed hands along with sacks of feathers, bowls and goblets, pairs of tongs, malt, hams and cheeses, and barrels of salt haddock brought in from neighbouring

---

[7] E. W. Moore, *The Fairs of Medieval England: An Introductory Study* (Toronto: Pontifical Institute of Mediaeval Studies, 1985); *Select Pleas in Manorial and Other Seignorial Courts*, ed. F. W. Maitland (Selden Society, vol. 2, London, 1989), pp. 130–60, for the records of the St Ives fair court in 1275, with a valuable introduction; *Select Cases concerning the Law Merchant*, vol. I, ed. C. Gross (Selden Society, vol. 23, London, 1908), has the records of the court from 1270 to 1324: see pp. xxxix–li (for lists of stalls), 23, 26, 59, 62–4; *Select Cases concerning the Law Merchant*, vol.. II, ed. H. Hall (Selden Society, vol. 46, London, 1929), pp. 64, 72; J. A. Raftis, 'Rent and Capital at St Ives', *Medieval Studies*, 20 (1958).

counties, perhaps by water along the Ouse. There were also booths where cooked sea-bass were sold; and Thomas of London hired a bakehouse to make bread for the benefit of merchants coming to the fair, where Maud Woodfull assaulted his wife, calling her a whore and sorceress, and poured yeast over the flour.[8]

In the proceedings of the St Ives fair court an international community of merchants can be seen adapting the processes of common law to its particular needs, and developing its own 'law merchant'. Maintaining order, punishing harlots and the receivers of lepers 'to the great peril of merchants and neighbours', and ordering the removal of muck heaps in the streets and the cleaning of wells and ditches were normal functions of a local court. The extra concerns of a fair court were the enforcement of royal edicts on weights and measures and catching the users of false ells, rods, gallons, pottles and quarts. Commercial practices which the communities of merchants seem to have evolved themselves were also enforced in the court in litigation employing professional pleaders. Legal partnerships were recognized at St Ives; and a strange rule was followed that a third merchant was entitled to intervene, cry 'halves' and participate in a bargain that was being struck (e.g. by a butcher purchasing a carcase). 'Obligatory writings' payable to the bearer were in general use.[9]

The practice of transferring a 'God's penny' to seal a bargain was given royal sanction in the *carta mercatoria* which Edward I granted to foreign merchants in return for new customs duties in 1303: neither of the parties might thereafter go back on the contract, and if a dispute arose concerning it there should be an inquiry 'in accordance with the usages and customs of the fairs and towns

---

[8] Moore, *Fairs of Medieval England*, cap. 1, and pp. 303–5, for the king's purchases in 1300; P. Chorley, 'English Cloth Exports during the Thirteenth and Early Fourteenth Centuries: The Continental Evidence', *Historical Research*, 61 (1988); *Select Cases Concerning the Law Merchant*, I. xxxiii–xxxiv, 3, 14–15, 21, 25, 28, 41–2, 46, 47, 49, 50, 55, 56, 60–1, 63, 64, 65, 68, 69, 86; G. A. Williams, *Medieval London: From Commune to Capital* (London: Athlone Press, 1963), pp. 126–9, for the London drapers; Raftis, 'Rent and Capital', p. 80; E. M. Carus-Wilson, 'An Industrial Revolution of the 13th Century', in her *Medieval Merchant Venturers: Collected Studies* (London: Methuen, 1954); *Walter of Henley and Other Treatises*, ed. Oschinsky, p. 399; *Select Pleas in Manorial Courts*, ed. Maitland, pp. 141–3, 160.
[9] *Royal Justice and the Medieval English Countryside: The Huntingdonshire Eyre of 1286*, ed. A. R. and E. B. DeWindt (Toronto: Pontifical Institute of Mediaeval Studies, 1981), no. 459; *Cases concerning the Law Merchant*, I. 18, 19, 40, 42, 83, 84; *Select Pleas in Manorial Courts*, ed. Maitland, pp. 154–5; Moore, *Fairs of Medieval England*, pp. 132–7.

where the said contract happens to have been made'. Edward had shown his eagerness to persuade foreign merchants to do business in England in statutes of 1283 and 1285 which offered forceful procedures for the recovery of debts where these had been enrolled before the mayors or chief wardens of London, York, Lincoln and Bristol and some other main towns, and of the fairs of Winchester, Boston, Stamford and St Ives. In 1287, 'the community of London and the other communities at the fair of St Ives were assembled to hear the command of the lord king in accordance with the new form of his statute touching merchants frequenting English fairs', and to witness the delivery of the two seals required for the registration of a debt; one of these was placed in the custody of a clerk named by the king, the other entrusted (in the absence of a mayor) to two merchants chosen from amongst the Londoners. Edward's statutes seem in fact to have followed local precedents, and lagged behind the methods the 'communities of merchants' had devised for themselves, such as payment of debts by install-ments at other fairs, and holding members of a 'community' responsible for the unpaid debts of a colleague. In 1270 the latter custom allowed Gottschalk of Almaine, burgess of Lynn, to sue the communities of Ghent, Poperinghe, Douai, Ypres and Lille in the St Ives court for 200 marks damage done to him by the seizure of fourteen sacks of his wool in Flanders on the orders of the countess of Flanders, about which a complaint to the king of England had been ineffective.[10]

The greater fairs had one foot in the world of international commerce, but the other remained in the seignorial – even manorial – economy. The fair from Easter Monday to the Tuesday of the following week on the spot where the relics of the Persian bishop St Ivo were discovered in 1001 was granted to the abbot of Ramsey in 1110 like just another piece of landed property, with the jurisdictional rights of 'sake and soke, and toll and team, and infangenetheof'. In the Hundred Rolls survey of 1279, the fair was described as part of the manor of St Ives, which was itself a very small part of the abbot of Ramsey's great estate. The abbot had his fair 'in the street of St Ives', where there were sixty-three tenants

---

[10] *Select Pleas in Manorial Courts*, ed. Maitland, pp. 132–7, 149, 152, 153, 159; *Cases concerning the Law Merchant*, I.3, 5, 8–9, 26, 39–40, 46–7, 59, 62, 65, 70, 71, 81, 86, 87; *Select Cases concerning the Law Merchant*, vol. III, ed. H. Hall (Selden Society, vol. 49, London, 1932), pp. xx–xxvii, lxxxii; *EHD*, III, nos. 54, 58, 91; T. F. T. Plucknett, *The Legislation of Edward I* (Oxford: Clarendon Press, 1949), pp. 138–43.

each holding from him a messuage or house-plot for the service of a day's work at haymaking and another in the autumn, and 8d. a year rent. Since they are not recorded as possessing land, these tenants must have lived by renting their houses out as lodgings for the merchants, and the harlots and others who provided the merchants with services. Tenants from surrounding manors owed the services of constructing booths and providing constables to police the fair. The fair court emerged at the same time as other seignorial courts and was presided over in the same way by the lord's steward. Its records are preserved amongst the public records because the abbot's deeds were confiscated along with his lands at the dissolution of the monasteries.[11]

The cycle of fairs of which the high points were St Ives at Easter, Boston in June, Winchester in August, Westminster in October and Northampton in November was the hub of a lively 'pioneer economy' which was separate from that of the settled towns, and sometimes in conflict with it. During the fairs at Winchester, Bristol and Nottingham the normal markets were required to shut up their stalls, except for the sale of foodstuffs. In an ultimately vain attempt to protect the profits of his fair of St Giles on the site he developed for it outside Winchester, the bishop had to fight a runing battle against the burgesses of Southampton, who wanted to keep the trade of foreign merchants arriving at their port, and royal officials who sought to collect dues from traders who remained in Winchester after the scheduled end of the fair. In 1248 Henry III insisted that London shops shut and all other fairs in Engald be suspended for the fortnight of the October fair of St Edward which he had granted to the monks to help finance the rebuilding of Westminster Abbey. But on its cramped site in the abbey churchyard in the October rains, St Edward's fair could not divert foreign merchants from the year-round trading facilities of the city, and after 1300 the Londoners themselves ceased to attend. It seems that from the 1260s, partly because of the turbulent relations with the Flemings but more because of the challenge of the towns, fairs generally began to decline, and in succeeding centuries they played a minor role in the trade of England. Though

[11] *Cases concerning the Law Merchant*, 1.xxviii–xxxv, xxxix–li, 7, 8, 10, 11, 32, 34, 42, 11.lxxxvii, 72; *Cartularium Monasterii de Rameseia*, ed. W. H. Hart and P. A. Lyons, 3 vols. (Rolls series, London, 1884–93), 1.240, 11.69; Paris, *CM*, v.296–7; *Rotuli Hundredorum*, 2 vols. (Record Commission, London, 1812–18), 11.603–5; *Select Pleas in Manorial Courts*, ed. Maitland, pp. 130–2; Moore, *Fairs of Medieval England*, pp. 250ff; Raftis, 'Rent and Capital', pp. 81–2.

they might contribute to suburban development they were unable on their own to create new urban settlements: at St Ives the temporary influx of merchants swamped a village which saw little permanent expansion from its one trading street. But in the end it was the inability of the seasonal fairs to develop the permanent institutions which merchants and craftsmen came to need that led to their decline before the towns: manorial organization seemed enough for St Ives, which never achieved municipal status.[12]

BURGESSES

On the other hand, some weekly markets were the nuclei of permanent settlements which prospered enough for Edward I to use 'merchant towns' (*villae mercatoriae*) as a distinct category, to be represented along with cities and boroughs in the Easter parliament of 1275. This was his first parliament and he wished it to be representative of the local communities of the realm as no parliament had been before. But to judge from the few counties for which we have names in 1275, many of these market towns, such as Biggleswade in Bedfordshire, Uxbridge and Staines in Middlesex, and Alcester, Birmingham, Nuneaton and Stratford in Warwickshire, did not return another member to parliament in the middle ages, if ever; and their claim to send 'four good men' on that occasion may not always have been their commercial importance so much as their position as the head townships of hundreds, accustomed (through a similar group of their leading men) to present criminals and sue as communities in the king's courts. Another measure of commercial importance becomes available from the last decade of the century, when the king began to tax cities and boroughs along with his own demesne lands at a higher rate than rural districts. (In 1296 an eighth of movable wealth was taken from the inhabitants of towns and the demesne, as opposed to a twelfth from the rest of the country.) The taxers automatically selected boroughs with royal charters for the higher rate, but less than half those with seignorial charters, and they also listed a number of unchartered towns. The line must have been drawn

---

[12] *Calendar of Charter Rolls*, 1.445; Moore, *Fairs of Medieval England*, pp. 18–20, 50, 204–22; *Select Pleas in Manorial Courts*, ed. Maitland, p. 132; *Cases concerning the Law Merchant*, I.xxx; *EHD*, III, no. 217; Paris, *CM*, v. 28–9, 333, 485; G. Rosser, *Medieval Westminster*, 1200–1540 (Oxford: Clarendon Press, 1989), pp. 97–8, 106–14; M. W. Beresford and J. K. S. St Joseph, *Medieval England: An Aerial Survey*, 2nd edn (Cambridge: CUP, 1979), pp. 182–3.

according to a town's market activity, and that relative to the trade of other towns in the same county, since prosperous eastern counties have remarkably few names in the list of 196 towns (outside the Palatinates of Chester and Durham) which were taxed at a higher rate in Edward's reign, while some very small communities in the west country are included. Devonshire has twenty-two towns listed; Rutland none at all; Carlisle is the sole representative of Cumberland, and Appleby of Westmorland, but so is Cambridge of Cambridgeshire. For Kent there are Canterbury, Rochester and Seasalter; for the much poorer Lancashire, Lancaster, Liverpool, Preston, Wigan and Dalton in Furness.[13]

If Coventry, which certainly had charters, could get itself omitted from a list which included Alcester, Birmingham and Stratford, on the grounds that it was not a borough, official ideas of urban status must have been uncertain. A good number of unchartered boroughs may have been left out despite their possession of the basic urban characteristic: inhabitants holding their messuages by burgage tenure. Linton in Cambridgeshire was a market centre for which William de Say, its manorial lord, obtained a market and fair in 1241; in the 1270s, according to the Hundred Rolls, it contained 200 or so households with 'free tenements by the name of burgages' – of bakers, salters, tailors, a tanner, a clothier, a cobbler, several 'merchants', and a Jew named Adam Caiaphas – forty-five of them described as having 'shops'. Without a charter to make it a borough, a fair-sized town like this (it probably had around 800 inhabitants) could remain much as it was, a lively centre of a largely self-sufficient rural economy, right down to the time when it was listed by the Royal Commission on Market Rights and Tolls in the 1880s.[14]

---

[13] F. M. Powicke, *The Thirteenth Century: 1216–1307* (Oxford: Clarendon Press, 1953; 2nd edn, 1961; issued in paperback, 1991), pp. 343, 532; H. Jenkinson, 'The First Parliament of Edward I', *EHR*, 25 (1910); *EHD*, III, no. 212, for the representation of Peatling Magna in a lawsuit of 1265 by Thomas the Reeve and Philip the Clerk; W. L. Warren, *The Governance of Norman and Angevin England, 1086–1272* (London: Arnold, 1987), pp. 219–20; D. Crook, *Records of the General Eyre*, PRO Handbooks, no. 20 (London: HMSO, 1982), pp. 195–252, for lists of the boroughs, hundreds, parishes and vills which presented crown pleas to the justices in eyre in each country; *Roll and Writ File of the Berkshire Eyre of 1248*, ed. M. T. Clanchy (Selden Society, vol. 90, London, 1973), p. xli, for the use of these terms; J. F. Willard, 'Taxation Boroughs and Parliamentary Boroughs, 1294–1336', in *Historical Essays in Honour of James Tait*, ed. Edwards, Galbraith and Jacob.

[14] Willard, 'Taxation Boroughs', p. 420; J. H. Clapham, 'A Thirteenth-Century Market Town: Linton, Cambs.', *Cambridge Historical Journal*, 4 (1933).

Burgage tenure began as the tenure of traders who lived for protection within the 'burgus' or enclosure of a castle or monastery. (Place-names like *Bury* St Edmunds and Dry*burgh* abbey in Scotland recall this original meaning of 'borough'.) Durham had no less than four such boroughs, the Old Borough, the (dominant) bishop's borough, the prior's borough of New Elvet and the borough of St Giles, which were integrated into a single community by the building of bridges over the Wear and by an agreement of 1229 to standardize weights and measures in the four areas and treat offenders in the same way. The peculiarity of these communities, whose commercial functions required that their members should owe minimal labour services, pay standard rents (commonly 12d. for boroughs founded in the thirteenth century), dispose of their tenements more freely than most tenants, and share equally in collective dues, is already clear in Domesday Book's descriptions of York, Shrewsbury and other towns in 1086. England was a part of a general movement by the kings and lords of western Europe to define and enlarge the special freedoms of townsmen, a movement well advanced by 1200 in which towns copied liberties from one another. In royal charters of the thirteenth century grants of 'free burgage' (*liberum burgagium*) became grants of 'free borough' (*liber burgus*), indicating the recognition of the borough as a distinct sort of community with a coherent set of institutions. Thus in 1200 John made Dunwich 'our free borough', and granted the townsmen the right to sell their burgage tenements without seeking permission; to have their own court or *portman-moot* and not attend the courts of shire and hundred; to have a merchant gild; to account directly to the Crown for the farm or dues of the borough and not have the sheriff come in to collect them; and to be free from tolls throughout the land. In the same year, William Brewer was granted 'free borough' status for his town of Bridgwater, though as the inhabitants of a seignorial borough the townsmen got only burgage tenure and right to a market and a fair.[15]

The early part of the century was the time when lords were following the king most enthusiastically in the planting of new towns, and (if they were more powerful or simply more ambitious

---

[15] Margaret Bonney, *Lordship and the Urban Community: Durham and its Overlords, 1250–1540* (Cambridge, CUP 1990), p. 31; Susan Reynolds, *An Introduction to the History of English Medieval Towns* (Oxford: Clarendon Press, 1977), pp. 93–4; J. Tait, *The Medieval English Borough* (Manchester: Manchester UP, 1936), pp. 96–108, 194–220; *BBC, 1042–1216*, pp. 3, 23–4.

than the lord of Linton) endowing old towns as well as the new with standard sets of liberties. The plotting of town foundations geographically and over time (done superbly by Professor Beresford, though others are still adding to his lists), combined with the analysis of the liberties conferred in borough charters, has enabled economic history and the old-fashioned constitutional history of towns to reinforce each other. The new towns planted by thirteenth-century kings often had strategic purposes: John's Liverpool (1207), providing another crossing-place to Ireland; Edward's ill-fated Wavermouth and Skinburgh on the Solway (1300–1), intended to assist the provisioning of forces against the Scots; his New Winchelsea (1288), replacing an eroded port, and his Kingston upon Hull, supplementing an existing one. Edward worked to acquire two other port towns founded by magnates in the middle years of the century, Newtown or Francheville in the Isle of Wight and Ravenserod at the mouth of the Humber (another injudiciously planted town long lost in the sea). But the military town-building of the Angevin kings had been largely relegated to Wales by the thirteenth century, and the association of all plantations in England with castles, standing at 75% of new towns in the period 1000–1140, was down to 23% in 1201–50, and to 4% in 1251–1368.[16]

It was in the south-west of the country that the plantation of new towns, often detectable on the map by the grid pattern of their lay-out and distance from the parish church, and the granting of borough charters to both new towns and towns that had grown 'organically', were most widespread. The Cornishmen tried to convince the government in 1295 that 'there are not many market towns in the county of Cornwall, nor is there any city'. But the extraordinary number of small boroughs recognized for taxation purposes there and in Devon reflect at least the aspirations of these less developed portions of England, where lords and communities exploited whatever trading opportunities their situations offered, in a way that the rich east with its few big towns, regional fairs and many rural markets had never needed to. In Cornwall, Earl Richard, King Henry's brother, gave borough charters to seven townships between 1230 and 1260: Bodmin, Dunheved, Liskeard,

---

[16] Powicke, *The Thirteenth Century*, pp. 634–7; Beresford, *New Towns of the Middle Ages*, pp. 11, 83, 102–4, 124, 183, 295, 337, 343; Beresford and St Joseph, *Medieval England*, p. 238, for Winchelsea.

West Looe and Tintagel, Camelford and Helston, the last two being new plantations.[17]

In Devon, Professor Beresford lists fourteen towns which seem to have been planted in the course of the thirteenth century. For instance, the earls of Devon planted Honiton sometime before 1217, and made their late twelfth-century foundation of Plympton Erle a borough by a charter of 1242. They were also lords of the Isle of Wight, where they had founded Yarmouth and Newport in the 1170s; in mainland Hampshire they founded New Lymington before 1216 and made Christchurch a borough between 1245 and 1262. Hampshire was an old-settled and rich county (Winchester was the ancient seat of the king), and the high number of eleven new plantations there between 1170 and 1256 must represent an attempt to exploit the growing trade through the Solent. In the wake of Richard I's foundation of Portsmouth, the bishop of Winchester planted five inland towns at some distance from his city and suburban fair, at New Alresford (1200), Downton on the Avon in Wiltshire (1208–9), Overton and Newtown in the north of Hampshire (1217–18) and Hindon, again in Wiltshire and well to the south-west (1219–20). The bishop also created Newtown/ Francheville in the Isle of Wight in 1255–6, and made his 'organic' towns of Witney in Oxfordshire and Farnham in Surrey into boroughs, the latter in 1247. The destinies of these ventures were mixed. The 'burgus' of New Alresford prospered, becoming in the fourteenth century one of the ten great wool markets of the kingdom, and already in the mid-thirteenth century yielding about £16 a year in rents (suggesting some 160 burgages) and £3–£4 in market tolls. This was only a fifth of the profits of the manor out of which it was carved, however, and most towns were no more than a useful supplement to manorial incomes, though they could serve other purposes. The bishop built himself a house in the *Novus Burgus* of Newtown, which had perhaps 140 burgesses in 1283–4; but it decayed and had disappeared from sight by the end of the seventeenth century. Francheville, where Edward I stayed for ten days in 1285 just after wresting it from the bishop, was worth about £29 at that time: it too had disappeared by 1800.[18]

[17] Beresford, *New Towns of the Middle Ages*, pp. 46, 79, 151, 245, 270ff, and maps, 399–414, 417–26, 443–4, 449–50; N. Denholm-Young, *Richard of Cornwall* (Oxford: Blackwell, 1947), p. 134; *BBC, 1042–1216*, pp. xxvi, cxxxviii; *BBC, 1216–1307*, pp. xxv–xxxiii, xc–c.
[18] Beresford, *New Towns of the Middle Ages*, pp. 417–26, 442–7, 449–50, 505–6; *BBC, 1042–1216*, p. xxvi; *BBC, 1216–1307*, pp. xxvii–xxviii, xxxii.

Other examples of town development by ecclesiastical lords are the bishop of Salisbury's very successful foundation of Chelmsford (1199–1201), which became the county town of Essex; the bishop of Salisbury's famous creation of New Salisbury as a site for his cathedral (1219); Abbot Adam of Eynsham's grant of a charter to 'the commune of all those who shall have tenements' in the town he planted on his demesne in 1215; and the bishop of Lincoln's creation of New Thame (1219–21), also in Oxfordshire. In the far north, the priors of Tynemouth and Durham founded North Shields and South Shields at the mouth of the Tyne, to the fury of the burgesses of the ancient borough of Newcastle (1225–35). Before 1253, Airmyn on the River Aire in the West Riding was founded by the north's richest monastery, St Mary's, York. The prior of Burscough gave a charter to Ormskirk c. 1286. Exceptionally, Abbot Peter of Whitby paid King John 100 marks for the revocation of his predecessor's charter to Whitby as contrary to the rights of the Church. (This was twenty marks more than the burgesses could offer in order to keep their liberties.)[19]

One of the most notable town plantations in the north by a layman occurred in the same year as John's foundation of Liverpool. By a charter dated the morrow of St Martin in the ninth year of the Coronation of King John (12 November 1207), Maurice Painell granted to his 'burgesses of Leeds and to their heirs, freedom and free burgage, and their tofts (house-sites), and with each toft half an acre of land to cultivate', to be held of Maurice and his heirs in fee and inheritance, for a rent of 16d. a year payable half at Whitsuntide and half at Martinmas. Those who were attracted by these terms and by a promise of the same 'free laws' given the burgesses of Pontefract by Maurice's overlord, Roger de Lacy, in 1194 seem to have been allotted burgages on a new site at a distance from the parish church, thirty on each side of a wide street leading down to the Aire later known as the Briggate.[20]

The king himself gave the first charters to many old boroughs on his own behalf or for their lords: King John to Grimsby, Hartlepool and Corbridge (all in 1201), and to Stafford (a Domesday borough still lacking a charter in 1206); Henry III to Lynn, along with the bishop of Norwich, (1233), to Newcastle-under-

---

[19] Beresford, *New Towns of the Middle Ages*, pp. 429–30, 433–4, 435, 436–7, 439–41, 474–5, 476–8, 506–8, 521; Beresford and St Joseph, *Medieval England*. pp. 212–13; *BBC, 1042–1216*, p. xliii; *BBC, 1216–1307*, pp. xxv, xxxi.

[20] Beresford, *New Towns of the Middle Ages*, p. 524; G. Wooledge, 'The Medieval Borough of Leeds', *Miscellanea XI* (Thoresby Society, vol. 37, Leeds, 1945).

Lyme (1235), to Wigan at the instance of its lord, John Mansell (1246), to Chipping Camden with Roger de Somery (1247) and to Bamburgh (1255). A tight-knit group of earls then took up the spreading of urban liberties in the north. Ranulf, earl of Chester, gave charters to his burgesses of Leek in Staffordshire (1207–15) and Frodsham in Cheshire (1208–15), and (as earl of Chester and Lincoln) a more extensive one to Salford (1231). The de Lacys, who were hereditary constables of Chester and succeeded Ranulf in the earldom of Lincoln, granted borough liberties to Clitheroe (1272–91) and Congleton (1272–*c*. 1274). Macclesfield's charter was granted in 1261 by Prince Edward, successor to the earldom of Chester itself. Ranulf of Chester's brother-in-law, William de Ferrers, was remembered still in the sixteeth century as one of the earls of Derby who, seeking

to make the Honour [of Tutbury] more populous and statelie erected three burroughes within six myles of the Castle, One at Tutburye, One other at Agardsley called Newburghe and One other at Uttoxeter . . . and to make men more desirous to plant ther habytacions in those places procured for them marketts and ffayres and graunted to the burgesses dyvers lyberties of common of pasture, panage and estover in the forest of Neadwood.

Other northern lords who granted borough charters in the thirteenth century included William Brewer at Chesterfield (1204), Peter de Bruce at Kendal (1247), Hamon de Massey at Altrincham (1290), Thomas de Furnival at Sheffield (1297) and William le Botiller at Warrington (1300).[21]

The proportion of landlord initiative to the enterprise of traders in the foundation of a borough must have varied greatly from place to place. It could just have been de Ferrers who decided to turn ninety villagers of Higham into burgesses in 1251. A king or lord might grant a charter to burgesses who failed to materialize. Forty-six of Beresford's new towns appear amongst the 240 or so towns assessed at the higher rate of tax between 1294 and 1336, but sixty-six did not reach that category. Nevertheless, the numbers of burgages taken up and built upon in new boroughs, and the spontaneous appearance of burgage tenements in old townships

---

[21] *BBC, 1042–1216*, pp. xxviii–xxix; *BBC, 1216–1307*, pp. xxv–xxxiv, lxxvii; *The Charters of the Anglo-Norman Earls of Chester, c. 1071–1237*, ed. G. Barraclough (Record Society of Lancashire and Cheshire, vol. 126, Liverpool, 1988), nos. 349, 371, 435; Beresford, *New Towns of the Middle Ages*, pp. 80–1, 105, 486; J. Tait, *Mediaeval Manchester and the Beginnings of Lancashire* (Manchester: Manchester UP, 1904), pp. 114–19.

which never received charters, indicate a real change in the economic and social texture of the country which the proliferation of markets on its own did not. Burgage tenure spread readily in some of the hitherto most backward areas: not only in Cornwall but also in Lancashire, where on this criterion at least a dozen boroughs achieved a modest existence in the thirteenth century. Lords did not mean to create new communities: all most of them can have intended to grant was burgage tenure, with the advantages to themselves of a whole batch of rents for little land; and to the tenants, of the free disposition of their burgages, perhaps including the precious right (which applied to no other landed property) of leaving the burgage by will outside the family. The breakthrough for the trading community came when it gained the right from the landlord to appoint its own reeve, to have its own portmoot separate from the existing manor court or court leet, and not have its members brought into court elsewhere – at least to answer civil pleas.[22]

It is within the buoyant economy of the west midlands that groups of townsmen can be best observed taking responsibility for their own affairs under the wary eyes of their landlords. The strained relationship between the men of the vill and its monastic lord did not prevent Halesowen being a significant member of the group of twenty-five or so small market towns that were growing up along the trade routes leading from Coventry and the Birmingham plateau down the Avon, Stour and Severn valleys to Worcester, Gloucester and ultimately Bristol. The abbot apparently obtained a market and fair for the township in the 1220s, and in the 1260s granted it the same liberties as were enjoyed by Hereford. What allowed the town a measure of independence was the possession of a separate 'hundred court' meeting about every four weeks to deal with admission to burgages and complaints of

---

[22] Beresford, *New Towns of the Middle Ages*, pp. 81, 105, 256–7, 297ff, 446, 460, 505; *Borough Customs*, ed. M. Bateson, 2 vols. (Selden Society, vols. 18, 21, London, 1904–6), I.34–5, 278–9, II.78, 90–102; Beresford and St Joseph, *Medieval England*, pp. 242–7; *Court Rolls of the Manor of Wakefield*, vols. I (1274–97), and II (1297–1309), ed. W. P. Baildon (Yorkshire Archaeological Society Record Series, vols. 29, 36, Leeds, 1901, 1906), I.130, II.145, 200; Tait, *Medieval English Borough*, pp. 352–3; R. A. Philpott, *Historic Towns of the Merseyside Area: A Survey of Urban Settlement to c. 1800* (Liverpool: National Museums and Galleries on Merseyside, 1988), pp. 12, 42, 47; Pollock and Maitland, *HEL*, I.643ff, 673–4, II.330–1; *BBC, 1216–1307*, pp. ix–xiv, lxxviii–lxxxi, xc–cii, and Beresford, *New Towns of the Middle Ages*, p. 205; for an analysis of the terms of borough charters, *Charters of the Earls of Chester*, ed. Barraclough, p. 434.

broken agreements as well as to punish a mixture of commercial and agricultural offences – forestalling, giving short weight, grain-stealing, fence-breaking, soaking flax (for linen-making) in the lord's fish-ponds, spreading rumours about neighbours, verbal abuse (frequently of a sexual nature) and unjustly raising the hue and cry (even by husbands and wives against their spouses). It appears from the records of this borough court, which begin in 1272 and run through to the sixteenth century alongside but separate from the manor-court records, that the liberty of the borough could be purchased from year to year in order to follow a craft such as linen-maker or to put up a stall in the market. It was not necessary to have a permanent tenement, and at least half the population of about 600 at the end of the century were incomers, often remarkably independent women of the sort who seem to have carried on much of the retailing in every medieval town. The resident community came together in the court to make ordinances against the pollution of streams by dyers, butchers and tanners, refine the details of the assize of ale and try to keep out the foreigners. Despite this defensiveness, Halesowen operated a lively market in grain, malt and livestock, and the court held occasional 'piepowder' sessions to settle the disputes of the pedlars coming to it with *pieds poudres* ('dusty feet'). Between the 1270s and the 1340s the number of debt cases in the borough court involving money alone (as opposed to goods) increased almost eightfold.[23]

Twenty miles away, on the bishop of Worcester's manor of Stratford, there was the same separation between the manor court with its villein suitors and the court of the borough laid out in the 1190s and given the customs of Bristol: but everything here was on a bigger scale, reflecting the bishop's ambitions and the links of the new borough with the rich wool trade of the Cotswolds and the fast-developing area of the forest of Arden. When a survey was made in 1251–2, the total population of the manor had increased sixfold in half a century, and three-quarters of it was in the borough, which contained 250 burgages (held by 234 tenants), 14 shops, 2 ovens and 2 dyepans, and must have had at least 1,000 inhabitants – more than its ancient neighbour, Warwick. Surnames derived from places (for example, 'John of Clopton') indicate that

[23] R. H. Hilton, 'Small Town Society in England before the Black Death', *Past and Present*, 105 (1984): reprinted in *The Medieval Town: A Reader in English Urban History, 1200–1540*, ed. R. Holt and G. Rosser (London: Longmans, 1990); for piepowder courts, see Salzman, *English Trade in the Middle Ages*, pp. 172–5, and *Select Cases concerning the Law Merchant*, I.xxxvii–xxxviii.

a third of these were people who had recently immigrated from villages within Stratford's 'market area' (a six or eight mile radius). By the end of the century migration to towns and the apparently higher mortality within them was helping a little to relieve the pressure of population in the countryside; and Stratford had the special attractions of a fine bridge, the broad streets of a planned town, separate markets for corn, sheep, pigs and cattle, a fullers' quarter and the beginnings of a civic consciousness represented by the gild or fraternity of the Holy Cross, with its hospital and charitable activities.[24]

Like almost every sizeable English town, Stratford had a preponderance of cloth-workers but nothing that could be called a specialized manufacture. All sorts of trades were carried on for a quite restricted area. Droitwich was the only purely industrial town in the region, its burgesses secure in their monopoly of the production of salt and its distribution far and wide along an ancient system of saltways, and therefore growing hardly at all. Birmingham was growing as a market for cattle from Wales and the north and as a centre for iron-working. But Coventry, the fastest-growing and most populous town in the west midlands, was different from Stratford only in the even greater variety of its occupations and wider provenance of its traders. Among its population in 1280 the Hundred Rolls show locksmiths, needlers, goldsmiths, brooch-makers, girdlers, mirrorers, soap-makers, butchers and bearwards, as well as the predictable cloth-workers; and there were merchants from Flanders as well as 'of Gloucester' and 'of Worcester', and vintners importing wine through Bristol. Coventry provides a striking example of a group of traders which managed to prosper as a community under two lords who divided the town down the middle. Early in the century one part belonged to the earl of Chester, who took as much care of it as of Chester itself and in 1199–1202 confirmed 'to his burgesses of Coventry' the previous grant, confirmed by Henry II in 1182, of a portmoot for the settlement of mercantile disputes and all the liberties enjoyed by the burgesses of Lincoln. The other lord was the prior of the cathedral, who held a court leet in his part as the earl also did in his for non-commercial matters. But by 1249 there was a

[24] E. M. Carus-Wilson, 'The First Half-Century of the Borough of Stratford-upon-Avon', *EcHR*, 2nd ser., 18 (1965), reprinted in *The Medieval Town*, ed. Holt and Rosser; R. H. Hilton, *A Medieval Society: The West Midlands at the End of the Thirteenth Century* (London: Weidenfeld and Nicolson, 1966), pp. 183–4.

chief bailiff who stood up to the prior on behalf of the whole town, when the priory became the principal lord. Already by 1280 the lesser landlords from outside had begun to give up their interests in Coventry, while the pressure of incomers had caused about 80 of the 260 burgages to be divided, two of them into no less than thirty cottage-plots, and the population of the town to rise to perhaps 5,000 people. By 1377 Coventry would be the fourth town in the kingdom, after London, Bristol and York. Like most towns, however, it kept its common fields and pasture round about, and had barns, orchards and even arable ridges within it.[25]

Bristol, at the other end of the trade route from Coventry, may have been three times as large as Coventry at the end of the thirteenth century. Each year 2,000 to 3,000 tuns of wine from La Rochelle and Bordeaux came into the country through Bristol, and the records of tolls taken there for the paving of the town's streets and quays and the upkeep of its four sets of walls show corn, hides and wool going out in quantities (though Cotswold wool was mostly taken overland to Southampton for export to Flanders). Woad was imported as a dye for the city's large-scale cloth industry, and in the next century Bristol would be seen as the country's leading exporter of cloth. Yet it too had grown as a seignorial borough within the honour of Gloucester, until John married the countess of Gloucester and kept hold of Bristol when he divorced her. Of the other ancient towns of the region, Worcester had an unspecialized economy typical of English towns, striking only in the number of victuallers and garment-makers needed to serve its high number of clerics and administrators. Gloucester was another royal borough of ecclesiastical and administrative importance, well endowed with charters and advantageously placed on the river system leading to Bristol; but it was given greater economic significance than Worcester by its community of fullers and dyers and position as an outlet for the iron production of the Forest of Dean (source of nails for the king's ships and crossbow bolts for his army, and of the metal needed for the multifarious implements of an agricultural economy). In the

[25] Hilton, *A Medieval Society*, pp. 167ff, 185; *The Early Records of Medieval Coventry*, ed. P. R. Coss (London: OUP for the British Academy, 1986), pp. xxxvi–xxxix, xli, 22–3, 366; R. H. C. Davis, *The Early History of Coventry*, (Dugdale Society Occasional Papers, no. 24, Oxford, 1976), p. 8; Joan Lancaster on Coventry in *The Atlas of Historic Towns II*, ed. M. D. Lobel (London: Scolar Press with the Historic Towns Trust, 1955), pp. 3–6 and maps 3–4.

tax assessment of 1334 Gloucester would come third in wealth in the region behind Bristol and Coventry.[26]

The planting of new towns; the chartering of new boroughs; the increasing commercial activity of many small towns that were never formally boroughs; the growth of rural industry such as coal-mining and the iron-smelting of the independent miners of the Forest of Dean; and the spread of cloth-making in the country-side of the west which was made possible by the application of the watermill to fulling – all this was an achievement of human endeavour which went some way to redressing the economic balance with the east of the country. Nevertheless, the imbalance remained. Estimates of the urban population in the thirteenth century are changing all the time, with changing views (for instance) of the size of the poorer element and of how many people the plague killed before the first detailed figures become available in the poll taxes of 1377 and 1381. The tax assessments of 1334 at least offer a ranking of towns by wealth. Only six towns in the whole of the west were assessed at £400 or above (leaving aside Chester, for which we have no figures): Bristol (£2,200, with a suggested population of 15,000), Shrewsbury (£800), Coventry (£750), Hereford (£605), Gloucester (£541) and Plymouth (£400); and their collective wealth was £5,296. Lincolnshire and East Anglia alone had nineteen, with a collective wealth of £11,820, the four leading towns being Boston (£1,100), Lincoln (£1,000), Great Yarmouth (£1,000) and Norwich (£946). Outside this area but drawing on its wealth, London was in a class of its own: it was assessed at £11,000 in 1334, and its population in the early fourteenth century has recently been put at 80,000–100,000 (in 1381 it would be down to not much more than 45,000). At £1,620 York lagged behind Bristol in estimated wealth though probably not in people, its trade and administrative importance having been stimulated by the Scottish wars, when it became a second capital. Far away on the north-east coast lay the town with the fourth largest assessment in 1334, Newcastle upon Tyne (£1,333), another beneficiary of the Scottish wars. In the south midlands, Oxford (with a population of perhaps 5,000 in 1300) was assessed at £914. (Cambridge's assessment was £466.) At £750, Salisbury's wealth was on a par with Coventry's. Canterbury (£599), Winchester

---

[26] E. M. Carus-Wilson on Bristol, in *Atlas of Historic Towns II*, pp. 6–10; Hilton, *A Medieval Society*, pp. 174, 197–9, 204; *BBC, 1216–1307*, p. lxxv; R. E. Glasscock, 'England *circa* 1334', in *New Historical Geography of England*, ed. H. C. Darby (Cambridge: CUP, 1973), p. 181.

(£515, despite a population which has been put at more than 10,000) and Southampton (£511, to be compared with a pre-plague population estimated at only 2,000–3,000) had the other largish assessments in the south. Exeter (£366) was another cathedral city which may have ranked higher in population than in its assessed wealth. Sussex, Dorset, Cornwall, Worcestershire, Staffordshire, Lancashire and Westmorland had no towns assessed above £225; Derbyshire only Derby itself (£300) and Cumberland only Penrith (£398). For the palatinate boroughs of Chester and Durham there are no data, but they would have ranked fairly high.[27]

The older boroughs (including most of the county towns), which had acknowledged no lord but the king since their foundation in Anglo-Saxon times because many lesser lords held property within them, were often well endowed with charters by 1200, but they were always looking to advance themselves by the purchase of further liberties from the Crown. King John, 'the great charter-monger', granted the farms of many boroughs to populations of burgesses whose aspirations had been raised by the example of the sworn communes of the continent. This potentially revolutionary institution got a foothold in England with the establishment of a commune in London in 1191. But the communal movement was kept in check by a watchful Crown, and its manifestations in England were limited to the introduction of sworn town councils with mayors to preside over them, and a renewed vigour in municipal affairs.[28]

The grant of the fee-farm, or in London's case its regrant at John's accession in 1199 for the enormous fee of 3,000 marks, forced the groups of burgesses to organize themselves. Money must already have been collected to purchase the charter. A common fund would now need to be set up, not only in royal but also in seignorial boroughs where the burgesses had been granted this essential right to pay a lump sum to their lords and not have officials come in to collect revenues. The money and the initiative

[27] J. C. Russell, *British Medieval Population* (Albuquerque: University of New Mexico Press, 1948); Hilton, *A Medieval Society*, pp. 167–8; R. H. Hilton, 'Towns in English Medieval Society', *Urban History Yearbook* (1982), reprinted in *The Medieval Town*, ed. Holt and Rosser, p. 22; Derek Keene, 'Medieval London and its Region', *London Journal*, 14 (1989), pp. 100, 107; Glasscock, 'England *circa* 1334', pp. 180–2; Colin Platt, *Medieval Southampton* (London, 1973), p. 262.

[28] *BBC, 1216–1307*, p. lvi; Tait, *Medieval English Borough*, pp. 177–93, 248–56, 263–301; C. N. L. Brooke and Gillian Keir, *London 800–1216: The Shaping of a City* (London: Secker and Warburg, 1975), pp. 245–57.

came from the ubiquitous gilds – fraternities with all sorts of religious, social and charitable purposes (periodic feasting in a gildhall was a usual feature), but particularly suited to the promotion of their members' trading interests. Once again, the Crown's approval was sought for the institution of a hanse or gild merchant to protect the burgesses' monopoly of trading within their town and any freedom from tolls they were granted outside, as well as to help raise the borough farm. A merchant gild with monopoly of trade was one of the four privileges regularly bestowed in the early charters of Henry III, along with the exclusion of the sheriff from town pleas, the freedom of villeins who remained in the town for a year and a day and a general quittance from tolls. The oldest town records are the gild registers, which for Leicester survive from 1196. This was an ancient borough which remained under the sole lordship of the earls of Leicester until Simon de Montfort's death in 1265, after which it was given to Henry III's younger son, Edmund of Lancaster, so that it eventually became part of the duchy of Lancaster. In this greatest of seignorial boroughs, where the burgesses did not have the fee-farm and the earl's manor court operated alongside the portmoot, the importance of the gild merchant is evident. The gildsmen showed their loyalty by dating their records from such events as the death of one of their lords at Damietta in 1220, but they stood up to these lords when the interests of the merchant community were at stake. The gild financed the upkeep of the gates and bridges, and the negotiation of remarkable charters from the earl which granted the burgesses inheritance by the eldest sons, in place of ultimogeniture with its implications of servile status. More important still, gild association opened the way to borough self-government, the alderman of the gild becoming by mid-century the mayor of Leicester, and the gild's 'morning-speech' in the gildhall providing a more flexible organ than the portmoot for the transaction of borough affairs (not least because the lord's steward did not have the same right to be there).[29]

---

[29] *BBC, 1216–1307*, pp. xvii, liv, lvi, lix, lxviii, lxx, lxxv, lxxxii–lxxxii; *Records of the Borough of Leicester, 1103–1327*, ed. Mary Bateson (London: Leicester UP, 1899), pp. xv, xxiv, xxvii, xxxviii–xxxix, xliii, xlvii; G. H. Martin, 'The English Borough in the Thirteenth Century', *TRHS*, 5th ser., 13 (1963), reprinted in *The Medieval Town*, ed. Holt and Rosser, pp. 37–9, 43; Charles Gross, *The Gild Merchant*, 2 vols. (Oxford: Clarendon Press, 1890), I.7–8, II.21, 114–25; Hilton, *A Medieval Society*, pp. 206, 221–2; J. W. F. Hill, *Medieval Lincoln* (Cambridge: CUP, 1948), plate 15, for the hall of St Mary's Guild at

The gild merchant was not identical in membership and purpose with the group of burgage holders, let alone the whole body of inhabitants, however, and it became subordinate to the borough as the institution favoured and regulated by the Crown. The gild's alderman, who bore an Anglo-Saxon name with noble or at least patrician connotations, needed to change character to become the mayor whose job was to represent the whole community of townsmen. The heyday of the gilds coincided with that of the great fairs and the two institutions declined in importance together. Leicester gildsmen aspired to control the internal trade in wool, and claimed exemption from attendance at the portmoot when they needed to be at the fairs of Boston, Lynn, Northampton, St Ives and Stamford. In the fairs members of the gilds of English and Flemish towns made up the 'communities' held corporately responsible for debts, but many a trader wanted to deny that he was 'of the community' of his fellow townsmen. The men of Leicester were as keen as those of Ypres, Ghent, and Douai to purchase royal grants that they should not be distrained for debts unless they were the principal debtors or the named sureties; and a royal statute of 1275 extended this liberty to all Englishmen.[30]

By *c.* 1250 those who dwelt (rather than traded) together were coming to be seen as the true communities. At Leicester, rules concerning trade in wool or cloth were generally passed 'by the community of the gild in full morning-speech': but the clerk writes of 'the community of Leicester' as the body which settles the wages of the wool-packers, who were humble people (often women) and not members of the gild; as the body, too, which is offended against by those who avoid tronage (weighing dues), breach the assize of ale, malign Leicester fish, or damage the town wall; and before which petty thieves are made to abjure the town. In 1251–5 William Ordriz granted land 'to the Mayor of Leicester and the Burgesses and Commune of Leicester and their successors', and in 1277 Edmund, earl of Lancaster, and his council reformed the procedure of the portmoot with 'the assent of the mayor, sworn officers and all the commons of the same town'. Burgesses

Lincoln; Platt, *Medieval Southampton*, pp. 17–23; M. D. Lobel, *The Borough of Bury St Edmunds* (Oxford, Clarendon Press, 1935), pp. 72–82.

[30] Hill, *Medieval Lincoln*, p. 187; *Records of the Borough of Leicester*, ed. Bateson, pp. xvii, xxviii, xxx–xxxii, 33; Platt, *Medieval Southampton*, p. 20; Miller and Hatcher, *Rural Society and Economic Change*, p. 78; *Select Pleas in Manorial Courts*, ed. Maitland, pp. 134–5; *Cases concerning the Law Merchant*, I.9–10; Stat. Westminster I, c. 23.

remained separately and individually responsible for the payment of the fee-farms of their boroughs to the Crown, but their acquisition in many places of 'a common and authentic seal wherewith are sealed the charters of feoffment' of the towns implied the corporate holding of property. In 1298 Edward I gave the burgesses and good men of Newcastle upon Tyne lands which were to be joined in perpetuity and at the previous farm to the rest of the town, and to constitute with it 'a single vill and one borough'.[31]

But the main impetus for the incorporation of boroughs, which began to be made explicit in charters of the next century, came from the joining together of burgesses in the purchase and defence of group liberties. When he declared himself of age in 1227, and again when he was under political and financial pressure in 1255–7, Henry III imitated his father's wholesale distribution of borough rights. In 1227 the four standard privileges granted to Hereford in 1215 (exclusion of the sheriff, gild merchant, freedom for villeins and quittance of tolls) were extended to Shrewsbury and Bridgnorth, then to Liverpool and on to Wigan; and there began a stream of confirmations of the charters of other towns which reached over a hundred by 1307 (by Edward's reign there were few new privileges left to give).[32]

The burgesses' attachment to their liberties was tempered in the fire of the *quo warranto* inquiries, and boroughs had all the time to be vigilant in defending their privileges against each other as well as in justifying them to the king. In the eyres of 1218–22 the burgesses of Bridgnorth complained that the burgesses of Shrewsbury prevented them from buying untanned hides and undyed cloth as their charter allowed; the burgesses of Shrewsbury that the abbot of Shrewsbury deprived them of their market; and the men of Evesham that the citizens of Worcester took tolls of their sheep and pigs whereas they should take them only of oxen and horses. Everyone complained of the burgesses of Droitwich, made assertive by their new charter, who were alleged to take a new toll from

[31] *Records of the Borough of Leicester, 1103–1327*, ed. Bateson, pp. xl–xli, 51, 150; *BBC, 1216–1307*, pp. lxvii, lxxii; *EHD*, p. 875, for the rules for the use of Winchester's seal; Hill, *Medieval Lincoln*, pp. 196, 215; M. Weinbaum, *The Incorporation of Boroughs* (Manchester: Manchester UP, 1937), pp. 19–22; Pollock and Maitland, *HEL*, II. 645, 654.

[32] Pollock and Maitland, *HEL*, II. 668, 685; *BBC, 1216–1307*, pp. xvii–xviii, liv–lv, lxi–lxiv; Hill, *Medieval Lincoln*, p. 206.

the knights who purchased food in their town; they were also said to go to Worcester's market on a Sunday, buy up goods privately while the citizens were in the Minster and resell them at a profit. Another example of the hundreds of disputes about liberties is a case heard by Hugh Bigod, the baronial justiciar, sitting at Bermondsey late in 1258. The sheriff of Surrey and the bailiffs of the king and Earl Warenne, the two lords of the town of Southwark, complained that the sheriffs of London were taking a toll of 'a fish and a halfpenny from laden horses beyond the drawbridge in the middle of London Bridge on the Southwark side and within the borough of Southwark' and 'quayage dues at St Olave's hithe in Southwark from ships and boats mooring there', and distraining men in Southwark to answer pleas in London: all to the loss of £100 to king and earl. The sheriffs and many citizens of London came and asserted that the whole bridge and width of the river from quay to quay belonged to London, but that they could not answer outside the city's boundaries to a plea affecting its rights. As individuals, the sheriffs were found not guilty of taking the tolls and dues, and the question whether the county of Surrey extended to mid-bridge and mid-stream was remitted to king and council for discussion.[33]

URBAN GOVERNMENT AND POLITICS

Disputes about the internal government of towns occasionally appeared in the king's courts. The defendants to a plea in king's bench in 1292 claimed to be the mayor and bailiffs of Northampton, and that it was 'by the consent of the twenty-four of the same town who have the community of the aforesaid town in their keeping' that they had seized the goods which the plaintiff was preparing to take to Stamford fair: he was 'for a long time mayor of the town of Northampton so that he received from the com-

---

[33] *Placita de Quo Warranto*, ed. W. Illingworth (Record Commission, London, 1818), p. 241, for the inquiry into Gloucester's liberties; *Rolls of the Justices in Eyre for Lincolnshire 1218–9 and Worcestershire 1221*, ed. D. M. Stenton (Selden Society, vol. 53, London, 1934), pp. lxxi, nos. 1127, 1149, 1157, 1268; *Gloucestershire Eyre*, nos. 1129, 1328, 1342, 1344; *Rolls of the Justices in Eyre for Yorkshire 1218–19*, ed. D. M. Stenton (Selden Society, vol. 56, London, 1937), p. xxxv, no. 1139; *CRR*, XVI, no. 1252; *Rotuli Hundredorum*, I. 61; *Select Cases in the Court of King's Bench*, ed. G. O. Sayles, 7 vols. (Selden Society, London, 1936–71), III.cviii; *Cases of Procedure without Writ*, ed. Richardson and Sayles, p. clxxiv, no. 80.

munity of the town about five hundred marks for which he refused to render account, although he had often been asked to do this'.[34]

The king did not at first concern himself with how towns were governed internally, so long as his law and peace were kept. The mayoralty and town council spread without the aid of royal grants: only three of Edward's charters included the power to elect a mayor, those to Nottingham in 1284, Northampton (clearly after the fact) in 1299 and Berwick in 1302. Yet the election by the commonalty of a mayor and twelve or (more often) twenty-four sworn councillors, whose first obligation was 'the saving and sustaining of the franchise', was the essence of communal government as it was established in England around 1200. The custumal of Ipswich gives a vivid description of how a town's constitution might be worked out. Its first chapter is King John's charter of 1200, its second begins to describe the charter's implementation, 'as it is contained in a roll in the town's common chest'. The charter is dated 25 May. On the Thursday after the feast of the Nativity of St John the Baptist (29 June), an assembly of all the people of Ipswich first elected two reeves and four coroners in St Mary's churchyard, who then named the Sunday after the feast of the apostles Peter and Paul (2 July) for the election of twelve chief portmen sworn 'to govern and maintain the said town and all its liberties, render the town's judgements, and guard, ordain and execute in that borough all that needs to be done for the town's state and honour'. In fact what happened was that the reeves and coroners chose four good men from each parish and swore them to the choosing of the portmen. Two custodians of the royal charter were appointed, and at the same time the portmen and officers were summoned to a meeting on the Thursday after the feast of the Translation of the Blessed Thomas the Martyr (13 July) to draw up further ordinances. Those they made concerned the payment of the town's farm to the royal exchequer, the appointment of two beadles to execute the council's orders, the making and custody of a common seal, the setting up of a gild merchant and the election of its alderman and the collection of tolls from burgesses who did not 'scot and lot' in the town's levies and transactions. Chapters 14 to 17 of the custumal describe the reading and implementation of the ordinances at meetings of the whole

[34] *Cases in King's Bench*, ed. Sayles, II. 113–15; cf. *Select Cases of Procedure without Writ under Henry III*, ed. H. G. Richardson and G. O. Sayles, (Selden Society, vol. 60, London, 1941), p. clxxv, no. 26.

community in the churchyard or the church itself on the Sunday after the Nativity of the Virgin Mary (10 September) and the Thursday after the feast of St Fides (12 October); chapter 18 records the town's agreement to the rewarding of the portmen with a meadow to graze their horses; and the final chapter orders that the laws and customs be written down in a roll called 'the Domesday'.[35]

The seed of the momentous idea of legislation for the welfare of the community and with its assent was planted early in the towns. But the king did not grant towns power to make their own laws: he required from them enforcement of his laws. The councillors of the tamed communes of England swore to keep the peace of the lord king rather than in the continental manner to stick together against the feudal world. Royal boroughs were classed as part of the king's demesne, to be administered by reeves like any other lord's. In 1200 the ancient city of Lincoln paid King John 300 marks for a charter allowing the citizens to choose two of their number in common council, and present them to the king's chief justice at Westminster for appointment as reeves of the town; and to choose another four to be coroners to keep the king's pleas in Lincoln (this only six years after the office of coroner had been created for the counties). Like seignorial reeves, Lincoln's officers were chosen in the borough's court leet. When the alderman of the gild merchant assumed the mayoralty (which he had done by *c.* 1206), he continued to be termed 'our bailiff' as well as 'your mayor' in royal letters.[36]

That leet jurisdiction simply became more elaborate to police urban populations is seen most clearly in Norwich. The five bridges over the River Wensum, more than in any other English city, testify to the vigour of Norwich's businesses, and the four over the River Yare to the south of the city to the importance of its consumption and its fishmongering to the countryside around. The new ditch with nine timber gates dug by the municipality in 1250 and the stone wall begun in the 1290s enclosed extensive greens where tenting frames were set up for the drying of cloth,

---

[35] *BBC, 1216–1307*, pp. lvii, lix, lxxiv; *EHD*, III.870–1, 878 (late thirteenth-century usages of Winchester and provisions for the government of Lincoln *c.* 1300); Hill, *Medieval Lincoln*, pp. 293–9; Gross, *The Gild Merchant*, II.114–23.

[36] Norman Doe, *Fundamental Authority in Late Medieval English Law* (Cambridge: CUP, 1990), pp. 20–1; *BBC, 1216–1307*, pp. lxxxiii–lxxxiv; Hill, *Medieval Lincoln*, pp. 193–200, 206.

and the quarters where the various orders of Friars had settled, demolishing existing properties and closing lanes. There was also at Norwich the largest Jewry outide London, perhaps 200 strong at one point; there was a big, though apparently neglected, royal castle; and there was the cathedral with its priory. The prior possessed a great segment of the city, in which he disputed the right of the city bailiffs to take distresses and hold inquests. This and the refusal of the inhabitants of the prior's fee to contribute to the city's taxes led to a mass attack on the priory and the cathedral itself on 11 August 1272; the descent of King Henry upon the town and the execution of thirty-four males and one female citizen; and in 1276 King Edward's sentencing of the burgesses to provide a golden pyx worth £100 'because of the damage they had done to the body of Christ', to pay 500 marks a year for six years for the damage to the priory and to send evidence of the settlement to the pope at their own expense.[37]

Acquiring neither gild merchant nor mayor, this turbulent city continued to be governed by reeves, and then from 1223 by four bailiffs, one for each of the four hundreds or 'leets' into which the city (outside the prior's fee) was presumably already divided for the exercise of view of frankpledge. By the time the records of proceedings begin in 1288, the bailiffs were sitting together almost daily during Lent in the 'city court' in the tollbooth (so distinguished from the shire court in the castle), to hear pleas, record recognitions of bonds and deeds of conveyance and punish offences presented by juries from eleven subdivisions of the four leets. These smaller units, formed out of combinations of the city's fifty or more parishes, corresponded to the wards of London, York, Wallingford and some other towns, and like them were needed to exercise the peace-keeping functions of the hundred in an urban environment. The Norwich court of the last years of the century was presented with the normal run of breaches of the assize of ale, cases of the use of false weights and measures, encroachments of buildings and muck heaps on public highways and waterways ('purprestures'), the vindictive raising of the hue and cry and miscellaneous anti-social behaviour. Sprowston men were said to have knowingly bought measly pigs and sold sausages and puddings 'unfit for human bodies' in Norwich market, and a whole

[37] James Campbell, 'Norwich', in *Atlas of Historic Towns*, II, pp. 8–15; *The Chronicle of Bury St Edmunds, 1212–1301*, ed. and tr. Antonia Gransden (London: Nelson, 1964), pp. 37, 50–52, 59.

list of cooks to have warmed up meat and pasties for sale after the second or third day; one Thomas was wont to receive goods stolen at Yarmouth and bring them into Norwich to sell, 'and sometimes he says that the goods are feathers'; Robert the fowler spent 'much and has nothing to spend from, and roves about by night'; John of Weston dug 'turves out of the city ditch to raise the floor of his tenting-frame' (fine: 2s.); and John de Scotia had an awning which was a nuisance to riders. More general ideas of commercial morality were involved in the presentment of John the chaplain as an 'excessive usurer'; of John the bleacher and Ranulph the fishmonger for riding out 'to meet a vessel laden with oysters' and buy them up so that prices rose in Norwich market; and of Thomas Gooseonthegreen and eighty-four other fishmongers for the forestalling of fish in that they bought 'before the hour of prime contrary to the common proclamation made in the city'.[38]

Measures against forestalling reflect a suspicious and restrictive attitude to hucksters shared by town oligarchies and the Crown. Taking a cue from the Church's condemnation of forestallers as 'manifest oppressors of the poor', a statute issuing from the royal marshalsea in 1274–5 gave firmer definition to the offence. The forestaller and regrater, it said,

hurries out before other men, sometimes by land and sometimes by water, to meet grain, fish, herring or other kinds of goods coming for sale by land or water, thirsting for evil profit [and contriving] to carry off these goods unjustly and sell them much more dearly. He gets around outsiders coming with goods for sale, offering himself for the sale of their goods and suggesting to them that they could sell their goods more dearly than they proposed.

The penalties the statute set increased progressively from a fine and forfeiture of the goods for the first offence, to abjuring the town for a fourth.[39]

The belief that profit-making was a breach of natural law and a

---

[38] *Leet Jurisdiction in the City of Norwich in the XIIIth and XIVth Centuries*, ed. William Hudson (Selden Society, vol. 5, London, 1892), pp. xxiii–xxxiv, xxxvi, 2, 4, 8, 14–16, 30–2, 35, 47, 53; Pollock and Maitland, *HEL*, I, 657–8; Tait, *Medieval English Borough*, pp. 60 n. 3, 63, 292 n. 4, 322, 334; Williams, *Medieval London*, p. 80, for London wards; *Berkshire Eyre*, ed. Clanchy, nos. 1035, 1044, 1048, for wards in Reading and Wallingford; cf. *Records of the Borough of Leicester*, ed. Bateson, p. xlix, for Leicester's four policing townships.

[39] R. H. Hilton, 'Lords, Burgesses and Hucksters', *Past and Present*, 97 (1982); R. H. Britnell, 'Forstall, Forestalling and the Statute of Forestallers', *EHR*, 102 (1987), p. 94; *BBC, 1216–1307*, p. lxxxvii.

cause of dearth reinforced the Crown's inclination to maintain a close control over the towns with their growing resources, both financial and administrative. The emergence of town government was marked in the second half of the century by the replacement of the gild register by the borough court roll as the typical urban record – the essential working document of the borough community. The oldest surviving London record is of a roll of deeds registered in the hustings court in 1252, but there is a Burghmoot roll recording land transactions in Wallingford in 1229, and portmoots were certainly operative long before the records begin. The king's judges made it clear that borough law was subordinate to the common law of the land. Claims that writs of mort d'ancestor did not run in boroughs because of the right to devise burgages outside the family met with judicial scepticism. Towns might send officers to the eyre to exhibit charters conferring on them the franchises of London and claim that persons appealed of homicide must therefore be tried within their walls and by oaths, not duels or juries, but the most they normally enjoyed was the right to have special sessions of the justices in eyre, and their own coroners to record the preliminaries of the cases that would be tried at it.[40]

Even the citizens of London had to appear before the king's justices in eyre at the Tower, and have the felons they imprisoned Newgate 'delivered' (that is tried and hanged) by royal commissioners. The judges rejected their claim that the city was a collective lordship and they themselves barons entitled to trial by the lords of the land as their peers. At the eyre of 1244, the citizens were told how their hustings court should operate, for instance that no alderman should give judgement in a case if he had been involved in it as counsel. Expressing themselves dissatisfied with the presentment of purprestures, which was vital to keeping a great

---

[40] Martin, 'The English Borough in the Thirteenth Century', pp. 42, 47; Hill, *Medieval Lincoln*, pp. 187, 294; *The Earliest Lincolnshire Assize Rolls*, ed. Stenton, p. lxxvii, nos. 249, 251; *Cases in King's Bench*, ed. Sayles, 1.63–4 (a case brought from Oxford borough court on a writ of error); *Shropshire Eyre*, ed. Harding, p. xxviii, no. 222; *Lincolnshire and Worcestershire Eyre*, ed. Stenton, no. 875; Pollock and Maitland, *HEL*, 1.643–4, 661; *Introduction to the Curia Regis Rolls*, ed. Flower, pp. 29, 115, 305, 357; *CRR*, 1.293; *Calendar of the Early Mayor's Court Rolls of the City of London*, ed. A. H. Thomas (Cambridge: CUP, 1924), pp. xxxi–xxxiii, for the London oath-helping procedures which other boroughs sought to follow; *Berkshire Eyre*, ed. Clanchy, pp. xxviii–xxx, for special eyre sessions; *BBC, 1216–1307*, pp. lviii–lxii; R. F. Hunnisett, *The Medieval Coroner* (Cambridge CUP, 1961), pp. 92–4, 156–62, 171, 196–7; *Select Cases from the Coroners' Rolls, 1265–1413*, ed. C. Gross (Selden Society, vol. 9, London, 1896), pp. 127ff, for London coroners in the thirteenth century.

city moving and lucrative to the king (something traditionally done in London by each alderman and his ward), the justices went on a tour of inspection along with the mayor and discovered (amongst other things) a forge standing in the middle of road opposite the New Temple, and willows planted by the Templars by the great channel of their mill to the obstruction of ships coming to a watergate on the Thames. The buildings on London Bridge had to be justified on the grounds 'that for the most part the fabric of the bridge was maintained by the alms of the citizens of London, and the wardens and brethren of the bridge built mostly from those alms upon the same bridge shops for the maintenance and improvement of the fabric'. The justices of 1244 went to the extreme of taking the city into the king's hand for the technical offence of harbouring Walter Bukerel, a member of one of its leading families, who had abjured the realm during Henry III's minority and then been restored to the king's peace – but without obtaining a royal confirmation of his pardon when the king came of age: this experience and the 'common fine' of £1,000 which the justices exacted from London for the restoration of its liberties are representative of the perils in which all boroughs lived, and of their value to a straitened royal treasury.[41]

London had already long counted as a shire in itself, with not one but two sheriffs to preside over its hustings courts, before the commune of 1191 added the mayoralty to its constitution. London's (and England's) first mayor was Henry FitzAilwin, who held office for at least nineteen years until his death in 1212, but after him the restive citizens established the principle of annual election to the mayoralty and took care that no one served continuously for more than seven years. The council and rulers of the city were its aldermen. London's gildhall is mentioned as a notable drinking-place in the late twelfth century, but instead of a single gild merchant the city by then possessed a great variety of gilds, ranging from the rich and powerful goldsmiths', drapers', mercers' and vintners' organizations; through charitable fraternities like that of St Lazarus and several gilds formed to raised money for the new bridge completed around 1209; to the lowly craft gilds of the cloth-workers. In early lists, both gilds and wards may be designated by the names of their aldermen, who came from a

[41] Williams, *Medieval London*, pp. 3, 26, 44, 74–5, 207, 324–5; *The London Eyre of 1244*, ed. H. M. Chew and M. Weinbaum (London Record Society, vol. 6, London, 1970), pp. x, xvii–xviii, xx, xxi, nos. 211–12, 221, 233–8, 298, 300, 304, 349; Pollock and Maitland, *HEL*, 1.678.

handful of dynasties of landowners, royal servants and merchants, and 'exercised an almost hereditary authority'. The necessities of policing in London attached the aldermen to twenty-four wards: territorial units derived in some way from older seignorial jurisdictions (or 'sokes') or from parish groupings, each with a hundred-moot presided over by an alderman for the enforcement of city regulations.[42]

The 'good men' of the wards chose their aldermen, who in the thirteenth century served for life unless the king intervened in a political crisis to order a general re-election; and the aldermen provided and effectively chose the mayor who personified the city. Most significant of their power was their displacement of the sheriffs from control of the city courts. It was agreed with the justices in eyre of 1221 that 'henceforth the Mayor and Sheriffs, associating with them two or three Aldermen' might hear 'the pleas of persons called "pepoudrous" [i.e. itinerant merchants] passing through the City' and unable to wait for the hustings in order to proceed against their debtors. In the course of time a mayor's court meeting later in the week than the Monday hustings became the city's dominant tribunal: by mid-century it heard commercial actions between foreign merchants and to some extent between citizens, and cases arising from disobedience to city ordinances; by an ordinance of 1280 it added complaints of error in the old hustings where the sheriffs still presided; and it began to receive complaints of a vast range of personal trespasses – all sorts of cases of assault, defamation and fraud. Amongst the first few cases from the earliest surviving records of the mayor's court, at the very end of the century, a cooper charges other coopers with taking a breach of contract before the archdeacon, when it belonged to the city's jurisdiction; Richard Horn is accused of driving away Adam Harewe's cart with two quarters of sea-coal in it; the Lady Blaunche, queen of Navarre, complains by attorney that Richard de Hacumby will not account for £1,500 which he received on behalf of her dead husband, Lord Edmund the king's brother, whose executrix she is; and two merchants of Lucca sue for a debt of fifty marks, the purchase price of a horse. The 'commonalty of London' complains of German merchants who operate as wholesale drapers and woolmen, trading beyond the privileges of their hanse and depriving the city of its customs; of a sworn broker of

---

[42] Brooke and Keir, *London 800–1216*, pp. 96–9, 245–57, 278ff; Williams, *Medieval London*, pp. 32–3, 50–75.

ships who has 'acted as a common broker in all kinds of merchandise against the custom, forestalled merchandise and procured it for others not of the Liberty'; and of a freeman of Candlewickstreet who deals with foreigners (that is, merchants of Bristol), and avows their goods, against his oath. Various persons appear to answer presentments before an alderman in his ward-moot that they made 'a great roistering with unknown minstrels, tabor-players and trumpeters to the grave damage and tumult of the whole neighbourhood and against the prohibition' or that they maintained 'a low haunt of prostitutes and depraved men who go about the City by night'; and Walter of Maidstone, carpenter, is charged with 'gathering together a parliament of carpenters at Mile End, where they bound themselves by a corporal oath not to observe a certain ordinance or provisions made by the Mayor and Aldermen touching their craft and their daily wages, which was enrolled in the "paper" of the Guildhall'.[43]

London's courts and peace-keeping ordinances (the latter most frequent in the early 1280s, when there was an attempt to compile a dossier on everyone living in the city) constituted a powerful engine of municipal government, but one jealously watched over by the royal justices. The conspiracy of the carpenters points to new types of conflict which invited a more direct and brutal intervention by the king in municipal affairs. The communal regime established in London at the end of the twelfth century was a patriciate under which the richer gilds, operating collectively as a merchant gild, ran the city to their own economic advantage, provoking from the first the resentment of the poorer craft gilds. As the chief centre for the manufacture of cheap cloth, London had many weavers whom the patriciate feared to the extent that in 1202 it paid the king sixty marks to have the weavers' gild forbidden – at a time when there were similar moves against organizations of textile-workers in Winchester, Oxford and other towns. The enormous expansion of London's commerce (from perhaps only 16% of the trade of the realm in 1203–5 to a third of the entire wool trade in 1300, much of the cloth trade and a quarter to a third of the wine trade) brought into existence new 'misteries' such as the furriers and skinners who were fostered by the opening up of the Baltic. Immigration from the English provinces, especially

[43] Williams, *Medieval London*, pp. 4, 27–34, 40–3, 80–1; *London Eyre of 1244*, ed. Chew and Weinbaum, no. 235; *Mayor's Court Rolls*, ed. Thomas, pp. vii–xxv, 1, 3–4, 6, 9, 12, 23–4, 25, 28.

from the east midlands, and at the end of the century of clothiers from Norfolk, contributed to the doubling of the population between 1200 and 1300. Rents rose by a half between 1234 and 1307, food prices by two-thirds between 1212 and 1280, and the victualling trades boomed. Fraternities of saddlers, lorimers, cord-wainers, chaucers, chaplers, cofferers, joiners, cauldron-makers, smiths and many other occupations – all the crafts of the Lord Mayor's show – organized themselves, perhaps around a church and even using excommunication to discipline members of the craft. The city authorities' belief in the minute regulation of all economic activity, so as to ensure an adequate food supply at reasonable prices and protect the citizens' trading monopolies, did not automatically conflict with the gilds' need to control their own members, though the bakers must have resented seeing allegedly fraudulent colleagues drawn through the streets on hurdles at the orders of the mayor's court in 1282. What new crafts constantly challenged was the monopoly of city government by a patriciate of older gilds and crafts.[44]

The craft gilds with their own hall-moots were in fact indispens-able instruments for the detailed trade regulation which the city government desired, but the court of aldermen sought to keep the crafts in subjugation, just as the dyers and burellers sought in their turn to control the weavers whom they employed, the skinners to control the curriers, and the mercantile gilds generally to dominate the journeymen who worked the material they supplied. The middling people resented the way the aldermen ('to avoid tumult') managed the election of the mayor, when the petition of 1215 had been for annual election by the folk-moot or general assembly of the citizens, and they denounced the personal privileges such as tax exemption which the patricians secured; and the *populares* resented the way the *mediocres* suppressed any competition from below and even, in the interests of trade, regulated what their inferiors wore. The danger for the city came when the people were willing to provoke the king's confiscation of the patrician commune's liber-ties. London's time of troubles after the middle of the century was the painful resolution of the struggle between the patricians and the bourgeois crafts, which was completed in favour of a new

[44] Williams, *Medieval London*, pp. 60, 79–80, 106, 138–41, 159, 170, 173–4, 181, 188; *The London Eyre of 1276*, ed. M. Weinbaum (London Record Society, vol. 12, London, 1976), pp. xxxiii–xxxv, for the special articles of inquiry the king's justices used in London; Keene, 'Medieval London and its Region'; *Mayor's Court Rolls*, p. xx.

bourgeois oligarchy during Edward's direct rule of the city between 1285 and 1298.[45]

London's political importance was shown by the confirming of its liberties and free customs in Magna Carta, the inclusion of its mayor in the committee of twenty-five barons to enforce the Charter, and its provision of a base for Prince Louis in his attempt to conquer England. It was shown again in July 1258, when according to FitzThedmar, the city chronicler, an undertaking to observe the baronial provisions was presented at the Guildhall for the seals of the mayor, aldermen and chief citizens to be added to those of King Henry, Prince Edward and the leading barons; and by the panic of the king in 1260 when it was reported that Earl Simon and Prince Edward planned to hold a parliament in London in his absence. But Henry had shown how kings dealt with recalcitrant cities in 1239, when he suspended the Londoners' liberties and dismissed the mayor for rejecting his nomination of a sheriff; and again in 1245 and 1248, when he intervened in quarrels between aldermen and people, at one moment putting in his own mayor, John de Gisors. In 1255 Ralph Hardel, son of the mayor of Magna Carta, led the city into a stubborn but inevitably losing battle with king and exchequer over the payment of a tallage of 3,000 marks: the city claimed that it should not be tallaged as part of the royal demesne, like other boroughs, but pay feudal aids. Henry's counter-attack was devastating. He had leant a sympathetic ear to the petitions of the weavers against their oppressors; now in 1258 he answered a probably contrived appeal of the populace by assembling the folk-moot and getting its noisy assent to the overriding of city custom in order to investigate aldermanic fraud. The whole body of aldermen was replaced and John de Gisors, the royal vintner, resinstalled as mayor; but almost immediately after this king-inspired revolution, the baronial justiciar, Hugh Bigod was at the Guildhall, hearig the complaints of the *populares* against their rulers with equal disregard of the laws of the city. It was a demoralized patriciate that was swept away in 1263 in the stream of national politics.[46]

In July 1263, Earl Simon displaced King Henry from the Tower and formed an alliance with the city which was crucial to the

---

[45] Williams, *Medieval London*, pp. 38–43, 169, 181–9, 196–201, 209–10.
[46] *EHD*, III.318 for cap. 13 of Magna Carta; *De Antiquis Legibus Liber: Cronica Maiorum et Vicecomitum Londiniarum*, ed. Thomas Stapleton (Camden Society, vol 34, London, 1846), pp. 38–40; Williams, *Medieval London*, pp. 7, 173–4, 203–14; Powicke, *The Thirteenth Century*, pp. 8, 10–11, 14, 135.

baronial cause. On the orders of a radical mayor, Thomas Fitz-Thomas, the great bell of St Paul's summoned the citizens to the folk-moot to swear allegiance to a 'commune of the middling people' (*communa mediocris populi*). Led by the rising mercantile misteries – cordwainers, girdlers, ironmongers, above all fishmongers – the movement brushed aside the aldermen and the hustings, and had the ordinances of the crafts confirmed. Arrayed militarily under their own constable and marshal Londoners fought and suffered heavy casualties in the baronial victory at Lewes, and were rewarded for their support of Earl Simon by the quashing (to papal fury) of the liberties of Westminster Abbey, and by the summoning of the first parliament with burgess membership. After the battle of Evesham came the inevitable punishment in the shape of a fine of 20,000 marks, but no return to a patrician regime. A settlement of the countrywide grievances of the Disinherited in the civil war was achieved only by their focussing on London, which the earl of Gloucester held against the king for two months in 1267.[47]

The dominant figure in London at the end of Henry's reign was Walter Hervey, the royal bailiff of the city after Evesham, and then mayor, another champion of the crafts against the aldermen. As the king lay dying in 1272 Hervey secured re-election by denouncing patrician avoidance of the great fine and rousing the populace to riot. The next year the aldermen got Hervey out by choosing a vintner and king's man, Henry le Waleys, who was appointed mayor of Bordeaux before his year of office in London was up. It was for King Edward that le Waleys repudiated Hervey's charters to the crafts and swept away the butchers' and fishmongers' stalls cluttering the Cheap. There followed the seven-year mayoralty of the last patrician, Gregory de Rokesle, during which the king became ever more impatient of London's judicial peculiarities, patrician arrogance and simmering feuds, as they were revealed by the Hundred Rolls inquiry and by the eyre of 1276. In 1281 le Waleys was re-elected, to launch a concerted drive for order and efficiency with a series of peace ordinances requiring among other things the registration of the members of trades and the inmates of inns and hostels. New weigh-beams were set up to catch fraudulent corn merchants, millers and bakers, and a new prison, the Tun on Cornhill, was created for curfew-breakers. In 1285 King Edward

---

[47] Williams, *Medieval London*, pp. 221–39; *Cronica Maiorum*, ed. Stapleton, pp. 55–96 (*EHD*, III.170–97); Powicke, *The Thirteenth Century*, pp. 188–90, 205–14.

tightened the screw further: John Kirkby, the treasurer of England, was sent to hold a judicial inquiry into the government of the city, and when Rokesle, once again mayor, protested, London was taken into the king's hands and administered for thirteen years by a warden. The courts continued to function, but a set of 'establishments' was made to bring the city fully under Edward's modernized common law, and especially under his provisions for foreign merchants, towards whom London's attitude was crucial. Abruptly it was commanded that aliens should be admitted to full citizenship. It was the king's treasurer rather than the warden who bore most heavily upon London: aldermen now had to go to the Exchequer to seek appointment and swear to enforce the ordinances made for the City, and in 1289 the court of the exchequer itself moved into the Guildhall.[48]

Resentment at the affront of 1285 to the city's liberties became difficult for the king to resist in the political crises which beset Edward in the 1290s. In 1298, the year after the Londoners gave their mass support to a protest of the earls of Hereford and Norfolk at the exchequer and a demand for the confirmation of the national charters, the mayoralty was restored. For 2,000 marks, borrowed from Italian companies, the city bought a new charter, the settlement of the fine imposed after Evesham and the removal of le Waleys's Tun prison. But the king's intervention had finally broken the power of the old established dynasties, and created a truly bourgeois capital city – one in which the great numbers of new citizens entering through the crafts were swamping the citizens by inheritance and preparing to frame the city's constitution to their liking. The rebellious gilds of 1263 had by now achieved economic power and respectability: via the Yarmouth fisheries and the Baltic trade, the fishmongers had become predominant in shipping, and in 1295 they were engaged in the building of the king's galley.[49]

TOWNS IN THE HISTORY OF THIRTEENTH–CENTURY ENGLAND

London epitomized the growing political importance of the towns. Some of them were key-points in baronial struggles with the

[48] Williams, *Medieval London*, pp. 21–2, 240–56; *Cronica Maiorum*, ed. Stapleton, pp. 148–53, 166–9; Powicke, *The Thirteenth Century*, pp. 626–30; *London Eyre of 1276*, ed. Weinbaum, no. 146.
[49] Williams, *Medieval London*, pp. 45–6, 159–67, 259–84.

Crown, not just on account of their castles and walls, but also because boroughs were natural advocates of chartered liberties. Lincoln was the scene of the decisive battle of the war between the supporters of Louis of France and the barons loyal to the infant King Henry in May 1217. After the Barons' War and a short-lived occupation by the Disinherited in 1266, the town suffered a fine of 1,000 marks, and when it was slow in payment, seizure into the king's hands and an increase of the penalty to £1,000. As in the case of London, the poorer citizens complained that their betters were not contributing their share. In 1290 the king responded by placing Lincoln too in the hands of a royal warden, where it remained for a decade. King Edward had come to recognize that the towns were one of the main foundations of his state. The control of lawless fullers and dyers, the tensions between rich and poor in the towns, the way the gild merchant was 'drunk' at Winchester, the price and quality of bread and ale, the punishment of forestallers and the state of pavements and city walls – all were of vital concern to royal government. This was demonstrated once more in 1298, when Edward moved his administrative capital to York to facilitate his campaigning in Scotland, as during the Welsh wars he had moved it to Shrewsbury. The numbers of people arriving in the city on the king's business, along with the purveyance of supplies in Yorkshire for the army, gave the citizens an excuse to push up the price of victuals and necessities, and in August 1301 the mayor and bailiffs were called before the king's council (then in York) to agree to a comprehensive set of ordinances for the trades of the city, from bakers to physicians, and apothecaries to innkeepers and prostitutes. The poorer burgesses of York, and those of Newcastle upon Tyne, continued to complain of profiteering by the gilds of the rich, whose machinations may have evoked the definition in 1305 of the crime of conspiracy.[50]

The Angevins moved from the simple exploitation of the towns by the sale of urban liberties, and treating them as royal demesne to

[50] Hill, *Medieval Lincoln*, pp. 196, 205–16; Platt, *Medieval Southampton*, p. 59, for the king's seizures of that town; M. C. Prestwich, *York Civic Ordinances, 1301* (York: Borthwick Papers, no. 49, 1976); *Cases in King's Bench*, ed. Sayles, II.cxlix–cli; *EHD*, III, nos. 228, 229, for the late thirteenth-century laws of Winchester and Lincoln; for royal grants of tolls to finance the building or repair of the town walls, C. T. Allmand, 'Taxation in Medieval England: The Example of Murage', in *Villes, Bonnes Villes, Cités et Capitales: Mélanges offerts à Bernard Chevalier* (Tours, 1989); *BBC, 1216–1307*, p. lxxiii, for paving as a municipal duty.

be tallaged at will, to employing them as the executants of the fiscal policies and diplomacy of an aggressive monarchy. In Edward's hands the incorporation of the burgesses into parliament begun by Earl Simon was an integral part of the mobilization of every part of the community to the supply of the king's 'necessities'. From the beginning of the century the old feudal revenues of the Crown (maximized though they were intended to be by exchequer reforms) were increasingly outweighed by direct and indirect taxes, till in Edward's reign as a whole these and the loans secured upon them brought in more than £1m. But the level of John's extraordinary aids, which yielded an astonishing income of £57,000 in the one year of 1207 and allowed the treasury to accumulate a reserve of £100,000 by 1213, could not be sustained. After 1237 Henry III was never able to obtain sufficient aid from the barons on acceptable terms, and resorted to loans from wherever he could get them: bishops and monasteries, the Templars and the Hospitallers, the occasional magnate, Londoners and foreign merchants who happened to be trading in England. Of Edward's £1m, general parliamentary taxation amounted to only half, and the taxing of the Church to another £200,000, leaving the rest to be provided by the merchants. The biggest lender to Henry III before 1254 had not been a merchant but his own brother, Richard of Cornwall, with resources from tin-mines; in 1247 Richard undertook a complete recoinage of the English currency and provided 10,000 marks for the initial stock of silver, receiving in return the farm of the royal mint and making an overall profit of £11,000 on the transaction. But professional bankers, the Riccardi of Lucca, were engaged to carry out the next recoinage of 1279 in conjunction with the London merchant and mayor, Gregory de Rokesle.[51]

King Henry turned to the Tuscan companies employed by the papacy in 1254, when he was offered the chance to win the Sicilian crown, and he borrowed at least £54,000 from them before the barons brought the venture to an end in 1258. Edward quickly learnt the uses of the Italian financiers drawn to England (often via Paris) by the wool and wine trades and as papal tax collectors; but he also knew that to realize their potential he must give them

[51] Williams, *Medieval London*, pp. 7, 251; E. Miller, 'The Economic Policies of Governments: France and England', in *Cambridge Economic History of Europe*, vol. III: *Economic Organisation and Policies in the Middle Ages* ed. M. M. Postan, E. E. Rich and E. Miller (Cambridge, CUP, 1963), pp. 301, 304–6; E. B. and M. M. Fryde, 'Public Credit', in *ibid.*, pp. 453ff.

security for their loans and special facilities for the recovery of their debts – both of which required the willing or unwilling co-operation of the towns. The successes of the first half of his reign, including the conquest of Wales, depended heavily on the Riccardi, from whom he had borrowed almost £400,000 by 1294. At the same time a customs system was being created to repay the loans. In 1266 power had been given to Edward to license foreign merchants to trade in England, and also to levy a general duty on imports and exports (as John had done briefly in 1203). With the imposition of this 'new aid' or 'custom' (*consuetudo, custuma*), 'customs' began to take on a new meaning in an urban context. The duties were resisted (the Londoners bought exemption from them) as contrary to the customary freedom from tolls many towns enjoyed, and in 1275 they were replaced by more precise customs of half a mark on a sack of wool of twenty-six stone or 300 woolfells, and a mark on a last of leather. Like the customs of Bordeaux, which had been used as security for a loan from the French crown to help defray Edward's crusading expenses, the 'great custom' of 1275 in England, yielding about £10,000 a year, was security for foreign loans; it was indeed handed over to the Luccans to collect from the local officials appointed in London and other chief ports. Then, in the crisis year of 1294, apparently on the advice of the English merchant, Laurence of Ludlow, Edward abruptly took control and seized the Riccardi's assets and the whole wool-crop of the land, which he released only on payment of a supplementary custom five or six times that of 1275. The king's actions may have got him the money he needed for the Scottish war – for instance, the £10,000 required to be sent to Newcastle by 1 March 1296 and £1,000 a week thereafter, to pay 1,000 men-at-arms and 60,000 foot and other expenses of the king's household – but they also bankrupted the main source of his loan finance and provoked the political confrontation of 1297, for the 'bad custom' was seen to fall on the large number of wool-producers in the shape of lower prices.[52]

The Crown subordinated the merchants ruthlessly to the requirements of war and diplomacy. The granting of freedom

---

[52] *Cronica Maiorum*, ed. Stapleton, p. 109; *Cambridge Economic History of Europe*, ed. Postan, Rich and Miller, III.304, 449–58; Powicke, *The Thirteenth Century*, pp. 281, 619, 628–31, 662–3; N. S. B. Gras, *The Early English Customs System* (Cambridge, Mass.: Harvard University Press, 1918), pp. 48–54; M. C. Prestwich, *War, Politics and Finance under Edward I* (London: Faber, 1972), pp. 195ff, 268.

from tolls to the burgesses of particular towns was partly to break down the fearful, restrictive attitudes of borough authorities, and to make a single trading area of the scattered Angevin dominions. Wholesale protections were sold to foreign merchants, beginning with the Flemings, who paid John 400 marks in 1204. The barons, who were both toll-takers and suppliers of commodities, joined with the Londoners in getting the free and safe passage of foreign merchants written into Magna Carta (cap. 34) – 'except in time of war and if they are of that land that is at war with us', when they should be held until it was known how 'merchants of our land' were treated there. In fact, King Richard and King John had already set a pattern of forcing the Flemings into coalitions against the king of France by confiscating the goods of Flemish merchants in England and (even more drastically) banning the export of wool to the county of Flanders. It was the seizure of the goods of English and Gascon merchants by the Countess Margaret in 1270, ostensibly to make up the arrears of a pension owed her by King Henry but possibly also out of resentment at the new customs policy, which provoked another eight-year embargo from the English side, taught Edward the use of export licences and let the Italians into the wool trade (still mainly to France and Flanders). In the Anglo-French war at the end of the century, Flanders was cajoled by both sides through its merchants. In contrast the Dutch and the Brabantines were attracted by grants of commercial privileges; and even more so the Germans, to whose hanse Edward instructed the Londoners to allow a mayor of its own and a court for the settlement of pleas of debts and contract. On behalf of favoured merchants the king had no qualms about overriding a town's cherished control of admission to its freedom. Equally, he took no account of the actual interests of the towns as he tightened the screw on the Jews by tallages and charges of coin-clipping, up to the final confiscations and expulsion of 1290.[53]

Edward left royal finances in a disorder: when he died in 1307 his household owed at least £60,000 for services rendered. For many reigns to come the Crown remained in a state of 'disguised bankruptcy' which bore heavily on the multitude of humbler creditors without the power of the Frescobaldi of Florence or the

---

[53] *Cambridge Economic History of Europe*, ed. Postan, Rich and Miller, III.308–13; Powicke, *The Thirteenth Century*, p. 621; T. H. Lloyd, *The English Wool Trade in the Middle Ages*, (Cambridge: CUP, 1977); *idem, Alien Merchants in England in the High Middle Ages* (Brighton: Harvester, 1982), caps. 1 and 2; H. G. Richardson, *The English Jewry under Angevin Kings* (London: Methuen, 1960), pp. 213–25.

wine merchants of Bayonne to get preferential repayment from the customs of Boston or Kingston-upon-Hull. But Edward did leave behind in the greater towns the customs machinery which lasted till the sixteenth century, with officials for the collection and enrolment of duties; and the system created by the statutes of 1283 and 1285 for the registration and more effective recovery of mercantile debts, employing two seals in each of the designated towns, one applied by the town authorities and the other by the clerk or 'controller' assigned by the king to keep a counter-roll. He had reinvigorated the mints and exchanges at the Tower of London, Canterbury, Newcastle, Exeter and Dublin and added new ones at Hull, which he used to put into circulation the new farthings and (four-penny) groats, and along with the customs officials to attempt to drive out the bad foreign money called 'pollards' and 'crockards'.[54]

And from his first parliament of 1275, to which he summoned representatives of the market towns as well as cities and boroughs and where he instituted the great custom, King Edward had brought the townsmen and their concerns into the centre of English politics, so that by the end of his reign he was having to evade attempts to make all taxes and duties subject to parliamentary consent and not negotiable separately with the merchants (as happened in the case of the *carta mercatoria*). The results of Edward's dealing with the towns were the ability of the Commons in his son's reign to advance a whole legislative programme concerning weights and measures, the wearing of furs, forestalling, strict adherence to the procedures of the Statute of Merchants and the location of staple ports so crucial for the cloth trade; and the eventual establishment of the constitutional principle that neither the merchants nor the lords, but the Commons alone, assented to taxation.[55]

---

[54] *Cambridge Economic History of Europe*, ed. Postan, Rich and Miller, III. 457–8; R. W. Kaeuper, 'The Frescobaldi of Florence and the English Crown', *Studies in Medieval and Renaissance History*, 10 (1973); Gras, *Customs System*, pp. 55, 223–56 (q.v. for the customs account of Hull for June 1275 to April 1276, which shows that 67 shiploads went out on 47 days, containing 13 shipments by English and 188 by foreign merchants, amounting to 4,058 sacks, 123 pokes and 11 1/2 stones of wool, 39 1/2 lasts of leather, 75 1/2 dickers and 103 hides, and 4, 704 woolfells; £1,431 7s. was paid in customs duties); *EHD*, III, nos. 54, 58, 226; Powicke, *The Thirteenth Century*, pp. 625, 630–7.

[55] M. C. Prestwich, *Edward I* (London: Methuen, 1988), p. 530; W. M. Ormrod, 'Agenda for Legislation, 1322 – c.1340', *EHR*, 105 (1990); B. Wilkinson, *The Constitutional History of Medieval England, 1216–1399*, 3 vols. (London: Longmans, 1948–58), III.338.

4

PROFESSIONAL PEOPLE

———— · ————

Perhaps the towns' most important contribution of all to thirteenth-century history was their concentration and nurturing of the professional skills of law and administration which made thirteenth-century advances in government possible. From the tenth century the county towns from which the sheriff and his bailiffs operated had been the focal points of the system of territorial administration, and they were reinforced in that role by the visits of the justices in eyre to the shire court. The Normans' patronage of Benedictine monasteries and enthusiasm for cathedral-building; the settlement of schoolmen at Oxford, Cambridge and Northampton even though they lacked the prestige of cathedral cities; and the coming of the friars to the towns – all this gave urban communities an extra cultural significance and a source of intellectual justification for their activities.

ESTATE MANAGERS

There was as yet little sense that professional administrators were divided into the public officials of the Crown on the one hand and the private servants of the lords on the other: the lord king's first requirement, like any other lord's, was the administration of his estates; and the bailiffs of liberties exercised powers of government just as much as the sheriffs' officers. From the beginning of the century estate officials would have needed lists of plough-teams in order to pay royal taxes, and by Edward I's reign written records of seignorial profits had reached down to village level. The detailed particulars of the revenues of the royal demesne lands which the king's bailiffs were accustomed to take with them to exchequer audits survive from Henry III's reign as 'Ministers' and Receivers' Accounts', which were soon joined by the manorial accounts of other lords. By 1258, Robert Carpenter of Haslett or Hareslade in the Isle of Wight, the man of business of Sir William de Lisle, was writing down advice for unscrupulous bailiffs, instructing them for instance how to make sheepskins look worthless and then sell them for much more than their enrolled value. An ever-growing corps of professional bailiffs and receivers was indispensable to the lords of the land, who began to employ them to manage groups of manors, and sent them as attorneys to defend their property in the king's court. At the same time, dishonest and oppressive officials became a major concern of government and barons and provoked elaborate systems of audit and control. Magnates like Isabella de Forz, countess of Devon and Aumale, in Holderness in Yorkshire, Roger Bigod, the earl marshal, in Norfolk and Suffolk and in Chepstow, and Edmund, earl of Cornwall, in the Stannaries, appointed sheriffs and stewards to administer their estates, and other stewards, marshals, chamberlains, treasurers and keepers of the wardrobe to oversee them from their households.[1]

The greater monasteries had long possessed central officials called 'obedientiaries', such as cellarers and kitcheners, who were responsible for particular departments of their houses' revenue and expenditure, and some of whose accounts survive from the 1260s. Magnates generally began to appoint *computatores*, experienced men headed by the household steward, to 'view' the estate accounts in the spring and 'audit' them finally around Michaelmas – much as the exchequer did for the king's revenues, except that seignorial auditors usually went round the manors rather than wait for the bailiffs to come to them. After the end of the financial year the protracted task of recovering 'arrears' commenced. In the same parliament of 1285 which produced the Statute of Merchants, the

[1] N. Denholm-Young, *Seignorial Administration in England* (Oxford: OUP, 1937; reprinted London, 1963), pp. 32–85, 121; P. D. A. Harvey, *A Medieval Oxfordshire Village: Cuxham, 1240 to 1400* (Oxford: Clarendon Press, 1965), p. 10–11, 63, 96–8; M. T. Clanchy, *From Memory to Written Record, England 1066–1307* (London: Arnold, 1979), pp. 31–2, 51, 53, 56, 71; *Guide to the Contents of the Public Record Office*, vol. 1 (London: HMSO, 1963), pp. 191–2; Kate Mertes, *The English Noble Household 1250–1600* (Oxford: Blackwell, 1988); *Britton*, ed. and tr. F. M. Nichols, 2 vols. (Oxford: Clarendon Press, 1965), 1.305.

right to attach the person of a defaulting bailiff was conceded by the Statute of Westminster II. At the end of the accounting process the lord's auditors could henceforth send the official to the nearest royal prison, whence he might be released on bail until the rehearing of the account before the barons of the exchequer. The king's court thus found itself sorting out complex professional issues. In 1286, Walter de Reygni was attached to answer an action of account concerning the period that he was keeper of the wardrobe and steward of the household of Bogo de Clare, a rich cleric and brother of the earl of Gloucester. Walter protested that his accounts had been cleared before Bogo's auditors, and that the jewels which he was alleged to have removed he had in fact (as ordered) 'pledged to certain Merchants of London from whom he received on loan . . . 4 score and 15 pounds and 8 shillings, as well in money as in other necessaries for the same Bogo'. After scrutinizing copies of William's accounts made in the exchequer and viewing the jewels deposited there in two sealed coffers, Edmund of Cornwall the king's lieutenant, the treasurer and barons, and other members of the king's council there present, absolved Walter and found that Bogo indeed owed him and others £375 3s. – a debt which Walter was instructed to certify in detail in the hustings court of London, before the royal keeper of the city.[2]

As they became more elaborate, magnate households were drawn to the towns and particularly to London. Just as the king kept his treasure in the Tower, so magnates kept theirs in castles often located in towns (or sometimes, like the earls of Arundel at Shrewsbury, in urban monasteries). Before he was king, Edward had four local exchequers at Bordeaux, Bristol, Chester and Dublin: at Bristol the constable of the castle, a steward and a treasurer received all the revenues of the Lord Edward's English lands, but his household expenses were accounted for by one John of London. The earl of Lincoln had receipts or treasuries at Lincoln, Pontefract and other places, including Holborn; and Roger Bigod, the earl marshal, had his central receipt and wardrobe in London, not at Framlingham or Chepstow. The bishop of Salisbury pos-

---

[2] D. Knowles, *The Monastic Order in England* (Cambridge: CUP, 1950), pp. 433–9; Clanchy, *From Memory to Written Record*, p. 71; Denholm-Young, *Seignorial Administration*, pp. 68, 131–61, 165; H. L. Gray, 'The Household Administration of Henry Lacy and Thomas of Lancaster', *EHR*, 42 (1927); T. F. T. Plucknett, *The Legislation of Edward I* (Oxford: Clarendon Press, 1949) pp. 152ff; Pollock and Maitland, *HEL*, II.221; *Select Cases in the Exchequer of Pleas*, ed. H. Jenkinson and B. E. R. Formoy (Selden Society, vol. 48, London, 1931), no. 170.

sessed a house in Fleet Street. Early in the fourteenth century the bishop of Hereford leased his London house in the parish of St Mary Mounthaw to Hamon of Chigwell, citizen of London, on the understanding that it would be available if he had to come up for a meeting of bishops or for a parliament, and that a room and stabling would be provided when his steward or other members of his household were in the city on business. Edward I's brother Edmund acquired the manor of the Savoy between the Strand and the Thames which was to become the headquarters of the duchy of Lancaster: earlier in the thirteenth century a royal judge who haled from the Isle of Wight had been building a house there.[3]

Lords needed townsmen for their professional services as much as for their merchandise. In 1287, the bishop of Hereford retained Master Warin de Boys 'advocate of London' at a fee of six marks a year to plead his cases in the archbishop of Canterbury's court of arches. (London, Westminster and Lambeth House across the river were at the centre of the archbishop's public world.) As well as lawyers, physicians were to be found in towns (by the York ordinances of 1301, they were bound to inform the civic authorities if they were treating anyone who was wounded in a fight); and (not least in the cathedral towns of Lincoln, Norwich and Canterbury) there were Jewish and by now Christian money-lenders. The great days of the Jewish financiers of the land market had been in the second half of the twelfth century, when Aaron of Lincoln had on his books the king of Scotland, the earls of Northampton, Leicester, Arundel, Aumale and Chester, nine Cistercian monasteries and a sprinkling of bishops and archdeacons, as well as the towns of Winchester and Southampton and several Lincoln merchants. The thirteenth century was a time of growing persecution and royal exploitation of the Jews, accompanied by stories of their forcible circumcision of Christian children or even ritual murder

[3] M. W. Labarge, *A Baronial Household of the Thirteenth Century* (London: Eyre and Spottiswoode, 1965), pp. 189–201; Clanchy, *From Memory to Written Record*, pp. 71–2, plate XI; *Records of the Borough of Leicester, 1103–1327*, ed. Mary Bateson (London: Leicester UP, 1899), pp. 36, 38, 46, 49, 51, 53, 57, 124–8, 175, 187, 191, 208; Denholm-Young, *Seignorial Administration*, pp. 8–14, 20; C. Given-Wilson, 'Wealth and Credit, Public and Private: The Earls of Arundel, 1306–1397', *EHR*, 106 (1991), pp. 3, 8; Gray, 'Household Administration of Henry Lacy', p. 183; W. Page, *London: Its Origin and Early Development* (London: Constable, 1923), pp. 156–8; *A Roll of the Household Expenses of Richard de Swinfield, Bishop of Hereford 1289–90*, ed. J. Webb (Camden Society, vol. 59, London, 1853), pp. 209–10; *Ministers' Accounts of the Earldom of Cornwall, 1296–97*, ed. M. Midgley (Camden Society, 3rd ser., vol. 66, London, 1942), p. xxxiii.

of such as Little St Hugh of Lincoln, but three hundred or so borrowers from the Norwich Jews were still recorded in 1225–7 in the Day Book of the chest where the bonds were registered, the majority of them ordinary gentry and yeomen.[4]

The financial officials of the magnates were drawn from or aspired to be gentry, but their urban links are apparent. The earl of Chester's steward in Lincolnshire till his death *c.* 1221 was Walter of Coventry, a town where the earl's patronage was a key to success. Countess Isabella de Forz's steward between 1268 and 1274, John de la Warre, came from a family which owned property in Bristol and Dublin; he entered Isabella's service after serving as steward of Earl Warenne and fighting valiantly in the baronial cause; he was rewarded with the manor of Whitchurch in Oxfordshire, and his son became Lord Delaware by personal summons to parliament. From very small beginnings in Wiltshire, Adam de Stratton had already built up considerable estates before he became the most notorious of Isabella's stewards in 1277, and he had done it as a clerk in the exchequer, master of the king's works at Westminster and a Christian usurer on a grand scale, working from a London office in Smalelane near the Fleet Prison. His evil reputation was acquired by the purchasing of debts owed to the Jews and the merciless pursuit of the debtors such as Bermondsey Priory. By 1289 he had overstretched himself. When King Edward stormed into Westminster in 1289 to launch his investigation of official corruption, he is pictured searching that bureaucratic paradise with cries of 'Adam, Adam, where art thou.' After this Adam's fall, almost £13,000 in cash was found in his house. A normal steward could hope to gain from his job no more than the salary of £60 a year enjoyed by Earl Edmund's steward in Cornwall – and also the professional experience which allowed rustic gentry to become shrewd knights of the shire in parliament, 'competent to judge of matters relating to the government of the country'.[5]

---

[4] *Household Expenses of Richard de Swinfield*, pp. 201–2; W. Urry, *Canterbury under the Angevin Kings* (London: Athlone Press, 1967), pp. 110, 119; M. C. Prestwich, *York Civic Ordinances, 1301* (York: Borthwick Papers, no. 49, 1976), p. 5; J. W. F. Hill, *Medieval Lincoln* (Cambridge: CUP, 1948), pp. 217–38; V. D. Lipman, *The Jews of Medieval Norwich* (Jewish Historical Society, London, 1967), pp. 59–64, 79–94, 187ff; R. C. Stacey, '1240–60: A Watershed in Anglo-Jewish Relations', *Historical Research*, 61 (1988).

[5] Denholm-Young, *Seignorial Administration*, pp. 16, 75–9, 164, App. 5; *Records of Coventry*, ed. Coss, pp. xxxviii, 31–2; F. M. Powicke, *The Thirteenth Century: 1216–1307* (Oxford: Clarendon Press, 1953; 2nd edn 1961; issued in paperback, 1991), pp. 363–6; *Accounts and Surveys of the Wiltshire Lands of Adam de Stratton,*

LOCAL OFFICIALS

Sheriffs controlled the bailiffs of the hundreds by the same processes, such as the action of account, that private lords used to
control their estate bailiffs. Sheriffs too had central offices and staff
to supervise the execution of the king's writs and the reporting
back which held together the whole of royal administration. The
following items were handed over to his successor by the outgoing
sheriff of Herefordshire on the Wednesday after the feast of All
Saints in 1278: Hereford castle with its appurtenances; a clutch of
royal statutes (which it was the sheriff's job to proclaim), and
letters patent about the keeping of the statutes recently made;
fifteen writs to be returned to the appropriate royal courts endorsed
with the action taken, another writ of novel disseisin and some
writs of mort d'ancestor; two prisoners – a man waiting to be tried
for homicide and a woman convicted in the hundred court of
Irchenfield of complicity in homicide; goods taken in distraint for
debts to the exchequer, namely three beasts taken for an unpaid
amercement and the purchase price of a writ, four beasts for a
Jew's debt (i.e. a debt to a Jew taken over by the exchequer), seven
pieces of cloth and a horse taken for tallage; and the rolls of the
county court and of the hundred court of Irchenfield with the writs
touching them. Without the sheriff and his officers no criminal
could have been presented, arrested or outlawed, and no jury
empanelled; more than that, no legal writ and no summons of the
exchequer could have been served, no law-suit or enforcement of
a debt could have proceeded. The right to receive and execute
royal orders was one prized by franchise holders, but the Statutes
of Westminster of 1275 and 1285 made it clear that the ultimate
responsibility was always the sheriff's, through whose hands the
returned writs had to pass.[6]

Ultimately it was down to the hundred bailiff and his mounted
sub-bailiffs to serve writs and round up the great numbers of

---

ed. M. W. Farr (Wiltshire Archaeological Society Record Branch, vol. 14,
Devizes, 1959), p. xi.

[6] *Select Cases in the Exchequer of Pleas*, ed. Jenkinson and Formoy, nos. 172, 222,
230; H. M. Cam, *The Hundred and the Hundred Rolls* (London: Methuen, 1930),
pp. 54–6, 65–6, 74ff, 88–9; W. A. Morris, *The Medieval Sheriff to 1300* (Manchester: Manchester UP, 1927), pp. 146, 188–191, 211; Plucknett, *Legislation of
Edward I*, pp. 30–4; R. C. Palmer, *The County Courts of Medieval England,
1150–1350* (Princeton: Princeton UP, 1982), pp. 277–9; *Select Cases in the Court of
King's Bench*, ed. G. O. Sayles, 7 vols. (Selden Society, London, 1936–71), II, no.
2, for the operation of *non omittas* in the liberty of Bury St Edmunds.

animals taken in distress. The hundred officials also included clerks – local priests might be employed – to write formal replies to the sheriff's mandates (the earliest extant sheriffs' precepts date from the 1240s and 1250s), and to keep the rolls of the hundred courts with their lists of fines imposed in them, and the counterfoils of the tally-sticks given as receipts for any debts collected. At the county level similar clerical services were required but on a larger scale, for the sheriff was acutely conscious of the scrutiny of the exchequer and the royal justices. The county court handled significant civil litigation and its rolls, though not an authoritative legal record like the plea-rolls of higher courts, might be wanted for examination by the justices, and were in any case important fiscally. The sheriff of Yorkshire from 1285 to 1291 was fairly representative in having a central staff of fifteen: an undersheriff, ten roving bailiffs and four clerks. One of the clerks would have been a keeper and returner of writs (from 1285 a receipt had to be given by the sheriff's office for every writ brought to it for execution), another perhaps the receiver of the plaints by which small claims were brought to the county court and the remaining two keepers of the money and the tallies which the sheriff would take to the exchequer. Much money was paid out for the king in the counties without passing through the treasury, and the receipts for it had to be shown.[7]

The best measure of the extent and complexity of local administration is the variety of the complaints of maladministration brought against the sheriff, usually after the end of his term of office. Although he was expected to give notice of the day of his accounting at Westminster, so that the bailiffs of liberties and others could attend to see that they were duly acquitted of the debts they had paid, he and his officers were frequently accused in the court of the exchequer of not paying the money in. In 1300 a former sheriff of Devonshire was confronted with seven tallies he had given as receipts for debts which were still outstanding in the rolls and for which the debtors continued to be distrained, but he claimed that he was an unlettered man and unable to read the

[7] Cam, *The Hundred and the Hundred Rolls*, pp. 132–6, 155–7; Clanchy, *From Memory to Written Record*, p. 220, and *passim* for the use of tallies; Morris, *The Medieval Sheriff*, p. 252; idem, *The Early English County Court: An Historical Treatise with Illustrative Documents* (Berkeley: University of California Press, 1926), for the reading of charters, including the Great Charter, letters of protection and administrative orders in the county court; Palmer, *County Courts*, pp. 37–8, 42–8.

writing on the tallies: he could not answer without the clerks who had been his receivers. Another type of corruption appears in 1293 in the allegation that a Lincolnshire undersheriff extorted money for deleting names from the returns to an inquiry about £40 landholders who had not assumed the responsibilities of knighthood, and wrote in the names of 'such as it pleased him should be accused hereupon'. The sheriff of Yorkshire accused his own clerk of breaking the seals of writs given him to keep and changing the endorsements, in one case substituting 20s. for £60 5s. as the value of lands in dispute in king's bench, and in another removing five names of persons indicted for trespasses in the park of the archbishop of York. The conduct of local officials emerged as one of the great political issues of the century. An administrative class of small landowners and clerks which was capable of handling a huge amount of legal procedure and innumerable executive orders had to live from what it could get from the people of the shires by way of fees or by simple extortion. If the opportunities of extortion had not been large it is difficult to believe that anyone would have accepted the hazards of the sheriff's and bailiff's jobs – the violent rescue of distresses and disruption of courts by the people, and the heavy amercement and even imprisonment by the Crown. The hundred bailiff rented or 'farmed' his office from the sheriff as the sheriff often rented his from the Crown. In answer to a question put by the Hundred Rolls inquiry of 1274–5, many juries said that farms had lately been raised, and a Hertford jury found that 'W. de Roothing gave ten pounds more than other bailiffs have usually given, to flay the countryside, which he has done.' Shire bailiffs enjoyed rights of hospitality on their official journeys; in some places they received customary fees – 4d. for every prisoner accommodated and every distraint made, and 3s. 4d. for every 6d or 8d of the king's debt collected; and small gifts were showered upon them by ordinary people seeking to escape the trammels of officialdom. The drinking-parties called *scotales*, at which bailiffs compelled villagers to buy beer made from sheaves of their own barley seized at harvest time, were a general abuse.[8]

A growing corps of officials was essential to the developing state, and the control of it became the test of good government.

---

[8] *Select Cases in the Exchequer of Pleas*, ed. Jenkinson and Formoy, pp. vii, cvii, nos. 16, 117, 176, 177, 225, 238, 250, 257; Palmer, *County Courts*, pp. 48, 50–4, 279; *EHD*, III, no. 113; Morris, *The Medieval Sheriff*, pp. 243–6; Cam, *The Hundred and the Hundred Rolls*, pp. 87, 93, 143–4, 150–2; *Britton*, ed. Nichols, 1.91.

Henry III recognized the problem even before the baronial reformers took it up. In the period 1246–54 a dozen new questions
concerning official abuses were introduced to the list which the
justices in eyre put to presenting juries, asking for instance about
ambidextrous (or rather 'ambisinister') officials who took bribes
from both sides in any dispute, extorted gifts of crops at harvest
time and held ale-drinkings at the hundred court, exacted the same
amercements twice over, distrained everyone they could find with
a similar name to the actual debtor and imprisoned people arbitrarily in order to extract money for their release. Administrative
reform was a chief aim of the baronial movement. In October 1258
the king was made to proclaim to the people, in French and English
as well as Latin, that counties and hundreds should no longer be
farmed: the king would 'give of his own' for the expenses of the
sheriff and his servants, because he did 'not wish that they have
occasion to take anything of another'. In the event, regular
payment of shire officials did not prove practical. But the other
measure announced in the proclamation, the appointment of four
knights in each shire to collect complaints of abuses by officials so
that they could be dealt with by the baronial justiciar on his eyre,
was part of a momentous development leading ultimately to
parliamentary scrutiny of the administration. At least from the
1220s royal justices had made a practice of accepting oral complaints against officials from individuals and from village communities; and such *querelae* must also lie behind many of the
presentments made by juries in answer to the new chapters of the
eyre about false imprisonment, extortion and other corrupt practices lumped into the category of 'trespasses'. Bigod's eyre in 1258
was to hear 'complaints of trespasses, whoever had committed
them', and in 1261 special sections of *querelae de transgressionibus*
began to appear in the eyre rolls. The Hundred Rolls contain
detailed complaints from individuals which are also drawn on by
presenting juries. And from 1278, the writ of summons to the eyre
announced that the justices would hear trespasses and plaints
concerning the king's ministers and bailiffs and the ministers and
bailiffs of others.[9]

---

[9] *The Roll of the Shropshire Eyre of 1256*, ed. A. Harding (Selden Society, vol. 96,
London, 1980), pp. xvi–xxvi; for the articles or chapters of the eyre: H. M. Cam,
Studies in the Hundred Rolls, Oxford Studies in Social and Legal History, VI
(Oxford: Clarendon Press, 1921), pp. 92–101, and *Crown Pleas of the Wiltshire
Eyre*, ed. C. A. F. Meekings (Wiltshire Archaeological Society Records Branch,
Devizes, 1961), pp. 19–20; for plaints and bills against officials: *Select Cases of*

Though there was an attempt to prevent hundred bailiffs from simultaneously serving as the stewards of private lords, thus making it difficult to secure impartial juries, officials moved freely between royal and private employment. By hearing complaints of the trespasses of baronial and municipal as well as royal ministers the justices in eyre established that they were all answerable for how the king's people were governed. A constant of Simon de Montfort's politics, to which he held even at the cost of dividing the baronial party, was that the barons' officers should be no less subject than the king's to reforms like those set out in the Provisions of Westminster of 1259. The scrutiny of this single administration under the Crown became one of Parliament's first and most enduring concerns. Parliamentary bills indeed originated along with bills in eyre in the early years of Edward's reign, when plaints against officials came to be written down and presented to whichever court was perceived to exercise most effectively the king's responsibility for his people's welfare.[10]

THE KING'S MINISTERS IN THE EXCHEQUER AND THE WARDROBE

The headquarters of the administrative class lay in the town which had grown up around the king's abbey and palace of Westminster and enjoyed easy access to the great market of London and by water to the Tower. That the two towns jointly constituted the capital is shown by their very similar patterns of immigration from a much wider area of the country than other towns could boast. By 1200 the Mauduit family, the king's hereditary chamberlains, had transferred their professional base from the old capital of Winchester to a house at Westminster previously occupied by the usher of the abbey; and the king's treasurer had established a semi-official residence along the river to the north (for a stretch past Westminster, the Thames flows almost northwards) in property

Procedure without Writ under Henry III ed. H. G. Richardson, and G. O. Sayles (Selden Society, vol. 60, London, 1941), esp. pp. ccxii–ccxv; A Harding, 'Plaints and Bills in the History of English Law', in *Legal History Studies 1972*, ed. D. Jenkins (Cardiff: University of Wales Press, 1975), pp. 68, 75ff; Cam, *The Hundred and the Hundred Rolls*, pp. 42–3, 67–9, 150; *EHD*, III, no. 39; *The Lincolnshire Assize Roll for 1298*, ed. W. S. Thomson (Lincoln Record Society, vol. 36, Lincoln, 1944).

[10] Denholm-Young, *Seignorial Administration*, p. 40; D. A. Carpenter, 'Simon de Montfort: The First Leader of a Political Movement in English History', *History*, 76 (1991), p. 5; Harding, 'Plaints and Bills'.

which had also belonged to lay officials of the monastery. The treasurer's mansion in what became York Place passed in about 1222 to the justiciar, Hubert de Burgh, and after his death to the archbishop of York whose London palace it remained until the downfall of Wolsey; but the keepers of the wardrobe still had their houses in York Place at the end of the century, and the great wardrobe itself was nearby for a while before moving into London. Closer to the palace on its north side was the mansion of Richard of Cornwall, who was granted thirty oaks from the royal forest in 1234 for its construction: this house was wrecked by the London mobs in 1263–4. Nearer still to the palace lived Odo the Goldsmith, much involved in Henry III's lavish building works, and his son, Edward of Westminster, also clerk of the works; another Odo of Westminster, probably the first Odo's grandson, became a melter and remembrancer of the exchequer. In 1272 Robert Burnel, Edward I's friend and soon chancellor, obtained a house from this family. A near neighbour of Burnel's was another of Edward's confidants, Sir Otto of Granson, whose house was big enough for a royal council to be held in it in 1292. The space between these great houses was quickly filled up. When a royal clerk called John of Langtoft was granted a messuage 'between the royal street [leading towards Charing and London] and the wall of the archbishop of York' in 1257, he was careful to get a protection from the king against the requisitioning of any of his property as lodgings for royal servants, such was the demand generated by the Crown. Two artisans questioned in 1235 about the famous murder of a royal clerk named Henry Clement apparently lived in tents at the gate of the palace.[11]

People were drawn to Westminster by the frequent residence of the king and his household. Many came as pilgrims to the shrine of St Edward in the abbey on which Henry III lavished huge amounts of money, or to receive royal charity in Henry's new almshouse and in the palace itself: some of the 6,000 poor applying in January 1243 were fed in the king's own 'painted chamber', the children in the queen's. The king's councillors and liveried servants provided custom for a prosperous group of tailors. But it was the accommodation for administrators in the great hall of the palace, and in the hall's and abbey's outbuildings, that made Westminster the centre to which all men of note must gravitate. At the

---

[11] G. Rosser, *Medieval Westminster, 1200–1540* (Oxford: Clarendon Press, 1989), pp. 10–32, 36, 39–41, 145, 186, 296.

beginning of the thirteenth century, the exchequer to which the sheriffs came twice-yearly was a two-storey building on the east side of the hall overlooking the river, the receipt into which the money was paid below, the exchequer proper above; by the time of a serious fire in the palace in 1263 the exchequer chamber had joined the exchequer of the Jews on the west side of the hall, where it remained till the nineteenth century. To the exchequer King Henry himself came with his council in 1250 to exhort 'all the sheriffs of England there present . . . in his own voice', to safeguard the liberties of holy church and arrest blasphemers, protect orphans, widows and the weak and see that peasants were the last to be distrained for their landlords' debts. They were further to correct the trespasses of magnates against their men, and be careful themselves to farm hundreds and bailiwicks only to those who would treat the people justly; to inquire into the setting up of unlicensed markets; and last, but certainly not least, to make sure that no lords exercised view of frankpledge, sheriffs' tourns or other liberties belonging to the Crown without the warrant of a royal charter or by use from antiquity. Six years on, the king came again to prescribe to the barons of the exchequer the amercement of a sheriff at five marks for every day he was late in appearing at Michaelmas with 'the king's money', and the forfeiture of the liberties of any town accounting through its own bailiffs which was as much as four days late.[12]

By then it would not have been possible to attempt to overhaul the king's finances by appointing the same household official, as Peter des Rivaux had been appointed in 1232, to the sheriffdoms of twenty-one counties; to the custody of the king's wardrobe, chamber and treasury of the household, and of the king's personal seal; and to the offices of chamberlain of London, buyer for the king in all markets and fairs, chief justice of the forests, controller of the mint and the Jews, and finally treasurer of the exchequer. The exchequer had 'gone out of court' to be the hub of a largely routine administrative department, and the sheriffs were knights of the shire, not court officials. The complex of financial procedures and records is illustrated by a case of 1236, in the first plea-roll of the exchequer as a court for the hearing of revenue disputes. In answer to William de Ambeley, the clerk Jordan de Winton

---

[12] *The History of the King's Works*, vol. I: *The Middle Ages*, ed. R. A. Brown, H. M. Colvin and A. J. Taylor (London: HMSO, 1963), esp. cap II: 'Westminster Palace'; M. T. Clanchy, 'Did Henry III have a Policy?', *History*, 53 (1968), pp. 208–10, 215–16; Paris, *CM*, v.588–9.

acknowledges the tally he gave to William for the payment of an amercement of one mark imposed by the justices in eyre in Norfolk, but says that it is not his fault that successive sheriffs of Norfolk have continued to distrain for the mark, since he has an exchequer tally to show that he paid it in. The barons of the exchequer inspect the Great Roll of the Pipe and the estreat sent in from the eyre, and discover that Jordan did *not* acquit William of the debt: they find that at the Norfolk accounting, the date of which they establish from the Memoranda Roll, he denied being given the mark, and from the Receipt Roll that he did in fact pay it in, but later got the exchequer tally changed for one referring to 'another person and another matter'. Jordan clearly received two marks one of which went into his pocket, so 'he is handed over to the Marshal as prisoner according to the Rules of the Exchequer'.[13]

The treasurer and barons of the Exchequer who had once been the king's all-purpose counsellors became more clearly financial officials, and they were reinforced in that role by the clerks, the chancellor of the exchequer at their head, who had originally been deputed by the chancery to provide the barons with a secretariat and now became a permanent part of the exchequer establishment. The significant new officials (first mentioned in 1248) were the two remembrancers who kept the collective memory of the exchequer. The memoranda were essential to the smooth running of what was now almost a year-round accounting procedure, which developed in pace with a growth of 'foreign accounts' presented by others than the sheriffs, such as household officials, military commanders and tax collectors. The king's remembrancer had custody of the rolls concerning lay and clerical taxes and reference books like the Book of Fees (listing feudal landholders); the lord treasurer's remembrancer annotated estreats of fines needing collection and was responsible for summonses to the exchequer. Recognizances of debt would be enrolled on the Memoranda Rolls (at a price), making the exchequer court available for private actions against defaulters. The remembrancers used this facility to advance the money-lending business they themselves carried on, in common with other exchequer clerks.[14]

---

[13] T. F. Tout, *Chapters in the Administrative History of Medieval England*, 6 vols. (Manchester: Manchester UP, 1920–33), I. 146–7, 216–18; W. L. Warren, *The Governance of Norman and Angevin England, 1086–1272* (London: Arnold, 1987), pp. 72–4, 184–9; *Select Cases in the Exchequer of Pleas*, ed. Jenkinson and Formoy, no. 16, I. 146–7.

[14] D. Crook, 'The Early Remembrancers of the Exchequer', *BIHR*, 53 (1980); and

In step with the conversion of the Exchequer into a workaday department went the reorganization of the royal household into the effective agency of government: the immediate agency demanded by a king who, after the loss of Normandy in 1204, was usually in the country, not directing affairs from abroad by letters to the justiciar. The heart of the household was the king's wardrobe. The placing of Thomas Bek, treasurer or keeper of the wardrobe, a controller (keeper of the counter-roll) of the wardrobe and eight wardrobe clerks and ushers (one intriguingly a surgeon and another a physician) towards the end of the Household Ordinance of 1279, after the steward, marshals, ushers, pantlers, cooks and porters, belies the pre-eminence the office was achieving by the time of the Welsh wars of Edward I. Men subsequently bishops in Ireland and a bishop of Hereford were already amongst the keepers of Henry III's reign; Bek would go on to be bishop of St David's, William Louth, keeper from 1280 to 1290, to be bishop of Ely and Walter Langton, keeper from 1290 to 1295, to be treasurer of the exchequer, and Edward's leading councillor. Between 1286 and 1289, Tout calculated, Louth received for the king more than £107,000 of money loaned by Italian bankers. The wardrobe was Edward's 'war office and admiralty'; the great bulk of the national expenditure passed through it and one of the two columns of the Issue Roll of the exchequer was taken up with payments of the wardrobe's debts. The scarcity of actual money, meaning that goods supplied and services rendered were frequently not paid for, seems only to have made wardrobe book-keeping more detailed and complicated. By chancery writs of *liberate*, the wardrobe was credited with as much as £20.000 at a time at the exchequer, sometimes long after the money had been spent. As treasurer, Walter Langton, once keeper himself, tried to assert exchequer control and to limit the diversion of cash straight to the wardrobe, but there was no way the spending of an office subject to the immediate demands of the king could be controlled. For the wardrobe mostly paid in 'bills' or 'debentures' cashable (in theory)

the introduction to his edition of *The Great Roll of the Pipe for the Fifth Year of the Reign of Henry III* (Pipe Roll Society, NS, vol. 48, London 1990); D. A. Carpenter, *The Minority of Henry III* (London: Methuen, 1990), pp. 64–6, 109–12; Mabel Mills, 'The Reforms at the Exchequer, 1232–42', *TRHS*, 4th ser., 10 (1927); *The Pipe Roll for 1295, Surrey Membrane*, ed. Mabel Mills (Surrey Record Society, vol. 21, Guildford, 1924), for a description of exchequer procedure at the end of the century; P. Chaplais, *English Royal Documents: King John – Henry VI, 1199–1461* (Oxford: Clarendon Press, 1971), plates 4, 7, 8.

at the exchequer or, increasingly, at the point of collection of revenue by a sheriff or mayor: spending of £43,589 16s. 2d. was recorded in 1302–3, but only £8,082 9s. 10d. of that ever went from the exchequer to the wardrobe in cash. Unpaid wardrobe bills came to be used as paper money, and creditors became so clamorous that the exchequer was forced to pay for some services in Scotland directly.[15]

Yet through all this the wardrobe clerks had been recording the cost of the king's 'necessities' day by day with growing professionalism. The Household Ordinance of 1279 had required a nightly account to be made of the number of messes served in the hall, and the spending of pantry, buttery and kitchen (the marshals were separately instructed to clear the hall of 'ribalds that ought not to eat'); the consumption of wine was to be measured, and the wax and tallow, including the candle ends, to be reweighed by the usher of the wardrobe, every day; and the steward of the household and the treasurer or keeper of the wardrobe were to deduct wages as punishment for any transgression of the rules 'not so heinous that it need be reported to the King'. Once or twice a year the treasurer was to audit the accounts of the chamberlain of wines and of the keeper of the great wardrobe, the department for the bulk purchase of the household's supplies including within it the sub-department of the king's tailor. The various sub-accounts were summarised in the *necessaria* rolls in which the wardrobe accounted to the exchequer, and by the end of the century these were drawn up with the help of detailed wardrobe books, one kept by the treasurer and the other by his controller, the second-in-command of the wardrobe. These books give a better picture of government spending than the whole complex of exchequer accounts (which were devised simply to show what remained owing to the Crown). The controller's 'daily book' (*Liber Quotidianus*) for 1299–1300 lists expenditure of around £52,000 under the following headings: *alms* (£1,166 14s. spent over the year, on 666 free meals a week, oblations at mass etc.); *necessaria* (£3,464 13s. 1¾d. in miscellaneous

[15] Warren, *Governance of Norman and Angevin England*, pp. 126–7, 172–4, 184–92; F. J. West, *The Justiciarship in England 1066–1232* (Cambridge: CUP, 1966); Tout, *Chapters*, I. 160–9, 188–205, 214–38; *Handbook of British Chronology*, 3rd edn, ed. E. B. Fryde, D. E. Greenway, S. Porter and I. Roy (Royal Historical Society, London, 1986), pp. 78–81, for lists of keepers of the wardrobe; *EHD*, III, no. 118; Tout, *Chapters*, II. 121–45; C. Johnson, 'The System of Account in the Wardrobe of Edward I', *TRHS*, 4th ser., 6 (1923), pp. 54–6; M. C. Prestwich, 'Exchequer and Wardrobe in the Later Years of Edward I', *BIHR*, 46 (1973), pp. 3, 7.

payments: the expenses of clerks sent to raise troops, the cost of military engines, horses and tents, and of parchment and fees for notaries); *the victualling and garrisoning of castles* (£18,638, much of it in wages); *gifts* (£4,386 4s. 5d. for minstrels, soldiers returning from French prisons and those who had lost war-horses); *knights' fees* (£3,077 19s. in wages for household troops, principally knights and esquires serving in Scotland); *wages of crossbowmen, sergeants-at-arms and esquires* (£1,038 16s. 7d, at 8d. a day, or 1s. with their own horses); *wages of foot-soldiers* (£4,446 9s. 11½d. for infantrymen and pioneers raised by commissions of array); *wages of sailors* (£1,233 9s. 11½d., including wages of a Fleet chaplain); *expenses of messengers* (£87. 11s. 1d. for those who carried departmental messages under the great or privy seals); *wages of falconers and huntsmen* (£77 6s. 11½d. only, this year); *robes for knights and clerks* (£714 3s. 4d.); *jewels and plate* (£253 15s. 6d.); *the great wardrobe* (£4,391 19s. 4½d.); *the king's butler* (£4,982 10s. for wholesale purchases on behalf of household and army); *the queen's household* (£3,667 9s. ½d., for the time she was away from the king); and finally, *outgoings in applying the great seal* (the chancellor's fee of £500, plus £81 9s. 9d in food and clothing for his staff).[16]

The last item shows that the chancery still counted as part of the household. The king could not govern without the chancellor to send out his letters under the great seal, for instance to instruct the exchequer to settle the bills for Henry's intensive programme of building works at Westminster. A chancellor's household still travelled with the king; when the court was at Woodstock in 1245 the king's bailiff was ordered to assign two oaks from the grove at Handborough to make stables for the horses of the clerks in the *hospicium cancellarie*, and in 1293 several inns at Canterbury were set aside for the different sections of the chancery when the king was there. Yet, perhaps because the chancellor was too often away from court on other business and the chancery clerks were becoming absorbed in formal (but lucrative) business which drew them like their exchequer cousins to permanent quarters near Westminster, the wardrobe officials sought an alternative means of communicating royal orders and turned the king's private seal into a second seal of state. In John's reign notes begin to appear on the

---

[16] *EHD*, III. pp. 584–6; *List of documents relating to the Household and Wardrobe, John to Edward I*, PRO Handbooks, no. 7 (London: HMSO, 1964); *Records of the Wardrobe and Household, 1285–1286*, ed. B. F. and C. R. Byerly (London: HMSO, 1977); *Book of Prests of the King's Wardrobe for 1294–5*, ed. E. B. Fryde (Oxford: Clarendon Press, 1962); Johnson, 'System of Account', pp. 64–71.

chancery rolls that particular great seal documents were issued on the warrant of writs *de privato sigillo*; it was only then that the royal seal kept by the chancellor needed distinguishing as 'the great seal'. Peter des Rivaux had custody of the privy seal between 1232 and 1234. When, six years later, the chancellor Ralph Neville was deprived of the great seal because of his acceptance of election to the bishopric of Winchester against the king's preferred candidate, confidential clerks in the wardrobe wrote privy seal letters denouncing him to the pope, 'the chancery clerks being kept in ignorance of it'. The use of the privy seal as an independent seal becomes noticeably more frequent with the intensification of governmental activity after the landmark year of 1290: to authenticate the king's orders to his ministers, and personal letters to members of his family, or to foreign rulers asking after their health; to issue letters of protection (the forerunners of passports) to his emissaries; and to seal bipartite indentures engaging (for instance) custodians of castles during the Scottish war. It is significant that privy seal letters were by then usually in French, the vernacular of the king's knightly lieutenants, the language of action and management. If a formal letter under the great seal to a foreign potentate was required, it was drafted in French in the wardrobe and translated into Latin in chancery. Diplomatic and other state documents were deposited for ease of reference in the treasury of the wardrobe, which was situated under the Chapter House at Westminster until after a famous burglary there in 1303, when it was transferred to the Tower. The privy seal was the instrument of such independent initiative as the king's council was beginning to acquire. By 1295 the controller of the wardrobe was its custodian, and there may already have been a privy seal office made up of the four clerks who for long were normally adequate for its business. Though it kept bulky files, now lost, the office did not enrol copies of its out-letters; it was a place for getting things done, not for storing up authoritative records. In the 1290s, all that *Fleta* knows about the privy seal is that it is not under the chancellor's control, but soon after Edward I's death its effectiveness as an instrument of government caused the barons to insist that the privy seal office should have as its head a keeper of the privy seal who was as publicly identified as the other ministers of state.[17]

---

[17] *Building Accounts of Henry III*, ed. H. M. Colvin (Oxford: Clarendon Press, 1971), pp. 190–201; T. F. Tout, 'The Household of the Chancery', in *Essays in*

CLERKS, JUSTICES AND LAWYERS

Like the exchequer, but unlike the wardrobe, chancery was a department serving the general public, to which it dispensed a vast range of great seal documents for all sorts of purposes – grants of lands and franchises, orders for payment from the exchequer, above all legal writs and judicial commissions. Many of these may be called 'formal', but then as now public transactions depended on getting the right forms. 'Fleta', writing in the 1290s his treatise on the courts and processes of the common law, not surprisingly makes his chapter on chancery a disquisition on the framing of writs, and the enrolment of recognizances and contracts on the back of chancery rolls as bases for litigation. Writs 'of course' which 'have been approved by the council of the whole realm' and cannot be altered without its consent are prepared 'for the convenience of the people' by 'young clerks of inferior rank': these *cursitores* (a hundred years later there will be twenty-four of them) must write their names on the writs they frame, thus acknowledging their responsibility to the purchasers, who should pay no more than a penny a writ. Senior clerks, forerunners of the twelve 'masters in chancery', are responsible for their juniors, some (as *preceptores*) prescribing which writs fit which cases and examining the writs before they go out, others (as 'protonotaries') apparently exercising some discretion in writing new 'writs appropriate to the various plaints'. All the chancery clerks, says Fleta, used to be members of the king's household. But they have now clearly moved into the public realm, and feeding and clothing them is the responsibility of the chancellor, who has become a paid official. Early in the century he ceased to farm his office at anything up to 5,000 marks. From 1244 or soon after a 'keeper of the hanaper' (the hamper in which the documents awaiting collection were stored) accounted to the wardrobe for the fees (12 marks and 5s. for a new charter, 18s. 4d. for a confirmation, 2s. for letters patent of protection) collected in chancery. The chancellor was then given

History Presented to Reginald Lane Poole, ed. H. W. C. Davis (Oxford: Clarendon Press, 1927); *idem, Chapters*, 1.217–25, 287; Chaplais, *English Royal Documents*, pp. 23–34, 41–2, plates 3a, 4–8, 13b, 19b, 20c; *Fleta*, ed. H. G. Richardson and G. O. Sayles, 3 vols. (Selden Society, vols. 72, 89, 99, London, 1953–83), II.123; Warren, *Governance of Norman and Angevin England*, pp. 187–8; Clanchy, *From Memory to Written Record*, pp. 152–4; *Records of the Wardrobe and Household*, ed. Byerly and Byerly, pp. 133ff; G. P. Cuttino, *English Diplomatic Administration, 1259–1339* (Oxford: Clarendon Press, 1971), pp. 13, 31, 171ff.

a fixed allowance which remained at £500 from the thirteenth century to the nineteenth.[18]

Yet his control of public documents continued to make the chancellor the chief figure among the king's councillors. The processes of English justice were embodied in the registers of writs, which grew from some sixty to several hundred items in the course of the century. The surviving manuscript registers vary in detail because they were working handbooks of lawyers and litigants, but there was an authoritative register kept in the chancery; sometimes the invention of a particular writ was attributed to a named protonotary or chancellor, and periodically the accumulating forms in the register were rearranged by the chancery clerks into a more logical order. In 1244 the barons complained of the unjust writs issued in the absence of a chancellor and a justiciar, who ought to be permanent members of the king's council. In Edward's reign many new writs were provided by statutes, which must, however, have been drafted by the chancellor along with the judges.[19]

The register of writs went far beyond instruments of litigation: it was a comprehensive 'formulary' containing examples of letters between the courts and other branches of government, and concerning the king's affairs generally (e.g. letters of protection for merchants, or seeking an audience with the pope for royal messengers). Similarly, the rolls of out-letters which it was the other main task of the chancery to keep, under the direction of its senior clerk, the master of the rolls, recorded the whole range of government. To the Charter, Close, Fine, Liberate, Patent and Scutage Rolls dating from the reign of John, Gascon and Treaty Rolls were added under Henry III, and Scotch, Parliament and Statute Rolls under Edward I. The Patent Rolls and Close Rolls in particular follow government activity day by day. On the face of the Close Rolls, which have been transcribed in seventeen volumes to 1272 and calendared in another five from 1272 to 1307, were enrolled letters 'usually of an executive nature, conveying in the sovereign's

---

[18] Chaplais, *English Royal Documents*, pp. 1–23, plate 2; *Fleta*, ed. Richardson and Sayles, II, 123–6; Tout, 'Household of Chancery', pp. 53–4; *Early Registers of Writs*, ed. E. de Haas and G. D. G. Hall (Selden Society, vol. 87, London, 1970), pp. xiii–xiv, cxxv, 38, 117, 126, 314.

[19] *Early Registers of Writs*, ed. Haas and Hall, pp. xiii, xv, xx–xxi, cxvi–cxxiii, cxxvi, 91, 212, 213, 218, 297, 309, 427; R. C. Stacey, *Politics, Policy, and Finance under Henry III, 1216–1245* (Oxford: Clarendon Press, 1987), pp. 216, 248; *EHD*, III.443 (Westminster II, c. 24).

name, to royal officers and others, orders and instructions about matters ranging in importance from major constitutional decisions to the daily economy of the royal household' – writs of summons to parliaments are a notable example. But as the tendency increased after 1300 to use the privy seal to send such instructions directly (rather than by warranting the great seal), the authoritative enrolment of private deeds on its dorse (which continued till 1903) became the Close Rolls' more important function. The Patent Rolls, which have been transcribed in three volumes to 1232 and calendared in another eight to 1307, had enrolled upon their face proclamations, royal grants of all kinds and licences which needed to be shown open; on the back are to be found the commissions under which the king's government was exercised in the countryside – for instance to commissioners to array troops, to justices of assize, gaol delivery and oyer and terminer, and eventually to justices of the peace.[20]

General eyres, one of which might last intermittently for eleven years though spending no more than a month in any one county, were directed from the chancery by writs patent and close, for justices might die or be withdrawn for other business; the parties of four or five justices periodically needed supplementing or splitting up, and always moving on; and counties had to be forewarned of their arrival. Early in 1282, the justices in eyre in Devon wrote to press the chancellor, Robert Burnell, to prorogue the eyre till after Michaelmas, because a parliament was coming up, which as he knew involved much delay; the journey from London to Cornwall, the next county on their list, was long; and the corn in the south-west had failed, so if they went there in summer they would 'bring back meagre cheeks'. (In fact they did not get to Cornwall till 1284.) Regular inquiries *post mortem* (surveying the lands of a deceased tenant-in-chief) and *ad quod damnum* (to discover whether a proposed grant of a market, fair or other privilege was prejudicial to the interests of the Crown or others) issued from the chancery; there too injured persons could obtain commissions to special justices to hear their complaints and either determine them (as justices of oyer et terminer) or return their findings to chancery. The judicial system supervised by the chancellor exhibited the characteristics of true government: that it should be seen to operate for the people in the name of the king.

[20] *Guide to the Contents of the Public Record Office*, I.14–26; R. B. Pugh, *Imprisonment in Medieval England* (Cambridge: CUP, 1968), p. 258.

And to service it and live from it a body of men fused the skills of clerks and the experience of royal administrators into the practice of lawyers – the first true profession in working for the general public as much as for Church or Crown.[21]

The system of common law founded by Henry II depended on a set of bureaucratic procedures and required a corps of specialist clerks to service it. Archbishop Hubert Walter, Richard I's justiciar till 1198, has been credited with setting up a judicial bench separate from the exchequer board, though justices continued to bring to their job experience in various aspects of exchequer work: inquiry into the possessions of the Jews, custody of crown lands and vacant bishoprics, and financial work in the counties as sheriffs or sheriffs' clerks, in which capacities they would have learnt the running of the county courts in which the king's itinerant justices sat. The significantly named Walter Mauclerc ('bad clerk') received livings from King John in both England and Normandy, served as a *clericus* in the administration of Lincolnshire and in the Irish exchequer, and was sent as a royal messenger to Flanders and France, before he was appointed a justice in eyre in 1219; soon after that he was given custody of the shire of Cumberland and while there secured election to the bishopric of Carlisle, but he was still able to return to be the king's treasurer. Richard Duket served in the exchequer, as sheriff of Norfolk and Suffolk, and then in the 1220s as a justice of assize and in eyre, and he appears in Bracton's treatise *On the Laws and Customs of England* seeking the advice of his fellow justices, Martin Pateshull (d. 1229) and William Raleigh (elected bishop of Norwich in 1239), about how litigants' *essoins* (excuses) for absence should be checked, so that cases were not prolonged indefinitely. Bracton may have had people like Duket in mind when he gave the purpose of his treatise as the instruction of 'the unwise and unlearned who ascend the judgement seat before they have learned the laws'. The common law, like the processes of the exchequer, was becoming too specialised to be handled entirely by men-of-all-work. The real legal expertise was transmitted by an apostolic succession of judges and the personal clerks who succeeded them as judges in the court of common pleas established at Westminster by the terms of Magna Carta, and in the parallel court with the king (*coram rege*) revived at the end of

---

[21] *Shropshire Eyre*, ed. Harding, pp. xi–xvi; *Cases in King's Bench*, ed. Sayles, i.cxlii; Powicke, *The Thirteenth Century*, p. 335; D. Crook, *Records of the General Eyre*, PRO Handbooks, no. 20 (London: HMSO, 1982), pp. 162–3; *Guide to the Contents of the Public Record Office*, i.27–8; Harding, 'Plaints and Bills', pp. 78–9.

Henry III's minority. Martin Pateshull was the clerk of Simon Pateshull, Raleigh probably Martin's, and Roger Thurkelby, another leading judge, had been Raleigh's. Bracton reverences Pateshull and Raleigh as the 'just men' whose judgements he cites to the exclusion of everyone else's, and on the evidence of his writings he himself was probably Raleigh's clerk from the early 1230s. *Bracton's Note Book* sets out a run of cases heard by Raleigh *coram rege* between 1234 and 1240, and the treatise *On the Laws and Customs of England* gives an expert account of how the assize of cosinage, invented by Raleigh in 1237, was set alongside mort d'ancestor in order to protect the inheritance of land within wider degrees of kinship. When Raleigh ceased to be a justice in 1239, Bracton was made a royal clerk with a grant of forty marks for his maintenance; and he went on to be a justice in eyre in 1245 and *coram rege* in 1247.[22]

Justices and other officials who received benefices like the deanery of St Martin-le-Grand in London, the almost hereditary preserve of the keepers of the wardrobe, or sought promotion to bishoprics, were necessarily clerics; and so must John of Lexington have been, to attend university and become 'expert in both canon and civil law'; and Bracton himself, to end as archdeacon of Barnstaple and chancellor of Exeter. One of the reasons for the king's wholesale employment of clerics was that he could reward them with 'livings' in the Church, though he might have to seek papal indulgences for their non-residence in their benefices and confront the anger of such as Bishop Grosseteste when he made them judges. But many of those who moved between the service of King and Church were in minor orders only, and there are examples of successful royal clerks who gave up their clerical status and benefices to become knights.[23]

---

[22] F. Pegues, 'The *Clericus* in the Legal Administration of Thirteenth-Century England', *EHR*, 71 (1956); *Rolls of the Justices in Eyre for Lincolnshire 1218–9 and Worcestershire 1221*, ed. D. M. Stenton (Selden Society, vol. 53, London, 1934), pp. xv–xxiv; R. V. Turner, *The English Judiciary in the Age of Glanvill and Bracton, c. 1176–1239* (Cambridge: CUP, 1985), pp. 65–107, 290ff; *Pleas before the King or his Justices*, ed. D. M. Stenton, III (Selden Society, vol. 83, London, 1966), app. 1; *Bracton on the Laws and Customs of England*, tr. S. E. Thorne, 4 vols. (Cambridge, Mass.: Harvard UP, 1968–77), II.19, 354, 360, III.317–28, IV.126; Pollock and Maitland, *HEL*, I.169, 189, 205–6; for the keepers of writs and rolls, see *Fleta*, ed. Richardson and Sayles, II.138; C. A. F. Meekings, *Studies in Thirteenth-Century Justice and Administration*, (London: Hambledon, 1981), caps. 11, 12 and 14; *Shropshire Eyre*, ed. Harding, p. xv.

[23] Pollock and Maitland, *HEL*, I.205–6; *Fleta*, ed. Richardson and Sayles, II. 138–9.

THE LEGAL PROFESSION, LEARNING AND LIFE

The law was becoming a profession in which laymen could compete with clerics, and would quickly supersede them. Matthew Paris acknowledged that, of Henry III's justices, Thomas Multon was a knight 'skilled in secular laws', and Henry of Bath and Roger Thurkelby both knights *and* literate. Some lay justices, perhaps experienced as sheriffs, were essential because high ecclesiastics could not impose blood-punishments. But eight of the fifteen justices who sat (usually three at a time) in Edward I's court of king's bench, including the two chief justices in the period after Hengham's dismissal in 1290, were laymen for a more fundamental reason: the king was beginning to choose his judges not from the clerks of the courts but from among the legal agents of the landlord classes. From the twelfth century onwards lords had regularly sent servants, and abbeys monks experienced in business, to act as their essoiners and attorneys, and the courts evolved careful procedures for the appointment and control of these legal agents. In John's reign, the essoiners at least seem to have been humble men given nicknames like 'Obbe Corne' in the court records. The man of business of a Lincolnshire monastery is styled 'Prester John', an attorney 'Groaning and Sighing'. But a respected group of professional attorneys, comprising both clerks and laymen, was emerging; in some cases they even had the academic background which conferred the title of 'master'. In the Bench at Westminster there practised a close-knit group of Londoners who had no inclination to follow the justices in eyre round the country.[24]

In addition to the attorney who stands in the place of an absent litigant, the plea-rolls begin to reveal another figure: the 'narrator', 'counter' or 'serjeant-counter' (serjeant simply means 'servant') who makes the statement of the case for a party 'who is here', answers the other side's 'exceptions' to the form of action and engages in the pleading-battle by which lawsuits were brought to the point of jury trial and judgement. Since the Church set its face against clerics' living by the argument of secular cases, these were the leaders of an unmistakably new lay profession. Matthew Paris

---

[24] For Multon, see R. V. Turner, *Men Raised from the Dust* (Philadelphia: University of Pennsylvania Press, 1988), cap. 6; for Thurkelby, see Meekings, *Studies in Thirteenth Century Justice and Administration*, article III, p. 262; *Shropshire Eyre*, ed. Harding, pp. xii–xvi; *Cases in King's Bench*, ed. Sayles, I, pp. xlix–lxiv, xci–civ, cxxix–cxli; *Pleas before the King or his Justices*, ed. Stenton, III, pp. xxxiii–xliv, ccxcv–cccxix.

is the first to mention 'forespeakers of the Bench, whom we commonly call "counters"', whom he describes arguing the king's case against Hubert de Burgh in 1235. A London ordinance of 1280 probably followed regulations in the king's courts when it required the estates of counter, essoiner and attorney to be kept distinct, and counters to swear on admission to the mayor's court to exercise their 'mystery' faithfully. Every court would soon acquire its bar of pleaders, right down to the county court, though almost all the hundred or so counters who have been identified practising before 1307 did so in the common bench.[25]

But the king wanted serjeants of his own to plead his cases, and in 1290 one of these, Gilbert of Thornton, succeeded Hengham as chief justice *coram rege*, when there was a clean sweep of that court. Before very long it would be regarded as obvious that the king should choose his judges from those whose arguments they would have to umpire. Pleaders and judges were now seen as members of one profession. A wealthy client, like the monastery of St Augustine's, Canterbury, would retain ten or more serjeants at a time on yearly or termly 'pensions'. Judges too were regularly retained as counsel by the great men of the land. Stephen Segrave, who briefly succeeded Hubert de Burgh as justiciar in 1232, was very much the client of Earl Ranulf of Chester. Hengham, the last of the great clerical justices, and Sir William Bereford, a serjeant who became judge in 1294 and died as chief justice of the common bench in 1326, both had large incomes from private patrons. Hengham was given an annual pension of £5 in 1284 to assist Christ Church, Canterbury, in its business affairs, especially when a legal action concerning the monastery came before him; Bereford was retained by the abbeys of Westminster and Ramsey, and by Merton College, Oxford, from which he received numerous gifts of robes and silver cups, and furs and spices for his wife. Counters and judges were not mere court practitioners; they were the valued advisors of the great men of the land – and from another point of view members of a tricky profession which stirred up trouble for profit, so that strenuous efforts were made to debar them from manorial courts and from the exchequer court.[26]

---

[25] J. H. Baker, *The Order of Serjeants at Law* (Selden Society, supp. ser., 5, London, 1984), pp. 3–27, 140–9; Paris, *CM*, III.619; Palmer, *County Courts*, pp. 89–112.

[26] *Cases in King's Bench*, ed. Sayles, I, pp. lvii–lviii, civ–cxv; J. R. Maddicott, *Law and Lordship: Royal Justices as Retainers in Thirteenth- and Fourteenth-Century*

The growth of the new profession was reflected in a new record: reports of actual pleadings contained in Year Books. During the swift development of common law procedures in the first half of the century, collections of entries on the plea-rolls were what justices and their clerks needed, and Bracton's collection was not the only one. The 'attorneys and apprentices' learning their trade by observing cases from their 'crib' in Westminster Hall (we first hear of them in 1292, when the king tried to limit their numbers to 140) had a different need: collections of pleadings in notable cases, which began to be written down in such compilations of the third quarter of the century as *Brevia Placitata* (writs pleaded), *Casus Placitorum* (cases of pleading) and *Placita Corone* (pleadings in criminal cases). Well before the end of the century a tradition of law-reporting was established in the Year Books, one of which describes Hengham, restored to favour as chief justice of the court of common pleas, explaining a case to the students in 1302. There is revealed a tradition of lively debate in the courts about substantial issues. Thus in 1309 William of Goldington is reported as bringing a case in the common bench against John of Bassingbourn and others by the recently created writ of conspiracy. The defendants were said to have 'conspired' that an acknowledgement of debt had been made at Winchester in 1297, in accordance with which two manors held by William were awarded to them until the alleged debt should be paid. Scrope, the serjeant-at-law pleading for the defendants, said that it was not a count they must answer, 'for every conspiracy and alliance ought to be precedent to what is conspired and devised'; Herle, for the plaintiff, replied that the conspiracy and evil had been to allege (in the future) that a non-existent acknowledgement had been made, whereupon Chief Justice Bereford demanded that the defendants 'say something else'. Scrope then argued that the writ was inconsistent in that it sometimes talked of 'conspirators' and sometimes of 'procurers'. At that point the irascible Bereford launched into a story of King Edward's impatience when Justice Hengham had questioned a writ summoning Isabella de Forz, countess of Aumale, to answer unspecified charges in parliament: 'then arose the king, who was very wise, and said: "I have nothing to do with your disputations, but God's blood! you shall give me a good writ before you arise

England (Past and Present Supplement 4, 1978), esp. pp. 14–15; for Segrave, see Turner, *Men Raised from the Dust*, cap. 7.

hence." So say I here.' Scrope asked for an adjournment to consult with his clients, and when John of Bassingbourn was called into court next morning, 'he came not'. The case had been won and lost in the pleading.[27]

The language of the law reports marks the shift in legal practice that has occurred: it is not the Latin of the clerks but the vernacular of the thirteenth-century aristocracy – the French which was used also in letters from the wardrobe under the privy seal, in the bills of complaint which helped to turn chancery and the king's council into new courts of justice, in bills to Parliament, and in the Parliament Rolls which recorded them. But the serjeants built the new profession on the foundations laid by the clerks. Lawyers obtained instruction in the science of writs at Inns of Chancery. In legal records there was a continuing interplay of English, Latin and 'Law French', which was from the first a technical instrument not necessarily reflecting what was actually said in court. It must have been the clerks of the courts who made the transition from collecting plea-roll cases to collecting pleadings, compiling books like *Brevia Placitata* which were always known by their Latin names though their contents were in French. Legal argument mirrored the disputations which were a medium of clerical education in the universities. Instruction in the elements of legal procedure in the courts of both Church and King, along with conveyancing and letter-writing and the keeping of accounts, was indeed available at thirteenth-century Oxford for young clerks hoping to gain employment in the households of landowners; and about 1272, one John of Oxford wrote a treatise on *How to Hold Pleas and Courts*, for the benefit of seignorial stewards. On a different plane, Gilbert of Thornton, serjeant and chief justice of king's bench, and the first layman to write on English law, composed his abridgement of Bracton as a scholastic *Summa*. In 1290, the year of Thornton's elevation, a parliamentary petition from the abbot of St Mary's, York, bracketed the distasteful methods of the lawyers prosecuting the king's *quo warranto* pleas with 'the subtlety of the moderns' in the schools.[28]

---

[27] *Bracton on the Laws and Customs of England*, tr. Thorne, III.xxxiv–xxxix; *RP*, I.84; P. Brand, 'Courtroom and Schoolroom: The Education of Lawyers in England Prior to 1400', *Historical Research*, 60 (1987); S. F. C. Milsom, *Historical Foundations of the Common Law*, 2nd edn (London: Butterworths, 1981), pp. 42–8; A. Harding, *The Law Courts of Medieval England* (London: Allen and Unwin, 1973), pp. 163–5.

[28] Harding, *Law Courts*, pp. 98–110; Brand, 'Courtroom and Schoolroom',

A greater contribution of the towns to social change in thirteenth-century England than Adam Smith's pursuit of wealth and
David Hume's political alliance of the 'more industrious classes'
with the king against the barons was this fostering of the professional groups studied by administrative and legal historians. A
new sort of career was opened to ambitious young men from
merchant or (more often) small landholding families, blurring the
distinctions between them. Towards the end of his life a Nottingham merchant called Ralph Bugge, who died between 1242
and 1248, bought land in Willoughby-on-the-Wolds to endow his
younger son, Richard, when his trading interests should pass to his
elder son; Richard Bugge prospered with a foot in both gentry and
commercial worlds, and it was as Richard of Willoughby that his
son appeared as a serjeant in the common bench in 1293, made a
good living from commissions of oyer and terminer and lending
money to his gentry neighbours, and became chief justice in
Ireland; this man's elder son, Richard Willoughby II, would be
chief justice of king's bench, his younger son an Oxford doctor of
theology and a canon of York. Eventually a Willoughby of
Wollaton Hall, Nottingham, would become Lord Middleton.[29]

Through the professions the experience and learning of churchmen in the human sciences were applied to affairs of state. Those
who made their way in royal service came from the same families
as those whose careers were in the Church. In the king's wardrobe
clerics and laymen worked side by side. Archbishops and bishops
– Hubert Walter, Robert Burnell, John Kirkby, Walter Langton –
served the king in the offices of chancellor and treasurer. There
was no barrier to the dissemination in the secular world of the long
experience of churchmen in the administration of their dioceses
and estates, or in the workings of the legal system of the universal
Church. Jocelin of Brakelond's account of Abbot Samson's rule of
St Edmundsbury at the beginning of the century shows the
complexity of a monastery's business. So too does the *Liber
Memorandum* of Barnwell Priory outside Cambridge, written in

pp. 157, 162; H. G. Richardson, 'The Oxford Law School under John', *Law
Quarterly Review*, 57 (1941); Clanchy, *From Memory to Written Record*, pp. 159–62,
224–5; *idem*, 'Moderni in Education and Government in England', *Speculum*, 50
(1975).
[29] J. C. Holt, 'Willoughby Deeds', in *Early Medieval Miscellany for D. M. Stenton*,
ed. P. M. Barnes and C. F. Slade (Pipe Roll Society, NS, vol. 36, London, 1960);
Baker, *Order of Serjeants*, p. 545; M. R. Bloom, unpublished DPhil thesis on the
rise of the Willoughbys (Oxford, 1985).

1295–6 by Prior Simon de Askellis, who is described as Professor of Civil Law in the university; with its wealth of transcripts from the rolls of the king's courts about such matters as the priory's conflict with the town of Cambridge over Stourbridge fair it was an armoury for litigation at a time when the house felt itself under threat from royal lawyers, but it could also have been a teaching book. Around 1240, with his authority as a bishop and his experience as the head of a great household, Grosseteste wrote for the countess of Lincoln a set of rules as to how she should 'guard and govern her lands and house: whoever will keep these rules well will be able to live on his means, and keep himself and those belonging to him'. In their dioceses bishops were experienced in legislating in great detail, and also knew the uses of public notaries appointed by imperial or papal authority to draw up official documents, particularly those requiring international validity; the home-grown methods of conveyancing in England left little scope for notaries in domestic business, but Edward I would need them to copy out papal bulls, and to prepare the public instruments of the Great Cause' of 1291–2, in which he adjudicated the claims to the Scottish Crown after consulting the civil and canon lawyers of the University of Paris about rules of succession.[30]

The king's clerical councillors and judges were able to see the English state in terms of traditional political theory, which began from the mutual responsibility of Church and Crown in the government of a Christian country, and proceeded to the responsibility of the king for his people. Bishops were called upon to excommunicate breakers of the king's peace, and sheriffs to imprison excommunicates who refused to submit to the Church; papal legates were received to assist in restoring peace to the land: Guala after the death of John, and Ottobuono after the battle of Evesham. But it was the inevitable conflicts between the canon law

---

[30] M. T. Clanchy, 'Power and Knowledge', in *England in the Thirteenth Century*, ed. W. M. Ormrod (Grantham: Harlaxton College, 1984); D. M. Owen, *The Records of the Established Church in England* (British Records Association, Archives and the User, no. 1, London, 1970), gives a good impression of the extent of ecclesiastical administration; *The Chronicle of Jocelin of Brakelond*, ed. H. E. Butler (London, 1949); *Liber Memorandum Ecclesie de Bernewelle*, ed. J. W. Clark (Cambridge: CUP, 1907); J. E. Sayers, *Papal Judges Delegate in the Province of Canterbury, 1198–1254* (Oxford: OUP, 1971); C. R. Cheney, *Medieval Texts and Studies* (Oxford: Clarendon Press, 1973), caps. 7, 9; *idem, Notaries Public in England in the Thirteenth and Fourteenth Centuries* (Oxford: Clarendon Press, 1972), p. 100; G. J. Hand, 'The Opinions of the Paris Lawyers upon the Scottish Succession c. 1292', *The Irish Jurist*, NS, 5 (1970).

of the universal Church and the laws developed for a particular national community which generated political argument. The king resented the excommunication of his officials when their enforcement of English law seemed to infringe the rights of the Church; the bishops resented the king's writs of prohibition which stopped property cases from being heard in court christian. But prohibitions were often sought by parties who were clerics themselves, and writs of consultation could be obtained to send back cases rightly within ecclesiastical jurisdiction. It was William Raleigh, a cleric who was also a royal judge, who led Henry III's councillors and barons at the Council of Merton in 1236 in refusing to change the laws of England at the behest of bishops, and to allow sons born out of wedlock to succeed to property even when they were legitimized in the eyes of the Church by their parents' subsequent marriages.[31]

In this connection Bracton declared: 'Just as the pope can dispose of spiritual ranks and dignities, so can the king dispose of temporal inheritances according to the custom of the kingdom; for each kingdom has its own customs, and there may be one rule of succession in England and another in France.' As a result of the work of Professor Thorne, Bracton's treatise on *The Laws and Customs of England* can now be seen, through the corruptions of a reviser, to have been the work of a university-trained jurist in Raleigh's circle, intent on ordering the judgements made in English courts according to the principles and distinctions of Roman jurisprudence; doing this to prove that England had true laws 'though they are unwritten, since whatever has been rightly decided and approved with the counsel and consent of the magnates and the general agreement of the *res publica*, the authority of the king or prince having first been added thereto, has the force of law'. The professional understanding of the sources of law had real political implications. For Bracton the king's only superiors were God, who promised all the torments of the fiery furnace to unjust judges – and the law, 'because law makes the king'.[32]

The great Bishop Grosseteste employed the same mixture of biblical authority and legal reasoning as Bracton, but in order to challenge Raleigh over the law of succession, and to assert the rule

---

[31] R. H. Helmholz, 'Writs of Prohibition and Ecclesiastical Sanctions in English Courts Christian', *Minnesota Law Review*, 60 (1976).

[32] *Bracton on the Laws and Customs of England*, tr. Thorne, i.xxxiii–xlviii, ii.33, iv.298; F. Schultz, 'Bracton on Kingship', *EHR*, 60 (1945); B. Tierney, 'Bracton on Government', *Speculum*, 38 (1963).

of a higher law. Back in 1223 the future bishop of Lincoln may just possibly have acted as the young king's secretary and keeper of his privy seal. Two decades later, as the stern ruler of a large diocese, he found himself having to refuse the king benefices for royal officials whom he thought unlikely to be satisfactory pastors. In 1231, he had been archdeacon of Leicester when Simon de Montfort became lord of the town, and joined with the earl in driving out the Leicester Jews with violent language about 'those murderers of our Saviour'. On his return in 1250 from the papal curia, where he had called the pope and cardinals worse things for intruding unworthy men into benefices and undermining the pastoral authority of bishops, he sent a speech he had delivered about the difference between just rule and tyranny to Earl Simon, himself on trial for his oppressive governorship of Gascony.[33]

Grosseteste was a patron of the Franciscans of Oxford, who arrived when he was *magister scholarum* in the university and continued to look to him as their diocesan bishop. He communicated his concern for the integrity of canon law to the Friars, who were gaining influence with the great men of the land by becoming their confessors. Grosseteste's closest disciple and friend, the Franciscan Adam Marsh, was also the confidant of Simon de Montfort, whom he regarded as a sort of political saint. The most interesting political statement of the century may have been written by a Franciscan and seems to reflect Adam Marsh's attitudes. The Song of Lewes celebrates the barons' victory in 1264 and England's new hope of liberty. Surrounded by much talk of Gideon, Goliath, David dancing with his handmaids and Earl Simon, 'like unto Christ', giving himself to death for the many, two essential and related themes appear in the Song. First, it was no shame to the king to be bound by the 'canonical constitutions and . . . catholic ordinances' agreed at the Oxford parliament, for 'every king is ruled by the laws which he makes'; by laws kings reign, and Saul and David were punished for breaking the laws. And secondly, it 'concerned the community' that the king should choose the right men to be his councillors – not foreigners but natives who knew and respected the laws of the country.[34]

---

[33] R. W. Southern, *Robert Grosseteste: The Growth of an English Mind in Medieval Europe* (Oxford: Clarendon Press, 1986), pp. 81–2, 192, 246–7, 254–7, 267–8, 288–9; W. A. Pantin, 'Grosseteste's Relations with the Papacy and the Crown', in *Robert Grosseteste, Scholar and Bishop*, ed. D. A. Callus (Oxford: Clarendon Press, 1955).

[34] Southern, *Robert Grosseteste*, pp. 13, 18, 290n; D. Knowles, *The Religious Orders*

The Song makes Simon tell those deputed after the battle to choose a new royal council to appoint men 'whose faith is lively, who have read the decretals [the laws made by recent popes], or have becomingly taught theology'. The author of the Song acknowledges that the king's knights resented the philosophy which it attributes to Simon's movement as 'the sayings of clerks'. But in Edward's reign the clerical belief in the rule of law became the ideology of the servants of the Angevin state. At one point it was proposed to sell English law to the native Irish, to replace laws that were 'detestable to God'. By a comprehensive set of laws contained in the Statute of Wales of 1284 Edward undertook to civilize the conquered Welsh, who (so Archbishop Peckham of Canterbury, Adam Marsh's old pupil, was telling the king) were a savage and unprofitable people because they did not live together in towns; in framing the statute the king claimed to be guided only by Divine Providence, but the statute transferred English criminal law wholesale to the Welsh, along with the famous rule of property law excluding bastards from succession. English law itself was being systematically developed by statute, from the base described by Bracton and with some deference to Bracton's claim that in England laws were not only made in accordance with God's law but 'approved by the consent of those who use them'.[35]

---

in England, vol. I (Cambridge: CUP, 1948), pp. 136, 138, 181–2, 205, 209–10, 214; Powicke, *HLE*, pp. 216, 219, 247, 391, 469–72; *EHD*, III, no. 232.

[35] J. Otway-Ruthven, 'The Native Irish and English Law in Medieval Ireland', *Irish Historical Studies*, 7 (1950); R. R. Davies, *Conquest, Coexistence and Change: Wales 1063–1415*, (Oxford: Clarendon Press and University of Wales Press, 1987), pp. 367–70; L. Beverley Smith, 'The Statute of Wales, 1284', *Welsh History Review*, 10 (1980–1), p. 140; *Statutes of the Realm*, II vols. (Record Commission, London, 1810–28), I.5, 55; *Bracton on the Laws and Customs of England*, tr Thorne, II.21.

5

KNIGHTS

Professional people, like the peasantry and tradesmen, existed to serve the lords of the land, who were themselves being drawn into administrative roles. The lords were united by their own ideas of honourable service within a hierarchy leading up to the king as lord paramount, and by the practicalities of the land tenure which sealed relationships of vassalage. Because the service of the lay lords was originally that of the knights who gave the Conqueror his throne, the relationship was also the source of politics. By 1200 the knight's fee had become hereditary property, and the development of a land market was weakening the connection between the hierarchy of lordship and the distribution of wealth. As landholders, moreover, the lords were subject to the economic pressures of the thirteenth century, at the same time as their military service was being transformed into the exercise of territorial authority in the name of a developing state. The two sorts of change combined to force the magnates to rebuild their relationships with the knights of the shires on a new footing.

KNIGHTS AT WAR

The early thirteenth century was the great age of the chivalric romances about King Arthur's court, which glorified the military prowess of knights in the service of their lords and ladies and of the Church founded by Our Lord, in supreme works of European literature such as Wolfram von Eschenbach's *Parzival* and Gottfried von Strassburg's *Tristan*. In England, Grosseteste obeyed the injunctions of the Fourth Lateran Council to instruct the laity in the faith and wrote 'The Castle of Love', a poem of 1,800 lines in French which, despite its difficult theology, was presumably intended to appeal to the interests of knightly retainers. Soon after mid-century there was composed a more earthy and exciting work, the last of a series of 'ancestral romances', which relates the legends of the Fitzwarin family of Whittington in Shropshire. The exploits of the rebel knight, Fulk Fitzwarin III, in which it culminates have a basis in history; unjustly deprived of his inheritance, Fulk resists the power of King John, in between rescuing damsels from giants and Welsh dragons. There is no great difference in values between this story and the Robin Hood legends, which may already have been current in the same gentry circles.[1]

Edward I was an enthusiast for the Arthurian legends which were part of the knightly culture of his day, perhaps using them intentionally to counter a Welsh claim that Arthur was theirs and would return to save them. 'Round table' feasts accompanied by jousting were held at Nefyn 'in the furthest limits of Snowdonia by the sea' in July 1284, and at Falkirk in 1302 during the attempt to conquer Scotland. Edward's crusade and his Welsh campaign both entered chivalric legend. Ceremonial knightings of young nobles took place on all great royal occasions. Twenty were knighted at the marriage of the king of Scots with Henry's daughter Margaret at York in 1251 – according to Matthew Paris in the presence of a thousand English and sixty Scottish knights. In October 1261 the Lord Edward knighted Henry and Simon, the sons of Simon de Montfort, at court; in a more warlike setting, Earl Simon knighted Gilbert de Clare, earl of Gloucester, Robert de Vere, earl of Oxford, and others before the battle of Lewes. The greatest of royal investitures accompanied the knighting of King Edward's eldest son, Edward of Caernarvon, in 1306, when the king and his knights swore upon two swans that they would 'avenge on Robert Bruce the wrong which he had done to God

---

[1] M. D. Legge, *Anglo-Norman Literature and its Background* (Oxford: Clarendon Press, 1963), pp. 171–3, 223; R. W. Southern, *Robert Grosseteste: The Growth of an English Mind in Medieval Europe* (Oxford: Clarendon Press, 1986), pp. 225–30; M. Keen, *The Outlaws of Medieval Legend*, 3rd edn (London: Routledge, 1987), pp. 39–52; J. Meisel, *Barons of the Welsh Frontier: The Corbet, Pantulf, and Fitz Warin Families, 1066–1272* (Lincoln: University of Nebraska Press, 1980), cap. 3; D. Crook, 'Some Further Evidence concerning the Dating of the Origins of the Legend of Robin Hood', *EHR*, 99 (1984), pp. 530–4.

and the church, but after that would bear arms no more against Christian man, but would go to the holy land never to return'. In theory, any knight could make another, but knighting by the king was sought after because knighthood was coming to be seen as a matter of social rank as much as personal service.[2]

The evolution of heraldry bears this out. It certainly had a military function: 'a man expert in arms' identified the opposing banners for Earl Simon at the battle of Evesham. (In fact Prince Edward, with a typical lack of chivalry in actual conflict, deceived by parading banners he had previously captured from the Montfortians.) But the herald's primary purpose seems always to have been to establish the social worth and precedence of the aristocrats mustered for battle or in some other context. In the margins of his chronicles, Matthew Paris painted scores of shields with their distinguishing devices, reversed beside his reports of the deaths of their bearers: for instance, the azure shield with three golden wheatsheaves of Ranulf, earl of Chester, on his death in 1232. His account of Henry III's voyage to Brittany has against it the king of England's red shield with three lions *passant*. Matthew was so taken with the pictorial qualities of shields that he invented them for King Canute and William the Conqueror, but the forty-five shields of the king of Jerusalem, Henry III, his earls, a number of other English barons, the counts of Flanders, Aumale and Toulouse and the duke of Brabant which are set out on a leaf of the *Liber Additamentorum* are likely to have been based on an actual herald's roll of arms. The first two such rolls to survive contain something under 270 families between them. Glover's roll of *c.* 1255 appears to reflect the state of Henry's court before it broke apart; the king, the Lord Edward and the earls are followed by nine stewards of the household, a butler, chamberlains and English, Breton and Poitevin knights. During Edward's wars the rolls do become more military. Minstrels called 'kings of arms' set out the coat of arms of the knights around Edward's 'great captains'. The great Ragman Roll, a notarial record of homages and fealties made to King

---

[2] T. Borenius, 'The Cycle of Images in the Palaces and Castles of Henry III', *Journal of the Warburg and Courtauld Institutes*, 6 (1943); *Age of Chivalry: Art in Plantagenet England 1200–1400*, exhibition catalogue, ed. J. Alexander and P. Binski (London: Royal Academy, 1987), pp. 341–2; R. S. Loomis, 'Edward I as an Arthurian Enthusiast', *Speculum*, 28 (1953); Paris, *CM*, IV.318–19, for a 'round table' at Walden Abbey in 1252; N. Denholm-Young, *History and Heraldry 1254–1310* (Oxford: Clarendon Press, 1965), pp. 25–9; M. Keen, *Chivalry* (New Haven: Yale UP, 1984), pp. 79–80, 135, 213, 215.

Edward at Berwick in 1296 during the Scottish war serves as the first armorial of the Scottish gentry. A minstrel or king of arms of Sir Robert Clifford, captain and warden of the west march, will have composed the chivalric Song of Caerlaverock, describing in verse the magnificent trapping, feats and coats of arms of the ninety bannerets and sixteen knights who captured the castle in 1300. (Bannerets were leaders of squadrons and paid at twice the rate of knights; their arms are represented on banners rather than the normal shields, in the margins of the Song.) The Falkirk Roll of 1298 lists the arms of the 111 bannerets whose troops, drawn up in four divisions, won the major battle of the war on 22 July 1298.[3]

Different from these rolls is the 'Parliamentary Roll' of 1312, which contains the arms of 1,110 knights, 914 of them grouped by shires, and almost seems an official census of the greater gentry. Many of them must have wanted a coat of arms largely for the social distinction it conferred. Soon it would be the bearing of arms in the heraldic sense which made a man an *armiger* or esquire, and certified him as a member of the aristocracy. But in the thirteenth century, to obtain arms he still had to be seen as a 'strenuous knight', and not just one of the 'literate knights' Matthew Paris described among the judges. Attendance at tournaments, which it was a first duty of heralds to organize, was a means of asserting the continued military role of an aristocracy which was being absorbed into administrative duties in the shires.[4]

The tournament as it emerged in the twelfth century was the confused marauding of small groups of knights typical of feudal warfare. William the Marshal made money and a reputation as what Dr Crouch calls 'player-manager' of a team of knights that went around competing against the 'national teams' of French principalities and exacting ransoms from those they captured – on his death-bed the Marshal claimed to have taken 500 prisoners on the tournament field. It was a matter of prestige for rulers to hold tournaments on state occasions, but they were also anxious to regulate these turbulent events which had very little chivalry about them, except that the participants rode heavy war-horses; they

---

[3] Richard Vaughan, *Matthew Paris* (Cambridge: CUP, 1958; reissued with supplementary bibliography, 1979), pp. 250–3; Paris, *CM*, III.77, 229, VI.469–77; A. R. Wagner, *A Catalogue of English Mediaeval Rolls of Arms* (Harleian Society, vol. 100, London, 1948), pp. 27–34; *Rolls of Arms: Henry III*, ed. T. D. Tremlett and H. S. London (Harleian Society, vol. 113–14, London, 1961/2); Denholm-Young, *History and Heraldry*, pp. 16, 23, 42, 61, 64–119.
[4] Denholm-Young, *History and Heraldry, pp. 103–7.*

could lead to the deaths of important people and boil up into full-scale revolts, so that the Church disapproved of them completely and excommunicated the knights who took part. After their use by the barons as rallying-points against King John, there were attempts to ban them altogether in the reign of Henry III, who had the ambivalent attitude to tournaments of a king who was not himself much of a warrior. But many 'private' tournaments were held. Some vicious encounters between English barons and the king's foreign relations and their men culminated in the 'rout of Rochester' in 1251. This was to be the last of the old mass tournaments, for the Lord Edward combined enthusiasm for jousting and a sense of its military value with a determination to enforce some rules, particularly after William Longsword, another crusader and claimant to the earldom of Salisbury, was fatally wounded at the prince's first taste of the sport on the tournament field of Blyth in 1256. Edward's very first piece of legislation was a statute of arms, which mainly concerned the squires, footmen and spectators, the people who really got out of hand at tournaments; combatants were to have no more than three squires each, and none but his own squire was to assist a fallen knight, under penalty of three years in gaol. Only at the end of his reign did Edward revert to an attempt to stop tournaments, because bored knights were deserting his armies to attend them during lulls in the fighting in Scotland.[5]

Chivalric stories, ceremonial knightings, heraldry and tournaments belonged to a society in which the original significance of feudal tenure had been destroyed by the procedures of the common law that made the knight's fee hereditary property. Great lords looked to their households and retinues for their men-at-arms, not to their feudal tenants. William the Marshal, whom Earl Ranulf of Chester called 'one of the finest knights of the world' when he was chosen, more than eighty years old, to be regent in Henry III's minority, normally had seven to ten knights in his retinue. Of the eighteen who were in his entourage for considerable periods, twelve had no feudal connection with him. They were not drawn from tenants in his honours of Striguil (Chepstow) in Wales or

[5] D. Crouch, *William Marshal: Court, Career and Chivalry in the Angevin Empire, 1147–1219* (London: Longmans, 1990), pp. 174–8; N. Denholm-Young, 'The Tournament in the Thirteenth Century', in *Studies in Medieval History Presented to Frederick Maurice Powicke*, ed. R. W. Hunt, W. A. Pantin and R. W. Southern (Oxford: Clarendon Press, 1948); Keen, *Chivalry*, pp. 86–7, 97; Paris, *CM*, III.88, 135, V.265, 557.

Crendon in Buckinghamshire, but from the 'affinity' he built up by a subtler patronage in his home 'country' from the Thames valley westward through north Wiltshire and Gloucestershire to Somerset. His followers were barons like John of Earley in Berkshire, who was put into William's guardianship as a young tenant-in-chief of the Crown, stayed with him when he became a knight, preferred 'the love and honour' which existed between them to his patrimony, which he forfeited on his disobedience to John's order to return from the Marshal's service in Ireland in 1208, and was one of his master's executors. It was John who put 'his heart, thought and money' into the compilation of the *History of William the Marshal*, which was unique in its time as a biography of a laymen who was not a king, and reflects contemporary standards of knightly behaviour – the dying Marshal is concerned only for his people and insists that his knights must have their robes.[6]

Feudal knight service for forty days in the year could not have provided the men to fight along with the Marshal for his lands in Leinster, nor the ninety-odd men (and a few women) who are known to have left England in 1218–21 on the fifth crusade, along with Earl Ranulf of Chester, his brothers-in-law the earls of Derby and Arundel and the earls of Winchester, Hereford, Oxford and Salisbury. That among them were a serf, a carter, a tanner, a franklin, a teacher (*grammaticus*), a physician and two stewards; and that twenty-seven of those identified came from Yorkshire, where John de Lacy, Ranulf's nephew and constable of Chester, was the dominant figure, and four more were townspeople from the Earl of Chester's Coventry: these facts indicate the importance of local and household connections in the recruitment of crusaders; at Damietta in the Nile delta, Lacy would make a donation to the church of All Saints, Pontefract, to enlarge the burial ground and build a chapel in honour of the Holy Sepulchre and Holy Cross, all for the welfare of his family and people. On Edward's crusade in 1270 there are apparent East Anglian, Welsh marcher and northern groupings of knights, united by land tenure, certainly, but more by clientage and by the sharing of administrative responsibilities in the shires. Chivalric romances helped to foster crusading enthusiasm, and so, despite the Church's official disapproval, did tournaments and heraldry, which mobilized regional

[6] Crouch, *William Marshal*, pp. 133–42, 151–4; extracts from the *Histoire de Guillaume le Marechal*, in *EHD*, III.81–103.

and national loyalties against the Saracens as they did against the French. Dynastic tradition sent families such as the Bohuns and Furnivalls on crusade, and the Song of Caerlaverock evoked the Arthurian past and the crusading achievements of William the Marshal, Clifford's ancestor. In turn, crusading sealed rifts within the knightly class. The leading rebels against King John, Robert Fitzwalter, the earls of Winchester and Arundel and John de Lacy, went on the fifth crusade in 1218 along with the great loyalist, Ranulf of Chester. It was probably on crusade that the marriage was arranged between John de Lacy and Margaret de Quincy, the daughter of Earl Ranulf's sister and the earl of Winchester's brother, which led eventually to John's succession to the earldom of Lincoln, obtained by Ranulf after the defeat of the rebels in the city of Lincoln in 1217.[7]

A *miles strenuus* like Richard Siward, who looked for action wherever he could find it, sometimes following the king in Gascony, Brittany and Wales, and serving on the king's council, sometimes landing up in prison for rebellion, would have needed maintenance when he took the cross with Richard of Cornwall in 1236. (A good war-horse alone cost up to £100.) John de Neville negotiated with Philip Basset, probably in 1239, that Philip should take two knights to the Holy Land at his own expense, but that, once there, all three should fight as members of John's household, at John's expense. There is evidence of large-scale contracting by Edward in the accounts of the receivers of the twentieth granted in England for the crusade of 1270; eighteen crusaders, trusted companions of Edward through the difficult years, are listed as having undertaken to provide contingents amounting to a total of 225 knights, for which they were paid 100 marks a man. The two original contracts which have been discovered are as yet rudimentary, saying nothing of other ranks below the knights, or of compensation for lost horses, or of the sharing of the spoils of war; Adam of Jesmond simply agrees to remain in Edward's service with five knights for a year starting at the September passage to the Holy Land (from Aigues Mortes, on the Mediterranean coast of France), in return for 'six hundred marks in money and

---

[7] J. M. Powell, *Anatomy of a Crusade 1231–1221* (Philadelphia: University of Pennsylvania Press, 1986), pp. 77, 81, 209–46; S. Lloyd, *English Society and the Crusade, 1216–1307* (Oxford: Clarendon Press, 1988), pp. 79, 80, 82, 96–9, 105–9, 125, 127, 161–2, 209; Denholm-Young, *History and Heraldry*, pp. 29, 93; Keen, *Chivalry*, pp. 135–9; D. A. Carpenter, *The Minority of Henry III* (London: Methuen, 1990), pp. 84, 103.

transport, that is to say hire of a ship and water for as many persons and horses as are appropriate for knights'. Most of the knights provided by the contractors were probably already in their households, and there was no great advance in sub-contracting till Edward made new demands on his barons for his wars at home, though men had long been retained in England for military purposes. King John had his retinue of 'bachelors', young knights who might be supported by annual fees from his chamber, and in the course of time the king's household knights became the officer-corps of a professional army.[8]

By 1200 the usefulness of feudal service to the king had been drastically weakened by the fragmentation of knights' fees in the property market, and by the unwillingness of barons throughout western Europe to acknowledge any obligation to provide men for service outside their own countries. The crisis of John's reign was precipitated by the refusal of the northern barons to serve overseas in 1214 on a last attempt to recover Normandy. In any case, a feudal army such as William the Conqueror used to defeat Harold would have been almost as useless in the wars of John against Philip Augustus as the armies of Wellington would be to fight twentieth-century wars. To defend the country against the threat of a French invasion in 1205, the king went behind the barons and ordered the mobilization of all burgesses and 'rustics'; and in 1213, earls, barons, knights and all free men and sergeants, 'whoever they are and from whomsoever they hold, provided they ought to or are capable of bearing arms', were ordered to muster at Dover for the defence of the realm. From 1181, when the assize of arms required all free men to have armour according to their means, the Angevin kings can be seen constructing a militia of crossbowmen and archers, organized for major operations into companies of foot-soldiers about 500 strong, each led by a few mounted sergeants and commanded by a knight as constable or 'master'. To obtain effective forces for service overseas, the Crown resorted to requiring only a proportion of a baron's feudal obligation (say one

---

[8] Lloyd, *English Society and the Crusade*, pp. 80–8, 103–5, 118–25, 136 and app. 5; N. Denholm-Young, *Richard of Cornwall* (Oxford: Blackwell, 1947), pp. 28–9; R. H. C. Davis, *The Medieval War-Horse* (London: Thames and Hudson, 1989), p. 67; B. Beebe, 'The English Baronage and the Crusade of 1270', *BIHR*, 48 (1975); H. G. Richardson and G. O. Sayles, *Governance of Mediaeval England from the Conquest to Magna Carta* (Edinburgh: Edinburgh UP, 1963), pp. 463–5; *CRR*, VIII.393; J. M. W. Bean, '"Bachelor" and Retainer', *Medievalia and Humanistica*, NS, 3 (1972).

knight in ten), and demanding that they serve for the duration of a campaign, equipped and maintained out of money levied from the remaining feudal tenants. The baron paid a fine in lieu of his own service and a scutage which he recovered from each of the knights who did not serve in person; in 1205, 4,000 knights commuted their service to a cash payment. Militarily, the feudal levy was being eclipsed by a profession of 'soldiers', so-called from the wages they received; for a *miles solidarius* these rose from 8d. a day in 1162 to 2s. in John's reign; for a mounted sergeant they then stood at 4d. or 6d., for an infantryman at 2d. or 3d. Politically, raising an army became largely a wrangle about how wages were to be paid. Success for a thirteenth-century king was a matter of building up an effective army based upon the household while maintaining the warrior traditions of the whole aristocracy, which must both finance the professional troops and continue to supplement them on major expeditions and in defence of the realm.[9]

Henry III's administration increased the pressure on the baronage to provide resources, but the king himself did not have the military competence to lead the aristocracy in successful ventures overseas. By the middle of the century many individual magnates, unable to get military service themselves from the tenants of fragmented fees, seem to have recognized only a vastly reduced obligation to the king based on the land they kept in demesne: the abbot of Peterborough's due service came down from sixty knights to five; the earl of Winchester owed sixty-six knights on the old assessment, but appeared with ten on the Welsh campaign of 1245, and admitted an obligation to produce only three and a half (a sergeant would count as the half, or a knight serving for twenty days). The actual number of fighting knights available to the king seems to have amounted to no more than 300–400. In the 1220s the king began to issue writs to the sheriffs to distrain men holding at least one knight's fee to assume the status and functions of a knight, originally perhaps just to make feudal service work at the reduced level. But Henry's expeditions in 1225 and 1230 to relieve the pressure on his remaining lands in France showed the need for a larger pool of knights. Disturbed by the poor response to his

[9] J. C. Holt, *Magna Carta* (Cambridge: CUP, 1965), pp. 64–6, 134, 220; *idem The Northerners* (Oxford: Clarendon Press, 1961), pp. 89–92; A. L. Poole, *Obligations of Society in the Twelfth and Thirteenth Centuries* (Oxford: Clarendon Press, 1946), pp. 35–56; M. Powicke, *Military Obligation in Medieval England* (Oxford: Clarendon Press, 1962), pp. 57–62; I. J. Sanders, *Feudal Military Service in England* (London: OUP, 1956), pp. 50–6.

summons to his tenants-in-chief to assemble with their retinues at Winchester on 27 April 1242 ready to accompany him to Poitou, the king introduced a purely economic qualification for service by ordering the distraint to knighthood of every man possessing £20-worth of land, however and from whoever he held it. In less than a month, the king was compelled to make another appeal for reinforcements of 200 knights, 100 sergeants and 500 Welsh foot-soldiers, since he was 'insufficiently provided with the good men and most powerful men of our realm of England, on whom we specially rely to fight the king of the French'.[10]

As his problems with the magnates intensified, Henry abdicated feudal leadership and relied on his household, in which even a clerk like John Mansell (much later the emissary who obtained from the pope absolution from Henry's oath to observe the Provisions of Oxford) could attract Matthew Paris's admiration for his fighting qualities. Between 1236 and 1245, around seventy-five knights were maintained in the household, at annual fees from the exchequer of £5 to £20 a man and a total cost, excluding robes, of £1,000 a year. Knights commanding the garrisons of royal castles on daily wages probably raised to a hundred the number employed by the king. There were also thirty to fifty mounted sergeants and at least as many foot-sergeants (the garrisons were largely made up of sergeants, under no more than one or two knights, even at Windsor); and based at Westminster there was a company of crossbowmen, whose Gascon constable in the 1240s lent the king money and was an influential figure at court. The household was becoming 'dangerously isolated' from the majority of magnates at this time, says Dr Stacey, as Henry turned to hired men for his councillors as well as his troops. After Henry returned from France on St George's day 1260 with 200–300 knights – probably a much larger force than Simon de Montfort and his friends could have assembled – the king's government and military household were one. His chief councillor, Philip Basset, and magnates like Roger

---

[10] Powicke, *HLE*, pp. 61–5; Carpenter, *The Minority of Henry III*, pp. 360–70; Sanders, *Feudal Military Service*, pp. 60–90; H. M. Chew, *The English Ecclesiastical Tenants-in-Chief and Knight Service* (London: OUP, 1932), pp. 30–4, 52–6; M. C. Prestwich, *War, Politics and Finance under Edward I* (London: Faber, 1972), p. 79; N. Denholm-Young, 'Feudal Society in the Thirteenth Century: The Knights', in his *Collected Papers on Mediaeval Subjects* (Oxford: Blackwell, 1946); Stubbs, *CH*, II.294–6; Michael Powicke, 'Distraint of Knighthood and Military Obligation under Henry III', *Speculum*, 25 (1950); R. C. Stacey, *Politics, Policy, and Finance under Henry III, 1216–1245* (Oxford: Clarendon Press, 1987), pp. 191–3.

Mortimer were retained as members of the household, and even his sheriffs were spoken of as his 'bachelors'.[11]

A civil war was inevitably a war of households. The force that would be decisive in the war between king and barons was that of Edward's household and marcher friends, once the headstrong, unreliable and vicious prince depicted in the Song of Lewes as a mixture of lion and leopard made up his mind what he wanted, beyond revenge for the Londoners' insult to his mother. Matthew Paris tells how Henry's officials warned the king in 1256 that Edward was usurping his authority by listening to the complaints of Gascon merchants against the royal buyers of wine; how Henry feared that the times of Henry II had come again when the king's sons rebelled against their father; and how the prince took the precaution of building up his household to what sounds the improbably high number of 200 knights. In 1259, the Burton annalist reports Edward swearing that he would see satisfied 'the community of the bachelors of England' which complained that the barons had not kept their promises of reform as the king had kept his; it looks as though the knights in the great households had found a common interest in seeking better conditions from their masters, and that the young Edward sympathized with them. By the Dictum of Kenilworth of October 1266 which attempted to settle the state of the realm, landless (presumably household) knights and squires were to pay a ransom of half their goods if they plundered in the war. In the list of those pardoned for their participation in the earl of Gloucester's occupation of London in the spring of 1267 to get better terms for the rebels disinherited after the battle of Evesham, there were several of the earl's 'bachelors', along with other knights, yeomen, clerks and citizens. The Barons' War was a time when the knights showed they had become a power to be reckoned with.[12]

Edward returned to his kingdom from crusade in 1274 with a

---

[11] Stacey, *Politics, Policy and Finance*, pp. 36, 178–86, 192, 250–3; Paris, *CM*, IV.236–7, 366–8; C. R. Cheney, 'The "Paper Constitution" preserved by Matthew Paris', in his *Medieval Texts and Studies* (Oxford: Clarendon Press, 1973); Powicke, *HLE*, pp. 413–14, 419, 433, 635–6.

[12] *EHD*, III.905; Paris, *CM*, v.538–9; R. F. Treharne, *Baronial Plan of Reform, 1258–1263* (reprinted with additional material, Manchester: Manchester UP, 1971) pp. 160–4; *Documents of the Baronial Movement of Reform and Rebellion, 1258–1267*, selected by R. E. Treharne, ed. I. J. Sanders (Oxford: Clarendon Press, 1973), pp. 326–9, cap. 14; *Calendar of Patent Rolls, 1266–72* (London: HMSO, 1913), pp. 145–7.

military reputation such as his father had never been able to achieve: a reputation which allowed him to lead armies into Wales and Scotland combining household professionalism with the service of a wider national community. Contractual, feudal and communal troops were mobilized behind the royal banner. In the wars of 1277 and 1282 the arraying of forces of infantry for local defence was turned to offence for the destruction of the native Welsh princedom (though 8,000 of the 15,000 raised in 1277 were themselves Welsh). Along with the spearmen and crossbowmen, and the longbowmen whose use in war had begun to be learnt from the Welsh, axemen were needed to cut their way through the forests, and carpenters and masons to build the castles with which Edward ringed subjugated Gwynedd. Men with slings from Sherwood Forest would be recruited for the Scottish war, and 445 workmen for the siege of Stirling in 1303, some to construct the engine called 'the Warwolf' which Edward determined on using against the castle before he would accept its surrender. Commissions of array to sheriffs or special commissioners emphasized the duty of all men to be ready 'not only to preserve the peace of our realm but also to repel the Scots our enemies and rebels'. Although the local community could be expected to provide initial expenses and basic equipment, it was realized that arrayed men could not be made to serve without pay, which was provided (at 2d. a day for the ordinary foot-slogger) from the muster point or the border of their county and for the number of days and no more that it was calculated to take them to march to the scene of operations (e.g. five days from Yorkshire to Roxburgh). By the efforts of the chancery which issued the commissions or array, the exchequer which was required to find the wages and the wardrobe which had to supervise the muster, concentrations of troops not exceeded till the seventeenth century were assembled in the 1290s in an attempt to overwhelm the Scots by sheer weight of numbers. The £5,000 a week demanded by King Edward in 1296 was for the wages of 1,000 men-at-arms and 60,000 foot-soldiers, together with the expenses of the household, but probably only 25,000 infantry were raised, 2,500 of them Irish, and conscripted men melted away quickly. For the campaign of 1298 which culminated at Falkirk, 10,500 men were ordered to be arrayed from Wales and 2,000 from Lancashire, and large numbers were recruited from other northern counties, so that the king had almost 26,000 in arms at the time of the battle. The reduction of the 14,800 English (and

some Irish) on the pay-roll on 20 July to 12,600 a week later may
be an indication of actual losses on the field rather than desertions.[13]

Nottinghamshire and Derbyshire in particular could provide
experienced troops to serve in platoons of twenty men led by
vintenars, which were brought together in larger groupings under
mounted *centenars*, in turn perhaps gathered into county or lordship
units. Among the 64 horse and 261 foot in the Edinburgh garrison
in 1300, and the 300 horse and 1500 foot whom Aymer de Valence
raised in the north in 1306 and led to the defeat of Robert Bruce at
Methven, the killing of the Scottish 'traitors' they captured and the
burning of their property, there are likely to have been many
hardened professional soldiers. In warfare of this sort the bannerets
and knights of the king's household formed 'a permanent headquarters staff', members of which could be detached to array men,
bring up relays of infantry and workmen, superintend transport,
escort prisoners or hostages and command garrisons. From the
horse rolls, kept to value the war-horses of the king's men-at-arms
which might have to be replaced, the household can be seen
becoming the nucleus of a paid army in time of war, when extra
knights would be enrolled and bannerets detached to 'seed' the
forces of the magnates. As the decisive campaign against the Welsh
progressed in 1282, the numbers of household troops rose to 245.
For the Falkirk campaign there were almost 800 household troops
on the horse-valuation rolls and 564 other paid cavalry; for the
Caerlaverock expedition two years later, 522 on the household list
and more than 300 other cavalrymen paid by the wardrobe – there
was now no practical difference between the two groups. At the
end of the reign household bannerets like John Botetourt (supposed
by some to be Edward's illegitimate son) were leading raiding
parties of dozens of horsemen and 1,000 or 2,000 foot-soldiers into
southern Scotland, under indentures which specified that none but
the listed troops should be taken, for fear of infiltration by enemy
spies. Earlier, Botetourt had commanded a fleet of ninety-four
vessels manned by 3,578 sailors from east coast ports; another
household knight, Roger of Leyburn's son William, was styled
admiral of the king's fleet in 1297. But an increase in these years in
the importance of bannerets (who received £24 a year in fees and
robes, to the ordinary knight's £12, the sergeant's £2 6s. 8d. and

[13] Powicke, *Military Obligation*, pp. 97, 118–33; J. E. Morris, *The Welsh Wars of King Edward I* (Oxford: Clarendon Press, 1901), pp. 138–9; Prestwich, *War, Politics and Finance*, pp. 92–113; B. C. Keeney, 'Military Service and the Development of Nationalism in England, 1272–1327', *Speculum*, 22 (1947).

the squire's £2) masks the beginning of a decline of numbers in the military household caused by financial stringency.[14]

The challenge to Edward's leadership was how to integrate a conscripted infantry and a professional household force with the service of the feudal aristocracy on which he still depended. While continuing to ask the magnates to provide knights on account of 'the fealty and esteem' they owed him, Edward sought to increase the supply of cavalrymen by mass knightings and the distraint of individuals of a certain substance. All those holding £30-worth of land were ordered in 1282 to 'meet the scarcity of the great horses suitable for war, by procuring such a horse with appropriate horse-armour'. In 1285, £100-worth of land was decided to be a realistic qualification for compulsory knighthood. For the Welsh and Scottish campaigns of 1295 and 1296 all £40 landholders were told to be ready to serve at three weeks' notice. By then a war across the Channel was once more providing the main test of the king's military leadership. Fourteen magnates contracted to take retinues to Gascony in 1294 at royal wages; Edmund of Lancaster, for instance, engaged to serve for a year with 140 men-at-arms for the sum of 4,000 marks. But the grand plan of 1297 to deploy the feudal host on two fronts, the marshal and the constable (Roger Bigod, earl of Norfolk, and Humphrey de Bohun, earl of Hereford) leading an army in Gascony and the king launching an attack on France through Flanders, provoked a political crisis. Bigod and Bohun revived the claim that there was no feudal obligation to serve overseas (even with a quota in Bigod's case which had been reduced from 169 to 5 knights), and insisted that in any case as marshal and constable they should serve alongside the king. Bigod's defiance – 'By God, Sir King, I shall neither go nor hang' – forced Edward to limit the feudal summons to the quotas owed by churchmen and women, and order a muster in London of all £20 landholders (whether knighted or not) and 130 magnates summoned individually for 'the salvation and common utility of the realm'. This was an attempt to put military obligation on to a new footing and was seen as 'disinheriting' the king's subjects of their customary rights, so that the marshal and constable simply refused to enrol the £20 men. The cavalry force Edward got to Flanders consisted of just 140 knights and bannerets and 755 squires. Of these, 550 were household men, 59 Irishmen provided

[14] Prestwich, *War, Politics and Finance*, pp. 54, 57, 111–12; Morris, *Welsh Wars*, pp. 84–5; Denholm-Young, *History and Heraldry*, pp. 35–40.

by the lord of Offaly for advantageous rates of pay, and 35 Scots serving as conditions of their release from prison. Similarly, two-thirds of the 7,810 archers who served in Flanders under 66 mounted constables were Welsh, despite the first extensive array-ing of infantry in the southern counties of England.[15]

His attempt to mobilize £40 landholders in 1300 once again resisted, the king gave up trying to introduce 'national' cavalry service; in 1301, 935 named individuals were summoned to serve for pay. Edward's army had ceased to be feudal without becoming a contractual or a national force. It was too reliant on Irish knights, Gascon crossbowmen, Welsh archers and pardoned felons to be the latter. Nor was it particularly effective. The infantry was of low quality, and the alleged innovation in tactics which combined crossbowmen and cavalry in one line at the battle of Maes Moydog in 1295 was probably accidental. The rise of the longbow which would be so potent in Edward III's reign was only beginning. The same may be said of the raising of armies by large-scale contracting with the magnates which Edward III would employ so successfully – the inducements his grandfather used were miscellaneous ones, such as the promise of conquered territory and the remission of debts to the exchequer, and many magnates were unresponsive. The most important military development of the thirteenth century was probably the separation of the 'strenuous' soldier-knight from the knight of the shire.[16]

KNIGHTS IN THE SHIRES

The change in feudal relationships in the shires is demonstrated by a case in the Shropshire eyre of 1256 involving Fulk Fitzwarin IV. 'Fulk Fitzwarin the younger' alleged that he had been disseised of 120 acres of arable land in Alberbury by his lord, Thomas Corbet, who replied that Fulk had renounced his homage to him for the fee 'in front of several magnates and faithful subjects of the king'. The

---

[15] Davis, *The Medieval War-Horse*, p. 88; Prestwich, *War, Politics and Finance*, pp. 76ff., 251; N. Denholm-Young, 'Feudal Society in the Thirteenth Century: The Knights', *History*, 29 (1944); idem, *History and Heraldry*, pp. 107, 112; N. B. Lewis, 'The English Forces in Flanders, August–November 1297', in *Studies Presented to F. M. Powicke*, ed. Hunt, Pantin and Southern; Powicke, *Military Obligation*, p. 123.

[16] Prestwich, *War, Politics and Finance*, pp. 91, 107–8, 238–9; Lewis, 'The English Forces in Flanders', p. 316.

jurors found that many lords of the marches had been present at a 'love-day' held by Corbet and his nephew, the great Welsh baron Gruffudd ap Gwenwynwyn, to settle a number of disputes between them. There Thomas had quarrelled with Fulk and called him a traitor like his father (the hero of the romance); whereupon Fulk, 'roused by this to violent anger', renounced his homage and said he would hold land from Thomas no more. But in answer to the justices' questions the jurors confirmed Fulk's plea that this had just been angry speech; he had continued to work the land till Corbet seized it, and he was still in occupation of Alberbury Castle. So the justices ordered that Fulk be reseised and paid 40s. damages. It may be that the romance was written down to sustain the Fitzwarin family in this lawsuit, for it emphasizes their emotional attachment to Alberbury. In expiation of his sins 'in killing people and other misdeeds' the hero builds an abbey there, and there the real Fulk Fitzwarin III was buried alongside his second wife in the very year of 1256 in which his son defended his honour. But the real meaning of the case is that even in the marches, where military feudalism lasted longer than elsewhere, the common law had deprived lords of the freedom to decide, in the company of their vassals in their honour courts and love-days, who should and should not hold lands from them.[17]

Among the thirteenth-century aristocracy economic relationships were becoming more important than military ties. A man's influence in his county came to depend on his landed estate and what he could make of it. Henry II's assizes, by preventing a lord from ejecting his tenant or stopping the succession of the heir without the judgement of a royal court, had effectively given the knight full ownership of his 'fee simple'. That ownership was quickly seen to imply a freedom to sell off the fee is shown by the king's attempts, culminating in the Statute of Mortmain of 1279, to limit alienations to the Church in whose 'dead hand' it would stay, and his insistence in the Statute of Quia Emptores of 1290 that all alienations must be by substitution not subinfeudation – the purchaser must take the place of the vendor in the landholding chain and assume his responsibilities, not come in as the vendor's tenant. The purpose of these statutes was to preserve the feudal

---

[17] *The Roll of the Shropshire Eyre of 1256* ed. A. Harding (Selden Society, vol. 96, London, 1980), pp. xxvii–xxviii, no. 335; Meisel, *Barons of the Welsh Frontier*, pp. 20–1; S. F. C. Milsom, The Legal Framework of English Feudalism (Cambridge: CUP, 1976), pp. 176–82.

dues which remained valuable to lords in cash terms, in a society where the free alienation of tenements had become the norm.[18]

By 1300 the number of estates held by knights had fallen far below the number of 6,500 or more knights' fees from which scutage could theoretically have been exacted. William, lord of Kentwell in Suffolk, owing the king the service of ten knights, was admitting in the 1240s that he had lost control of seven of the fees and did not know who held them. At the end of the thirteenth century the number of actual knights has been reckoned at about 1,250 – a few more than the number with coats of arms in the Parliamentary Roll of 1312, and perhaps twice as many as were useful to the king in war. Another 1,500–2,000 freeholders probably had the economic qualification to become knights. The knightly families of this time were the ones that remained when the growing cost of being dubbed a knight, the expense of providing for an excess of daughters and younger sons, and probably most of all failure to meet the challenge of 'the managerial revolution' which began late in the twelfth century, had weeded out the rest. The chief importance of the land market, which appeared first among the knights, was that it permitted over-stretched families to sink down the social scale in a relatively dignified way – and, as with the peasantry, new families (which did not automatically assume knightly status) to rise by reassembling fragments of their estates.[19]

Enough examples of declining families have been given to suggest a 'crisis of the knightly class' in the thirteenth century. The break-up of the original knights' fees of the Conquest seems to have begun in the last quarter of the twelfth century, exactly when the development of the land law and of the final concord as a conveyancing instrument made alienations easy, the normal dynas-

---

[18] T. F. T. Plucknett, *The Legislation of Edward I* (Oxford: Clarendon Press, 1949), pp. 96–108; P. A. Brand, 'The Control of Mortmain Alienation in England', in *Legal Records and the Historian*, ed. J. H. Baker (London: Royal Historical Society, 1978); J. M. W. Bean. *The Decline of English Feudalism, 1215–1540* (Manchester: Manchester UP, 1968), pp. 51–4, 79–97.

[19] Denholm-Young, 'Feudal Society in the Thirteenth Century: The Knights', pp. 56–7; C. Dyer, *Lords and Peasants in a Changing Society: The Estates of the Bishopric of Worcester, 680–1540* (Cambridge: CUP, 1980), p. 49; Sanders, *Feudal Military Service*, p. 55 (from the Memoranda Roll of 14 Henry III); R. H. Hilton, *A Medieval Society: The West Midlands at the End of the Thirteenth Century* (London, 1966), pp. 50–61; E. Miller and J. Hatcher, *Medieval England – Rural Society and Economic Change 1086–1348* (London: Longmans, 1978), pp. 171–4.

tic vicissitudes of too many or too few sons setting off the process. William of Clapton, whose ancestors had held two knights' fees in Northamptonshire since the Conquest, having provided for his four brothers (the youngest as priest of Clapton church), gave his only daughter and two virgates of land to the nuns of Stamford; 180 acres of demesne and nine virgates in the hands of peasants to two nieces as marriage portions; and at least three virgates to the abbey of Peterborough, where he died a monk between 1190 and 1194. (One of the niece's descendants would reassemble the estate of this family by purchase in the thirteenth century.) If a knight had no sons but a number of daughters his lands were divided between them, since none could perform knight service, and their husbands might then sell the shares off, especially if they were at a distance from their own fees. Abbeys acquired the lands of knights on the largest scale, often in return for life pensions or for the payment of debts which the knights had contracted to others. A widow in financial difficulties dispersed the estate of Stivichall in Warwickshire, releasing the last of her demesne to the priory of St Sepulchre, Warwick, in 1249, in return for a third of its produce annually. But lay magnates could also be the beneficiaries of the 'necessities' of knightly families. Probably in the 1260s, James Beauchamp rounded off the estate given him by his father at Acton Beauchamp in Herefordshire with purchases from local freeholders such as John son of Robert of Abetot, who received in return the payment of his debts to Isaac, a Jew of Worcester, and a pension for his mother of a tunic a year and as much grain as James's servants had. Taking the wrong side in civil war was one way of dissipating one's patrimony, as the Disinherited of 1265 knew; another was selling it to raise money for crusade. Hugh fitz Henry put his fee on the market before he took the cross in 1249, and the abbey of Abingdon determined to buy it though it stretched their resources: after all, it was held from the monks, and partly in Abingdon itself, and could not be allowed to pass to a magnate such as Richard of Cornwall.[20]

[20] Postan in *The Cambridge Economic History of Europe*, vol. I: *The Agrarian Life of the Middle Ages*, 2nd edn, ed. M. M. Postan (Cambridge: CUP, 1971), pp. 592–5; E. King, 'Large and Small Landowners in Thirteenth-Century England', *Past and Present*, 47 (1970); E. Searle, *Lordship and Community: Battle Abbey and its Banlieu, 1066–1538* (Toronto: Pontifical Institute of Mediaeval Studies, 1974), pp. 155–6; P. R. Coss, 'Sir Geoffrey de Langley and the Crisis of the Knightly Class in Thirteenth-Century England', *Past and Present*, 68 (1975); C. H. Knowles, 'Provision for the Families of the Montfortians Disinherited after the Battle of Evesham', in *Thirteenth-Century England*, vol. I, ed. P. R. Coss and S. D. Lloyd

Jewish money-lenders introduced abbeys, lay magnates (including the king) and the growing race of stewards and royal clerks to the opportunities of investment in the property of indebted knights. The dealings of such as Adam of Stratton, Master Simon of Walton, who rose to be a royal justice and a bishop ('the good shepherd of Norwich, who devours the sheep' the 'Song of the Barons' called him in 1263), and Walter of Merton, looking to endow his college, provoked the complaint in the 25th article of the Petition of the Barons: Jews, it said, transferred their debts and the lands pledged to them to magnates and powerful men in the kingdom, who held on to the lands even when the debtors were ready to pay. In 1269, the Provisions of Jewry forbade lending by the Jews on the security of the land, but not before Walter of Merton had acquired Cuxham and three other manors by paying the debts of Stephen Chenduit to three Lincoln Jews. The ferocity of Montfortian anti-Semitism against Jewish activities was caused by the fear that Christians, particularly the Crown and its officials, were learning the same techniques. Around 1276, indebtedness forced Geoffrey of Southorpe, the head of a family which had held knights' fees of the abbot of Peterborough from before 1100, to sell Gunthorpe, one of the two manors of his patrimony, to the abbey for 550 marks. The other manor, Southorpe itself, came into the hands of a London merchant, Stephen of Cornhill, foreclosing on its owner's debts, and was bought by the abbey while Geoffrey lay in prison on account of further debts to Queen Eleanor.[21]

However, the majority of landowning families failed within six generations – through lack of heirs, if not through debt – and the land market permitted other families to advance themselves and new dynasties to become established. Because he was a member of the royal household, Sir Geoffrey de Langley, the son of a fairly lowly Gloucestershire knight, had opportunities to acquire lands mortgaged to the Jews, particularly in Warwickshire, which had few religious houses to mop them up; and he brought stronger management to estates where rents had been low and demesnes unprofitable. By good management, but perhaps also because the

(Bury St Edmunds: Boydell, 1986); S. D. Lloyd, 'Crusader Knights and the Land Market in the Thirteenth Century', in *Thirteenth-Century England*, vol. II, ed. P. R. Coss and S. D. Lloyd (Bury St Edmunds: Boydell, 1988), pp. 122ff.

[21] Coss, 'Sir Geoffrey de Langley', pp. 12, 32–3; *EHD*, III.916; *Documents of the Baronial Movement*, ed. Treharne and Sanders, pp. 86–7; King, 'Large and Small Landowners', pp. 35–7.

abbot of Peterborough was his brother, Richard Hotot (d. *c.* 1250), the son of the niece whom William of Clapton had endowed with sixty acres of demesne and two virgates before he retired to the abbey, was able partly to reconstitute and considerably to extend the estate dissipated by his great-uncle. Hotot spent at least 1,000 marks on these purchases – the same as the abbey spent on acquiring Gunthorpe and Southorpe half a century later, and recorded his achievements in one of the earliest lay cartularies, which includes a history of his mother's family – his father's came from nowhere, and the Hotot's name will not be found in thirteenth-century surveys of knights' fees. Thurstan of Thorpe was a villein enfranchised in the reign of John; around the beginning of Edward's reign, Thurstan's grandson William build a new church for Longthorpe (the one that still survives) since the previous chapel was so far from the village that 'the old and infirm often die without the sacraments'. For himself William built a manor house, to which his son Robert added a three-storey tower, perhaps when he became the abbey's steward early in the next century. In 1356 the villein's great-great-great-grandson would become chief justice of the court of common pleas.[22]

Longthorpe tower symbolizes the arrival of a landlord class whose roots spread wider than the knights of the Conquest. In the fifteenth century the term gentleman (*generosus*) would become established for the head of a landed family, who might no longer be a knight or even bear arms as an esquire (*armiger*). In the thirteenth century the range of landholders later called the gentry are best characterized as the people who were able to use the procedures of the Common Law to protect, develop and exploit their family lands. Many knights had very small estates and merged into the ranks of the peasant farmers. The half of a knight's fee which Sir Hugh of Gillingham held of the archbishop of Canterbury in 1273 is described by Professor du Boulay as consisting of 178½ acres 'under wheat, oats, barley, peas and vetches, with numerous marsh-pastures, some meadow and a garden', centred on a thatched manor house, and worked almost entirely by hired labour supervised by a serjeant. However, some knightly tenants had from a very early point increased their holdings by taking on extra fees for a money rent, perhaps from a number of lords at the

[22] Coss, 'Sir Geoffrey de Langley', pp. 6–10, 13; *The Kniveton Leiger*, ed. A. Saltman (London: HMSO for Historical Manuscripts Commission, 1977), pp. viii–ix; King, 'Large and Small Landowners', pp. 44–5.

same time (so losing any exclusive feudal allegiance). Other land might be leased, or 'farmed' just for the tenant's life or for a term of years. Thus in 1237 the archbishop of Canterbury granted Tarring in Sussex to Godfrey le Waleys of Malling (but with no mention of his heirs), for a rent of £80 a year or the entertainment of the archbishop and his entourage at the manor to the same value, and on condition that the peasants there were treated fairly; the grant was a lease for life, though Godfrey's son and then his grandson got it renewed.[23]

Landlords possessing less than about 150 acres of often scattered demesne, and lacking villeins and the profits of jurisdiction, had little over for new purchases when they had paid their labourers and maintained their agricultural equipment. Kosminsky's theory that the minor landlords were the pioneers of agrarian capitalism has been questioned by Dr Britnell's study of the accounts of four Essex estates in the second quarter of the fourteenth century: a higher rate of investment was necessary on small estates simply to keep going. The consolidation of their holdings by legal agreements and lawsuits, not their extension using the profits of the market, was the limit of the ambition of the gentry. Legal actions which had been created to settle differences between feudal lords and tenants were now developed to serve a variety of concerns of landholding families. The main restraint on the landholder's disposal of his fee ceased to be the rights of his lord and became the right of his wife to the third part of his property set aside to support her after his death. The most common variant of the writ of right used in thirteenth-century courts was the writ of dower, which was brought by widows against strangers to whom their husbands had alienated property in their lifetimes as well as against the heirs to the estates. The provision for wives in their widowhood, and the settlement of property on younger sons and daughters when they married, were positive aspects of gentry society, and legal procedures were designed both to facilitate them and to guard against their abuse. An heir could obtain a writ ordering the sheriff to 'admeasure' the dower lands which his ancestor's widow was occupying and restore to him any excess. A father gave a *maritagium* or marriage-gift to a couple and 'the heirs of their

[23] F. R. H. du Boulay, *The Lordship of Canterbury* (London: Nelson, 1966), pp. 99–111; Barbara Harvey, *Westminster Abbey and its Estates in the Middle Ages* (Oxford: Clarendon Press, 1977), pp. 78ff, 107, 115; Miller and Hatcher, *Rural Society and Economic Change*, pp. 174, 180, 213–28; Dyer, *Standards of Living*, pp. 38–9.

bodies' in order to support a new lineage, a purpose which was frustrated if the land was alienated as soon as an heir was born, or if (as the Petition of the Barons complained in 1258) the woman sold it in her widowhood, having produced no children. In 1285 the Statute of Westminster II (c. 1: *De donis conditionalibus*, 'Concerning conditional gifts') ordered that the *maritagium* must descend to the issue of the marriage, apparently (though the statute is ambiguously phrased) to the fourth generation – only then could it be alienated. There already existed writs of 'formedon in the descender' by which the issue of the marriage might claim the land from the heir of the donor, if he tried to keep it from him; and in the case of failure of issue, writs of 'formedon in the reverter' and 'in the remainder' to take the land back to the donor's line or to a designated 'remainderman' (perhaps the heir of another of the donor's children). The invention of the 'fee tail' or 'cut-down fee', the descent of which was limited to a designated line, was of enormous importance for the future of English landed society, because it allowed the gentry to provide for all the members of their families without unnecessarily dissipating their lands and power.[24]

Legal processes served the basic attachment of families to their land in many other ways. 'Writs of entry' were framed to reclaim land which had been granted away by people who should not have done so – for instance, widows could use them to recover their property when it was alienated by their husbands, 'whom in their lifetime they could not contradict'; heirs, to reclaim lands granted away by dowagers, or by their guardians while they were under age; and, most commonly, lessors to get back tenements sublet by the holders of leases which had now expired. The existing tenants of these lands were not the wrongdoers: they 'vouched to war-

---

[24] R. H. Britnell, 'Minor Landlords in England and Medieval Agrarian Capitalism', *Past and Present*, 89 (1980); *The Kniveton Leiger*, ed. Saltman, pp. xii–xiii; Pollock and Maitland, *HEL*, II.422–3; S. F. C. Milsom, *Historical Foundations of the Common Law*, 2nd edn (London: Butterworths, 1981), pp. 121–5, 167–77; *Early Registers of Writs*, ed. E. de Haas and G. D. G. Hall (Selden Society, vol. 87, London, 1970), pp. 8 (18–19), 30 (46), 35 (6), 36–7 (9), 111–12 (15–18); *Berkshire Eyre of 1248*, ed. M. T. Clanchy (Selden Society, vol. 90, London, 1973), pp. 567–8; *Shropshire Eyre*, ed. Harding, p. 383; J. H. Baker and S. F. C. Milsom, *Sources of English Legal History* (London: Butterworths, 1986), pp. 37–53; S. F. C. Milsom, 'Formedon before *De Donis*', *Law Quarterly Review*, 72 (1956); P. Brand, 'Formedon in the Remainder before "De Donis"', *Irish Jurist*, NS, 10 (1975); R. M. Smith, 'Women's Property Rights under Customary Law', *TRHS*, 5th ser., 36 (1986), for family provision amongst the peasantry.

ranty' their grantors, who were obliged to make over equivalent property if the cases were lost. Because an advowson, the right to present a clerk to the bishop for examination and admission to the village church, was a valuable piece of property (a landlord would sometimes seek to make his son the parson) the assize of *darrein presentment* was designed to settle claims to it; the person a jury found to have 'presented last time' would be permitted to do so again – unless, as sometimes happened, the parties agreed to present alternately. The Statute of Westminster II (c. 25) extended the scope of the assize of novel disseisin ('there is no other writ in the chancery which gives plaintiffs so speedy a remedy') from the recovery of tenements and the pasture rights that went with them to claims to take 'reasonable estovers' of firewood and building and fencing material from common woodland. The cognate assize of nuisance had long been available against those who caused damage and injury to a neighbour's holding by obstructing a right of way, diverting a stream to a new mill or setting up a rival market for the produce of the land. A difficult problem was the temporary tenant who 'wasted' the assets of the manor: the dowager, guardian or leaseholder who cut down the woods, slaughtered the breeding stock and drove out or enfranchised the serfs on the heir's or lessor's land. Magna Carta (c. 4) proclaimed a general ban on waste by a guardian in chivalry, but until the Statute of Gloucester of 1278 (c. 5) an action for damages could be brought only after a specific prohibition of the waste had been issued by chancery and defied by the tenant.[25]

The writ of waste was one of an increasing number of writs which did not ask whether the defendant was keeping the plaintiff out of particular landed rights, but peremptorily summoned him to show why (*ostensurus quare*) he had done something forbidden by the king, or not done something the king had ordered him to do. Such writs allowed complainants to bring before the king's courts any injuries they could make out to be trespasses against the king's peace. The earliest example in the registers of writs is a summons to ecclesiastical judges to show why they had heard a

[25] Milsom, *Historical Foundations*, pp. 143–9; *Berkshire Eyre*, ed. Clanchy, pp. 284–5, 568–70; *Shropshire Eyre*, ed. Harding, pp. xxix–xxxi, 383–4, nos. 22, 111; *EHD*, III.317, 417, 443–5; *Early Registers of Writs*, ed. de Haas and Hall, pp. 53, 72, 149 (165); S. S. Walker, 'The Action of Waste in the Early Common Law', in *Legal Records and the Historian*, ed. J. H. Baker (Royal Historical Society, London, 1978); R. C. Palmer, *The Whilton Dispute, 1264–1380* (Princeton: Princeton UP, 1984) for the deployment of the whole range of legal actions.

case about a disputed advowson which the king had prohibited them from doing; the next, an order to justify waste in defiance of a royal injunction. The crucial type of prohibition for the development of the catch-all action of trespass was that of injury to the persons and property of the many people, royal servants and others, who had obtained special grants of protection from the king. Then, from the 1220s cases of personal assault, breaking into others' property and destroying or carrying off their crops began to be brought to the king's courts as breaches of a public order reckoned to bind everyone without specific injunctions. To make sure royal judges took notice, the plaintiffs in early claims for damages for personal injury added to the allegation of breach of the peace the statement that it was done 'by night', or 'violently', or by a gang of armed men with swords and axes, and the developed writ of trespass had to say *cum vi et armis* ('with force and arms') as well as *contra pacem domini regis* ('against the lord king's peace'). The complainant might also tell a story about the way the property trespassed upon had come into his hands (e.g. from one of the king's enemies after the battle of Evesham); or about the granting of the market which the defendant had prevented him from holding; or cite an Edwardian statute forbidding the type of trespass. But eventually *contra pacem* and *vi et armis* were just labels to bring even such civil injuries as the negligence of a doctor into the king's court.[26]

The knights of the shire were first brought into direct relationship with the king's government in the administration of the legal procedures developed for their benefit. Henry II had created not only the petty assizes of novel disseisin and mort d'ancestor to reverse specific and recent wrongs in the transmission of feudal tenements, but also a procedure by 'grand assize' to decide who had the better right to the land in the long term. A claimant by writ of right was required to trace the descent of the tenement to more remote 'dates of limitation' than those used in the petty assizes. The use of juries assembled by sheriffs on the orders of the

---

[26] *Early Registers of Writs*, ed. de Haas and Hall, pp. 5, 26, 53, 93, 138, 139, 142, 154, 241, 285–6; *Select Cases of Procedure without Writ under Henry III*, ed. H. G. Richardson and G. O. Sayles (Selden Society, vol. 60, London, 1941), pp. cviii–cxxxiv; *Shropshire Eyre*, ed. Harding, pp. xxxii–lviii; S.F.C. Milsom, 'Trespass from Henry III to Edward III', *Law Quarterly Review*, 74 (1958), pp. 201, 411–12, 429; *idem, Historical Foundations*, pp. 153–4; *Berkshire Eyre*, ed. Clanchy, pp. 492–3; *Royal Justice in the Medieval English Countryside: The Huntingdonshire Eyre of 1286*, ed. A. R. and E. B. DeWindt (Toronto: Pontifical Institute of Mediaeval Studies, 1981), nos. 189, 204, 205, 840.

king automatically took issues of landholding out of the lords' courts into the king's, but there was a sentiment that the basic right to a feudal tenement should still be decided by a jury of the claimant's fellow knights. The lists of knights summoned for the grand assize incidentally provide a check on the numbers available to run the local administration, seeming to confirm Denholm-Young's figure of 1,000–2,000 knights in the whole country. In some counties there appear to have been too few knights for their judicial and administrative needs. In 1258 the barons complained that the king was so free with grants of exemption from jury service that in many counties it was not possible to hold grand assizes for lack of knights. Knighthood had probably become restricted to a smaller circle since 1221, when complaints were made at the Worcestershire eyre of the exactions of the men of Droitwich from the (seemingly numerous) 'knights of the shire' who came to town to buy food. Soon after that time those who valued the rank and accepted the expense became careful to be designated *milites* in the witness-lists of charters, from which it can be calculated that in Edward I's reign there were about 200 knightly families resident in Gloucestershire, Warwickshire and Worcestershire, spread over some 1,100 villages.[27]

A fair attendance of landowners, whether or not they had assumed the rank of knight, was essential to the fulfilment of the manifold functions of the shire court. All free tenants were required to do suit to the usually monthly court, where the suitors acted as judges in the cases of debt, breach of contract, assault, seizure of crops and unjust distraint which were brought to it by oral complaint. Suit may have been a burden for individuals but it was a vital necessity for the community. In 1226, Lincolnshire knights

---

[27] Pollock and Maitland, *HEL*, I.147ff; Harding, *The Law Courts of Medieval England* (London: Allen and Unwin, 1973), pp. 60–2, 157; *Shropshire Eyre*, ed. Harding, nos. 13, 16, 30, 410, 459 etc.; above, p. 197 and n. 19; *Documents of the Baronial Movement*, ed. Treharne and Sanders, p. 89; *Parliamentary Writs and Writs of Military Summons*, ed. F. Palgrave, 2 vols. (Record Commission, London, 1827–34), I.417; *Royal Justice*, ed. DeWindt and DeWindt, pp. 155, 185, 202; *Rolls of the Justices in Eyre for Lincolnshire 1218–9 and Worcestershire 1212*, ed. D. M. Stenton (Selden Society, vol. 53, London, 1934), pp. 565 (no. 1149), 568 (no. 1157); P. R. Coss, 'Knighthood and the Early Thirteenth-Century County Court', in *Thirteenth-Century England*, ed. Coss and Lloyd, II, pp. 53–4; D. F. Fleming, '*Milites* as Attestors to Charters in England, 1101–1300', *Albion*, 22 (1990); Hilton, *A Medieval Society*, pp. 54–5; J. Quick, 'The Number and Distribution of Knights in Thirteenth Century England: The Evidence of Grand Assize Lists', in *Thirteenth-Century England*, ed. Coss and Lloyd, I.

and stewards refused, as contrary to the provisions of Magna Carta, the sheriff's request that they return the following morning to hear 140 pleas left over from the county court day for lack of daylight, whereupon the sheriff adjourned the cases (against protest) to the wapentake courts, 'so that the poor might have justice'. Plaints were judged by the suitors under the sheriff's presidency; of a wider range of cases brought by royal writs of *justicies* – claims for customs and services, rights of wardship, the return of title-deeds, the rendering of accounts to executors, pasture rights, the abatement of nuisances, the demarcation of boundaries between estates and remedy for a whole variety of trespasses – the sheriff was sole judge. The king expected cases of small value to be dealt with locally. In the Statute of Gloucester of 1278 (c. 8) Edward ordered that sheriffs should 'hold pleas of trespass in counties as they used to be pleaded', and that no one should have a writ before the king's justices unless damage of at least 40s. could be shown. (The purpose of the statute was not to limit the shire court to 40s. cases, though defendants soon interpreted it that way when it suited them.)[28]

Without an experienced group of suitors the sheriff could not have carried out the vast range of judicial duties loaded upon him. Historically, and still procedurally, cases got from the feudal courts to the courts of common law by way of the county. Since the early twelfth century it had been the rule that a dispute between the tenants of two different lords could not be settled in the honour court of either, but must go to the county court. A case in the seignorial court was brought to the county by a writ of *tolt*, and from there to the eyre or bench by a writ of *pone*, or if the tenant sought a grand assize, by a writ of peace. The sheriff might be ordered to take with him four knights and go to the lord's court to record a plea in which false judgement was alleged, so that it could be reconsidered by the king's justices; and since the county itself was not normally 'a court of record', the sheriff and four knights might have to execute a writ of *recordari facias loquelam* concerning

[28] Pollock and Maitland, *HEL*, I. 547–52; W. A. Morris, *The Early English County Court: An Historical Treatise with Illustrative Documents* (Berkeley: University of California Press, 1926); J. S. Beckerman, 'The Forty-Shilling Jurisdictional Limit in Medieval English Personal Actions', in *Legal History Studies 1972*, ed. D. Jenkins (Cardiff: University of Wales Press, 1975); *EHD*, III. 354, 417; *Documents of the Baronial Movement*, ed. Treharne and Sanders, pp. 85 (17), 89 (29), 127 (14); *Early Registers of Writs*, ed. de Haas and Hall, pp. xli–xlii, lxxii–lxxiii, 25, 70–4, 81, 215–17, 260; *Select Cases of Procedure without Writ*, ed. Richardson and Sayles, p. xlii.

its own proceedings. Parties of four knights (though sometimes they were found not to be properly knights) were also kept busy visiting litigants who had excused themselves from attendance, in order to certify their sickness and register their appointment of attorneys. But non-knightly freeholders were also called upon by the sheriff to make up juries for cases to be heard by the king's justices in eyre in the county or far away at Westminster. Pleas of right might be settled by the agreement of the parties to submit specific issues to jury trial (e.g. whether a man through whom land was claimed to have descended to the demandant had possessed an elder brother). The jurymen in these cases and in the petty assizes could not be exclusively knights because they had to be neighbours of the parties or (in assizes of nuisance) of the offending pond or obstruction – people 'who best knew the true facts'.[29]

Small groups of knights represented the landowners brought together in the shire court in their dealings with government. Magna Carta (c. 18) required four knights to be associated with the two royal justices who were to visit each county four times a year and hear petty assizes. According to Bracton, when the justices for all pleas came, they should call together in 'some private place . . . four or six or more of the greater men of the county, who are called "buzones" of the county and on whose nod the views of the others depend, and . . . consult with these men in turn'. (The only other known use of the obscure term *buzones* is to refer to the four knights held responsible for a false judgement in the shire court of Gloucestershire in 1212, and for bearing false record of the case to the king's court.) And in 1258 the first of the Provisions of Oxford ordered the choosing of 'four prudent and law-worthy knights' from each county, who 'on every day when the county court meets, shall attend to hear all complaints of any trespasses and injuries whatsoever by sheriffs, bailiffs, or any other persons', enrol them and take pledges for the appearance of the complainants and defendants before the baronial justiciar on his eyre. The outcome of this investigation into the abuses of all officials in the localities, both the king's and the magnates', was the promulgation of the Provisions of Westminster in October 1259, which restricted the right of lords to impose on tenants new

[29] *Early Registers of Writs*, ed. de Haas and Hall, pp. 45, 113, 117, 119, 124–5, 155–6, 187, 195, 276–7 (e.g. no. 723); *Lincolnshire and Worcestershire Eyre*, ed. Stenton, pp. 318–19, 522–4, 767; *Shropshire Eyre*, ed. Harding, nos. 128, 227, 283.

obligations of suit to their seignorial courts, and removed the need for prelates, barons, monks and women to attend the sheriff's tourn unless their presence was specially required; forbade itinerant justices to amerce townships because not all men of the age of twelve years had come before the sheriff and coroners for inquests upon dead men; reaffirmed the duty of the eyre to inquire into the behaviour of 'the rich men of the land' and their bailiffs, and report to the next parliament; and resorted again to four knights of each shire 'to review the wrongs committed by the sheriffs', and investigate abuses of forest pleas. The same combination of inquiry by four knights, complaints to the eyre and legislation in parliament was applied to local government by Edward I in the 1270s. Shire government turned the knights of the shire into a political force and provided the first consistent interest of the commons in parliament, not just in reaction to the fiscal exploitation of the counties by the government, but also, as David Hume realized, because the shire court had made the freeholders 'a kind of community' with positive interests to pursue.[30]

Some of the *buzones* no doubt owed their influence to stewardships in the service of magnates, but the operation of the machinery of comital justice gave them a certain independence of their betters, which the tendency of royal favourites to ignore both the sheriff's authority and the rights conferred on under-tenants by Magna Carta was a reason for using. In 1226–7 knights may have made common cause with the magnates in protests against the high-handedness of royal sheriffs, but the Provisions of Westminster were the culmination of something of a campaign against the magnates' oppressive use of their hundred courts and overriding of the gentry's rights; later, the magnates' exercise of their liberties was a main target of the Hundred Rolls and *quo warranto* inquiries. The first aim of the shire community was, however, to curb the arbitrary exercise of the sheriff's power, and to get local men with some regard for local interests appointed sheriffs. This is

---

[30] *Bracton on the Laws and Customs of England*, tr. S. E. Thorne, 4 vols. (Cambridge, Mass.: Harvard UP, 1968–77), II.327; Coss, 'Knighthood', p. 52; *Introduction to the Curia Regis Rolls*, ed C. T. Flower (Selden Society, vol. 62, London, 1943), pp. 62–4; *CRR*, VI.228; *Documents of the Baronial Movement*, ed. Treharne and Sanders, pp. 99, 112–15, 119–23, 137ff; J. R. Maddicott, 'Magna Carta and the Local Community 1215–1259', *Past and Present*, 102 (1984); *idem* 'Edward I and the Lessons of Baronial Reform: Local Government, 1258–80', in *Thirteenth-Century England*, ed. Coss and Lloyd, I; F. M. Powicke, *The Thirteenth Century: 1216–1307* (Oxford: Clarendon Press, 1953; 2nd edn, 1961; issued in paperback, 1991), pp. 144–6; above, p. 33, for Hume's view of the county court.

a theme which appears in the reign of John, who was driven by inflation to increase the Crown's financial demands on the sheriffs, and thus the sheriffs' pressure on their shires. The king might make some of his familiars custodians of shires for seven years at a time or even 'in perpetuity', but he also saw the advantage of selling the right to have local men as sheriffs to county communities which could find the price of 1,000 marks or more. Magna Carta (c. 45) promised that only justices and sheriffs who knew the law of the land and meant to observe it would be appointed (as the Song of Lewes would demand with regard to all the king's ministers); and more significantly ordered that the habitual abuses of sheriffs and foresters 'be investigated at once in every county by twelve sworn knights of the same county'. Chapter 42 of the 1217 reissue of the Charter, limiting the county court to one meeting a month and the tourn to two a year may have been a result of this investigation. Magna Carta and the Charter of the Forests, which were ordered to be read out in the county court, were the touchstones of local liberties until 1258, when the Provisions of Oxford (c. 17) set out the new requirement that sheriffs be 'loyal men and sound landholders' of their counties, chosen yearly, and paid by the king out of his own revenues sufficiently well for them not to need to oppress the people. The Provisions of Westminster (c. 22) laid down the procedure of appointment to a shrievalty: four 'vavassors' who would be 'useful in that office to both the king and the county' should be elected in the shire court and presented to the barons of the exchequer for them to choose the best.[31]

In practice it was usefulness to the king which was decisive in appointments to sheriffdoms, but this allowed for much bargaining with the men of the shires. The promises of Magna Carta that no increments would be charged on the ancient farms of the shires and that royal bailiffs would pay cash for corn and chattels were not of the sort that kings kept. For the twenty years up to 1258, Henry was driven back from direct taxation to reliance on judicial and county revenues, and from 1241 imposed swingeing new increments, which in turn forced the sheriffs to rely on extracting

[31] Maddicott, 'Magna Carta and the Local Community', pp. 27, 49; W. A. Morris, *The Medieval Sheriff to 1300* (Manchester: Manchester UP, 1927), p. 145; Holt, *Magna Carta*, pp. 53–4, 79–80; R. V. Turner, *Men Raised from the Dust* (Philadelphia: University of Pennsylvania Press, 1988), pp. 76–7; *Documents of the Baronial Movement*, ed. Treharne and Sanders, pp. 109, 119ff, 155; Treharne, *The Baronial Plan of Reform*, pp. 121ff, 205ff.

more from their tourns, fees and rights of hospitality. After the breakdown of the baronial experiment with annually apointed and paid custodians of the shires, Edward I reverted to a system of farmer-sheriffs. Yet Henry and Edward learnt that a harsh exploitation of shire revenues was conducted better by local men than by the *curiales* who held many of the sheriffdoms in Henry's minority and into the 1230s and were more like regional governors than revenue collectors. The break with this regime came with the king's marriage to Eleanor of Provence and the establishment of the queen's uncle, William, bishop-elect of Valence, as Henry's chief councillor. William had no commitment to the *curiales*, but equally no network of clients in England to put in their place. Quite quickly a new class of sheriff came into existence, which was answerable to an exchequer engaged in tightening up its control of shire revenues and in appointing new local officials, the escheators, to improve the management of crown lands. Both sheriffs and sub-escheators were now generally from knights of standing in the country rather than at court. Encouraging complaints against them by the people of the shires under the new articles of the eyre of 1254 or the Hundred Rolls inquiry was a way of controlling this growing corps of local administrators.[32]

The Provisions registered the emergence of the vavassors or under-tenants of the magnates as the real rulers of the counties under the Crown. A successor of Robert 'le Vavasour', a tenant of the houses of Percy and Lacy, and a notorious sheriff of Nottinghamshire and Derbyshire in the years 1246–55, would become a baron by receipt of an individual writ of summons to parliament at the end of the century. So would the successors of the first two sheriffs of Shropshire and Staffordshire of the new type, Thomas Corbet (1248–50) and Robert of Grendon (1250–5). Corbet, Fulk Fitzwarin's adversary, held the strong castle of Caus and a barony from which he acknowledged a service of five knights; connected by marriage to the Welsh princes and the powerful Mortimers of Wigmore, he was prominent in Anglo-Welsh wars and politics up to his death in 1274 at the age of ninety-two. To this 'quarrelsome, crafty, vindictive' man, 'the foe of his own relations and his own vassals', the office of sheriff was an additional weapon for use in private quarrels. At the eyre of 1256, the first after his term of

[32] Holt, *Magna Carta*, p. 325 (cc. 25, 28); D. A. Carpenter, 'The Decline of the Curial Sheriff in England 1194–1258', *EHR*, 91 (1976); Maddicott, 'Edward I and the Lessons of Baronial Reform'; Powicke, *The Thirteenth Century*, pp. 63–4.

office, he was fined twenty marks for disseisin, ten marks for several trespasses, five marks for many defaults and five marks for not producing a man for whom he had stood pledge; juries and individual complainants testified to his false imprisonment of people at Caus, in one instance of a shire bailiff who had failed to present a proper account.[33]

The wider class of gentry defined economically by distraint of knighthood was brought into the ruling of the shires at the instance of an increasingly ambitious royal government. As the king attempted to restrict the liberties of the great lords he found himself compelled to return power to the knights of the counties for the enforcement of his peace. What Bracton's *buzones* were to be lectured about by the justices in eyre was the king's ordinances for the pursuit of criminals. In the northern and western counties, where no tithings had ever developed to take responsibility for the criminous members of communities, sheriffs and private lords employed 'serjeants of the peace', who were hated for their powers of arbitrary arrest and right to demand their sustenance from the people. The communal militias which were formed, as William Lambard put it in the sixteenth century, 'to defend the coasts and country both from foreign and inward enemies', needed persons 'much like the Lieutenants of shires now in our days' to lead them 'in times of great trouble'. In 1238 the justice of forests was ordered to assemble his foresters and the knights and free men sworn to arms in Wiltshire, Gloucestershire and Northampton-shire to clear the forests in those parts of bandits, in conjunction with a force of ten serjeants from the king's household. Ad hoc commissions appointed wardens of coastal and border areas under threat: the constable of Dover to guard the Cinque Ports and prevent the export of ships and timber to the king's enemies; the constable of Colchester to keep the ports of Essex; the sheriff of Devon to keep the coast and the peace against the pirates of Lundy; commissioners to guard the coast of Northumberland and the northern borders against the Scots. From these 'captains and keepers of the peace' (*capitanei et custodes pacis*) were emerging by the end of the century the wardens of the Scottish marches and the admirals of the eastern and southern coasts. And from the com-

[33] Coss, 'Knighthood', p. 134; G. E. Cokayne, *The Complete Peerage of England, Scotland, Great Britain and the United Kingdom*, new edn by Vicary Gibbs and others (London: St Catherine Press, 1910–59); *Shropshire Eyre*, ed. Harding, pp. xxi–xxii; R. W. Eyton, *Antiquities of Shropshire*, 12 vols. (London, 1854–60), VII. 15, 22, 81.

missioners appointed from time to time 'for the preservation of our peace and of tranquillity' in particular inland counties was crystallizing the office of keeper, soon justice, of the peace, by which the gentry were to rule the counties of England until the nineteenth century.[34]

Such commissions were first marked in 1233–4, the winter of Richard the Marshal's rebellion against the regime connected with Peter des Rivaux, and were consolidated during the Barons' War, when both sides realized the necessity of controlling the county communities. The barons were the main innovators, needing to counter the power of the sheriffs over whom the king had reasserted control, and when they gained the upper hand in July 1263 they appointed a 'keeper of the peace' for each shire. Apart from confiscation of the property of the king's men, which they restored only when the owners swore to observe the Provisions, the keepers' primary concern was day-to-day policing. They appointed constables; they restored plundered goods and protected the property of the Church; and they proclaimed the coming of commissioners to hear and determine complaints against the peace and the Provisions, took security for prosecution, attached the accused persons and empanelled juries. In December 1263, as he left England for Amiens where King Louis was to give judgement on the barons' cause, Henry appointed *custodes* of his own in many shires. This was a more blatantly military arrangement: the southern counties each had one or two keepers, but in the north formidable bands of *custodes* were attached to groups of counties: eleven keepers, with Balliols, Bruces, Nevilles and Percies prominent, were assigned jointly to the five most northern shires. After the battle of Lewes, the barons reappointed a single *custos pacis* for each county, with instructions to prevent the carrying of arms, arrest marauders and see to the election of knights for the coming parliament; the keepers were prohibited from interfering with the sheriffs' administrative functions, but they were given control of castles and told to combine the levies of adjacent counties where necessary for defence against the growing power of the king's

---

[34] *EHD*, III, no. 51; *Bracton on the Laws and Customs of England*, tr. Thorne, II.327–8; R. Stewart-Brown, *The Serjeants of the Peace in Medieval England and Wales* (Manchester: Manchester UP, 1936); *Shropshire Eyre*, ed. Harding, pp. xvii, xxii, 196, 223; A. Harding, 'The Origins and Early History of the Keeper of the Peace', *TRHS*, 5th ser., 10 (1960); Powicke, 'Distraint of Knighthood', pp. 459, 462; *idem, Military Obligation*, caps. 5 and 7; *EHD* III, no. 33, for the important assize of 1242.

party; in Powicke's words, they were 'Simon de Montfort's commissars'.[35]

For the restoration of order after Evesham keepers were assigned to twenty-two shires at one time or another by the king. Again these were the products of military emergency, but they showed a basic continuity of function with the baronial keepers, and particular knightly families were by now becoming established in the office. Sir Richard de Tany was a baronial keeper in Essex in 1264, and therefore needed a pardon in 1267, though by that time Sir Richard de Tany the younger had been appointed to keep the county for the king; the latter was again a keeper when Edward I ordered the election of *custodes pacis* in all counties in 1277 from knights not accompanying the king to Wales, and he appears as a warden of the maritime parts of Essex in 1295, the year before his death. Though they long continued to be used to array troops, the *custos pacis* began to lose the functions of a military captain as civil war receded into the past and military operations departed to the marches and beyond. The emphasis shifted to the keepers' job of leading the shire levies to arrest malefactors made bold by the absence of the great men in the wars. Commissions were sometimes issued for the pursuit of particular criminals, but more often their names and those of their receivers would have to be discovered from local jurors. By chance there survives, alone from the thirteenth century, a single membrane of such inquests, 'made by Richard de Tany, keeper of the peace of the lord King in the county of Essex' in 1277. A jury of the county presents a steward of a Sir Ralph de Tany for arbitrarily arresting and hanging a free man from his master's lordship of Walthamstow, against the king's peace and the liberty of the abbess of Barking (who held the entire hundred from the king). The reeve and four men of Hatfield Peverel, who are the jurors of the vill, report housebreaking by three men of Richard of Colworth, their stealing of goods worth 30s. or more and their harbouring by a fourth man; the jurors of Fairsted present three housebreakers and a thief; the jurors of Hanningfield tell of housebreaking and assault 'with force and arms' by a servant of the Templars, for which the hue and cry was raised, and of another housebreaking in which a surcoat worth 12s. was stolen; and the jurors of Boreham accuse a serjeant, a reaper

[35] Harding, 'Keeper of the Peace', pp. 91–2; Calendar of Patent Rolls, 1258–66 (London: HMSO, 1910), pp. 271, 287; *Documents of the Baronial Movement*, ed. Treharne and Sanders, pp. 291–3.

and a carter of the abbot of Waltham of reaping and appropriating an acre of their master's oats.[36]

Treated as a lesser class of crime (later called misdemeanour) below the capital felonies, 'trespass' would prove as useful a concept for extending the JPs' control of local society as it was for bringing civil injuries within the scope of the common law courts. A major step in the development of the office of *custos pacis* was the appointment of keepers in 1287, this time usually two per county; two was the customary number for a judicial commission, and indeed the keepers of 1287 were appointed to enforce the provisions of the two-years old Statute of Winchester for watch and ward, the maintenance of arms according to income and the presentment and arrest of trespassers, because the justices of assize who were originally given the responsibility were not going on circuit as often as had been intended. Supervision of community policing under the Statute of Winchester would long remain the basis of the JP's authority, but inquests and arrests immediately generated pressure for power to try those indicted. Articles added to Magna Carta and the Charter of the Forests in the Lenten parliament at Westminster in 1300 ordered that there

be chosen in each county by the community of that county three men of standing, knights or other upright, wise and prudent men, to be sworn as justices and assigned by letters patent of the king under his great seal to hear and determine, without other writ than their common warrant, the complaints that shall be made of all those who contravene or offend in any of the said points of the aforesaid charters in the counties to which they are assigned, as well within liberties as outside them, as well as of the king's officers in their private capacities as of others; and determine the complaints heard day by day without allowing the delays that are allowed at common law; and that these same knights have power to punish all those convicted of offending against any point of the aforesaid charters, where as there has been said there was previously no remedy at common law, by imprisonment or by fine or by amercement, according to what the offence demands . . . And because many more evildoers are in the land than ever there were . . . because the statute which the king caused to be made but lately at Winchester has not been kept . . . let the three knights be charged to keep and maintain this statute who are assigned to correct infringements of the great charters.

[36] Harding, 'Keeper of the Peace'; H. M. Cam, 'Some Early Inquests before "Custodes Pacis"', *EHR*, 40 (1925), reprinted in her *Liberties and Communities in Medieval England* (Cambridge: CUP, 1933).

At least fourteen of the keepers of 1287 were chosen in 1300 also.[37]

The necessity and, as the eyre declined, the difficulty of controlling the gentry justices themselves was already apparent in 1305, when the king issued the first commission of trailbaston to parties of justices each comprising one or two professional judges and two or three barons who were usually veterans of Edward's wars, their job to tour the country on five circuits and punish the 'enormous trespasses' committed in England since the beginning of the Scottish war. Highway robbery and obstruction of justice had always been typical gentry crimes; conspiracy, the running of protection rackets, the laying of false complaints and the terrorizing of juries to their private advantage were now shown to be activities at which gentry-justices were particularly adept. At the Lincoln trailbaston sessions juries found for example that Sir Ralph of Friskney, 'a *custos pacis* by the king's writ', had promptly retained in his household malefactors indicted before him at Boston, and sent them to beat people in fairs and markets (presumably to extract protection money). He was also 'a common sustainer and maintainer of pleas and complaints', and for six years or more had been threatening jurors of assizes and inquests, so that they dared not come to court or tell the truth; in particular he terrorized the jurors who had indicted him, deriding them as 'rustics'. Friskney had been one of the justices of 1300 to enforce the charters and the Statute of Winchester. In 1303 he received a licence to crenellate his dwelling-house, and sat for Lincolnshire in the parliaments of 1306 and 1307. In the year that he was imprisoned for his misdeeds by the trailbaston justices, he ironically sat on a commission concerning trespasses alleged against one of them.[38]

The members of the 'county community' at the end of the thirteenth century ranged from knights experienced in the Scottish war to men qualified for knighthood who did not choose to take it

---

[37] Harding, *Law Courts*, pp. 95ff; *idem*, 'Keeper of the Peace', pp. 99–100; *EHD*, III, no. 59 (Statute of Winchester), and pp. 497, 500 (Articles upon the Charters, c. 1, 17).

[38] Harding, *Law Courts*, pp. 90ff; *idem*, 'The Revolt against the Justices', in *The English Rising of 1381*. ed. R. H. Hilton and T. H. Aston (Cambridge: CUP, 1984), esp. pp. 181–2; *idem*, 'Early Trailbaston Proceedings from the Lincoln Roll of 1305', in *Medieval Legal Records Edited in Memory of C.A.F. Meekings*, ed. R. F. Hunnisett and J. B. Post (London: HMSO, 1978), pp. 148–9 and cases 44, 45; cf. Charles Moor, *Knights of Edward I*, 5 vols. (Harleian Society, London, 1929–32); M. T. Clanchy, 'Highway Robbery and Trial by Battle in the Hampshire Eyre of 1249', in *Medieval Legal Records*, ed. Hunnisett and Post, pp. 42ff.

up, and lesser, sometimes obscure, people like Richard Pike, one
of the justices for Somerset in 1300, who could not even find
sureties for his attendance at a special parliament called in May of
that year concerning the observance of the charters. It is hard to
see any original bond between them except their looking to the
king for powers which they could use to their local advantage. At
the centre of county society were families like the lords of Harley
near Much Wenlock, from whom was descended Queen Anne's
great earl of Oxford. At the Shropshire eyre of 1256, a year in
which he was listed among the holders of £6-worth of land who
were not knights, Richard of Harley was a juror of Condover
hundred and one of the four men appointed to walk the disputed
boundaries between the land of John Fitzalan and the abbot of
Lilleshall, and he paid 20s. for a perambulation of the boundaries
of his own wood at Belswardyne. The family rose in the world on
the death before Michaelmas 1269 of Richard's son Robert, whose
son, another Richard, was an infant and at the disposal of Prince
Edward, custodian of the heir to the Cantilupe barony from which
the Harleys held a knight's fee. The prince entrusted the young
Harley to his clerk Robert Burnell, a Shropshire man who in a few
years time would become chancellor of England and bishop of
Bath and Wells. Whether or not by Burnell's agency, Richard of
Harley was married by 1283 to a Shropshire heiress, Burga of
Willey, who had been regranted the estates forfeited when her
father was killed on the baronial side at Evesham. Certainly further
property came to the couple by the grant of Philip Burnell, made
with the assent of his uncle the bishop and witnessed by a
sprinkling of Shropshire knights and squires.[39]

In 1297, Richard of Harley was a £20 landowner who received
the summons to serve overseas which caused such uproar, and in
the same year he had the first of a string of commissions to assess
taxes and to array troops (500 foot to be taken to Newcastle). By
1300 he seems to have been the representative figure in the county.
He was chosen as one of its two knights for the Lenten parliament,
and under the *Articuli supra cartas* promulgated there he was chosen
as one of the three justices for Shropshire. The Articles also

---

[39] *Return of the Name of Every Member of the Lower House of the Parliaments of England,
Scotland and Ireland* (Parliamentary Papers, 1878, vol. 52 in three parts), 1.12;
Parliamentary Writs, ed. Palgrave, 1.419; *Book of Fees*, part II (London: HMSO,
1923), p. 966; *Shropshire Eyre*, ed. Harding, nos. 138, 352, 670, 983; for the
parallel rise (though to greater heights) of the Etchinghams of Sussex, see N.
Saul, *Scenes from Provincial Life* (Oxford: Clarendon Press, 1986), p. 4.

conceded that the men of the shires could elect their sheriffs, and once again Richard was chosen and began two chequered years as sheriff of Shropshire and Staffordshire. In the Articles the king had commanded sheriffs to take care to choose impartial jurors; at assizes in Shropshire a case had to be adjourned when all the jurors were challenged on grounds that Richard, who chose them, was related to the defendant. His impartiality must also have been compromised in these years by his service as steward in Shropshire for the Fitzalan earls of Arundel and for King Edward's cousin Amadeus, count of Savoy. In April 1303 the king wrote to the coroners and community of Shropshire and Staffordshire, informing them that Richard of Harley was, 'as the king learns', insufficiently qualified to be their sheriff, and ordering them to choose another for presentation at the exchequer. On this the rifts in county society became apparent: a body of magnates, abbots and priors objected to the new name which was submitted as required under the seals of six knights, and asked the king to make the choice. Meanwhile his release without warrant of two people accused of homicide had landed Harley in Shrewsbury gaol in his turn. In January 1304 the king's sergeant was to take him to York to give an account of his tenure of the sheriffdom. Yet he was to receive further commissions as keeper of the peace and arrayer, and in 1305 he resumed a run of eight elections to parliament, henceforth as the first of the two knights named.[40]

Twenty-three knights and thirty other men-at-arms were summoned from Shropshire to a great council at Westminster in 1324. This was the dimension of a county community which was represented by thirty individuals from twenty-four different families in the thirty-four parliaments between 1290 and 1327 for which we have names. Two generations of the Rossall family which had been providing knights for the grand assize from early in the century served in parliament, along with new men like William of Ludlow, son of the great wool merchant. The fact that Harley went to eight parliaments, another Shropshire man to seven and a third to six suggests that people were not unwilling to be chosen. There was a shared interest to be promoted at court. That interest was not the moderation of the king's demands for money, to which the knight's assent was as yet purely formal, but the

---

[40] Eyton, *Antiquities of Shropshire*, II, 31, 51, 58, 60, III.17, IV. 99–101, 123, VI. 230; Morris, *The Medieval Sheriff*, pp. 184–5; *EHD*, III.499; *Calendar of Close Rolls, 1302–7* (London: HMSO, 1908), pp. 84, 113.

securing from the Crown of chartered rights and the administrative and judicial powers which would safeguard their social position. Their influence stemmed from their employment as 'the work-horses of thirteenth-century government', their representative role from the actions of four knights on behalf of the county court. In 1227 four knights from each of thirty-five counties were summoned to a meeting to settle disputes between sheriffs and the men of the shires about some articles of Magna Carta. In 1258 the Oxford parliament evolved the choosing of four knights to record complaints in each county. There followed the summons and counter-summons by the barons and the king in 1261 of three knights from each shire to attend political negotiations; Simon de Montfort's summons of two knights from each county along with two burgesses from each city and borough to parliament in the impasse after the battle of Lewes; and the calling of four knights from each county in 1275 to Edward's 'first parliament general after his coronation', at which was promulgated the Statute of Westminster I with its detailed reforms of the local administration of justice.[41]

If they wanted to, the magnates of a shire could usually dictate who was elected. Yet the multiplication of the knight's administrative and judicial functions was making the gentry a distinct and powerful interest-group, which the nobles would have to cultivate in more subtle ways. It was not the magnates but the knights who insisted in 1254 that the charters be confirmed. It was a knight, Henry of Keighley, that Edward took five years to track down as the person who had submitted a bill on behalf of those 'who pressed us outrageously' at the Lincoln parliament of 1301, and was ordered to be confined in the Tower without irons but in such a way that this 'courtesy' was not thought to come from the king. Keighley was one of the justices for Lancashire in 1300, and sat for the county for the third time in the Lincoln parliament. His bill, purporting to be 'on behalf of the whole community of the land',

[41] *Return of the Name of Every Member of the Lower House*; J. G. Edwards, 'The Personnel of the Commons in Parliament under Edward I and Edward II', in *Essays in Medieval History Presented to Thomas Frederick Tout*, ed. A. G. Little and F. M. Powicke (Manchester: Manchester UP, 1925), reprinted in *Historical Studies of the English Parliament*, ed. E. B. Fryde and E. Miller, 2 vols. (Cambridge: CUP, 1970), I; J. C. Holt, 'The Prehistory of Parliament', in *The English Parliament in the Middle Ages*, ed. R. G. Davies and J. H. Denton (Manchester: Manchester UP, 1981), pp. 16, 20–1, 23, 25, 27–8; *Documents of the Baronial Movement*, ed. Treharne and Sanders, pp. 51, 99, 113–15, 247, 303; *EHD*, III, no. 47.

asked that statutes contrary to the charters be annulled; 'that the authority of the justices assigned in the counties to keep the charters should be put beyond doubt, with the counsel of the prelates, earls and barons'; and that there should be new auditors of complaints against officials. More money should not be demanded of sheriffs, for this simply impoverished the people of the shires. Finally, nothing of the fifteenth granted by the people of the kingdom should be levied unless these matters were dealt with by the following Michaelmas; and when they had been dealt with, four knights should be chosen to assess and collect the tax. By the 1320s the commons in parliament, led by the knights, would actually seize the initiative from a nobility weakened by the struggles of Thomas of Lancaster and his supporters with the king, and begin by repeated petitioning to develop an agenda for legislation on such matters of vital importance to the gentry as the location of the wool staple, the wearing of clothes according to rank and the magnates' corruption of justice.[42]

During the formative years of Parliament in the late thirteenth and early fourteenth centuries the Crown attempted to bring the clergy and laity together into a single assembly for the granting of taxation. In January 1283 the experiment was tried of holding two assemblies of the knights and burgesses alongside councils of the clergy in the two provinces of Canterbury and York. From the 1290s to the 1330s the Church's method of representation of the diocesan clergy by proctors was brought into many meetings of Parliament itself. Thus in Edward's last parliament at Carlisle in January 1307, the clergy of the Shropshire archdeaconry of Hereford diocese were represented by William, rector of Silvington, and Walter of Lugwardine, rector of Munsley in Herefordshire. The parochial clergy might have been permanently joined to the knights in representing the interests of the counties to the king, as the prelates were joined with the lay magnates. If the laity learnt from the clergy how to petition, however, they used their knowledge to denounce the 'vexations, citations and exactions' of the church courts, which they declared more oppressive than all the *Curiae laycales.* So it is not surprising that the clergy (though not,

---

[42] L. Riess, *The History of English Electoral Law in the Middle Ages,* tr. K. L. Wood-Legh (Cambridge: CUP, 1940), p. 52; *Calendar of Patent Rolls, 1281–92* (London: HMSO, 1893), p. 266; J. R. Maddicott, 'Parliament and the Constituencies, 1272–1377', in *The English Parliament,* ed. Davies and Denton, p. 72; *EHD,* III, nos. 88, 94; W. M. Ormrod, 'Agenda for Legislation, 1322–c.1340', *EHR,* 105 (1990).

of course, the spiritual lords) effectively withdrew from Parliament in Edward III's reign, to grant taxes thereafter in provincial convocations. It is difficult to see that there was ever a place for the clergy as representatives of the shire community alongside the knights, whose chief interest in Parliament was to gain more powers for themselves as *custodes pacis*. By the fourteenth century the shires were coming to be ruled by amateur landlord-magistrates with little regard even for the now professionalized county court which had been their springboard. At the 1305 trailbaston sessions a tale was told of knights who had broken up the proceedings of the Lincoln court with force and arms, actually while the king was holding a parliament in the city four years earlier, because a case brought there by writ of right was going against them.[43]

[43] J. H. Denton, 'The Clergy in Parliament in the Thirteenth and Fourteenth Centuries', in *The English Parliament*, ed. Davies and Denton; Maddicott, 'Parliament and the Constituencies', pp. 71–2; J. H. Denton and J. P. Dooley, *Representatives of the Lower Clergy in Parliament 1295–1340* (Royal Historical Society, Woodbridge, 1987); *Memoranda de Parliamento*, ed. F. W. Maitland (Rolls Series, London, 1893), p. cviii, 21; *RP*, I.60 (nos. 180–2), 189–91, 219–23; R. C. Palmer, *The County Courts of Medieval England, 1150–1350* (Princeton: Princeton UP, 1982); Harding, 'Early Trailbaston Proceedings', no. 15.

6

MAGNATES

——— . ———

The judicial power achieved by the gentry in their individual
counties did not translate easily into political influence at the centre
of the country's affairs. There, a notion of representation derived
from feudal relationships remained dominant – that the tenants-in-
chief represented their tenants and the whole 'community of the
realm' in dealings with the king as 'lord paramount'. Chapter 14
of Magna Carta, though it was excluded from reissues, appears to
set out the accepted principle. Before levying an aid (beyond the
three to which every lord was entitled from his tenants: for his
own ransoming, his eldest son's knighting and his eldest daughter's
first marriage), and before imposing a scutage in place of knight
service in the field, the king would 'obtain the common counsel of
the realm,' by summoning individually the archbishops, bishops,
abbots, earls and greater barons, while the lesser tenants-in-chief
would be summoned generally through his sheriffs and bailiffs. In
all letters of summons the reason for it would be stated; the
business would then go forward on the day arranged, and by
implication all be committed by the outcome, 'even if not all those
summoned have come'.[1]

The provision in Magna Carta for the consultation of the lesser

[1] F. M. Powicke, *The Thirteenth Century: 1216–1307* (Oxford: Clarendon Press,
1953; 2nd edn, 1961; issued in paperback, 1991), pp. 540–1; J. C. Holt, 'The
Prehistory of Parliament', in *The English Parliament in the Middle Ages*, ed. R. G.
Davies and J. H. Denton (Manchester: Manchester UP, 1981), pp. 25ff; *idem*,
Magna Carta (Cambridge: CUP, 1965), pp. 321–3.

men matured into the election to Parliament of 'knights of the
shire', who were not, of course, usually tenants-in-chief of the
king, nor by the fourteenth century sometimes even knights in the
old sense at all. There was an equally important development in
the conception of the greater men who gave the effective assent.
The assembly that witnessed the reissue of Magna Carta in 1225
consisted almost exclusively of barons in a narrow sense, that is to
say of men who held clusters of knights' fees from the king in
chief, though the list of those said to have granted a tax of a
fifteenth of moveable wealth to the king in return for the charter
included ordinary 'knights and free tenants'. Even 'free men and
villeins' who can have had nothing to do with the transaction were
listed among the grantors of a fortieth in 1232, clearly because, as
beneficiaries of the charters, they were coming to be seen as
members, though subordinate ones, of a single political community. At the same time the looser term 'great men' was coming
into use as a substitute for 'barons' to refer to the people who dealt
with the king on the community's behalf. *Magnates* allegedly
presented a draft constitution to the king in 1244; and in 1258 'the
magnates of the realm' told the king, 'as though with one voice',
that his demands for money had become intolerable. 'Barons' is
still the preferred term in the Provisions of Oxford for those who
are to choose twelve sound men from their ranks to negotiate with
the king's council at regular parliaments, but they are now synony-
mous with 'the community of the land' or at least with the body
which speaks for it. Open 'letters of the barons' were sent out in
December 1263 under the names of Henry, bishop of London,
Walter, bishop of Worcester, Simon de Montfort, earl of Leicester
and steward of England, Hugh Despenser, justiciar of England,
and twenty others to announce that they were submitting the
baronial cause to the arbitration of King Louis of France. In the
mid-century struggles, the barons in Parliament assumed a representative role, as the commons were to do a little later.[2]

Prelates and lay magnates alone attended forty-two of the forty-
nine parliaments and councils of Edward's reign before 1295; ten
of the twenty-two parliaments from 1295 to 1307 they shared with

[2] L. Riess, *The History of English Electoral Law in the Middle Ages*, tr. K. L. Wood-
Legh (Cambridge: CUP, 1940), p. 65; Paris, *CM*, IV.185–7, 366, V.20–1, 680,
682, 688, 695; *Documents of the Baronial Movement of Reform and Rebellion,
1258–1267*, selected by R. E. Treharne, ed. I. J. Sanders (Oxford: Clarendon
Press, 1973), pp. 104, 111, 285; *EHD*, III.385–7, for the overmighty 'magnates'
whom the Statute of Marlborough instructs to cease their illegal distraint.

representatives of the knights, burgesses and lower clergy. In the later years of the reign, summonses to Parliament by individual writ thus began to mark off 'the lords' as a separate order from the mere gentry. Eight earls and ninety-four 'barons by writ' were summoned to the Lenten parliament of 1305, nine earls and seventy-seven barons to the parliament at Carlisle in 1307. At the front of the 'Parliamentary Rolls of Arms' 155 names (in addition to the earls') are given, before the mass of armigerous families is broken down by counties. This seems to be a comprehensive list of the people summoned to parliaments in the last years of Edward I's reign and the early years of Edward II's by individual writ – summoned in this way not so much because they were tenants-in-chief of the Crown but because their landed wealth and therefore military and political importance transcended the boundaries of any one county. If everybody had come in 1305, 102 earls and barons would have found themselves in the company of about 74 knights of the shire and 160 burgesses, and facing 70 to 80 spiritual lords (bishops, abbots and masters of the military orders) backed by 145 representatives of the lower clergy (deans, archdeacons and diocesan proctors).[3]

The magnates, lay and spiritual, shared ideals and preoccupations with the knights, leading burgesses, deans and archdeacons. For instance, they were all touched by 'the business of the Cross'. Many who purchased the status and privileges of crusaders did not fulfil their vows in person, yet deeds in the East were still a matter of national pride. There was less enthusiasm for the papacy's 'internal crusades' against its enemies: the barons' objections to King Henry's costly ambitions on the pope's behalf in Hohenstaufen Sicily were a main cause of the mid-century crisis. The expiation for the civil strife of that time was Edward's crusade, which was supported by the granting in 1270, after months of careful negotiation, of the first aid from prelates, magnates and free men for thirty years, and the only national tax (as opposed to a papal tax) ever levied for crusading purposes. Magnates and

[3] *Handbook of British Chronology*, ed. E. B. Fryde, D. E. Greenway, S. Porter and I. Roy (Royal Historical Society, London, 1986), pp. 545–52; *Memoranda de Parliamento*, ed. F. W. Maitland (Rolls Series, London, 1893), pp. cx–cxv; *RP*, 1.188–9; *Parliamentary Writs and Writs of Military Summons*, ed. F. Palgrave, 2 vols. (Record Commission, London, 1827–34), 1.410ff; M. C. Prestwich, *Edward I* (London: Methuen, 1988), pp. 446–7; G. O. Sayles, *The Functions of the Medieval Parliament of England* (London: Hambledon, 1988), p. 61, for the writ summoning the abbot of St Albans in 1258.

lesser men were also regularly drawn together in response to the demands of royal government. Like a knight or burgess, though by a different procedure, a baron was called to parliament 'to consent to those things' (in the matter of taxation) which happened 'to be ordained by the prelates and other magnates and captains' collectively. Finally, lords great and small were landowners, having to adapt to the same changes in the agrarian economy. The essential difference of the magnates was that they had to cope with both demanding kings and the increasingly confident gentry, to whom a developing relationship with the Crown was giving the more secure position in the country.[4]

The spiritual and lay magnates were alike in many ways. They came from the same landholding families and had the same preoccupations with landed rights. They all founded markets and fairs and new towns. They owed military service on the same scale to the king, and saw the same reductions in their quotas of knight service – in the cases of the bishops of Lincoln and Winchester and the abbot of Peterborough, as in that of Earl Warenne, from sixty knights to five. Differences between the political roles of the spiritual and the lay lords stemmed from an extra ideological element in the relationship of churchmen to king and realm. A prelate had three duties: the first to defend the land and liberties of his cathedral's or abbey church's patron saint quite as fiercely as any lay lord his dynastic lands; the second, to place the authority of the Church and the skills of clerks at the service of kings and temporal lords who in turn acknowledged their duty to protect the clergy's rights; and the third, to show obedience to the papacy, which was tightening its grip on the administration and resources of the Church. The different loyalties generated tensions. The clergy's defence of their rights to take tithes and to receive grants of land 'in free alms' (that is exempt from the usual feudal services), and the fact that in any case a church never died, so that its lands could not be subject to normal succession dues or escheat through lack of heirs – these things invited the jealousy of lay lords. Issues of jurisdiction over cases with both spiritual and temporal dimensions, such as the disputed ownership of tithes, and the argument about the property rights, or lack of them, of bastards, caused

---

[4] C. Tyerman, 'Some English Evidence of Attitudes to Crusading in the Thirteenth century', in *Thirteenth-Century England*, vol. 1 ed. P. R. Coss and S. D. Lloyd (Bury St Edmunds: Boydell, 1986); S. Lloyd, *English Society and the Crusade, 1216–1307*, (Oxford, Clarendon Press, 1988), pp. 72ff; Paris, *CM*, III.127; Powicke, *The Thirteenth Century*, pp. 222–3; *Parliamentary Writs*, ed. Palgrave, I.166.

trouble with the common lawyers. The king acknowledged a responsibility to protect the interests of feudal lords generally by legislating against grants of property into 'the dead hand' of the Church: by taking charge of the lands of bishoprics and abbeys during vacancies, he recognized a duty to the clergy analogous to his wardship of the heirs of tenants-in-chief. (He turned both obligations to his fiscal advantage, by selling licences for mortmain grants, and by the exploitation of the lands of vacant churches as his 'regalian right'.)[5]

Tensions were there between the prelates themselves. Many owed their position to the king, took the side of the common law in jurisdictional disputes, and resented the 'high church' doctrines of such as Grosseteste, who would have withdrawn them from royal service. The mutual co-operation of King and Church which was the medieval norm tested the political skills of the prelates to the hilt, for they were both the exponents of royal government and the natural leaders of the baronage in defence of the liberties it threatened. Their position was made more complicated by the interventions of popes over their heads to deny or support the king's wishes in the choice of archbishops and bishops; to absolve John, Henry III and Edward I in succession from their oaths to observe Magna Carta, the Provisions of Oxford and the Confirmation of the Charters, on the grounds that they swore under duress and in derogation of a king's essential right to appoint and dismiss his councillors; and to suspend Archbishops Stephen Langton and Robert Winchelsey at the king's instance for opposition to the royal will. Most disturbingly of all, popes forbade the king to include the clergy in general taxation, with far-reaching consequences in Edward's later years, while occasionally imposing a clerical tax for royal use. Though Henry of Keighley's bill in the Lincoln parliament of 1301 assured the king of a fifteenth if the people's grievances were met, the prelates dared not 'assent to a contribution being made from their goods or from the goods of the clergy contrary to the pope's prohibition'.[6]

[5] Powicke, *The Thirteenth Century*, pp. 458–60; E. G. Kimball, 'Tenure in Frank Almoign and Secular Services', *EHR*, 43 (1928); N. Adams, 'The Judicial Conflict over Tithes', *EHR*, 52 (1937); M. E. Howell, *Regalian Right in Medieval England* (London: Athlone Press, 1962).

[6] W. H. Bryson, 'Papal Releases from Royal Oaths', *Journal of Ecclesiastical History*, 22 (1971); F. M. Powicke, *Stephen Langton* (Oxford: Clarendon Press, 1928), p. 132; *idem*, *The Thirteenth Century*, pp. 220–4; S. K. Mitchell, *Taxation in Medieval England*, ed. S. Painter (New Haven: Yale UP, 1951), pp. 196–200; *EHD*, III.512.

ABBOTS

Heads of religious houses made up the majority of prelates summoned to meet with the king. The authoritative reissue of Magna Carta in 1225 had among its witnesses the heads of nineteen monasteries, led by the abbots of the Benedictine houses of St Albans, Bury St Edmunds, Battle, St Augustine's Canterbury, Westminster, Peterborough, Reading and Abingdon, and of the richest house of Augustinian canons at Cirencester. In the parliaments at the end of Edward's reign the representatives of these ancient monasteries, all holding lands from the king in chief, had come to be outnumbered by abbots from the new orders which had established themselves in England since the early twelfth century, twelve Premonstratensians and seventeen Cistercians (or forty-two Cistercians if an extra group summoned in 1305 appeared). By comparison, bishops from seventeen English and four Welsh dioceses were summoned in that year.[7]

But none of the large body of abbots played the role in thirteenth-century politics that several of the smaller group of bishops did. Monks were held back by their rules from involvement in secular business (Henry and Edward conspicuously made no use during their reigns of the fourteen bishops of English dioceses who were monks or canons), and abbots did not have the experience bishops acquired in the administration of their dioceses. The most prominent monks in public life were probably the priors of cathedral monasteries. (In ten of the seventeen dioceses the cathedral was an abbey church, the bishop the titular abbot.) Henry of Eastry, prior of Christ Church, Canterbury, from 1285 to 1331, was not only a famous builder and manager of the priory's estates, but also possessor of a wide knowledge of diplomatic affairs, advisor of Archbishop Winchelsey at the time of his battle of wills with King Edward, and later the archbishop's vicar-general. John de Caux, prior of St Swithun's Cathedral at Winchester and then abbot of Peterborough, scandalized Matthew Paris by becoming a justice in eyre, and from 1260 till his death in 1263 served as treasurer of England. The one other monk to hold a major office, Richard Ware, abbot of Westminster, was also treasurer between 1280 and 1283 – he would not have needed to stir very far to do his work. Ware's predecessor in office was Sir Joseph Chauncy,

---

[7] Holt, *Magna Carta*, p. 357; *Memoranda de Parliamento*, ed. Maitland, pp. cxi–cxii; *RP*, I.188–9.

prior to the Hospital of St John of Jerusalem in England. Abbots and priors were important to the king for their standing in the country (which must have been a reason for using abbots as itinerant justices), the wealth they commanded and their financial expertise (that of a Chauncy, the head of military order used to managing crusading funds, no doubt especially useful).[8]

The abbots of some monasteries – Glastonbury, Battle, Reading, Bury St Edmunds, Ramsey, Ely, Tynemouth – enjoyed a comprehensive jurisdiction over cases both civil and criminal within their precincts, which in Battle's case extended for about a mile and a half around the abbey and in Bury's over a fair-sized town. Sometimes, as at Reading, this only meant that the king's justices held separate sessions on the abbey's lands with the abbot or his steward on the bench and receiving the fines, but at Bury the abbot seems to have appointed his own justices in eyre, as did the bishop-abbot at Ely. For the king the abbots' extensive jurisdictions were the exercise of government on his behalf and consequently as subject to the supervision and challenge of the king's lawyers as the franchises of any layman.[9]

Houses of the newer orders never had franchises like the black monks, but the widening of the body of abbots at parliaments brought the king into contact with more subtle forms of territorial influence, which were of particular importance in those northern areas which were monasticized by the Cistercians in the twelfth century. Every monastery had links of business and fraternity with surrounding landholders, from whom its monks were very likely drawn. Wary as they were of the influence of princes and magnates, and forbidden to hold lands except in free alms, even the Cistercians had patrons, perhaps descendants of the lords who had

---

[8] *The English Parliament*, ed. Davies and Denton, pp. 89–91; D. Knowles, *The Religious Orders in England* vol. I (Cambridge: CUP, 1948), pp. 49–55, 321–2; Powicke, *The Thirteenth Century*, pp. 49–55, 261–2; Paris, *CM*, v.84, 466; *The Roll of the Shropshire Eyre of 1256*, ed. A. Harding (Selden Society, vol. 96, London, 1980), pp. xi–xiii; *Handbook of British Chronology*, 3rd edn, ed. Fryde, Greenway, Porter and Roy, p. 104.

[9] M. D. Lobel, 'The Ecclesiastical Banleuca in England', in *Oxford Essays in Medieval History Presented to H. E. Salter* (Oxford: Clarendon Press, 1934); H. M. Cam, 'The King's Government as Administered by the Greater Abbots of East Anglia', in her *Liberties and Communities in Medieval England* (Cambridge: CUP, 1933); E. Searle, *Lordship and Community: Battle Abbey and its Banlieu, 1066–1538* (Toronto: Pontifical Institute of Mediaeval Studies, 1974), pp. 225ff; *The Chronicle of Bury St Edmunds, 1212–1301*, ed. and tr. Antonia Gransden (London: Nelson, 1964) , pp. 23–4, 67, 125; *Reading Abbey Cartularies*, ed. B. R. Kemp, 2 vols. (Camden Society, 4th ser., vols. 31, 33, London, 1986–7), I.84, 90, 95.

provided the land and resources when the abbeys were founded. A monastery might act as the repository of its patrons' family traditions, as the Augustinian house of Little Dunmow in Essex was for the Fitzwalters, recording their births, deaths and marriages, and reporting in its annals the quarrel between Robert Fitzwalter and King John. An earl would visit his monastery with great ceremony, as Earl Richard de Clare visited Tewkesbury in 1259, and in a period of turmoil 'gave the kiss of peace to all, great and small'. The Clares were buried at Tewkesbury, the Bohun earls of Hereford usually at their foundation of Lanthony-by-Gloucester, until they became earls of Essex as well and inherited from the Mandevilles the patronage of Walden Abbey. When Henry de Lacy, earl of Lincoln, moved the abbey of Stanlow, which was threatened by flooding from the Mersey, north to Whalley, he stipulated that the bones of his ancestors should go along too.[10]

It was only natural that specific benefits should be expected in return for the prayers and other spiritual services of the religious, from casual gifts of vestments to major endowments and 'protection' against the many hazards facing rich corporations in their dealings with other lords and with the ecclesiastical authorities. Large resources were transferred to monasteries by the gift of advowsons and the appropriation of the tithes of parish churches, into which the recipients would put underpaid curates. The earl of Lincoln helped the Stanlow monks with money and advice to defend their rights at the papal court in Rome, and they regretted his absence when they were in trouble with Walter Langton, their bishop and the royal treasurer, over a debt of £1,000. Patrons would come to the aid of 'their' priories in disputes with mother-houses. (Many seignorial monasteries were dependencies, ruled over by priors, not abbots.) Earl Ranulf of Chester withdrew his assent to the appointment by the abbot of Angers in France of a prior for the Augustinian house of Spalding in Lincolnshire, when the monks disliked it. A patron had a duty to guard the estates of a monastery during a vacancy, like that of an overlord to protect those of a deceased feudal tenant till the heir came of age; to see also that an improvident abbot or prior did not alienate the convent's property. He expected to be consulted by bishops – all of whom would be patrons of one or two convents themselves –

[10] S. Wood, *English Monasteries and their Patrons in the Thirteenth Century* (Oxford: OUP, 1955), pp. 4, 124ff.

about matters such as the election of priors, in which they were not permitted to interfere directly.[11].

Once again, the patron's duties of wardship and protection became property rights to be exploited. Like parochial advowsons, the three hundred and more monastic houses in the hands of magnates were inherited, alienated and contested in lawsuits. Tenure of its lands in free alms did not remove expectations that a house would present its patron's sons to parish churches appropriated to it, take in his nominees as monks and nuns and provide hospitality to his family extending to the accommodation of their horses and dogs. Monasteries were called upon to make gifts and loans to patrons – above all to place their credit at the patrons' disposal. The Clare foundations regularly stood surety for loans to the earls of Gloucester from the Crown, other earls and the Jews. When the king's Poitevin relatives were expelled in 1258, their treasure was seized from various monasteries.[12]

The king himself was the patron of more than a hundred of the greatest houses which were of royal foundation, and when he wanted money from the Cistercians he claimed to be the patron of monasteries in general. Royal attitudes exemplify patronage in both its beneficent and its exploitative guises. Edward called his youngest son Edmund at the prayer of the abbot of Bury St Edmunds. The very first clause of the first Statute of Westminster is directed against the impoverishment of houses of religion, and the impairment of their accustomed charity, by the uninvited 'coming of the great who had means enough' to entertain themselves. While the Statute of Mortmain of 1279 forbade the receiving of lands by men of religion whereby the services 'due from such fees, and which were provided from the beginning for the defence of the realm, are unjustifiably withdrawn, and chief lords lose their escheats', the second Statute of Westminster of 1285 (c. 41) provided for the recovery by the king or other patrons of frankalmoign lands which had been alienated by abbots, priors and wardens of hospitals 'contrary to the form of the gift'. Reading Abbey's cartularies show the king's solicitude for one of his abbeys. In the first year of his reign, in a charter witnessed by William Marshal earl of Pembroke, William earl of Salisbury, Robert

[11] *Ibid.*, pp. 40–100, 139, 142, 144, 147, 150, 155, 156, 160; *The Charters of the Anglo-Norman Earls of Chester, c. 1071–1237*, ed. G. Barraclough (Record Society of Lancashire and Cheshire, vol. 126, Liverpool, 1988), nos. 426–31, for the relations between the earl and his monastery of Spalding.

[12] Wood, *English Monasteries and their Patrons*, pp. 118–19, 158–60.

FitzRoger and Hugh Bardulf, King John granted Reading a gold mark annually, inspired by the presence in the abbey of the Hand of St James (brought from Germany in the reign of its founder, Henry I, by Henry's daughter and John's grandmother, the Empress Matilda). The stream of royal benefactions to the abbey continued with a grant in 1205 of an annual fair at Reading for three days at the feast of St Philip and St James (1 May), to which Henry III added in 1265 a six-day fair at Leominster for Reading's daughter-house, and with repeated confirmations of grants of lands, churches and liberties. Henry supported the abbot in a dispute over liberties with the Reading townspeople; and in 1286 Edward put the abbey of Reading and the priory of Leominster into the hands of his clerk Ralph of Broughton to restore them to solvency, which after three years Robert Burnell was able to congratulate Ralph on achieving. At this time a new Cistercian monastery founded by Edward in his own earldom of Chester in 1270 as he prepared to leave on crusade was rising at Vale Royal.[13]

Yet it was the king whose travels put the greatest burden of entertainment on monasteries such as Glastonbury, Reading, St Albans, Bury St Edmunds and Dunstable; his men who were repeatedly alleged to have flouted St Edmund's liberties. The king's horses, sick and well, were stabled at abbeys; retired royal servants pensioned off and converted Jews required to be accommodated in them. Henry resorted constantly to the religious for money. In 1235 he toured the Thames valley and midland counties from July to September to drum up funds from groups of abbots and priors assembled by the sheriffs according to a carefully planned schedule. Thousands of marks were raised, but the Cistercians and Premonstratensians usually held out, and Matthew Paris describes how the Benedictines also defeated the king's favourite device of speaking to each abbot separately. Though the provincial chapter of the Black Monks had forbidden such practices, it was demanded of them in 1258 that they stand surety for the repayment of a loan of 2,500 marks towards the Sicilian enterprise, and the abbot of Westminster, 'infatuated with false promises', gave way; but Waltham, the next house visited by Simon Passelew, the king's

---

[13] *Ibid.*, pp. 101, 117, 126; Powicke, *HLE*, pp. 718–19; *EHD*, III.397; Barbara Harvey, *Westminster Abbey and its Estates in the Middle Ages* (Oxford: Clarendon Press, 1977), pp. 176ff, for the working of the Statute of Mortmain; C. R. Cheney, *From Becket to Langton: English Church Government 1170–1213* (Manchester: Manchester UP, 1956), p. 159; *Reading Abbey Cartularies*, ed. Kemp, I.69–122; Prestwich, *Edward I*, pp. 113–14.

agent, maintained that Westminster's obligation to the Crown was unique – and sent warnings of what was happening on to other abbeys.[14]

Monastic houses were at the forefront of economic activity, and some had enormous wealth: with an income probably rising to more than £3,000 a year the abbey of Glastonbury was the richest ecclesiastical lord in the country; and St Albans had 100 monks early in the century. The special character of large monastic communities demanded central organization of the flow of produce from their estates. Under abbots or priors who were often of local origin (Henry of Eastry was from one of Canterbury Cathedral Priory's manors), land was reclaimed from marsh and fen, and money beyond the resources of a single manor invested on drainage, fencing and the provision of dovecotes, granaries, sheepfolds and medicine for the livestock. The central management of great flocks of sheep was developed as at Croyland, and the bulk marketing of their wool as transacted by the abbey of Eynsham through a merchant of Witney. New towns were founded, like Newland by Eynsham and Airmyn by St Mary's, York. But investment in reclaiming land that was marginal anyway, and in buying up land mortgaged by knights, produced no agricultural revolution – indeed, combined with royal and papal exactions it was a cause of monastic indebtedness. The records of Canterbury Cathedral Priory show these other burdens: £1,160 paid in taxes in the 1270s, another £1,000 and more in fees at the election of a prior and the £1,300 expended on the election of Winchelsey as archbishop in 1293–4. In 1279 Reading Abbey set aside a gold casket enriched with precious stones (the gift of King John to contain the Head of St Philip), a gold chalice and three precious Bibles, as pledge for the abbey's payment of £370 18s. 11d. towards a papal tithe. The sort of financial dealings in which an abbey could become enmeshed is shown by a curious episode at Reading in 1290. In that year of the Jews' expulsion, two respectable neighbours of the abbey presented to its startled chamberlain three bonds bearing the abbey's seal for money which

---

[14] *Reading Abbey Cartularies*, ed. Kemp, 1.93; Prestwich, *Edward I*, pp. 156, 165; *Chronicle of Bury St Edmunds*, ed. and tr. Gransden, pp. 67, 96–7, 125, 135; Wood, *English Monasteries and their Patrons*, pp. 101ff, 118; Paris, *CM*, v.364, 553, 682–8; Powicke, *HLE*, pp. 307, 372–3; *Documents Illustrating the Activities of the General and Provincial Chapters of the English Black Monks, 1215–1540*, ed. W. A. Pantin, 3 vols. (Camden Society, 3rd ser., vols. 45, 47, 59, London, 1931–7), 1.56 (24a).

had allegedly been received by the house years earlier, mostly as advance payment for 400 quarters of wheat and 100 sacks of wool never delivered, for which all the lands and chattels of the abbey were said to have been mortgaged. Fortunately the bonds were adjudged in the king's court to be the forgeries of a Jew called Josce of Newbury. And in fact the assets of monasteries far outweighed their debts, so that indebtedness seldom lasted long. Investment never seems to have exceeded 5% of income, and more business-like accounting and calculation of returns meant, at least in the case of Bolton Abbey in Yorkshire at the end of the century, that a running debt could be carried in order to finance expanding activity.[15]

Lay neighbours appeared in the witness-lists of monastic deeds and were increasingly employed by them as professional stewards. Abbeys were integrated into gentry society, their abbots sometimes better landlords than they were churchmen. Their interests lay with magnates and knights such as those who dined in the great hall of St Peter's Abbey Gloucester in 1305 along with the ecclesiastical dignitaries of the county (but no burgesses), in a gathering seventy strong to honour the justices of assize. Yet monasteries were also members of privileged orders within the universal Church. Abbots and priors were often appointed as judges delegate to hear cases appealed to Rome back in their place of origin. Reading received a string of papal and episcopal grants. In 1201 the bishop of Salisbury confirmed the abbey in possession of fourteen churches and one chapel in his diocese, specifying in some instances the proportions of the tithes to go to perpetual vicars of the parishes. Five years later, Pope Innocent III instructed the abbots of Evesham, Gloucester and Wigmore to hear and decide a complaint by Reading Abbey against the bishop of Salibury of his unjust disturbance, despite a papal confirmation, of rights in two churches appropriated to the poor of the hospital before the abbey gates. In mid-century the Reading monks got permission from the pope to wear felt caps in the monastery since they asserted that the cold winter was so severe in their region that

[15] Wood, *English Monasteries and their Patrons*, pp. 8, 159; E. Miller and J. Hatcher, *Medieval England – Rural Society and Economic Change 1086–1348* (London: Longmans, 1978), pp. 55–6, 182–4, 200, 214, 218–19, 226, 228–9; Knowles, *Religious Orders*, I.32–77; R. A. L. Smith, *Canterbury Cathedral Priory: A Study in Monastic Administration* (Cambridge: CUP, 1943); *Reading Abbey Cartularies*, ed. Kemp, I.188–94, 197–200; cf. *EHD*, III, no., 171, for the affairs of Dunstable Priory, 1272–95.

they could not attend divine service without danger to their health.[16]

Cistercian and Premonstratensian abbeys enjoyed exemption from visits of inspection by diocesan bishops, having their own internal systems of visitation. The ancient Benedictine houses had until the thirteenth century no organization to maintain discipline among them, and often received with hostility visitations by diocesan bishops; in the early fourteenth century the monks of Bath and Glastonbury were accused of conspiring to maintain silence when the bishop came. Consequently the Fourth Lateran Council required the holding of triennial chapters by the black monks of every kingdom or province, to which all abbots and priors should come (with retinues of no more than six mounts and eight persons each); pairs of monks should also be appointed by the chapters to make a tour of inspection of black monk houses between meetings. The records of the chapter in the province of Canterbury show it producing detailed statutes – for instance, on monastic hospitality – and the two abbots who held the rotating presidency hearing complaints from monks against their abbots and writing to individual houses on matters of discipline. The comprehensive statutes made at the chapter which met at Reading in 1277 caused protest on a number of grounds. A ruling against standing surety for debts was said to imperil the lands and liberties of houses which were the lords of many fees, for defaulting tenants would be liable to forfeit their mortgaged lands to other magnates. Another statute abbreviating the divine service was alleged to have provoked the Statute of Mortmain in retribution for the slackness and ingratitude it displayed.[17]

Perhaps the best reflection of the monasteries' importance as corporate magnates in thirteenth-century society is the political concern of the monastic chroniclers. Matthew Paris describes the black monks standing together against the king's demands for money with a solidarity born of their new organization; and the Cistercians, doing the same when they were summoned to Reading in 1256 to meet the papal nuncio and collector, Rostand Masson, come with a retinue of subcollectors, clerks and foreign merchants

---

[16] Harvey, *Westminster Abbey and its Estates*, pp. 96–7, 100; Hilton, *A Medieval Society*, pp. 223–4; *Reading Abbey Cartularies*, ed. Kemp, 1.136–200; J. E. Sayers, *Papal Judges Delegate in the Province of Canterbury, 1198–1254* (Oxford: OUP, 1971), pp. 114–15, 296–301.

[17] Knowles, *Religious Orders*, I. 9ff; *EHD*, III.651–2; *Chapters of the Black Monks*, ed. Pantin, 1.58, 60ff, 65 (II,5), 85, 88ff, 92, 106, 120, 145, 162.

to gather in the papal tithe imposed for the Sicilian business. Told that 'all the world knows their wealth in wool', the Cistercians replied that they could agree to nothing without consulting the abbot and chapter of Citeaux. The political interests of the monasteries also appear in the Tewkesbury chronicle's enthusiastic account of the fight of their patrons, the earls of Gloucester, for the Provisions of Oxford. The Bury chronicle tells how in 1263 the hated bishop of Norwich fled to Bury for security, 'for at this time the Liberty of St Edmund [meaning the territory within which the franchises were exercised] was exceedingly precious in the eyes of the barons'. The strenuous defence of the liberties of Bury St Edmunds and Battle and other abbeys in the Quo Warranto inquiries was a part of the whole baronage's defence of its freedoms.[18]

BISHOPS

If there were normally three or four bishops (besides the chancellor and treasurer) in the king's council at the end of Edward's reign, when abbots were hard to find there, it was because they offered the king the experience of rulers of dioceses as well as the influence of great landowners. Even if many of them had not become bishops only after a career in royal service – the king having few other rewards available for his ministers than high office in the Church – they would surely have been looked to for advice. There were perhaps 30,000 'secular' clergy spread over some 9,500 parishes, as against 20,000 to 25,000 monks, nuns and friars living in some 530 major monasteries and 250 smaller establishments (for all of whom the bishop also had some canonical responsibility). The numbers of clergy were not enormous, but they embraced a rich variety of roles in the community, from the absentee rectors and pluralists who worked as civil servants and business agents, through the paid vicars and curates who served the parishes, to a proletariat of clerks without benefices or regular employment. The bishops ruled over them within territorial dioceses older-established than the shires, through a system of courts which had grown

---

[18] Powicke, *HLE*, pp. 373–4; Paris, *CM*, v.553–4, 682–8; Wood, *English Monasteries and their Patrons*, p. 123; *Chronicle of Bury St Edmunds*, ed. and tr. Gransden, p. 27; A. Gransden, 'John de Northwold, Abbot of Bury St Edmunds (1279–1301) and his Defence of its Liberties', in *Thirteenth-Century England*, vol. III, ed. P. R. Coss and S. D. Lloyd (Woodbridge: Boydell, 1989); Lobel, 'The Ecclesiastical Banleuca', p. 131; Searle, *Lordship and Community*, pp. 235–46.

to maturity in pace with the king's, and often with a state made possible by great landed endowments.[19]

The history of the bishopric of Winchester in the first half of the century shows the vital importance to the king of controlling rich dioceses. The 'regalian right' of custody of a diocese during a vacancy, when the king could tallage it as part of his demesne, take the agricultural profits and present to prebends in the cathedral (with the incidental advantage that the chapter was more likely to fall in with the king's wishes in future episcopal elections), was invaluable to a king as pressed as John was. In the nine months after the death of the bishop of Winchester in September 1204, £3,633 8s. 2d. was levied from the diocese, more than the king could get in an equivalent period from any see but Durham, and four times as much as from the diocese of London, most of it being expended directly on supplies for the war in Poitou. But more valuable still would prove the man whom John got elected and sent to Rome to be consecrated by Pope Innocent III himself before a rival candidate could protest. Peter des Roches was the son of a knight from the Touraine in the king's French dominions and a knight himself before he took orders and became a clerk in the royal household. In John's early years he was treasurer of the church of Poitiers, precentor of Lincoln Cathedral (which may have given him topographical knowledge useful in the siege of Lincoln in 1217) and a trusted financial official under Hubert de Burgh, the king's chamberlain. It was a reflection on the king's needs as much as a reward for Peter's loyalty as the only bishop to remain in England to the end of John's quarrel with the papacy, that the bishop of Winchester was made justiciar on the death of Geoffrey FitzPeter, earl of Essex, in 1213, while Hubert de Burgh was fighting in France. He was not the first episcopal justiciar, but the first from the financial department of the household rather than the bench of the exchequer; he was also the last justiciar to rule England while the king was absent across the Channel on a final attempt to recover Normandy. Hard, efficient and unpopular as an administrator, Peter was replaced by Hubert de Burgh when Magna Carta was granted in June 1215 and probably as a condition

---

[19] *Memoranda de Parliamento*, ed. Maitland, p. cvi; Prestwich, *Edward I*, p. 437; Sayles, *Functions*, p. 267, for the presence of the abbots of Westminster and Waverley among the king's councillors in September 1305; Powicke, *The Thirteenth Century*, pp. 445–6, 458–9; see the will of Richard of Chichester (d. 1251) in *EHD*, III, no. 173, for the possessions, connections and benefactions of a bishop.

of the agreement between king and barons. But the agreement fell apart, and in September it was the bishop of Winchester with the papal nuncio who suspended Archbishop Stephen Langton for his refusal to excommunicate the baronial leaders on the pope's instructions. Peter was an executor of John's will and, with the legate and the marshal, safeguarded the succession of Henry III, crowned the young king (since Langton did not return to his see until 1218) and was made his tutor.[20]

Peter des Roches became a figure of European stature. As bishop he escorted the first party of Dominican friars to England, and issued one of the first sets of diocesan statutes implementing the decrees of the Lateran Council, especially in relation to the behaviour of clerks. In the role of soldier and statesman, he was reported to have been elected archbishop of Damietta in Egypt, the target of the fifth crusade, and accompanied the Emperor Frederick on his crusade to the Holy Land in 1228. As late as 1235 he was summoned by Pope Gregory IX to put down the pope's rebellious subjects at Viterbo. His death at his episcopal manor of Farnham in 1238 was described by Matthew Paris as an irreparable loss to the councils of King and Church: the success of the emperor's crusade, which had recovered Jerusalem by diplomatic means, had been due largely to the bishop of Winchester; he was the founder and patron of monasteries in both the Holy Land and England, and left his diocese in a prosperous condition.[21]

Peter des Roches was a controversial figure. A truer political role for the bishops may seem to have been found in the crises of 1223 and 1233–4 by those who followed first Archbishop Langton and then Ralph Niger, bishop of London, and Edmund Rich, the new archbishop, in reconciling enemies and excommunicating the obdurate. But they could not stand aloof from the lay baronage in thirteenth-century politics; nor would Henry, once he had shaken off his tutelage, or Edward after him, concede an independent role to the episcopate, into which they intruded their servants with increasing vigour. By 'the custom of England' a chapter was

[20] Howell, *Regalian Right*, pp. 55–8, 229; F. J. West, *The Justiciarship of England 1066–1232* (Cambridge: CUP, 1966) pp. 178ff; *Councils and Synods, with Other Documents relating to the English Church*, vol. II: A.D. 1205–1313, ed. F. M. Powicke and C. R. Cheney (Oxford: Clarendon Press, 1964), pp. 41, 46.

[21] Knowles, *Religious Orders*, I.363; *Councils and Synods*, II, ed. Powicke and Cheney, pp. 48, 102ff, 125–37; M. Gibbs and J. Lang, *Bishops and Reform, 1215–1272*, (Oxford OUP, 1934), pp. 112, 127; Paris, *CM*, III.304, 489–90; *EHD*, III, no. 163, for the transactions surrounding Peter's foundation of the Augustinian priory of Selborne in 1233.

obliged to ask the king's permission to proceed to election, and this was the king's opportunity to press his candidate. Though it might prove costly, chapters could still resist, and in Henry's reign sixteen contested elections in which the king had an interest went on appeal to the pope, who either confirmed them or rejected people he found unsuitable, decided between rival candidates or appointed choices of his own.[22]

Of the seventy-nine bishops who ruled English dioceses at some time during the reign of Henry III, forty-two have been classified as 'administrators and magnates', a third of whom were also 'university graduates and teachers'. Sometimes they arrived in the king's service from obscurity: nothing is known of Walter Gray, bishop of Worcester (1215–16), archbishop of York (1216–55) and regent of England while King Henry was in Gascony in 1242–3, before he bought the chancellorship from King John in 1205, except that he had an uncle who was bishop of Norwich and willing to stand surety for his fine of 5,000 marks. On the other hand Walter Giffard, bishop of Bath and Wells (1264–6) and archbishop of York (1266–79), is known to have gone to the Cambridge schools from a baronial family with lands in Wiltshire and Gloucestershire. His father Hugh Giffard was appointed to keep the accounts and receipts of Prince Edward and the king's other children in 1241; a quarter of a century later Walter himself was made chancellor on the morrow of the battle of Evesham; his brother was also a bishop, and two of his sisters abbesses. One should not assume that the administrators were necessarily elected bishops because they were the king's men. After the death of Peter des Roches in 1238, the king kept the temporalities of Winchester in his hands for six years, not primarily for the sake of the £18,000 it netted him but because the chapter resisted his heavy-handed pressure to elect William of Savoy, the queen's uncle and from 1236 the king's chief councillor, and after his death, Boniface, another Savoyard uncle. Henry would not accept the chapter's choice of William Raleigh, though Raleigh was his chief justice and a leading councillor, retorting to the objection to William of Savoy as 'a man of blood' that he had slain fewer men with his sword than Raleigh with his tongue. When the chapter next postulated Ralph Neville, the bishop of Chichester and chancellor, Henry promptly took the great seal way from him, and the pope in any case forbade the translation. The chapter finally returned to Raleigh, but the king remained implacable even after Boniface was elected archbishop of Canterbury. Matthew Paris tells a story of years of victimization of Raleigh before Henry bowed to the protests of the other bishops and the pope's insistence (the latter bought, Matthew informs us in a typically malicious detail, at the cost of 8,000 marks and the diocese's long-term indebtedness).[23]

In 1253 a delegation of four bishops is reported to have begged the king to remember his oath to maintain the liberties of the Church as set out in the Charter, especially with regard to elections, for no one could look for promotion to cathedral and conventual churches unless he was put in by the king, from which followed enormous damage to churches, prelates and people. The four were Archishop Boniface of Canterbury, Bishop William of Salisbury, a former royal clerk and judge, Bishop Silvester of Carlisle, a former chancellor, and the bishop-elect of Winchester, the king's half-brother Aymer of Lusignan; and the king's cynical reply was that he would mend his ways if they would set an example of repentance by resigning the positions they had unjustly obtained from him. Matthew Paris could almost be suspected of inventing the story in order to include Aymer, and to have the king remind him how, lacking both in years and learning, he had been raised to the noble heights of the church of Winchester. Henry had taken no chances on Raleigh's death in 1250. Matthew reproduces a 'sermon' preached to the chapter by the king in person: as ruin came to the world by a woman and by a woman salvation, so the misfortunes the monks brought on themselves by rejecting his wife's uncle they could redeem by choosing his mother's son. The monks gave way, Matthew echoing their lament that the land was a prey to any plunderer who had the king and a mercenary pope on his side and their fears that England would soon be turned into another Poitou.[24]

The outrageous behaviour of Aymer de Valence at Winchester was one of the precipitants of the baronial protest in 1258. Amongst the supporters of Simon de Montfort were bishops of a

[23] Gibbs and Lang, *Bishops and Reform*, pp. 15, 90, 185–96; Powicke, *The Thirteenth Century*, p. 458; *idem*, *HLE*, pp. 270–3; R. C. Stacey, *Politics, Policy, and Finance under Henry III, 1216–1245* (Oxford: Clarendon Press, 1987), pp. 128–30; Paris, *CM*, III.493–4, 630, IV.15, 108, 159, 259, 263–6, 285–6, 294–8, 346–52, 390, V.179.

[24] Paris, *CM*, III.525,m 531–2, V.185; for bishops in the king's council in these years, see Stacey, *Politics, Policy and Finance*, p. 93.

very different sort, like Stephen Bersted. This bishop of Chichester
came from a tradition of scholar-bishops stretching back to Grosseteste and Archbishop Edmund Rich, men sometimes of humble
origin and praised for their 'wonderful simplicity and innocence',
who had risen through the Oxford schools and cathedral chapters
rather than by royal service. Not surprisingly, however, the real
episcopal leader of the baronial cause was himself from a west
midlands baronial family closely associated with the royal household as well as being a *magister*. Walter de Cantilupe's father and
eldest brother were both stewards of the king's household. William
de Cantilupe the father was reputed one of John's 'evil counsellors'
and fought for Henry at the Fair of Lincoln – probably in the
entourage of the earl of Chester, for he became a regular witness
of the earl's charters, sometimes the first in the list immediately
before Fulk FitzWarin. Walter de Cantilupe was elected bishop of
Worcester in 1236 and accepted 'without difficulty' by king and
pope; a loan, probably of 1,000 marks, was forthcoming from the
wardrobe to cover the expenses of his journey to Rome for
consecration. At a council called by the legate Otto in London in
1237, the new bishop showed the worldly wisdom that went with
his reputation for holiness by speaking up in the defence of the
holding of benefices in plurality; this was necessary, he argued, for
churchmen of noble birth like himself to live in proper state and
show hospitality and charity. He was zealous in the Grosseteste
mould in visitation and correction within his diocese, and the
leader with Grosseteste in contesting Archbishop Boniface's rights
of visitation throughout his province. With Grosseteste he remon-
strated with the king about his treatment of William Raleigh, and
with him he was a leader of the English bishops at the papal
Council of Lyons in 1245. Walter's brother attended the council
also, as one of the six proctors (Roger Bigod, earl of Norfolk, and
John FitzGeoffrey were others) sent by the king to complain on
behalf of 'the baronage of England' of the burden of papal taxation
in England. The bishops of Lincoln and Worcester apparently
supported the right of the pope to tax, though the English were
united in protesting against papal 'provision' of clerks to benefices
in England, in derogation of the rights of lords to present to
livings. Cantilupe took the cross, and at a meeting at Bermondsey
in April 1250, he was chosen 'captain' of a group of crusading
magnates, which included the earls of Leicester, Winchester and
Hereford, for a passage to the Levant in June. Their departure was
prevented by the king's insistence that none should go till he was

ready to lead them, but in 1263 the bishop of Worcester could still be commissioned 'executor of the cross', with comprehensive powers to preach and organize crusade in England. A bishop like Cantilupe was a natural leader in a movement which was concerned to defend the liberties of the baronage, appealed to the sanctity of oaths and called for the excommunication of infringers of Magna Carta and the Provisions. [25]

On the other hand, Boniface of Savoy, the archbishop of Canterbury throughout this period, was not fitted to be a Stephen Langton or Edmund Rich in mediating between the baronial party and the king's men, even if Henry had any longer been prepared to concede such a role to his archbishop. Yet Boniface was able to show his successors how to defend the rights of an English Church which was becoming ever more closely enmeshed, administratively and bureaucratically, with the Angevin and papal monarchies – a defence which admittedly often narrowed to the assertion of the rights of the church of Canterbury. Matthew Paris presents the image of a metropolitan who had to be advanced to the diaconate and priesthood after his election, and carried his rights of provincial visitation to the extreme of arriving at the recalcitrant London priory of St Bartholomew wearing armour under his vestments; but the chronicler acknowledges that Boniface was with Grosseteste in bringing pressure on the king on Raleigh's behalf and working to keep the royal servant Robert Passelew out of the see of Chichester. The first good man of business at Canterbury since Hubert Walter also thrashed out practical agreements with his monks about the division of jurisdiction between his own and the priory's seignorial courts; and with cathedral chapters throughout his province about the exercise of ecclesiastical jurisdiction in episcopal vacancies. [26]

---

[25] Gibbs and Lang, *Bishops and Reform*, pp. 4, 13, 15–16, 34–5, 37–40, 47–9, 151, 188, 194; Powicke, *HLE*, pp. 279–80, 356–8, 362, 458–9, 464, 484, 528; *Documents of the Baronial Movement*, ed. Treharne and Sanders. pp. 49, 289 (15, 16), 295; *Book of Fees*, part II (London: HMSO, 1923), p. 966; D. A. Carpenter, *The Minority of Henry III*, (London, 1990), p. 320; *Charters of the Earls of Chester*, ed. Barraclough, nos. 274, 310, 364, 382, 385, 390–1, 393, 416, 422, 439–41, 447, 453; *Councils and Synods*, II, ed. Powicke and Cheney, pp. 238, 402; Stacey, *Politics, Policy and Finance*, pp. 127–8; Paris, *CM*, III.528–9, IV.286ff, 420, V.98, 102–3, 282, 375; Powicke, *HLE*, pp. 279–80, 356–8, 362; Lloyd, *English Society and the Crusade*, pp. 47–50, 58, 68, 84, 149.

[26] Paris, *CM*, v. 122–3; Powicke, *HLE*, pp. 361ff; Gibbs and Lang, *Bishops and Reform*, pp. 19–23; F. R. Du Boulay, *The Lordship of Canterbury* (London: Nelson, 1966), p. 292; I. J. Churchill, *Canterbury Administration: The Administra-*

This was a time of crystallization of ecclesiastical courts and assemblies, just as it was of other institutions ranging from manorial courts to parliaments. Between the mid-twelfth and mid-thirteenth centuries, the exercise of the 'ordinary' jurisdiction of the Church which belonged to the bishop (remember that this included many matters of vital importance to the laity, such as marriage contracts, wills and defamation) had moved from the episcopal synod, which might (like the pope) simply refer cases back to local judges, to a 'consistory court' presided over by the bishop's 'official'. In Archbishop Boniface's time there also appears the 'Court of Canterbury' sitting at the archbishop's church of St Mary Arches in London to hear appeals from the courts of the bishops of the province; even cases from the province of York might come there through the procedure called 'tuition', by which cases appealed to Rome were put under the church of Canterbury's 'protection' and might be settled at that stage if the parties agreed. Boniface was the effective defender of the jurisdiction of the Church which Grosseteste had looked for but not found in Edmund Rich. Defence was necessary because the methods of pastoral visitation which Grosseteste taught other bishops outraged the corrected laity almost as much as the deposed abbots and purged chapters. Questions such as 'whether any layman is notoriously proud or envious or avaricious or liable to the sin of slothful depression or rancorous or gluttonous or lecherous behaviour' could not be answered 'without precise investigations', but the king, Grosseteste complained, sought to prohibit the laity from giving sworn testimony at the command of bishops and archdeacons, and stopped the hearing of any plea in court christian, even of breach of faith and perjury, if it involved money. Grosseteste had his official compile a systematic statement of clerical rights under canon law, which provided the subject-matter of a provincial assembly called by Boniface in 1257 and of the canons of Lambeth issued in 1261. Bishops, it was decided, were to refuse to obey writs of prohibition used outside their proper sphere, and to excommunicate royal officials who attempted to enforce the appearance of the litigants in a royal court. Boniface thus left to his combative successors like John Pecham a manifesto against the lay power – and one especially provocative because it emerged from something more representative of the Church in England than a

tive Machinery of the Archbishopric of Canterbury Illustrated from Original Records, 2 vols. (London: SPCK, 1933), I.169ff.

council of bishops. Provincial councils had never been held yearly in England as the Lateran decrees required. Clerical assemblies became frequent only when there were taxes to be opposed or grievances against the king's administration to be discussed. The meeting in August 1257 was not simply a council of bishops: deans, heads of monastic houses and archdeacons were summoned to attend with letters of proxy from the bodies of clergy they were deemed to represent. The king vainly forbade the meeting on the grounds that he needed the bishops on his Welsh campaign, doing so by writs which termed the offensive gathering an illegitimate *convocatio*. The name stuck, and this developing clerical parliament was thereafter known as 'convocation'.[27]

After the Barons' War the intrusion of royal relations into wealthy sees no longer disturbed the proper co-operation of the king and the spiritual magnates, but there was increasing tension between the high-minded men elected or provided to the see of Canterbury and the efficient but pluralist and not over-moral royal clerks for whom Edward sought episcopal endowment. Included in the armoury of powers which the legate Ottobuono came with in 1265, along with the removal from their ecclesiastical dignities and benefices of the sons of noblemen and nephews of prelates who fostered disturbance, was the reservation to the pope of all elections of bishops and abbots. (The suspensions of Montfortian bishops had left large parts of the country without pastoral oversight.) The election already made at York was quashed and the first friar provided to an English see: the minister-general of the Franciscan order, St Bonaventura. When York did not appeal to this great Italian theologian, Walter Giffard was translated there from Bath and Wells, as in 1268 another *curialis* who had behaved with moderation in the recent troubles, Nicholas of Ely (he had been chancellor in 1260–1 and again in 1263), was translated from Worcester to Winchester. [28]

These men were typical of the curial bishops of Henry's reign,

[27] C. Morris, 'From Synod to Consistory: The Bishops' Courts in England, 1150–1250', *Journal of Ecclesiastical History*, 22 (1971); Churchill, *Canterbury Administration*, I.460–2; *Select Canterbury Cases c. 1200–1301*, ed. N. Adams and C. Donahue (Selden Society, vol. 95, London, 1981), pp. 14–16, 64ff; *Councils and Synods*, II, ed. Powicke and Cheney, pp. 530–47, 568–85, 661–92; R. L. Storey, 'The First Convocation, 1257?', in *Thirteenth-Century England*, ed. Coss and Lloyd, III; E. W. Kemp, *Counsel and consent* (London: SPCK, 1961).

[28] Gibbs and Lang, *Bishops and Reform*, pp. 73–4; *Calendar of Entries in the Papal Registers relating to Great Britain and Ireland*, vol. I (London HMSO, 1893), pp. 426–31; Powicke, *HLE*, pp. 592–3.

men who were archdeacons when they were appointed to the chancellorship or the treasurership and left secular office before or soon after their promotion to the episcopal bench. Walter of Merton, Edward's first chancellor, conformed to the pattern. By 1240 he was a chancery clerk earning enough in fees to purchase the encumbered manors of Malden with Chessington and Farley from the royal escheators who had custody of them during the minority of Richard de Clare, earl of Gloucester. During Henry's absence in France between November 1259 and April 1260, accompanied by the chancellor, Nicholas of Ely, it was Walter of Merton that sent out the king's orders from the chancery which he seems to have taken to Malden with him. By then archdeacon of Bath, Walter was chancellor in name as well as fact in the interval of royal dominance between 1261 and 1263, and his lands suffered heavily from baronial partisans in the summer of 1263. In July 1264 he was one of the royal clerks offered immunity if they retired to their benefices. It was at this time that he turned to the project for which he is remembered: the application of his talent for amassing landed property (which he had previously used to marry off his sisters) to the foundation of the first true college at Oxford, the 'House of the Scholars of Merton', for the benefit of his eight nephews. In his old age he was made chancellor again by the council at Edward's accession, and his election to the bishopric of Rochester came only just before his replacement by Robert Burnell on Edward's return in 1274.[29]

In contrast to the Henrician bishops who were elected near their retirement from royal office, Burnell was bishop of Bath and Wells for all but six months of his eighteen years as Edward's chancellor; Anthony Bek, appointed keeper of the wardrobe on the same day that Burnell was given the great seal, continued to serve the king in various capacities long after his promotion to the see of Durham in 1283; John Kirkby hurried back from his consecration as bishop of Ely to complete another four years of the treasurership, ended only by his death; and Walter Langton, treasurer for the last twelve years of the reign, was elected bishop of Coventry and Lichfield within five months of his appointment. Edward tried hard to get Burnell the archbishopric of Canterbury, which only Hubert Walter (d. 1205) had ever combined with the chancellorship (and that at a time when the king's chief minister was not the chancellor

[29] *Fitznell's Cartulary*, ed. C. A. F. Meekings and P. Shearman (Surrey Record Society, vol. 26, Guildford, 1968), pp. lviii–lxxv.

but the justiciar). After the death of Boniface in 1270, when the Lord Edward first pressed Burnell's name on the Canterbury monks, the pope settled the matter by providing Master Robert Kilwardby, prior of the Dominican friars in England, to the see. Though possibly a Londoner by origin, Kilwardby moved in the world of the Paris and Oxford schools, and it was his great reputation as a theologian that brought his appointment to Canterbury. As archbishop he was an energetic and strict visitor, especially of abbeys, but was happiest on occasions like his return to Oxford in 1273 to be present at the inception of his old pupil Thomas de Cantilupe as master of theology. Perhaps because of the theological enemies he had made, or his summoning of a provincial council to appeal to Rome against the behaviour of the papal collector of taxes, or his own wish to retire, Kilwardby was removed from his archbishopric in 1278 by elevation to the college of cardinals; whereupon Edward tried again for Burnell. This time the chapter elected him (or rather postulated him from Bath and Wells to which he had been elected in 1275), and Edward sent a high-powered embassy to Rome to present his case. The pope proceeded to appoint three cardinals to examine it, called for more reports on Burnell and after much delay provided another friar: this time the recent minister provincial of the Franciscans in England, John Pecham, a native of Patcham in Sussex but currently in Rome as lector in theology at the papal court.[30]

Edward received Pecham with surprising lack of rancour, but in the next thirteen years found the qualities of yet another veteran of the great argument raging in France between the Friars and the other clergy an intense irritation at Canterbury. The primacy of this irascible and never popular man shows the full extent of the impact of the spiritual magnates on public affairs. On the negative side there was the clash of pride and ambition, at its most destructive when it appeared as the defence of ecclesiastical rights. Burnell had reason to think that Pecham secured a further disappointment for him when his postulation to Winchester was quashed in 1280, and the archbishop was compelled to ask the Curia to deny that he had written secretly to the pope about the chancellor's demerits. He certainly made inquiries about the man who was believed, 'after the order of Aaron rather than Melchize-

---

[30] Powicke, *HLE*, pp. 585–6, 591–3, 595, 696; *Cal. Papal Registers*, pp. 442, 456; Knowles, *Religious Orders*, I.106, 165–6, 168, 219–24, 228–9, 282; *Councils and Synods*, II, ed. Powicke and Cheney, pp. 801–4, 807–10, 820–7; D. L. Douie, *Archbishop Pecham* (Oxford: Clarendon Press, 1952), pp. 47–8.

dek' to provide for the illegitimate sons out of the revenues of Church and King, and whose estate at Acton Burnell in Shropshire was able in 1283 to accommodate an entire parliament – perhaps appropriately the one that saw the promulgation of the first Statute of Merchants. The age-old dispute between the archbishops of Canterbury and York about the latter's claim to have his cross carried before him anywhere in the kingdom reached new heights of scandal at this time; Pecham had scouts posted to see that no cross was raised when Archbishop Wickwane disembarked on his return from Rome, and Edward needed to make Pecham promise not to prohibit the sale of provisions to the household of the archbishop of York when he entered the southern province to see the king. A constitutional struggle between the archbishop and his suffragan bishops about the operation of the court of arches, particularly tuitorial appeals and Canterbury's claim to jurisdiction over the wills of persons who left property in more than one diocese, led to a personal tragedy. The opposition to Pecham on these issues was led by his old pupil Thomas de Cantilupe, the nephew of the great bishop of Worcester, a man educated in civil and canon law at Orleans and Paris, and a past chancellor of Oxford University and of England, now bishop of Hereford. When Cantilupe's official refused to serve citations to the court of Canterbury on the executors of the wills left by two members of the Hereford chapter, and resisted a tuitorial appeal by the abbot of Reading against the bishop's sequestration of Leominster Priory, Pecham ordered his excommunication. When Cantilupe refused to carry out the order, he too was excommunicated, and died within a few months at Orvieto, seeking redress from the pope. The miracles at his tomb at Hereford made Thomas de Cantilupe the most popular English saint after Thomas Becket, and his life is known in such detail because of the proceedings for his canonization in 1320.[31]

On the positive side was the transcending of these personal resentments in the endeavour by men as different in temperament as Pecham, Burnell and Bek to define the functions and relationship

[31] *Registrum Epistolarum Johannis Peckham Archiepiscopi Cantuariensis (1279–92)*, ed. C. Trice Martin, 3 vols. (Rolls Series, 1882–5), I.269–73, 290, 318–20, 382–3, II.393–5, 506, 680, 714, III.1032, 1057, 1061; Douie, *Archbishop Pecham*, pp. 192–234; *Select Canterbury Cases*, ed. N. Adams and C. Donahue (Selden Society, London, 1981), pp. 27–30; *Councils and Synods*, II, ed. Powicke and Cheney, pp. 921–6; R. C. Palmer, *The Whilton Dispute, 1264–1380* (Princeton: Princeton UP, 1984), pp. 137–44, for Burnell's land deals.

of royal and ecclesiastical jurisdiction, and make them work. Much more information becomes available on ecclesiastical administration in the second half of the thirteenth century because of the general keeping from that time of bishops' registers recording ordinations, institutions, court proceedings and the letters streaming backwards and forwards between the magnates of the Church, royal officials and the pope. Pecham's is the first Canterbury register to survive. It is possible to follow the friar archbishop's attempts to mend the ways of the black monks, particularly with respect to financial accountability, which brought him into conflict with the presidents of the provincial chapter. His determined campaign against pluralists in implementation of the decrees of the Council of Lyons of 1274 can be observed in detail. Royal officials, not least the last generation of clerical justices like Hengham, depended on the accumulation of benefices, and very often had papal dispensations to hold them in plurality. Pecham wrote to Pope Nicholas III in 1280, lamenting the need to reduce 'to modest poverty men of high birth, affluent and accustomed to honours', but drawing comfort from the fact that 'sir Anthony, called Bek, very trusty secretary of the king of England' had submitted to his will all his benefices in the province of Canterbury (no doubt Bek had to make this gesture if he was to be eligible for the bishopric which was his due). Four of these he had left in Bek's hands, said Pecham, until he received the pope's guidance, 'because I am publicly assured that your Clemency is disposed to grant grace of dispensation as well to him as to certain other royal clerks'.[32]

Pecham moderated his stand on pluralism, and in the interests of the Church he was even prepared to come to terms with the worldly chancellor over ecclesiastical jurisdiction. He had begun his primacy with a reaffirmation at the Council of Reading of Boniface's defence of the Church's liberties: the charters were to be posted up in public places, and eleven causes of excommunication were to be expounded to the people, beginning with the obtaining of writs from a lay court to impede cases which were known to belong by the sacred canons to the church courts. In his

---

[32] David M. Smith, *Guide to Bishops' Registers of England and Wales* (Royal Historical Society, London, 1981); *Registrum Johannis Peckham*, I.46–7, II.575, III.1032, 1041; *Councils and Synods*, II, ed. Powicke and Cheney, pp. 837, 865; *Select Cases in the Court of King's Bench*, ed. G. O. Sayles, 7 vols. (Selden Society, London, 1936–71), I, p. lxxiii; *EHD*, III, nos. 169 (Pecham's letter about Bek's benefices), 170 (account of a suit at the papal court from Cantilupe's register); Douie, *Archbishop Pecham*, pp. 166ff; Knowles, *Religious Orders*, I.58–9.

anger, the king had the charters taken down, and the archbishop was instructed at the Michaelmas parliament of 1279 to delete from the canons of the council, and hold never to have been pronounced, the sentences of excommunication against those who secured prohibitions, against royal officials who omitted to arrest obdurate excommunicates when called upon and against trespassers on the property of churchmen (since in this case the common law provided sufficient penalties). The conflict reached new heights with the sending of royal writs to the prelates, archdeacons and their officials on 1 July 1285, demanding observance of an edict that the church courts should hear only testamentary and matrimonial cases. A violent protest came from the diocese of Norwich, where the bishop, William Middleton, was a canon lawyer who had been the official of the Court of Canterbury. Special measures ordered against Norwich by the king led to the imprisonment of ecclesiastical judges. Then in June 1286 the government drew back: the writ *circumspecte agatis* told the justices itinerant to 'go carefully' in their dealings with the bishop of Norwich and his clergy, and gave such a precise (and apparently acceptable) list of the spiritual pleas the church courts might hear that it was soon cited in the royal courts as a statute. The settlement of 1286 was made workable by a mechanism which Burnell had suggested in 1280: if a prohibition was obtained in a case which was clearly spiritual, he would 'counsel' the ecclesiastical judge to proceed notwithstanding. The Statute of Consultation of 1290 made it the right of the plaintiff to submit a case stopped by prohibition in the church court to the chancellor or chief justice, who would decide whether to instruct the ecclesiastical judge to proceed in the way Burnell had envisaged. The royal lawyers thus kept ultimate control, but vigorous argument among the spiritual magnates serving Church and Crown had produced a working system of courts serving the whole community, clerical and lay.[33]

Robert Winchelsey, Pecham's successor, was a secular clerk and a Kentish man who had possibly been at school in Canterbury, and he was duly elected in 1293 by the cathedral chapter, not provided by the pope like the two friars who were his predecessors. But like

---

[33] *Councils and Synods*, II, ed. Powicke and Cheney, pp. 828–51, 856–7, 864–6, 932, 937, 955–75, 1090; D. F. Logan, *Excommunication and the Secular Arm in Medieval England* (Toronto: Pontifical Institute, 1968); *Registrum Johannis Peckham*, II.426–7; H. G. Richardson and G. O. Sayles, 'The Clergy in the Easter Parliament, 1285', *EHR*, 52 (1937); *EHD*, III, nos. 60, 62; *Canterbury Cases*, ed. Adams and Donahue, p. 101.

them he was a theologian, who had been rector of the arts faculty in Paris and chancellor of the University of Oxford, and had shown in these capacities the sort of skills, for example in settling conflicts between secular students and mendicants, which must have been a reason for his election as archbishop. His misfortune was to have to use his qualities, which included a courageous obstinacy, not in the years of Edwardian legislation but in a time of war and political crisis. The new archbishop tried to be co-operative towards the king's increasing demands for money from the clergy along with the rest of his subjects, to defend the country against the French. But when a parliament met at Bury St Edmunds in November 1296, and the clergy were asked to contribute a fifth, Winchelsey was obliged to publish the bull *clericis laicos* issued by Pope Boniface VIII in the previous February, which lamented the natural hostility of 'laity to clerks' and forbade the taxing of the clergy without papal permission. The clergy's dilemma was debated at no less than four convocations of the southern province in 1297, which first refused any grant and brought a furious response from the king – a sentence of outlawry and confiscation of property on any clerk who would not pay. Winchelsey acknowledged the needs of the king in opposing a perfidious enemy, and sympathized with clergy who submitted, but he was firm in his assertion of ecclesiastical authority. The excommunication was ordered of those who laid hands on church property or infringed *clericis laicos* in any way: in return, the king forbade excommunication. But the pope was softening his stance and allowing exemptions from the bull on grounds of 'urgent necessity', which could be assessed locally. In face of a threat from Scotland, and made more amenable by the king's concession of the Confirmation of the Charters, the fourth convocation of 1279 conceded a grant, though Winchelsey insisted that the Scots must not be pursued back across the border, and that the levy should cease when the necessity was over. In this last great political struggle of the century, Winchelsey appears as more the president of the clergy, in convocations grown brave enough since Boniface's time to arrogate to themselves decisions on the needs of royal government, than as a leader of the baronage in the mould of Stephen Langton. When the archbishop of Bordeaux, one of Edward's own subjects, was elected pope in 1305 as Clement V, the king sent his treasurer, Walter Langton, bishop of Coventry and Lichfield to the papal coronation at Lyons with the charge that Winchelsey was 'spiteful and perverse' and had brought the kingdom to the edge of rebellion, and the archbishop was suspended and summoned to the Curia. Yet the evidence is that Winchelsey tried to remain aloof from the opposition of the lay barons to the Crown. He was a sacerdotalist in the mould of Grosseteste, in a situation in which the king wanted Burnells. At a time of intense diplomatic activity between the English court and Rome, conducted by royal clerks like John of Pontoise, bishop of Winchester, who in 1297 actually obtained for himself an unprecedented papal grant of exemption from the jurisdiction of Canterbury, the archbishop's authority was inevitably diminished.[34]

The thirteenth-century archbishops of York were a different type from the scholars of European repute who were chosen for Canterbury. Apart from the abortive provision of St Bonaventura and the translation of Walter Giffard (1266–79) from Bath and Wells in his stead, there was no interference by pope or king in York elections, and the chapter chose long-serving canons from its own ranks. What the king wanted was men who were reliable in ways that Pecham and Winchelsey were not: who would act as regents and help to ensure the smooth accessions of kings, as Giffard did for Edward I and William Greenfield (chancellor 1302–4, archbishop 1304–15) did for Edward II, preach crusade, and pray for success against the Scots. He also wanted York's rich prebends for relations like the son of Amadeus of Savoy and ministers such as John of Droxford, keeper of the wardrobe and prebendary of Masham (1296–1309). For two generations the staff of the English chancery were rewarded to a large extent by the plunder of York's patronage, and clergy from south Yorkshire and north Lincolnshire directed the country's administration to a disproportionate degree.[35]

The futile obsession of York's archbishops with the right to carry their cross in the south may have come from feelings of inferiority in their own province. With only two suffragans, at Durham and Carlisle, the vigorous conciliar activity of the southern province was missing; but with all the apparatus of

---

[34] J. H. Denton, *Robert Winchelsey and the Crown, 1294–1313* (Cambridge: CUP, 1980), pp. 7–14, 19–20, 35ff, 136–9, 145–7, 171–3; *Councils and Synods*, II, ed. Powicke and Cheney, pp. 1148–85; *EHD*, III, pp. 237–42, and nos. 72, 74–7, 87; Richardson and Sayles, 'The Clergy in the Easter Parliament, 1285', p. 231; *Documents Illustrating the Crisis of 1297–98 in England*, ed. M. Prestwich (Camden Society, 4th ser., vol. 24, London, 1980), pp. 115–17.

[35] R. B. Dobson, 'The Political Role of the Archbishops of York during the Reign of Edward I', in *Thirteenth-Century England*, ed. Coss and Lloyd, vol III; *Cal. Papal Registers*, p. 578.

metropolitan jurisdiction, and the same frenzy of visitation, there was full scope for jurisdictional disputes, in which the archbishop was liable to be humiliated by his suffragan at Durham. Besides great wealth, the bishop of Durham possessed more extensive temporal franchises than any lord in the country except the earl of Chester (who in any case was from this time the king or his eldest son). Within the two 'shires' of Durham and Sadberge, he had his own sheriffs and his own justices in eyre, of assize and of the forest, and he possessed the rights, elsewhere the prerogative of the king, to grant wardships, mint coins and control the mining of coal and iron. This liberty was well established before the arrival of the king's clerk, Anthony Bek, as Bishop. Bek already included the archdeaconry of Durham and the precentorship of York among his many benefices when he was sent north by Edward in 1283 to arbitrate in a long-standing dispute about the archbishop of York's right of visitation in the bishopric of Durham, in which the appeals and counter-appeals to Rome had become 'a scandal in the sight of the clergy and people of England, and of many in foreign lands'. Bek had by this time served as keeper of the king's wardrobe, constable of the Tower of London, negotiator of treaties with the Welsh and ambassador to the kings of France and Aragon. It was no surprise that on the death of their bishop in June 1283, the Durham monks moved quickly to elect such a powerful advocate. Ironically, in 1300 they were to be subjected to an assertion by Bek of the bishop of Durham's rights to visit the priory which was more scandalous than most such disputes in its open and protracted violence.[36]

These things were not uncommon between bishops and cathedral priories. What is remarkable is the additions to his temporal power which the Scottish crisis gave Bek the opportunity to make. The custody of the Scottish Crown's manors of Wark in Northumberland and Penrith in Cumberland came as a reward for his negotiation of the marriage treaty between Edward's son and the Maid of Norway, the heiress of Scotland; and the Maid's death on the way to her realm only tightened Bek's hold of them. In a *quo warranto* plea of 1293, the bishop successfully claimed before parliament a liberty which included lesser liberties belonging to both the main claimants of the Scottish Crown, John Balliol and

[36] R. Brentano, *York Metropolitan Jurisdiction and Papal Judges Delegate* (Berkeley: University of California Press, 1959); C. M. Fraser, *A History of Antony Bek, Bishop of Durham, 1283–1311* (Oxford: Clarendon Press, 1957); Knowles, *Religious Orders*, I. 107, 260; *Cal. Papal Registers*, pp. 589–90, 599, 603.

Robert Bruce. He contributed 500 horse and 1,000 foot to Edward's army in Scotland in 1296, and led one of the three divisions at the battle of Falkirk in 1298. Alone of the bishops, 'the Bishop Anthony of Durham, and Patriarch' appears in the Parliamentary Roll of Arms, immediately after the earls. Jerusalem was firmly in Muslim hands, and what the acquisition of the patriarchate in 1306 conferred was extra prestige and formal exemption from the jurisdiction of a mere archbishop – but in fact his unique combination of spiritual authority and baronial liberty had long allowed him to ignore his metropolitan. For excommunicating Bek, a royal servant, in 1291, when his exasperation at the defiance of his mandates and the arrest of his messengers boiled over, Archbishop John le Romeyn was arraigned before the king and escaped imprisonment only by a fine of 4,000 marks. At Romeyn's trial the king's attorney decribed the bishop of Durham in terms never before used in England: he had 'a double status, namely, the status of a Bishop as to his spiritualities, and the status of an Earl Palatine as to his temporal holdings'.[37]

LAY MAGNATES AND THE CHANGING FACE OF LORDSHIP

The position of the ecclesiastical magnates depended on their relationship with the king, the pope and their own clergy; that of the lay magnates more exclusively on their relationship with the king. Though non-military forms of service were advancing new men, the 160–200 lay lords summoned to parliaments by individual writs were still largely the successors of the barons of the Conquest. Their fortunes still depended on their ability to cope with the various claims of their families, in terms of a law developed to govern the relationship between feudal tenants-in-chief and the king as lord paramount: a law which Edwardian legislation only began to adapt to the wider needs of aristocratic society. The accumulation and safe transmission of family lands needed to be reconciled with provision for widows and younger children. Succession by minors and, sooner or later, the failure of heirs needed to be anticipated. (Of course, ecclesiastical magnates also had a duty to provide from their personal wealth for their nephews and nieces and even illegitimate children, as did Walter of Merton and Robert Burnell, but under a law which excluded bastards from succession, they could not be so concerned about inheritance and

[37] *RP*, I. 102–5, 117–19.

the biological accidents which attended it.) Lay tenants-in-chief also had to take account of the Crown's right under feudal law to a succession tax called a 'relief', to the exploitation of the lands of heirs until they did homage ('primer seisin'), to the wardship of the infant heirs of tenants-in-chief and all their lands (even if most of them were held of others than the king) and to arrange or grant away the marriages of wards.[38]

The exercise of the king's feudal lordship helped to create a baronial community. With regard to the disposal of wardships and marriages royal lordship operated according to principles of mutual interest generally accepted by an aristocracy within which almost everyone had the rights and responsibilities of both vassal and lord. The king had an overriding interest in the stability of the military aristocracy: he normally respected the preference of magnates for marriage with their own kind, and did not tolerate the wasting of the lands of the wards he granted to baronial guardians, or the forcing on them of disparaging marriages. Wardships were an investment, and their granting redistributed wealth and power among the baronial families which ranged from the holders of two or three knights' fees to the earl of Hertford and Gloucester reckoned to hold 500 or more. The common stake in the fruits of royal lordship and the circulation of responsiblity for other lords' heirs and lands made for social solidarity and co-operative politics, which easily turned to a coherent opposition to the Crown when financial need caused the king to flout the norms of behaviour, as it did King John. The king's prerogative wardship then appeared as a naked exercise of power and patronage which ignored the interests of families and favoured upstarts in the royal household at the expense of established barons (though the aggrieved might in fact come from the previous generation's 'new men'). The loss of Normandy, Anjou and Touraine in 1204 left John with loyal servants to be supported from English lands. Robert de Vieuxpont, a household sergeant who was the younger son of a family holding ten fees in Normandy was granted a whole conglomeration of custodies – of the sees of York and Durham during vacancies as well as of lay fees and castles – and Brian de Lisle was not far behind. The king's agents acted together to purchase grants of feudal rights, which were both a source of revenue to the Crown

---

[38] What follows is heavily dependent on S.L. Waugh, *The Lordship of England: Royal Wardships and Marriages in English Society and Politics, 1217–1327* (Princeton: Princeton UP, 1988).

and an inducement to service. Even the loyalty of Earl Ranulf, Earl William de Ferrers and Earl William de Warenne, with their vast territorial power in the north, and that of William the Marshal himself, needed a continuous flow of material rewards to ensure it.[39]

No subsequent king used his feudal lordship so arbitrarily as John to bribe and discipline his magnates. Rather the barons were faced with a more systematic administration of the king's feudal rights, which drew away from the normal rights of a lord to become recognized as the first element of the royal prerogative. Kings kept in their own hands the disposal of the greater wardships, which were as important politically as fiscally. Henry complained bitterly to Louis IX in 1261 that the baronial council ignored his orders concerning wardships 'as though he were not king', which was 'prejudicial both to him and to his heirs'. In their counter-submissions to Louis, the barons complained of the dilapidations committed by royal custodians who sold plantations, destroyed parks and fish-ponds, permitted 'houses, park-fences, ditches and other things which could and should be kept in order by small repairs, to go to utter rack and ruin: even marrying such noble persons to obscure and unknown persons' and disparaging them against the terms of the Charter. Certain 'courtiers, aliens and others, leaguing together and pushing each other's interests', obtained 'escheats, wardships and other perquisites of the lord king, by means of which he ought [rather] to replenish his treasury.'[40]

In the area of marriage arrangements as well as of wardships there were rules respected by everyone with an interest: the king, the lord, the families and peers of contracting couples, and the couples themselves. To ensure the legitimacy of children the pope was called upon to grant dispensations to those who had contracted marriages in apparent ignorance that they were related within the prohibited degrees. In this the aristocracy showed the same determination to remove uncertainty from property arrangements

---

[39] Holt, *Magna Carta*, pp. 216; I. J. Sanders, *Feudal Military Service in England* (London: OUP, 1956), pp. 35, 39, 71, 136ff; J. C. Holt, *The Northerners* (Oxford: Clarendon Press, 1961), pp. 32, 76–7, 217, 220–5, 241, 254; M. Altschul, *A Baronial Family in Medieval England: The Clares, 1217–1314* (Baltimore: Johns Hopkins Press, 1965), p. 221.

[40] Waugh, *The Lordship of England*, pp. 131–43, 240–8; H. Ridgeway, 'The Lord Edward and the Provisions of Oxford', in *Thirteenth-Century England* ed. Coss and Lloyd, 1; *Documents of the Baronial Movement*, ed. Treharne and Sanders, pp. 219, 270–1, 276–7.

which caused them to oppose the inheritance by bastards even when they were legitimated by their parents' subsequent marriages. The development of the jointure (the joint enfeoffment of man and wife with all their lands), and of the entailing of property to couples and 'the heirs of their bodies', made the devolution of property through marriage settlements more flexible. The Petition of the Barons broke new ground in 1258 by asking for a legal remedy against childless widows who alienated the marriage-gifts entailed on them and their issue. On the other hand, provision was made for the sustenance even of the widows of rebels in the vengeful atmosphere after Evesham. Within these rules of feudal wardship and marriage, strategies could be developed for the accumulation and transfer of family property with minimum disadvantage to infant heirs and families faced with successive minorities. The marriage strategies of baronial families have been analysed by Professor Waugh. For example, the brothers Gilbert Basset, Fulk Basset, future bishop of London, and Philip Basset, Henry III's most constant advisor during the Barons' War, are shown using their connections with the king's households to acquire the wardships of their relatives and to get approval for marriage alliances with other courtier families. Intermarriage helped to forge the identity of the corps of royal administrators, especially while Edward's Queen Eleanor was engaged in matchmaking and property-dealing. But families like the Bassets and their Montague relations belonged both to royal administration and to regional society and used their court influence for the benefit of their country neighbours. The main effect of marriage strategies was to share among other baronial families patrimonies fragmented by the failure of male heirs. (Inheritances were divided equally among heiresses, rather than passing to the eldest.)[41]

Succession to the lands of the greatest lords was of special concern to the king, and the arrangements of marriages among the earls were with reason conducted like political negotiations. The terms of the marriage of Margaret Longspée, great-granddaughter and heiress of Earl William of Salisbury, the bastard son of Henry II, with Henry de Lacy, heir to the earldom of Lincoln (the couple then aged one and six) were agreed by two groups of barons

[41] Waugh, *The Lordship of England*, pp. 49–51, 57–63, 207–15; *Cal. Papal Letters*, pp. 278, 307, 331, 332, 358, 491, 503, 510, 514, 570; *Documents of the Baronial Movement*, ed. Treharne and Sanders, pp. 88–9, 328–9, 334–5; C. H. Knowles, 'Provision for the Families of the Montfortians Disinherited after the Battle of Evesham', in *Thirteenth-Century England*, ed. Coss and Lloyd, I.

including on the bride's side Philip Basset, a royal minister who was also Margaret's great-uncle, and on the husband's Simon de Montfort, earl of Leicester. The rise of the justiciar Hubert de Burgh was sealed by the creation, unique in the thirteenth century, of a new earldom for a person not of royal blood; but the grant to Hubert of the earldom of Kent had been prepared by the extension in that county of his territorial power, founded on the custody of Dover Castle, and by his marriage (shortly before her death) to Isabella, countess of Gloucester, divorced wife of King John and widow of Geoffrey de Mandeville, earl of Essex, and then to Margaret, the eldest daughter of the king of Scots. The earldom was to go to issue of the latter marriage, and since there was none, it expired with Hubert in 1243. The other new, or revived, earldom of Cornwall, granted in 1227 to the king's eighteen-year-old brother Richard, became the core of the most formidable accumulation of landed wealth in thirteenth-century England. When he died in 1301, Edmund of Cornwall, Richard's second son and successor, had an annual income of £3,800; Richard will have had more, from his brother's gifts and his own multifarious financial dealings, and would have needed it to gain election as king of the Romans in 1257.[42]

In the 1230s and 1240s, the two non-royal earldoms which had profited from their loyal support of John and the infant Henry, and might have rivalled Cornwall, came to an end in a major redistribution of land and power to the chief advantage of the Crown. In 1232, Ranulf, earl of Chester, and from 1217 also of Lincoln, for a time duke of Brittany and earl of Richmond in right of his wife, and custodian of the honour of Leicester, died childless, but not before he had contrived that in the inevitable partition of his vast territories the earldom of Chester should go to John the Scot, earl of Huntingdon, the son of the eldest of his four sisters and coheirs, and the earldom of Lincoln to John de Lacy, constable of Chester, another sister's son-in-law; a third sister's son, the earl of Arundel, received Coventry, and William de Ferrers, earl of Derby, the remaining sister's husband, had the land between Ribble and Mersey, including Liverpool. But on the death in 1237 of John the Scot, also childless, King Henry refused to allow 'the fair dominion' of the county of Chester itself to be divided among the

[42] Waugh, *The Lordship of England*, pp. 57–8, 212; for the earls in the following paragraphs, see G. E. Cokayne, *The Complete Peerage of England, Scotland, Great Britain and the United Kingdom*, new edn by Vicary Gibbs and others (London: St Catherine Press, 1910–59).

husbands of the earl's sisters and nieces. (Interestingly, these included representatives of the three families of Balliol, Bruce and Hastings which at the end of the century would claim the Scottish kingdom on the same genealogical grounds, John having been the king of Scots' brother; Edward would then judge Scotland as indivisible as his father had the English county-palatine.) With firmness and considerable political skill Henry III annexed Chester to the Crown, to become in 1254 the appanage of the Lord Edward and soon the headquarters for the conquest and annexation of the principality of Wales. The dismantling of Ranulf's earldom, 'the strongest bulwark of an independent baronage', was followed in 1241 by the death of Gilbert Marshal in a tournament, and the deaths in swift succession in 1245 of the last two of the five brothers who held one after the other the earldom of Pembroke which John had given their father at his coronation. The vast lands of the Marshal in England, Wales and Ireland were divided among five sisters and their issue; the office of marshal passed via the eldest of them to the Bigod earls of Norfolk; and the earldom reverted to the Crown. Immediately on his arrival in England in 1247 William de Valence, Henry's Lusignan half-brother, was given the hand of the coheiress who held Pembroke itself (this marriage outside the ranks of 'true-born Englishmen' may have been the source of the barons' complaint in 1258), and at the end of Edward's reign his son Aymer would be recognized as earl.[43]

The group of comital families amongst whom wives and lands circulated was tight-knit but not closed off from foreign connections. Earls went on crusade, and they might die overseas, like successive counts of Aumale and lords of Holderness. As a result of the marrige back in the twelfth century of Amice, daughter of the earl of Leicester, to the lord of Montfort in the Isle de France, the earldom of Leicester and the hereditary master stewardship of the king's household passed in 1204 to Simon de Montfort IV. This man's famous victory over the Albigensian heretics made him a potentate in Languedoc, but his English inheritance was placed by King John in the custody of Ranulf of Chester, and all claim to it was surrendered by Simon IV's eldest son Amaury, constable of France, to his brother Simon in exchange for all claim to the French patrimony. Simon de Montfort V came to England and by

[43] N. Denholm-Young, *Richard of Cornwall* (Oxford: Blackwell, 1947); S. Painter, *Studies in the History of the English Feudal Barony*, (Baltimore: Johns Hopkins Univ. Stud. 61, 1943), pp. 171, 174–7; Miller and Hatcher, *Rural Society and Economic Change*, p. 181; *Cal. Papal Registers*, p. 147.

1238 had so impressed Henry III that he not only recovered the earldom but became a dominant figure in the king's council and received the hand of the king's sister Eleanor, widow of William Marshal the younger, a disparaging marriage (though supported by a papal letter) which brought Richard of Cornwall and Gilbert Marshal out in revolt. For Simon there were to be further arguments with Richard over royal grants of wardships, the humiliation of the inquiry into his conduct as seneschal or steward of Gascony and a running battle with Henry over lands in Ireland due to Eleanor as dower from her marriage to William Marshal: this actually threatened to hold up the sealing of the Treaty of Paris with King Louis in 1259, since Simon wanted to withhold the required renunciation of any claims Eleanor might have in France as King John's daughter till he got satisfaction over the Irish lands. Despite (or perhaps because of) all this, and a certain contempt for English sloppiness, the formidable Simon established himself as the barons' leader.[44]

Earls had hereditary functions which go some way to explaining their political role. Simon de Montfort worked to make the earl of Leicester's stewardship of the household into a stewardship of England comparable in power with the stewardship of France which the French barons apparently offered him in 1253. Along with Simon on the barons' side in 1258 stood three other earls whose predecessors had all been among the twenty-five barons of Magna Carta: Humphrey de Bohun, earl of Hereford and hereditary constable of England, and also from 1236 earl of Essex by inheritance from his mother; Roger Bigod, earl of Norfolk, who, having unsuccessfully disputed Simon de Montfort's claim to the stewardship at the coronation of Queen Eleanor, inherited the marshalcy of England through his mother, the eldest sister and coheir of the great marshal's childless sons; but standing first in the list after Simon in 1258, Richard de Clare, earl of Gloucester, whose power was simply in his vast lands. A fortunate marriage in the twelfth century had led in 1217 to the Clares' inheritance of the earldom of Gloucester with its 260 knights' fees in England and the marcher lordships of Glamorgan and Gwynllwg, which, added to the old Clare earldom of Hertford, gave the Clares a yearly income of perhaps £3,700, the third highest in the kingdom after the Lord Edward's £8,000–£10,000 and the earl of Cornwall's

£5,000–£6,000. The wavering allegiances of Earl Richard de Clare and of the son, Gilbert, who succeeded him in 1262, would as much as anything determine the outcome of the Barons' War and the settlement that followed it.[45]

After Evesham all Simon de Montfort's honours were forfeit, and went along with the earldom of Derby, which the rebel Robert de Ferrers could not ransom on the punitive terms singled out for him, to create the appanage of Lancaster for Henry's younger son, Prince Edmund – one with the brilliant future which might have been predicted for the earldom of Cornwall until Earl Edmund died childless in 1301. By 1272 the eighteen holders of non-royal earldoms at the start of Henry's reign had been reduced by forfeiture and the failure of direct heirs to twelve. Two earldoms were revived in Edward's reign: Arundel for the FitzAlans and Pembroke for Aymer de Valence. But the king's dealings with his earls were marked by something nearer the rapacity and lack of scruple described by the Song of Lewes than the leadership of a band of companions pictured by Sir Maurice Powicke. John Ferrers's attempts until the end of the reign to recover his heritage in the courts were simply barred by royal order. When a magnate house failed in the direct line, there were always more distant heirs, but it was easy for the king to exclude them: in 1274, Edward obtained the inheritance of the counts of Aumale and lords of Holderness by the expedient of finding a bogus claimant and buying him out for a paltry sum. Arrangements with the Clares, Bigods and Bohuns opened up their property for the endowment of the king's children. In 1290 the forty-seven-year-old earl of Gloucester was persuaded to marry Edward's eighteen-year-old daughter, Joan of Acre, in an arrangement which disinherited the earl's children by his previous wife, gave Joan a jointure in all his property for her lifetime (and the earldom for a while to her penniless and obscure second husband) and would have given her the permanent disposal of twenty-five Gloucester manors worth 2,000 marks annually had the marriage proved childless. The royal family which was sustained by the plundering of the earldoms was increased by Edward's second marriage to Margaret of France in 1299. Three years later the financially embarrassed Roger Bigod, sixty years old and childless, was given assistance in return for the

[45] L. W. Vernon Harcourt *His Grace the Steward and the Trial of Peers* (London: Longmans, 1907), pp. 74ff; Stacey, *Politics, Policy and Finance*, pp. 118–21; *Cal. Papal Registers*, p. 172; Waugh, *The Lordship of England*, p. 240; *Documents of the Baronial Movement*, ed. Treharne and Sanders, pp. 194–211.

surrender of his earldom of Norfolk with the marshalcy, which he received back entailed upon the (improbable) heirs of his body, with reversion to the Crown; in 1306 they duly reverted, and in 1312 were given by Edward II to his half-brother, Thomas of Brotherton. In 1302 also, Edward I's daughter Elizabeth was provided for by a marriage (supported by a papal dispensation, since the couple were related within the prohibited degrees) to Humphrey de Bohun, a match designed to give the king the reversion of the Essex patrimony with the constableship if no children came (but they did). On the death in 1304 of the faithful John de Warenne, earl of Surrey, his grandson and successor was married to Edward's granddaughter, Joan of Bar. Of the thirteen earls extant at Edward's death in 1307, only the earls of Arundel, Oxford and Warwick were unrelated to the royal house.[46]

Edward seems to have had no policy towards the earls as a group; the purpose of these dealings was the endowment of his family, not political management. Opposition like that of the marshal and constable in 1297 was confronted by different means. Politically, the magnates were kept in check no longer by the disciplines of feudal land tenure (for a recalcitrant tenant could not be disseised), but by the use of judicial commissions. In the course of the *quo warranto* proceedings, which began in Henry III's reign and were generalized by the Statute of Gloucester in 1278, the king's lawyers learnt to deploy Bracton's teaching that liberties or franchises were powers of government belonging to the king, against the claims of the magnates, Gilbert of Gloucester at their head, that these were rights they had won by conquest along with their lands. In 1290 the Statute of Quo Warranto allowed pleas of the long use of franchises (defined as going back beyond the accession of Richard I in 1189) to be accepted, but only as an act of grace on the the king's part. Though their military importance as the king's *comites* may have declined, the earls' territorial power nevertheless continued to guarantee them representation on the king's council in roughly equal numbers to the bishops. In 1305, the earls of Lincoln, Gloucester, Hereford, Warwick and Lancaster

[46] Vernon Harcourt, *His Grace the Steward*, pp. 76, 120–4; Paris, *CM*, v.366; Altschul, *The Clares*, pp. 25, 201ff; Painter, *English Feudal Barony*, p. 174; K. B. McFarlane, 'Had Edward I a Policy towards the Earls?', *History*, 50 (1965), reprinted in his *The Nobility of Later Medieval England* (Oxford: Clarendon Press, 1973); for the treatment of Ferrers, see also *Cases in King's Bench*, ed. Sayles, II.lxix, cxxxi–cxxxv, III.lvi, 175–8; Denton, *Robert Winchelsey*, pp. 205–7; *Cal. Papal Registers*, p. 602.

appear alongside seven bishops and seventeen barons – a ratio of earls to other barons not very different from the 7:17 of the twenty-five magnates to safeguard Magna Carta. Baronial families such as the Despensers, Mortimers and Percys would acquire earldoms under Edward's successors. But the lack of new creations in the thirteenth century lost the earls a distinctive role in the developing administration of the shires; Hubert de Burgh's earldom of Kent did not last, and Roger Leyburn's dominance in the county brought him no title.[47]

The power of the magnates as a whole was integral to the government of the realm. In 1283 the sheriffs were ordered to swear the people to arms and pursue malefactors, because these were emboldened by the absence of the nobles (*proceres*) at the Welsh war. But a new basis had to be found for territorial lordship, as feudal tenure lost its binding power and royal administration bypassed the magnates and worked directly with the knights of the shires. This rebuilding of lordship has been seen too much through the eyes of historians looking for the origins of 'bastard feudalism': that retaining of service not primarily by fees of land but by more volatile forms of payment in money, kind and the exercise of influence on the retainers' behalf, which has often been blamed for the political and social turmoil of the fourteenth and fifteenth centuries. Other historians have pointed out that feudal tenure was never the whole of the relationship between lords and men: it was rather the most public and concrete of the variety of bonds which held together the 'affinities' of magnates. That should not lead one to the fashionable idea that there was never such a thing as a 'feudal society'. There was certainly a law of fee-holding, which grew into common law, progressively defining and developing methods to protect exactly those profits incidental to feudalism, such as wardships and annuities charged on land, which could be used to retain more varied services than those of armed knights.[48]

Nor should the perception that the magnates always relied on

---

[47] D. W. Sutherland, *Quo Warranto Proceedings in the Reign of Edward I* (Oxford: Clarendon Press, 1963), pp. 8–9, 73–4, 82, 149, 176–89, 194–7; *RP*, I.70–7; R. R. Davies, *Conquest, Coexistence and Change: Wales 1063–1415* (Oxford: Clarendon Press and University of Wales Press, 1987), pp. 377–9; *Memoranda de Parliamento*, ed. Maitland, p. cvi; Holt, *Magna Carta*, p. 338.

[48] J. M. W. Bean, *From Lord to Patron: Lordship in Late Medieval England* (Manchester: Manchester UP, 1989), pp. 1–9, 41–8, 121ff, 137, 175–6; P. R. Coss, 'Bastard Feudalism Revised', *Past and Present*, 125 (1989); D. Crouch, D. A. Carpenter and P. R. Coss, 'Debate: Bastard Feudalism Revised', *Past and Present*, 131 (1991).

their influence over a wider circle than their military tenants make one conclude that nothing really changed: there was a gradual but profound readjustment of aristocratic society. The scarcity of land to dispense to new retainers, the taking of several tenements by the same individuals from different lords, the common law's protection of tenants against seignorial power and the Crown's decreased reliance on feudal knight service – these factors had already done much by 1200 to destroy the honour as a military and social unit. In 1215 the rebel lords of the north were nevertheless followed 'almost to a man' by their knightly tenants. At the other end of the century, what little is known about the 'confederates' or 'allies' who supported Bigod and Bohun in their near-rebellion suggests that they were held together by more varied ties, sometimes sealed by formal indentures. The contract retaining one of the five barons who accompanied the earls to the exchequer on 22 August 1297 with 'many others, bannerets and bachelors' has survived. By this indenture 'Sir Roger Bigod, earl of Norfolk and Marshal of England on the one part and Sir John de Segrave on the other part' agreed that John would stay with the earl for the whole of his life with a band of sixteen knights, 'against all, saving his fealty to the king, as well in peace as in time of war, in England, Wales and Scotland'. If John was required in time of peace, his party would receive *bouche a court* (food and drink), and he and his bachelors have robes equal to those of any banneret or bachelor in the earl's livery. Finally John would be enfeoffed with the manor and advowson of Lodden in Norfolk, but return it as soon as his service terminated.[49]

Indentures were appearing which harked back to the temporary enfeoffments of early feudalism to provide the service demanded by the king for his wars, but which also set out the terms of peace-time service in the great lords' households. Other agreements show men who are more nearly equals granting annual rents rather than fees to one another in return for support and 'counsel': sometimes from widely separated parts of the country, they must have been brought together by military service in Wales or Scotland, but the

---

[49] Holt, *The Northerners*, p. 43; *EHD*, III.226–7, 482; Prestwich, *War, Politics and Finance*, pp. 249–50; N. Denholm-Young, *Seignorial Administration in England* (Oxford: OUP, 1937; reprinted London, 1963), pp. 167–8; K. B. McFarlane, 'An Indenture of Agreement between Two English Knights', *BIHR*, 38 (1965); Bean, *From Lord to Patron*, pp. 42–3; P. A. Brand, 'Oldcotes v. d'Arcy', in *Medieval Legal Records Edited in Memory of C. A. F. Meekings*, ed. R. F. Hunnisett and J. B. Post (London: HMSO, 1978).

agreements are for peace a well as war. It now seems likely that the indentures of military service which became frequent in the fourteenth century were just one aspect of a general contracting for service which developed from the late twelfth century, the common law providing the means of enforcing the agreements. It was administrative service that was first, and always principally, retained by contract, and the main impulse towards a contractual society was probably the shift to demesne farming, which brought a need for professional stewards, receivers and auditors. Magnates wanted the homage and fealty of such men, but did not wish to give them hereditary offices and fees – indeed, they might reduce previously inherited offices to life-contracts. Wardships were an ideal form of payment for temporary service, since they had a fixed expiry date at the heirs' coming-of-age. Most flexible of all was the annuity: thus in the reign of Edward I Hugh de Neville entered into an indenture to pay John Filliol 100s. a year in cash and to provide him with robes and equipment, for as long as John remained in his 'company'. (Hugh raised the money by leasing back the wardship of an infant tenant to the boy's widowed mother, but usually the annuity was a straightforward rent-charge on land.) The initiative must often have come from the client in this 'free market' for service. Gentry families seem to have welcomed the new forms of dependency, offering their service in return for the magnates' protection and assistance in arranging marriages for their children.[50]

Feudal tenants ceased to be an important element in a great man's retinue. From an analysis of the witness-lists of the charters or 'acts' of Roger de Quincy, earl of Winchester (d. 1264), Dr Simpson has identified an inner circle of twenty-seven retainers of this Anglo-Scottish magnate, each of whom witnessed between six and twenty-nine charters, and an outer circle of thirty retainers, each of whom witnessed five or less. In neither circle were the earl's tenants significantly represented. Seven of the fifteen knights in the inner circle were minor landholders, not necessarily of the earl, who would have included his land stewards. The other eight were 'household knights', supported in the case of Sir Robert of St

---

[50] See the fundamental article by S. L. Waugh: 'Tenure to Contract: Lordship and Clientage in Thirteenth-Century England', *EHR*, 101 (1986); Coss, 'Bastard Feudalism Revised', p. 40; Altschul, *The Clares*, pp. 226ff; H. L. Gray, 'The Household Administration of Henry Lacy and Thomas of Lancaster', *EHR*, 42 (1927), pp. 181–3; E. Gemmill, 'The Ecclesiastical Patronage of the Earls during the Reign of Edward I', in *Thirteenth-Century England*, ed. Coss and Lloyd, III.

Andrews by an annual fee of 100s. from the office of reeve of the earl's borough of Brackley in Northamptonshire. In Quincy's inner circle there were also five clerks, the men who wrote as well as witnessed most of his charters, and travelled with him between England and Scotland as did the household knights; whereas the clerk who held three of the earl's churches in Scotland was in the outer circle. The four burgesses in the inner circle and six in the outer circle presumably attended on the earl during his visits to Brackley. Much larger than Quincy's was the household of the earls of Gloucester. No less than 200 knights, esquires and maids of honour were said to have accompanied Earl Gilbert and Countess Joan on a visit to her brother, Prince Edward, in 1293. There were the same small landowners and salaried knights in Clare's retinue as in Qunicy's, but also professional men of great consequence who moved between the earls' salaried council and the king's government. Hervey of Boreham, Earl Richard's steward in 1259 and subsequently Earl Gilbert's confidant, was a member of the Montfortian regime in 1264–5, but also keeper of the peace in Essex and Hertfordshire in 1266 and from 1272 a baron of the exchequer, at which period he was listed along with other royal servants receiving annuities from Durham Priory. Hamo le Hautein, Earl Gilbert's steward in 1268, had been a royal escheator and twice sheriff of Lincolnshire between 1259 and 1262 and would later be sheriff of Norfolk and Suffolk; in 1279 he was appointed a justice in eyre for Kent, Sussex and Surrey but preferred to continue to work as a justice of the Jews. Besides these, the earl of Winchester could only show his steward John le Moyne, a future sheriff of Cambridgeshire and Huntingdonshire, and Northamptonshire, justice of the Jews and escheator south of Trent.[51]

The potency of the magnate retinue lay in its capacity for absorbing public officials. An eyre jury even found itself deciding on the entitlement to an annuity of an archdeacon who had left his contracted service with the abbot of Lilleshall to work for Robert Burnell. Lay magnates imitated the greater monasteries which early retained the counsel of royal judges, but they rebuilt their lordships above all on the retaining of county and borough

[51] G. G. Simpson, 'The *Familia* of Roger de Quincy, Earl of Winchester and Constable of Scotland', in *Essays on the Nobility of Medieval Scotland*, ed. K. J. Stringer (Edinburgh: John Donald, 1985); Bean, *From Lord to Patron*, pp. 175–6, for Bigod's household; Altschul, *The Clares*, pp. 118–19; 226–8, 233–41, 279–80, 336; J. R. Maddicott, *Law and Lordship: Royal Justices as Retainers in Thirteenth- and Fourteenth-Century England* (Past and Present Supplement 4, 1978), p. 7.

officials. The malign element in 'bastard feudalism' was not the monetary nature of the bond between magnate and client (though this was certainly more unstable, because more easily created and broken, than the tie of land in old-style feudalism); it was rather that what the retainer placed at his lord's disposal was no longer the strength of his sword-arm but the authority of his public office. To an extent, the magnates with pretensions to 'bear the rule' in their 'countries' became the suitors of the knights, because their power depended on the number of county justices and officials they could attract into their retinues – which further depended on the influence they could wield at court to get their retainers more offices. The 'corruption of local government', livery and the great lords' 'maintenance' of their clients' lawsuits were evils intrinsic to a changed aristocratic culture which also included the new law of trespass (protecting retainers' annuities and other perquisities, and curbing their excesses), and the new politics of petitions and parliaments. The king himself was part of this culture and could not avoid using its methods. On Henry III's return from France in 1260 with a strong force of knights, royal government and household became one; leading supporters like Philip Basset were retained as members of the household, and the sheriffs were even spoken of as the king's 'bachelors'. The troubles of later medieval England can be seen as the spreading of the darker aspects of retaining from the counties to the court, for as Sir John Fortescue would still remind the king in the fifteenth century: 'the people will go with him that best may sustain and reward them'.[52]

---

[52] Waugh, 'Tenure to Contract', pp. 822ff; Maddicott, *Law and Lordship*; D. A. Carpenter, 'Kings, Magnates and Society: The Personal Rule of King Henry III, 1234–1258', *Speculum*, 60 (1985); *idem, Minority of Henry III*, pp. 121–2; *Documents of the Baronial Movement*, ed. Treharne and Sanders, pp. 86–7, 122–7, 130, 132–41, 274–5, 298–9; Powicke, *HLE*, pp. 413–14, 419, 433; C. Given-Wilson, 'The King and the Gentry in Fourteenth-Century England', *TRHS*, 5th ser., 37 (1987); Sir William Fortescue, *The Governance of England*, ed. C. Plummer (Oxford: Clarendon Press, 1885), p. 129.

7

THIRTEENTH-CENTURY POLITICS

———— · ————

Thirteenth-century politics have two aspects: the relations of the English Crown with the European princes, with the kings of Scots and the princes of Wales, and with powerful vassals in the marches and in Ireland; and the dealings of royal government with communities and social groups within the land, dictated to a large extent by foreign ambitions and the demands they generated.[1]

ENGLAND, FRANCE AND THE PAPACY, 1199–1213

When Richard I was killed in April 1199 in a minor skirmish in the Limousin, the question of the relative status of the kingdoms of England and France was raised in an acute form. Richard wanted his younger brother John, count of Mortain, to succeed to all his lands, but feudal custom was not clear that John's claim was as good as that of his nephew, Arthur of Brittany, the son of Richard's and John's long-dead elder brother Geoffrey. King Philip Augustus accepted Arthur's homage for much of Richard's enormous territory in France; and when John took possession of the duchy of Normandy and refused homage, Philip retaliated by supporting Arthur's claim to the English Crown as well. Perhaps

---

[1] A comprehensive political narrative will be found in the two Oxford histories: A. L. Poole, *From Domesday Book to Magna Carta* (Oxford: Clarendon Press, 1951; 2nd edn, 1955), and F. M. Powicke, *The Thirteenth Century: 1216–1307* (Oxford: Clarendon Press, 1953; 2nd edn, 1961; issued in paperback, 1991).

through the advocacy of William the Marshal, John prevailed in England, despite the bad reputation his scheming had already earned him. And soon matrimonial difficulties, which incurred the threat of a papal interdict, compelled Philip to a settlement: for a massive relief, John was accepted as Philip's vassal for all the French lands. A significant aspect of this treaty was the transfer to John of Arthur's homage for Brittany – an overriding of Arthur's feudal rights which lawyers justified as in the public interest of the French state.[2]

The lands in France held feudally by the king of England would inevitably remain a source of friction between monarchies growing in ambition and administrative capacity. The annulment on grounds of consanguinity of his marriage to the childless Isabel of Gloucester allowed John to take as his wife a second Isabel, the heiress of the strategic county of Angouleme in the heart of the duchy of Aquitaine which he held in the right of his mother, but his insensitivity turned this political coup into a disaster. Isabel had been contracted to one of John's greatest continental vassals, Hugh of Lusignan. When Hugh's family showed their discontent, John charged them with treason, and they appealed to King Philip, who like his successor Philip IV in his dealings with Edward I at the end of the century, and like Edward himself in his dealings with Scotland, moved from the role of just overlord to that of aggressive sovereign. John prevaricated in the face of a summons to answer before a court of the French king's barons at Paris, and his fiefs of Aquitaine, Poitou and Anjou were declared forfeit and transferred back to Arthur; but Normandy, which had not technically been at issue, was simply annexed to the French crown.

'For the first time in the modern world', wrote Powicke, 'one highly organised state had annexed another . . . When the Normans became French they did a great deal more than bring their national epic to a close. They permitted the English once more to become a nation, and they established the French state for all time.' But it was less a sense of nationality than the administrative energy which mobilized English resources in the face of French aggression, that made the separation absolute. Though his barons refused to follow him there, John prevented the duchy of Aquitaine from going the same way as Normandy; and in the years 1209–11 he led

---

[2] W. Ullmann, 'Arthur's Homage to King John', *EHR*, 94 (1979); W. L. Warren, *King John*, 2nd edn (London: Eyre and Spottiswoode, 1978) is a good modern narrative of the reign.

triumphant expeditions to bring to heel William the Lion, king of Scots, pacify Ireland and (at least temporarily) subdue the Welsh. But fortification (which gave Dublin, for instance, a new stone castle) was becoming more elaborate and costly, and siege-warfare with it, at the same time that inflation was hitting the fixed revenues of the Crown particularly hard. After an attempt to increase shire revenues, John eventually fell back on a policy of direct taxation, demanding from his subjects a seventh of moveable wealth in 1203, a thirteenth in 1207.[3]

The use of the resources of the Church in defence of the realm embroiled John with another foreign jurisdiction – the pope's. In 1205, after exploiting the wealth of the vacant see for nine months, John obtained the bishopric of Winchester for Peter des Roches, his warrior-clerk from the Touraine. When Hubert Walter died in July 1205, the king sought the archbishopric of Canterbury for another of his servants, John de Gray, bishop of Norwich. The election was confused, however, by the claim of the bishops of the province to have a part along with the Canterbury monks, and Pope Innocent eventually decided to impose his own candidate, the Lincolnshire-born schoolman, Cardinal Stephen Langton. John would not admit the new archbishop to the kingdom. In 1208, the pope placed England under an interdict, so that no sacraments except the baptism of infants and the absolution of the dying should have taken place, and in 1209 the king himself was excommunicated. Many prelates left the country, but John made the most of the situation and simply used his increasingly formidable administration to divert the clergy's wealth into his treasury. Only the French threat and baronial unrest persuaded John to submit to the papacy in 1213. For both medieval chroniclers and sixteenth-century protestants like Bale the struggle of king and pope, not that of king and barons, was the significant event of the reign. The difference was that in the eyes of the chroniclers John's kingship was curtailed by his resignation of England to the pope to be received back as a fief of the Church, while for Bale in the sixteenth century the king was a 'faithful Moses' who 'withstood proud Pharaoh for his poor Israel'.[4]

---

[3] F. M. Powicke, *The Loss of Normandy*, 2nd edn (Manchester: Manchester UP, 1961), pp. 286–303, 306–7; S. Painter, *The Reign of King John*, (Baltimore: Johns Hopkins Press), pp. 130–6.

[4] *EHD*, III, no. 17, for John's surrender of the kingdom; *Radulphi de Coggeshall Chronicon Anglicanum*, ed. Joseph Stevenson (Rolls Series, London, 1975), p. 167; Paris, *CM*, II.535, 541, 546, 547; John Bale, *King Johan*, lines 1107–13.

THE ASSERTION OF BARONIAL LIBERTIES, 1213–27

In the period between John's submission to the pope and Henry III's full coming-of-age, the place of the barons in the Angevin state became the central issue of English politics. Already in 1212 John's exactions had provoked a baronial conspiracy, its purpose said to be 'to drive the king and his family from the kingdom and choose someone else as king in his place'. The struggle that emerged was essentially a feudal conflict between a demanding and unreliable overlord and a volatile group of his tenants-in-chief, but the circumstances of national peril and John's untiring government forced the barons to transcend merely feudal notions of right conduct. The king's accommodation with the Church proved its worth by depriving Philip Augustus of papal approval for his plans to conquer England for his son, and by ensuring papal condemnation of any further 'conspiracies and factions' on the part of John's subjects. The northern barons continued to refuse to join an expedition to Poitou, and Stephen Langton, now restored to Canterbury, persuaded the king that he should not coerce them before obtaining a proper legal judgement; so John had once again to show his ability to defend his patrimony without them, and even succeeded in recovering Angers, the cradle of his house, from the French. Hope of recovering Normandy also was ended only by the defeat of the northern prong of the attack on Philip Augustus, led by the Emperor Otto, the count of Flanders and the earl of Salisbury, at the decisive battle of Bouvines. John negotiated a five-year truce for Aquitaine and in October 1214 returned home personally undefeated, to face a baronage resentful at the rule of Peter des Roches and now determined to deny an obligation to pay the scutage needed to support war beyond the shores of England, let alone give personal service.

The more moderate of the barons, inspired by Langton, had begun to see an agreement with the king enshrined in a charter as a better protection than appeal to the nebulous 'laws of Edward the Confessor'. Charters were after all the normal way of conveying rights and privileges. Over a century earlier Henry I had actully set a precedent for the grant of a charter of liberties (meaning freedom from arbitrary and excessive feudal dues) to the baronage as a whole. What was needed now, however, was a document that would be proof against the abuse of the administrative power which had begun to be created in the reign of John's father. As Langton knew, England was more a monarchy than a commonwealth, and a monarch was to be restrained only by natural law and judicial custom. The crucial question was whether a king like John, dominant at least in Britain and Ireland and believing his kingdom the equal of the empire, would accept as a restraint upon himself the system of justice which his dynasty had fashioned and which he applied so diligently to others. Was the king above the law or made by it?[5]

John's brilliant counter to the demand for a charter of liberties came on 4 March 1215, when he took the cross. By assuming the role of a crusader he placed himself even more firmly under papal protection, and Langton further in the wrong for supporting baronial protest. A group of barons nonetheless broke out in open revolt, defying the king (that is withdrawing their fealty to him) in proper feudal manner, and going on under the command of Robert Fitzwalter, lord of Baynard's Castle in London and self-styled 'marshal of the army of God', to attack the royal castle at Northampton. To isolate these extremists, John promised to submit all grievances to papal arbitration and made the crucial undertaking (which would become c. 39 of Magna Carta) not to disseise the barons who were against him, 'nor go upon them with force and arms, except by the law of our realm or by the judgement of their peers in our court'. With the king at Windsor and the rebels ensconced in London, Langton and the moderates saw their chance to mediate. On 10 June 1215, John and the rebels met at Runnymede by the Thames; and by 15 June the draft set of liberties known as the 'Articles of the Barons' had been turned into the Great Charter, copies of which were ready for distribution four days later when the rebels restored their fealty.[6]

Magna Carta was about feudal liberties, not some abstract liberty for all subjects of the king. Particularly in the north, John had created a divide within the baronage, for on the other side from the king's men were drawn together the people who had lost out in the sale of royal lordship rights: the widows of tenants-in-chief forced to offer up to 200 marks and three palfreys a time not to be compelled to marry again, or at least not to marry below them; and men like Nicholas de Stuteville, made to pay 10,000 marks to

---

[5] See above, p. 55; W. Ullmann, *Principles of Government and Politics in the Middle Ages* (London: Methuen, 1961), pp. 158ff.

[6] J. C. Holt, *Magna Carta* (Cambridge: CUP, 1965), p. 344; Paris, *CM*, II.117; the copy of the Articles of the Barons quoted in the House of Commons by John Selden in 1628 was found in the Lambeth archives, where it may have been placed by Archbishop Langton himself.

succeed to his brother's lands, or like Robert de Vaux to pay 2,000 marks just to recover the king's good will. There is no surprise in the absence of the earls of Chester, Derby and Warenne, all beneficiaries of royal generosity, from the twenty-five barons listed in the final ('security') clause of Magna Carta who 'with the commune of all the land' were 'to distrain and distress the king' if he or his ministers failed to keep the Charter's provisions; or in the presence there of John de Lacy, constable of Chester, who had been required to pay a relief of 7,000 marks on coming-of-age, after his lands had already been exploited for twenty-two months in royal custody. At the head of the twenty-five along with the earls of Clare, Aumale, Winchester, Hereford, Norfolk and Oxford, is the poignant figure of Geoffrey de Mandeville, earl of Essex and Gloucester. This son of the justiciar Geoffrey FitzPeter had first been married to Maud, Robert Fitzwalter's daughter, whose attraction of King John's lustful attention the Dunmow chronicle makes the cause of the rebellion; she died childless, and in January 1214 he was cajoled by the king into marrying the latter's divorced wife Isabel, countess of Gloucester, for a fine of 20,000 marks. The Crown's ruthless pursuit of this ruinous fine, along with the denial of the custody of the Tower of London which his father had possessed, gave Geoffrey every reason to stand among the rebels. The priorities of the rebels in 1215 show clearly in the Articles of the Barons and in Magna Carta itself. The first chapter declared that the English Church should be free; the second restricted the relief for the heir to a knight's fee to 100s. 'at most', and set the relief for an earl or lesser baron at £100; and chapter 3 answered John de Lacy's grievance by providing that no relief at all should be payable by a ward on coming of age. Chapters 4 and 5 forbade the wasting of an heir's lands by guardians, and chapters 6 to 8 dealt with the marriage of wards and widows; heirs should be married off by guardians 'without disparagement' and with the foreknowledge of their nearest kinsmen; a widow should have her dower without delay or payment, might stay in her husband's house for forty days after his death and could remain unmarried as long as she wished on giving security that she would not eventually remarry without her lord's consent.[7]

---

[7] Holt, *Magna Carta*, pp. 46–7, 210, 331, 338; *idem*, *The Northerners* (Oxford: Clarendon Press, 1961), pp. 48–9, 73–6, 177–9, 230–1, 251, 253; S. L. Waugh, *The Lordship of England: Royal Wardships and Marriages in English Society and Politics, 1217–1327* (Princeton: Princeton UP, 1988), p. 160.

John cannot have seen the Charter as more than a settlement of his differences with a particular group of rebels: for him the real concessions were probably that he would at once restore all the hostages and charters given to him as securities for faithful service, along with the lands, castles and liberties of which he had deprived people without the lawful judgement of their peers; and that he would dismiss foreign captains, knights, crossbowmen, sergeants and mercenary soldiers who had come 'with horses and arms to the hurt of the realm'. But the whole of Angevin government and the rights of all the king's subjects came under scrutiny. By c. 53 John promised that when he returned from crusade justice would be extended to his predecessors' seizures of property without lawful judgement. The story that John was poisoned at Swineshead for threatening to increase the price of bread rather than his lusting after the abbot's sister shows that within a century a wider public good than simply baronial rights was seen to have been at stake in his reign. The barons needed the support of the knights and the merchants, both of which groups were gaining an independent sense of their rights. The knightly sub-tenants, to whom the charter required the tenants-in chief to grant the same customs and liberties as they themselves had been granted by the king, were gaining independent status as local administrators and beginning to received direct grants of liberties from the Crown: an example is the power conceded to the knights of the Devon shire court in 1204 'to give bail for men arrested by the sheriff, so that none should stay in prison because of his malice'. The clause of Magna Carta which ordered the individual summons of the prelates and greater barons to give 'the common counsel of the realm' concerning taxation also provided for the general summons of the lesser men through the sheriffs. The Great Charter granted 'the liberties written below . . . to all the free men of our realm for ourselves and our heirs for ever' – not just, as in previous coronation charters, to all the king's barons and free tenants. Clause 20 against arbitrary fines was more comprehensive still. People were to be amerced 'by the testimony of reputable men of the neighbour-hood', and not so heavily that a free man lost his livelihood, a merchant that he was left without merchandise and a villein that he had to give up his cart. The Charter was seen as laying down a law of the land (*lex terrae*) which belonged to all free men and perhaps to villeins also. The king promised that he would only make justices and sheriffs of people who knew the law 'and meant to observe it well'. The tradition of statute law takes its origin

from the detailed clauses of the Charter. There is even an anticipation of the judicial parliaments prescribed by the barons in 1258
in the provision that the twenty-five barons of the 'security clause'
should give judgement in case of disagreement about the restoration of a man's property or legal right.[8]

As a settlement between John and the barons, however, the
Charter was a failure. The idea of giving a sworn body of magnates
power to distrain the king to observe his promises was as unacceptable to John as the more elaborate checks devised in 1258
would be to Henry, and the rebel diehards showed no greater
intention of working the security clause. While John sent off to
Pope Innocent for the annulment of the agreement, his adversaries
reinforced their position in London. On 5 September the pope's
commissioners (the nuncio Pandulph, the bishop of Winchester
and the abbot of Reading) excommunicated the rebel barons and
their London supporters, and suspended Archbishop Langton who
refused to execute the papal mandate on the grounds that it had
been issued on out-of-date information. As Langton left the
country once more for Rome civil war was beginning. Expert
siege operations brought the surrender of the rebels who had
occupied the great castle of Rochester to bar the way to the capital
of the mercenaries John was expecting from the continent. But he
was then diverted to the harrying of his enemies in the north, and
allowed the barons and their French allies to consolidate their
poition in London, though they in turn were unable to dislodge
the new justiciar Hubert de Burgh from Dover Castle. The king's
agitated movement between the castles held by his mercenary
captains where his treasure was stored came to an end at last with
his death at Newark on 18 October 1216.

The firm establishment of chartered liberties was achieved by
the loyalist barons who safeguarded the succession of the nine-
year-old King Henry III. That a new feeling of nationality, fostered
by the cutting of the ties with Normandy, also played a part is
suggested by the strictures of the Marshal's biographer against the
French ribalds who boasted that England was theirs. At a great
council at Bristol in November 1216 the vital step was taken of
reissuing Magna Carta, shorn of some of its more radical clauses,
under the seals of both the Marshal and the papal legate Guala: it
effectively became Henry's coronation charter. Militarily the king

---

[8] Holt, *Magna Carta*, pp. 52–60, 317–37; A. Harding, 'Political Liberty in the
Middle Ages', *Speculum*, 55 (1980), pp. 430–2.

seemed desperately weak. The households of the Marshal, Earl
Ranulf of Chester, the earl of Salisbury and the bishop of Winchester provided the backbone of the force of 406 knights and 317
crossbowmen which won the decisive battle of 20 May 1217
known as the 'Fair of Lincoln', raising the siege by Louis's men of
the castle held for the Crown by the Lady Nicola de la Hay, and
capturing the earls of Winchester, Hereford and Hertford and most
of the rebel leadership. This and another defeat in a sea battle off
Sandwich in August forced the excommunicated Louis to make
terms. By the Treaty of Kingston, he was paid liberally to abandon
the rebels, restore the chancery and exchequer records, possesion
of which had symbolized his control of the government, and leave
the country. There was to be an amnesty for the rebels and a
restoration of their lands. There seems even to have been a
suggestion (which came to nothing) that Normandy might have
been restored to the Angevins in this feudal peace-making. And
Henry again promised to concede the liberties the barons asked
for. The Charter was reissued still further revised, and along with
it a Charter of the Forest, so that later demands would often be for
the confirmation of the Charters in the plural.[9]

Reissuing the Charters was becoming a method of refining law
and government. The 1216 version dropped the 'weighty and
doubtful' provisions of the original Charter which dictated how
the king should exact scutages and aids and what sort of men he
should choose as his officials: the baronial government did not
wish to shackle royal administrators while they struggled to get
the exchequer and the courts back into action, and – as the new
king wrote to the justiciar of Ireland – 'with the help of the divine
mercy to change the state of the realm for the better'. The 1217
reissue of Magna Carta and the Charter of the Forests were more
positive. Probably as a result of complaints to the inquiry into
shire administration ordered in 1215, there was a new chapter in
1217 curbing the sheriffs' abuse of power in shire courts and tourns
which provided the basis for future reforms of local government.
The promises in the Forest Charter to reduce the king's forests to
the dimensions obtaining at the accession of Henry II started

[9] Above, p. 10; D. A. Carpenter, *The Minority of Henry III* (London: Methuen,
1990), pp. 36–40; *EHD*, III.84, 87; J. W. F. Hill, *Medieval Lincoln* (Cambridge:
CUP, 1948), pp. 201ff; D. Crouch, *William Marshal: Court, Career and Chivalry in
the Angevin Empire, 1147–1219* (London: Longmans, 1990), pp. 121–4.

another century-long argument that 'helped to keep Magna Carta alive.'[10]

The pipe rolls which resume in the second year of Henry's reign demonstrate the resilience and determination of the officials who brought order and a yet more formidable exchequer machine out of the financial disruption of the civil war. A careful adherence by the exchequer to the rates of relief set out in the Charter and a remedying by the council of some of John's more blatant fiscal injustices were combined with a relentless pursuit of the rebels' debts to the Crown and even of sums owing from well before the war. Five years into the reign the huge and virtually untouched debt of Fulk Fitzwarin was parcelled into yearly instalments of eighty marks, which should have needed twenty-three years to pay off. Judicial revenues bulked larger in the pipe rolls as the journeyings of the king's justices round the country were resumed. In 1218 eight groups of judges were sent out on the most comprehensive eyre to be launched since 1176. It was faced with the difficult problem of finding a substitute for the ordeal, since the essential participation of the clergy in that method of trying criminals had been forbidden at the Fourth Lateran Council, and conviction by a fallible jury was only reluctantly accepted in place of 'the judgement of God'. But the eyre appears to have been a triumphant success. The dispensation of justice according to the principles of the Charter was what the community looked for. When the baronial council, seemingly for political reasons, allowed the reopening of a case of novel disseisin decided against the count of Aumale in the eyre at Lincoln, the shire rose up in protest and demanded the 'common liberty of the whole realm granted and sworn'. The real protection for liberties was passing from the Charter itself to the courts, where peasants learnt to assert their personal freedom, or their privileges as 'villein sokemen'; townsmen of Dunwich or of Lynn to claim their chartered liberty not to have to plead outside their borough; and barons, bishops and abbots to sue each other for the setting-up of fairs, gallows or weaving-looms to the damage of existing 'liberties'. The definitive reissue of the Charters in 1225 would be placed by Sir Edward Coke at the head of his exposition of statute law in the second part of his *Institutes*, because he held it to have been 'for the most part

---

[10] Holt, *Magna Carta*, pp. 271–5, 357; T. Rymer, *Foedera*, new edn, 4 vols. in 7 parts (Record Commission, London, 1816–69), I(i), p. 145.

declaratory of the principle grounds of the fundamental laws of England'; as they were expounded also by the great thirteenth-century legal authors, Bracton, Britton and Fleta; and above all as they were applied in the courts.[11]

On Whit Sunday 1220 Henry received from Langton the proper coronation in Westminster abbey not possible in 1216. The recovery of the king's fortunes was marked by the increasing numbers of his household troops: Henry granted robes to 25 knights at Christmas 1220, took 37 knights and 70 sergeants with him on a Welsh expedition in 1223, and by 1226 had some 123 knights available. The bishop of Winchester's nephew, Peter des Rivaux, was already at work in the king's wardrobe, which was in process of emerging from the chamber, as the exchequer had done long before, to become the most dynamic part of the royal household and government. In one ten-month period in 1223–4 the wardrobe received more than £9,000, over half from the exchequer but a significant proportion brought in from other sources by special mandates; and payed out, among 'the necessary expenses of the royal household', the wages of 'the knights, sergeants, and other workmen of *petrariae*, mangonels, and other necessities for the siege of the castle of Bedford', amounting to £1,311 18s. 2d.[12]

But incorporation of baronial energies into the running of the state could not be a short or easy task. When Langton proposed the 1225 confirmation, the old royal servant William Brewer protested that the Charter had been extorted from King John by violence. The tensions existed even within the group of ministers who had worked hardest to see that the Angevin crown survived.

---

[11] See four important volumes published by the Pipe Roll Society: the rolls for *2 Henry III*, ed. E. P. Ebden (NS, vol. 39, London, 1972), *3 Henry III*, ed. B. E. Harris (NS, vol. 42, London, 1976), *4 Henry III*, ed. B. E. Harris (NS, vol. 47, London, 1987), and *5 Henry III*, ed. D. Crook (NS, vol. 48, London, 1990); Carpenter, *Minority of Henry III*, pp. 96–103; *Rolls of the Justices in Eyre for Lincolnshire 1218–9 and Worcestershire 1221*, ed. D. M. Stenton (Selden Society, vol. 53, London, 1934), p. lii; above, p. 76; Harding, 'Political Liberty', pp. 434–5; examples in *CRR*, ix(1220), pp. 36, 124–5, 134, 193, 370; XIII (1227–30), nos. 406, 2199; Sir Edward Coke, *The Second Part of the Institutes of the Laws of England, Containing the Exposition of Many Ancient and Other Statutes* (London, 1797), third of the unnumbered pages of the Proeme; Holt, *Magna Carta*, pp. 2–10; J. G. A. Pocock, *The Ancient Constitution and the Feudal Law: A Study of English Historical Thought in the Seventeenth Century. A Reissue with a Retrospect* (Cambridge: CUP, 1987), p. 45.

[12] Powicke, *The Thirteenth Century*, p. 28–9; above, p. 216; Carpenter, *Minority of Henry III*, pp. 52, 227, 242, 317, 382; T. F. Tout, *Chapters in the Administrative History of Medieval England*, 6 vols. (Manchester: Manchester UP, 1920–33), I. 188–205.

Though a leading member of the government, Peter des Roches persistently refused to pay the tax imposed to buy off Prince Louis, apparently because his individual consent had not been obtained. As the justiciar Hubert de Burgh increased his grip, the bishop of Winchester no doubt resented playing second fiddle in the administration. In 1223 he backed the protest of the earls of Chester and Gloucester, Fawkes de Breauté and the mercenary captains, against Hubert's move to take from them control of the great castles and the counties they dominated. This was the crisis of the minority, brought to an end by the intervention of Langton and the bishops, and by the forcible ejection of Fawkes from the country after the siege of Bedford in the summer of 1224.

Hubert's action in 1223 was inspired by Pope Honorius's declaration (perhaps, ironically, secured by Peter des Roches) that King Henry was now mature enough to govern and should have the kingdom delivered to him. The king was eager to assert himself. When, nineteen years old, he declared himself of age in January 1227, and assumed full control of the great seal, the personality of the king and his concern for his state became the major factors in politics.[13]

THE AMBITIONS OF A KING, 1227–58

Chroniclers in following centuries gave short measure to the period between Henry's coming of age and the 'mad parliament' of 1258, for they found it difficult to make a coherent story out of the uncertain responses of king and barons to the rise of a professional administration.

Henry sought, with a mixture of obstinacy and evasion, to pass over the events of his father's reign and attempt to restore the Angevin monarchy to its old position. This meant first and foremost an effort to regain the lost territories in France (in 1224 Poitou had been lost as well), from which increased demands on the English administration followed. Hubert de Burgh was weakened by his inability to provide the resources for a successful Breton expedition, or even to keep out Llywelyn of Wales, and brought down by the animosity of Peter des Roches. As told by Roger of Wendover and Matthew Paris, the story of Hubert's downfall begins with the bishop of Winchester's return from

---

[13] Powicke, *The Thirteenth Century*, p. 28; *Pipe Roll for 5 Henry III*, ed. Crook, p. 21; Carpenter, *Minority of Henry III*, pp. 304, 321, 332, 360.

crusade to find Langton dead and the way clear to the destruction of his old rival; continues with des Roches's wielding of power through his creature Peter des Rivaux, and his procuring of the death of Earl Richard Marshal in Ireland for leading a baronial protest against the regime; and concludes with his dismissal by a remorseful king, who blames the bishop for alienating his vassals from him and making him forget his kingly duties.[14]

Peter des Rivaux's fall from grace in 1234, along with his patron, did not stop the development of the household. As the household clerks became more professional, the vice-regal justiciarship, made redundant by the majority of a king without the rule of Normandy to keep him from England, effectively came to an end with Hubert de Burgh, the last great lay magnate administrator. For thirty years after Henry's quarrel in 1238 with the chancellor Ralph Neville, bishop of Chichester, over his postulation to Winchester, the chancellorship, too, was in virtual abeyance as a great office of state. In 1234 Henry has been described as beginning his 'personal rule', but there is little to suggest that he relished it. The strains of government showed in his hectoring of the sheriffs at the exchequer, and of the men of Hampshire in the great hall of Winchester Castle about the robbery of Brabantine merchants. The very city where he was born was a den of murderers and thieves, Matthew Paris has him complaining on the latter occasion: how could such things be, when he had appointed wise men to help him rule. He was only one man and could not support the burden of the whole kingdom without the comfort of helpers. The exchequer was reinvigorated by the chief baron, Alexander de Swereford, archdeacon of Shropshire and later treasurer of St Paul's (d. 1246); and the extensive surveys of knights' fees and serjeanty tenure recorded in the *Red Book of the Exchequer* and the *Book of Fees* were made. Henry was determined in the assertion of his rights, but there is no indication that he would have been able to impose 'absolute rule', even if he could have envisaged it.[15]

---

[14] Above, pp. 18, 188, and chapter 4; B. Wilkinson, *The Constitutional History of England, 1216–1399* 3 vols. (London: Longmans, 1948–58), I, Introduction, is suggestive on Henry III's character; Powicke, *HLE*, pp. 75ff, 270–1; D. Carpenter, 'The Fall of Hubert de Burgh', *Journal of British Studies*, 19 (1980); Tout, *Chapters*, I.200, 214–32, 242–3; R. C. Stacey, *Politics, Policy, and Finance under Henry III, 1216–1245* (Oxford: Clarendon Press, 1987), cap. 3.

[15] Above p. 160; M. T. Clanchy, 'Did Henry III Have a Policy?' *History*, 53 (1968); Paris, *CM*, v.56–60: translated in *Chronicles of Matthew Paris*, ed.

In the counties, this was 'the irregular time of Henry III' described by Sir Edward Coke in the seventeenth century, when great men took distresses 'of the beasts of their tenants or neighbours . . . to enforce the owners of the beasts for necessity to yield to their desire'. The presentments in the eyre of lords who withdrew their tenants from the public hundred courts, and complaints in 1258 about their oppressive use of distraint of suit to courts leet, fit in with the multiplication of seignorial court rolls after the middle of the century; together they show that it was the magnates who harnessed the new administrative zeal to bolster their power in the countryside. The government introduced new articles of the eyre to curb the abuses of the king's officials in the counties, but there was no consistent royal interference in private lordships. The case made against Henry in 1264 was not that his rule had pressed directly on the magnates, but that they could not get justice against the king's favourites.[16]

In 1261, Henry would make the claim that during the forty-five years he had held the government all his labour had been to establish 'the peace and tranquillity of one and all' and that he had indeed achieved the avoidance of 'hostility and general war'. But his self-doubt made keeping the peace amongst the 'wise men' he needed to help him govern and fulfil his foreign ambitions a struggle. To cap the administration a sworn council made its appearance in 1236, meeting in the household (not the exchequer) and including the stewards of the household and other ministerial figures. But the most professional council could never be immune from the jealousies amongst the magnates and the king's extended family. A new generation of earls was coming to the fore, of an age with the young king and the queen he took from Provence in 1236; the Langtonian bishops who had helped the country through the minority had died off. With Eleanor came the 'Savoyard uncles': William, who became the king's chief councillor and his candidate for the bishopric of Winchester in competition with William Raleigh, who had been the minister responsible for reform of the accounting procedures of the sheriffs and the new county

---

R. Vaughan (Gloucester: Alan Sutton, 1986), pp. 169–72; Stacey, *Politics, Policy and Finance*, pp. 41–2, 257.

[16] Above, pp. 83–4, 157; Coke, *Second Institutes*, pp. 156, 193; D. A. Carpenter, 'King, Magnates, and Society: The Personal Rule of King Henry III, 1234–1258', *Speculum*, 60 (1985), pp. 46, 51–2; cf. Stacey, *Politics, Policy and Finance*, pp. 255–6.

escheators; Boniface, elected in 1241 to the see of Canterbury; and Peter, later count of Savoy, who also entered the king's innermost councils.[17]

In 1238 the marriage of Henry's sister and widow of William Marshal the younger to Simon de Montfort, newly arrived from France to claim his inheritance, provoked an angry reaction from Earl Gilbert Marshal and from the king's brother, Earl Richard of Cornwall. The latter's great wealth and international stature gave him an influence which would generally be exercised in a moderating fashion, however, and after their joint participation in a successful crusade, the king's brother and brother-in-law showed that they could work together in the council. It was Henry himself who quickly found it difficult to work with the formidable earl of Leicester, of whom he confessed himself more afraid than he was of thunderstorms. On his way back from crusade in 1242, Simon found Henry at Saintes on the west coast of France amid the ruins of his last effort to recover Poitou, and told the king that he ought to be shut up like Charles the Simple. Henry needed the military skill and political weight of a man sought at various times as the governor of the community of the kingdom of Jerusalem and as regent of France, but he did not forget the humiliating words of 1242. In 1248 he sent Simon to make safe the last Angevin lands in Gascony, apparently giving him complete freedom of action but continuing to interfere in details of the duchy's administration. The earl's uncompromising methods in fact set Gascony in turmoil, and in the end he was subjected to an inconclusive state trial at Westminister on charges of overriding the Gascons' customary rights.[18]

The king's ambitions turned away from the recovery of his lost French inheritance, first to the domination of Britain. In 1244 there was a show of force against the Scots in a dispute over the line of the border. The accession of the eight-year-old Alexander III as king of Scots in 1249 gave Henry the opportunity to settle the border issue and marry his daughter Margaret to the young king. Simon de Montfort and the archbishop of York were sent to Edinburgh in 1254 to instruct the Scottish king, and in 1255 Henry went to the march himself to impose an acceptable regime. Until the succession crisis of 1286 there was peace between England and Scotland. In Wales, the vital 'Four Cantrefs' between Dee and

---

[17] Carpenter, 'King, Magnates and Society', p. 60.
[18] Above, pp. 178, 255; Powicke, *HLE*, p. 215.

Conway were conquered in 1247 and annexed in 1254 to Edward's lordship of Chester, only to be lost again in 1256–8 with much else. Meanwhile larger ambitions beckoned in Europe. Henry lived somewhat in the shadow of Louis IX: he rebuilt Westminster Abbey in an attempt to emulate the king of France's Sainte-Chapelle. The French Queen Margaret and the English Queen Eleanor were sisters, and in 1243 Richard of Cornwall married Sanchia, another daughter of the count of Provence. Henry was in danger of being outshone by his own brother, who was a famous crusader and in 1257, seven years after the death of his friend the Hohenstaufen emperor Frederick II, went on to be chosen king of the Romans, that is emperor-elect, though 'Richard of Almaine' would never became emperor in fact nor establish himself in the empire's heartland of Germany. In 1252, Richard had refused the kingdom of Sicily, which the pope was seeking to wrest from the Hohenstaufen dynasty. Two years later Henry was glad to accept it for his younger son Edmund, and got the vows he had taken in 1250 commuted from a crusade to the Holy Land to a Sicilian expedition and the payment of 135,541 marks towards papal expenses from Michaelmas 1256. The penalties for non-performance were precisely those incured by failure to keep crusading vows: excommunication for the king and interdict for the land. The straining to avoid them and the disappointment of the hoped-for rewards were the background of the baronial coup of 1258. Unable to summon feudal troops in the numbers available to Louis IX, Henry had to seek the money to hire them, 'as though [in Matthew Paris's words at an earlier point of the reign] the king of England was a banker, exchanger or huckster, rather than a king and a noble leader and commander of knights'. These were years when Henry was falling back on his household for actual military resources.[19]

The reign of a king as ambitious and yet unsure of himself as Henry seems to have been was perhaps better soil for the growth of political institutions than the confident rule of an Edward. The baronial government of the minority was conscious of its responsiblity for 'the state of the king and the kingdom', and took care to inform foreign powers such as the king of Norway and the pope of it. The councillors who swore an oath in 1236 to serve the king,

[19] *Anglo-Scottish Relations 1174–1328: Some Selected Documents*, ed. and tr. E. L. G. Stones (Oxford: Clarendon Press, 1965), no. 10; A. Young, 'The Political Role of Walter Comyn during the Minority of Alexander III', *Scottish Historical Review*, 57 (1978); Powicke, *HLE*, cap. 9; Paris, *CM*, IV.191; above, p. 189.

and whose advice the king swore to follow, acted as a catalyst for the larger conferences of judges and magnates to which the term 'parliament' (parley) would soon begin to be applied. A new word was necessary to comprehend a new political institution perceived as beginning in 1215. In a writ of 1242 the sheriffs were ordered not to allow anyone in their bailiwicks to exercise liberties belonging to the Crown which they had not enjoyed at the time of 'the parliament of Runnymede' between King John and his barons. Matthew Paris first uses the term of a 'general parliament of the English realm' held in London in 1246, to which the whole nobility of prelates, earls and baron were summoned to 'treat effectively of the unstable state of the kingdom as urgent necessity required'.[20]

But the earliest uses of all have a judicial context: legal cases were adjourned (on the first known occasion in November 1236) to 'parliaments' which were clearly meetings of the justices 'with the king' (soon known as the court of 'king's bench') The building up of the court *coram rege* was part of the remaking of the king's council at the end of the crisis of 1232–4. It operated all the time, not just in law terms, and during the king's absence in France in 1242–3 its hearings were indistinguishable from sessions of the council. Cases of political importance would naturally come before judges reinforced by magnates and prelates present in the king's court. But eventually the existence of the two 'central' courts of king's bench and common pleas dividing the justice of England between them was bound to require another court of final resort beyond them: 'the king in his council in his parliaments'.[21]

The first business of parliament was therefore to guard and foster that law of England which Bracton, a clerk and justice of king's bench, was just then claiming as true law though unwritten, because it was promulgated by the king with the counsel of the magnates. At the great meeting of the king's court at Merton in 1236, the barons said that they would not change the law of England to conform with the Church's views on bastardy, not that it was incapable of change. Manifestly, it had been built up in the

[20] Rymer, *Foedera*, i(i), pp. 145, 149, 171; Powicke, *HLE*, pp. 153, 290ff, 336–7; *Close Rolls, 1242–7* (London: HMSO, 1916), p. 242; Paris, *CM*, iv.518.

[21] R. F. Treharne, 'The Nature of Parliament in the Reign of Henry III', *EHR*, 74 (1959), reprinted in *Historical Studies of the English Parliament*, ed. E. B. Fryde and E. Miller (Cambridge: CUP, 1970), i.73–4; see generally the introductions by Mr. C. A. F. Meekings to *CRR*, xv, 1233–7 (1972), xvi, 1237–42 (1979) and 1242–3 (1991); *CRR*, xv, no. 2047, for the 1236 adjournment; *CRR*, xvi, nos. 1493, 1625, 1659.

previous three-quarters of a century on the basis of Henry II's assizes, and continued to be made by the invention of new writs and the judgements of the courts. Matthew Paris recognized that Henry made 'new laws' at Merton, 'for the salvation of his soul and the amendment of his realm': laws about widows' dower, the working of the assizes of novel disseisin and mort d'ancestor, wardship and marriage, the date from which descent of land must be pleaded in actions of right, the power to appoint attorneys to do suit to local courts and the right of landlords to enclose common land not needed by their tenants. Retrospectively, the laws made at Merton were recognized as the first statute, and they appear as such at the head of the printed *Statutes of the Realm*. New terms were needed for new forms of law-making. In France, the language of statutes ('establishments' or statements of law) had already begun to replace the language of royal grants, particularly when the rights or disabilities of groups such as the Jews were in question. In England, 'provisions' rather than 'statutes' was the term used during much of Henry III's reign for the statements and refinements of people's rights beginning with 'the Provisions of Runnymede' (i.e. Magna Carta), though such phrases as 'we provide and establish' (*providimus et statuimus*) and 'it is provided and established by agreement' appear in the 1250s and continue into the legislation of Edward I. The feudal charter was no longer an adequate vehicle for the establishment of the personal liberties of knights, townsmen and villeins within the state of the realm.[22]

In Bracton's view, the king also was given his liberties and status by the law. King and barons acknowledged a mutual responsibility to prevent the alienation of the rights possessed by the king for his kingdom's sake, though Henry patently flouted this responsiblity to reward his favourites. Pope Gregory IX warned Henry in 1237 about the improvidence with which he had heard that the king was alienating to prelates and magnates liberties, property and dignities which belonged 'by right to the state and crown', alienations which threatened not only the subsistence of the kingdom but also the rights of the apostolic see to which it pertained. In 1256 it was King Henry who found 'the Crown and royal dignity . . . intoler-

---

[22] Above, pp. 167, 177; *EHD*, III, no. 30; Powicke, *HLE*, pp. 148–53; Paris, *CM*, III.341; A. Harding, 'Legislators, Lawyers and Lawbooks', in *Lawyers and Laymen*, ed. T. M. Charles-Edwards, M. E. Owen and D. B. Walters (Cardiff: University of Wales Press, 1986), p. 248; *idem*, 'Aquinas and the Legislators', in *Théologie et droit dans la science politique de l'Etat moderne* (Rome: Ecole Française de Rome, 1991).

ably damaged' by the alienation of lands held of the king in chief, which the sheriffs were not to allow without his specific licence. When Prince Edward was invested with Ireland and Gascony two years earlier, these lordships were declared inalienable from the Crown.[23]

Already in 1244 the magnates felt the need to press their advice on the king. In that year they insisted on replying as a body to his demand for an aid and chose a committee of twelve, four bishops (Archbishop Boniface, Robert Grosseteste, William Raleigh and Walter de Cantilupe), four earls (including Cornwall and Leicester) and four barons (including William de Cantilupe) to speak for them. A draft 'constitution' which seems to have circulated during this episode (though it can hardly have been an agreed view of this respectable body) proposed that four 'conservators of liberties' should be elected 'by common consent to the king's council and sworn to handle faithfully the affairs of the king and the kingdom, doing justice to all without respect of persons'. They should 'hear each one's complaints' but also manage the funds granted by the whole community to the king. These were presumably justices *coram rege*, for two justices of the (common) bench, a justiciar and a chancellor were also to be chosen. Writs sued out contrary to law and custom should be revoked. There should be a judicial eyre; a mutual oath should be sworn against opponents of the scheme; and suspect councillors should 'be removed from the king's side' – all of which would happen in 1258.[24]

A new dimension entered politics in 1254. When the magnates refused in the community's name an aid for one more Gascon expedition, Henry's regents in England were driven to appeal over the heads of the tenants-in-chief to the feudal sub-tenants, ordering each shire to send two knights to say what aid they would give. They were unlikely to give anything, the king was advised, unless he first confirmed the great charters of liberties. But the danger to Gascony passed without the help being needed: the high-point of the expedition was Edward's knighting at Burgos and marriage to Eleanor of Castile. In 1257, at about the time that Walter Cantilupe

---

[23] *Bracton on the Laws and Customs in England*, tr. S. E. Thorne, 4 vols. (Cambridge, Mass.: Harvard UP, 1968–77), II. 33; Powicke, *The Thirteenth Century*, pp. 5–6; Rymer, *Foedera*, I(i), p. 234: cf. *Calendar of Entries in the Papal Registers relating to Great Britain and Ireland*, vol. I (London: HMSO, 1893), p. 167; *Close Rolls, 1242–7*, pp. 65–6; *CRR*, XVII, no. 90; *EHD*, III, no. 35.

[24] *EHD*, III, no. 34; Powicke, *HLE*, pp. 231–6, 298–300, 336–8; Stacey, *Politics, Policy and Finance*, pp. 249–54.

of Worcester, since Grosseteste's death the longest-serving of the bishops, was admitted to the king's permanent council, its increased responsibility was marked by the councillors' swearing of an oath not to reveal the secrets of government; not to accept gifts from suitors in the king's courts, nor from the king himself, without the consent of the whole council; and not to approve grants of royal demesne lands and liberties except by common agreement. If personal animosities at court had not got beyond his control, Henry might have emerged from the Sicilian mess relatively unscathed.[25]

ATTEMPTING TO PUT THE KING IN HIS PLACE, 1258–65

The Lord Edward was fifteen in the year that he married Eleanor of Castile and was endowed with Chester, Ireland and Gascony. The growth to manhood of the self-willed prince, who chafed under the limitations imposed on his disposal of his lands, and whose behaviour and imposing retinue scared his father as early as 1256, was inevitably a disturbing factor in the politics of the following years. But the immediate cause of divisions at court was another group of King Henry's foreign relations, the children of his mother's second marriage to Hugh of Lusignan, who were settled in England from 1247. A particular source of offence was Aymer, the half-brother whom Henry pressed on the cathedral chapter of Winchester after Raleigh's death. Matthew Paris's story of the behaviour of the bishop-elect (though the pope immediately confirmed the election, Aymer was not consecrated till shortly before his death) reads like a brief for the barons' actions in 1258: his persecution of the monks and display of contempt for all things English; outrages such as the seizure of the official (chief legal officer) of the see of Canterbury at the archbishop's manor of Lambeth and his imprisonment at Farnham; and even the drugging of nobles dining with him at his Southwark house in order to rob them.[26]

If the Sicilian business aroused the barons' concern, the resentment against Aymer of Lusignan and his brothers precipitated their revolt. In April of that year the king called the prelates and magnates to London, where he was told that if he would 'reform

---

[25] Above, pp. 190, 238; *Royal and Other Historical Letters Illustrative of the Reign of Henry III*, ed. W. W. Shirley, 2 vols. (Rolls Series, London, 1862–6), II. 101–2.

[26] Paris, *CM*, V. 55, 178–85, 224, 348ff, 359–60, 373–4, 698, 702, 708, VI. 401–9.

the state of his realm . . . they would loyally use their influence
with the community of the realm so that a common aid should be
granted' for the Sicilian project; and on 2 May Henry swore that
'the state of the realm should be put in order, corrected, and
reformed' by twelve loyal men of his council (including the three
Lusignan brothers) and twelve elected by the magnates, who were
to meet together at Oxford one month after Whitsun. But at that
same assembly a complaint was made by John FitzGeoffrey, the
son of King John's justiciar Geoffrey FitzPeter, that Aymer of
Lusignan's servants had launched an attack on his manor of Shere,
the advowson of Shere church being in dispute between them. It
was the king's denial of justice against his favourites in cases like
this which inspired the first action of the barons at the momentous
Oxford parliament in June: the appointment of Hugh Bigod as
'justiciar of England' and the swearing of him to 'show justice to
all complaints', not failing in this 'for the lord king or the queen or
their sons, or for any living person, or for anything, neither for
hatred nor love, for prayer or price'.[27]

Hatred was fostered most by the coercion of the king's side to
join in the reformers' oath. Some of the king's men refused to
swear, with 'unrepeatable oaths' of their own, and the Lusignans
resisted the order that the alienations which had so impoverished
the king should be revoked, whereupon their castles were besieged
and they were driven from the land. The barons then proposed (so
a member of the king's household at Oxford reported) 'nothing
less than to embark upon the deposition and deprivation of the
bishop-elect of Winchester'. It was an objective which compelled
the barons to produce a reasoned justification of their whole
enterprise, as the simple expulsion of some magnates would not
have done. A manifesto was sent by the baronial council to the
pope in July 1258, explaining that the aliens had been driven out as
unruly members of the commonwealth, which was a body nour-
ished by God and moved by equity and reason; they had infatuated
the king and his son so that justice was denied those they harmed,
and the *communitas* would not allow Aymer back, even if the
greater men were willing. The pope nevertheless consecrated him
bishop at last, and by supporting him came down on the king's

[27] D. A. Carpenter, 'What Happened in 1258?', in *War and Government in the Middle
Ages*, ed. J. Gillingham and J. C. Holt (Woodbridge: Boydell, 1984), pp. 110–15;
Powicke, *HLE*, pp. 387–8; *Documents of the Baronial Movement of Reform and
Rebellion, 1258–1267*, selected by R. E. Treharne, ed. I. J. Sanders (Oxford:
Clarendon Press, 1973), pp. 91–7, 101.

side against the barons. Aymer died in Paris on his way back to Winchester in December 1260, threatening an interdict if he was not received.[28]

The Provisions of the twenty-four (twelve from the barons' side and twelve from the king's) who were appointed to carry out the reform, sought to make the parliaments *coram rege* as they had developed since 1234 the basis of a plan of government. There were to be three *parlemenz* during the course of the administrative year, in early October, early February and early June. To these should come the elected councillors of the king 'to review the state of the realm and to deal with the common needs of the realm and of the king together'. A further twelve sound men should be chosen to attend the parliaments on behalf of the community, the rest of which would be spared the cost of attendance by accepting as established whatever its representatives did. The set terms for the parliaments, permitting the systematic references of cases from other courts, indicate the judicial nature of the arrangements. But one other provision opened the way to an indefinite widening of the parliamentary administration of justice. Oral complaints were, in certain circumstances, already acceptable instead of writs as a way of initiating suits in the king's courts: they had a vital role in the development of the action of trespass. The Provisions of Oxford made the process of general application. They began with an order for the election of four knights in each shire court 'to hear all complaints of any trespasses and injuries whatsoever, done to any persons whatsoever by sheriffs, bailiffs, or any other persons, and to make attachments arising from these complaints, until the first visit of the chief justiciar to those parts'. A month later the four knights were told to bring the records of their inquisitions to Westminister at the octave of Michaelmas (when the first parliament scheduled in the Provisions would have been due) and deliver them personally to the king's council. On the 18 October 1258, King Henry sent 'to every county, to remain there in its archives', his grant that whatever the council elected by the community had done or would do 'for the honour of God' should 'be confirmed and established in all things for ever'. Out of essentially judicial arrangements was being forged a means, of unlimited political significance, for bringing to governments the grievances of the whole people of the realm and providing a remedy for them.[29]

[28] *Documents of the Baronial Movement*, ed. Treharne and Sanders, pp. 101, 105, 111.
[29] A. Harding, 'Plaints and Bills in the History of English Law', in *Legal History*

In May 1258, even before the Oxford parliament met, a series of
articles had been brought forward by 'the magnates of the realm,
both high and low, together with the clergy . . . as matters
requiring correction in the kingdom'. It has been shown by Dr
Brand that the 'petition of the barons' (not a contemporary name)
collected grievances from various sources, and constituted just the
first of several stages in the preparation of the so-called 'Provisions
of Westminster', which lasted from the summer of 1258 to the
autumn of 1259. Some were indeed complaints from the 'earls and
barons', but c. 19 was about the sheriffs' arbitrary amercement of
'knights and freeholders' who absented themselves from assizes,
and c. 26 about the sufferings of London citizens from the usurious
merchants of Cahors. In the late summer of 1258 the Earl Marshal,
Earl Simon, John FitzGeoffrey and others were reported to be
having daily discussions at the New Temple and elsewhere 'on the
reform of the usages and customs of the realm'. Perhaps at this
time a committee of 'justices and other wise men' was set up to
consider the reforms of 'ill laws' in readiness for the next parliament. A further group of provisions, principally concerning suit
of court, and reflecting grievances expressed by the clergy in
provincial councils and complaints presented over the winters of
1258-9 in the justiciar's eyre, were worked out in French and then
translated into what was still a tentative Latin Draft: this is the
document known as the 'Provisions of the Barons', which the
reformers, needing to show that they were making progress,
published at the New Temple in March 1259. (Matthew Paris,
who died in 1259, stopped writing half-way through copying it
into the *Liber Additamentorum*.) Futher reworkings in French preceded the emergence of the final version of the reforming legislation as the Latin Provisions of the Westminister parliament in
October 1259.[30]

The Provisions made at Westminster were regarded as an
extension of the Provisions of Oxford. Justices were ordered to 'be
appointed to go throughout the land' to see 'that the *établissements*

    Studies 1972, ed. D. Jenkins (Cardiff: University of Wales, 1975), p. 67; *idem*,
'Aquinas and the legislators'; *Select Cases of Procedure without Writ under Henry III*,
ed. H. G. Richardson and G. O. Sayles (Selden Society, vol. 60, London, 1941),
pp. 85ff, for plaints before the baronial justiciar; above p. 206; *Documents of the
Baronial Movement*, ed. Treharne and Sanders, pp. 99, 107, 113-15.

[30] *Documents of the Baronial Movement*, ed. Treharne and Sanders, pp. 77-90,
123-57; P. Brand, 'The Drafting of Legislation in Mid-Thirteenth Century
England', *Parliamentary History*, 9 (1990); *Select Cases of Procedure without Writ*,
ed. Richardson and Sayles, nos. 70b,f,j, 78; above, pp. 158, 207-8.

made for the good of the realm, both those already made and those still to be made' were observed in the counties along with the Charters. As for parliaments, 'two or three councillors of middle rank' were to be in constant attendance on the king from one parliament to the next' to carry forward their business. These provisions, then, were part of the programme embarked on sixteen months before, but others made at Westminster carried on a process of defining the rights of the different social estates which stretched back to Magna Carta and forward to the statutes of Edward I. The men of 'middle rank' and the ordinary free men were now demanding of the magnates that they observe towards them the chartered liberties they had received from King John. The quarrel on account of which Matthew Paris describes a disillusioned Earl Simon storming off abroad in the spring of 1259 probably arose from the earl of Gloucester's reluctance to see applied to his lands the 'wholesome statutes' that were being drawn up to limit the powers of seignorial courts.[31]

If it was hard to get the magnates to honour their promise to reform 'the state of the realm', it was harder still to hold them to the regulation of 'the state of the king'. A consecrated king was not to be ruled by his subjects, yet permanent constraints on the king's actions were implicit in the baronial plan. 'The state of the king and of the kingdom' were inseparable: the character of the territorial state was seen to depend on the nature of the regime at its heart, but that regime had independent sources of strength which made it hard to contain. In July 1258 the Lord Edward was 'persuaded only with the greatest difficulty' to submit 'himself to the ordinance and provision of the barons, who appointed for him four counsellors' and began to 'make arrangements for the state of his household and of the household of the lord king'. The real test of the barons' commitment to the plan of reform came early in 1260. On 4 December 1259 the treaty between the kings of England and France which had been negotiated in 1258 as part of a general peace in the West was finally ratified when Earl Simon and the Countess Eleanor gave belated consent to it. Henry surrendered all claims to the lost lands, and Louis accepted his homage for Gascony and undertook to pay the cost of 500 knights 'for the service of God and the Church and to the profit of the realm of England'. In January Simon was back in England ready for the meeting of

---

[31] *Documents of the Baronial Movement*, ed. Treharne and Sanders, pp. 149–51; Paris, *CM*, v.744 (*EHD*, III, p. 151); Powicke, *HLE*, pp. 406–9.

parliament due in February. But from King Henry in France there came a stream of letters, first to Hugh Bigod as justiciar, then to Archbishop Boniface, Bishop Walter de Cantilupe, Earl Simon and other councillors, with the message that he was delayed by negotiations about the expense of the 500 knights, and that there must be no thought of holding a parliament in his absence. He also expressed disgust that he had not been kept informed of 'the state of his kingdom'. On 1 April he announced his imminent return, and 'on the same day at table', Walter of Merton received at his manor of Malden the king's order to summon seven named earls and ninety-nine lay tenants, conspicuously excluding Earl Simon and his supporters, to appear in London three weeks after Easter with their due service of knights. The king's chief fear at this time seems to have been of an alliance between Simon and Prince Edward; the justiciar and the Londoners were ordered to bar Edward from the city, for he was believed to be coming with horses and arms for a parliament which was meeting against the king's will. After an appeal for help to King Louis, to whom he promised that when he got back he would report 'our state and the state of our kingdom . . . and be ready to do what we know fits in with your wishes', Henry returned to England on 30 April 1260 with a force of 300 knights.[32]

Open war was avoided on this occasion, but the ideological conflict became clear in the July parliament, when Henry made the earl of Leicester answer a series of charges. Simon was accused first of all of obstructing the French negotiations by insisting on his wife's rights, and then of making threatening alliances in England, holding a February parliament when it had been explicitly prohibited and telling the justiciar not to send the king the money he requested; by which the kingdom was greatly troubled, and the king 'forced to return to England with a large following' and at heavy expense. Earl Simon replied that he had done nothing to justify the king in bringing armed men into the land, so the expense was the king's affair; that he had made no alliances, 'except for the common enterprise'; that he and 'other sound councillors' had assembled for the Candlemas parliament, because that was one of the three parliaments a year in 'the common provision' sworn to by the king and council (it had in fact been adjorned from day to day for three weeks, awaiting the king's promised return); and

[32] *Documents of the Baronial Movement*, ed. Treharne and Sanders, pp. 82–3, 95, 165–79; Powicke, *HLE*, pp. 247–57, 411ff.

that what the king charged him with saying to the justiciar, he had said to the council, before which he should answer. Simon's steadfastness, and probably King Louis's restraining hand, once again produced an inconclusive result.[33]

But by March 1261 Henry had found the resolution to articulate his objections to the whole operation of his council under the provisions. He complained that the councillors had been negligent over the business of Sicily and Apulia, so that the king was indebted in this matter for 100,000 marks or more, and had been no more effective in supplying aid to save his land of Wales; Edward was allowed to squander his possessions and had been seduced from his father's friendship and obedience 'by the counsel of a certain man'; justice was not done, England was impoverished and the king's right perished daily through the wickedness of the bailiffs the barons appointed; matters would get much worse in the future, because the three things by which the land was governed – the law, the great seal and the exchequer – had also been placed in bad hands. Henry's real grievance, however, was the taking away from the king 'of his power and dignity, so that no one carries out his orders'; he had no power over his seal; pleas were heard before the justiciar in remote places, and people ceased to look to the king's court for redress; his orders concerning wardships were ignored 'as though he were not king'. By reason of his unforced promise to abide by the councillors' advice on the restoration of the state of the king and the realm, they had stripped him of all honour and royal dignity, in contravention of their oath as councillors. The latter replied point by point to the thirty-odd complaints. They could not help the dreadful weather; Sicily had always been a bad bargain; but yes, something needed to be done about the marches of Wales, and they heartily wished the king's justices would cost less to maintain. As to the working of the council, it met frequently but openly; they had no intention of taking away the dignity of the king; it was indeed right that he should be listened to – when he talked sense.[34]

The king agreed on the necessity of consultation 'for the reform of his own state and of the realm, and for his own great needs which he had to satisfy'. But traditional views of the king's state were simply incompatible with the permanent share in government which some barons thought the situation required. A royal clerk,

[33] *Documents of the Baronial Movement*, ed. Treharne and Sanders, pp. 194–211.
[34] *Ibid.*, pp. 211–39.

John Mansel, was already in Rome, and on 12 April 1261 he got the papal bull absolving Henry and others from the oaths to the provisions they had taken 'under the pretext of reforming the state of the realm', except where these were advantageous to the Church; to rational minds, said the pope, it was absurd that princes, who were the lords of laws, should be constrained by the will of their subjects – it was as though a woodsman was turned on by his axe.[35]

For the barons, the only legal resort left to them was an appeal to King Louis. At the arbitration which eventually took place in January 1264 the barons, led by Henry of Sandwich, bishop of London, Walter de Cantilupe, bishop of Worcester, and Simon de Montfort, earl of Leicester, related to the French king the whole course of their reform movement, asserting that they had acted throughout 'for the honour of the king and for the common advantage of his kingdom', whereas 'the opposing party' were 'seeking to pull him into confusion, which heaven forbid, and his kingdom into ruin'. They were intent on explaining in practical terms why they had sought to elect the king's ministers. The choice of chancellor was crucial, since he not only originated the writs on which the entire system of justice depended, but also sealed the king's grants. The barons recalled to Louis that the Provisions of Oxford, which the king had sworn to observe, commanded the chancellor not to seal a gift of a greater wardship without the full council's approval. They had made the 'honest' provision that the king's advisors should be chosen only from men of sufficient means who could meet their own expenses, and would swear not to seek gifts of wardships or escheats. Central to Henry's submission, on the other hand, were demands that the free appointment of his ministers be restored to him, and that he himself be returned by Louis's arbitration to that state in which he was before the making of the provisions, statutes, obligations and ordinances already quashed by papal authority. It was inevitable that Henry's overlord would come down on the side of his brother king. By the Mise of Amiens. given on 23 Janurary 1264, the provisions were annulled once again, and specifically any statute which declared 'that the realm of England should in future be governed [only] by native born men'.[36]

Louis's arbitration ended with an injunction to king and barons

---

[35] *Ibid.*, p. 237, and all nos. 32, 33, 34, 36.
[36] *Ibid.*, nos. 37A, 37B, 37C, 38.

that they should renounce all rancour to each other, but the battle lines were by this time too firmly drawn. Both king and barons had been seeking the support of the knights and the townsmen. Knights were the foundation of magnate power and the key to the control of the shires. The military history of the Barons' War is encapsulated in the career of Roger of Leybourne, who had gained notoriety by using a sharpened lance at the Walden 'round table' of 1252, and killing a knight of the king's household who had broken his leg in a previous encounter. In the following year Roger was himself in the king's household in Gascony, but soon he was Edward's steward and campaigning with the prince in Wales. At some point he fell under the spell of Earl Simon, and encouraged Edward in his brief alliance with the earl which so agitated King Henry. In 1262, however, he was convicted in the exchequer court of misconduct as steward, his lands were seized, and he went off with other lords of the marches, tourneying and spreading to his native Kent a spirit of unrest which Earl Simon would exploit. From a meeting at Oxford in May 1263 of the earl of Leicester with a group of his supporters which included Gilbert de Clare, the new earl of Gloucester, Henry of Almain, Richard of Cornwall's son, and the marchers came a demand for the strict observance of the Provisions, and a renewal of the declaration of five years before that any who opposed them would be treated as public enemies. The baronial party seized the Tower and made an alliance with radical Londoners which forced Henry to submit to the restoration of the constitution of 1258, which a new council moved quickly to protect by the appointment of 'keepers of the peace' in the shires. But the Lord Edward would not accept humiliation by a baronial government a second time, and the royal cause was bolstered in the autumn of 1263 when he was reconciled with Roger Leyburn and the marchers. As he left England for Louis's arbitration the king appointed military keepers of his own in many counties. Leyburn soon appears in that role in Kent, Surrey and Sussex.[37]

In a last attempt to prevent full-scale war, Walter de Cantilupe of Worcester, Stephen Bersted of Chichester and two other bishops went to the king's headquarters in Oxford in March 1264, and on the barons' behalf offered to accept every other article in the French king's award if Henry would only waive the right to rule through others than 'native-born men': meeting with no response, they

---

[37] *Ibid.*, pp. 247, 291; Paris, *CM*, v.318–19; Powicke, *HLE*, pp. 435–8; *EHD*, III.915 (Song of the barons); above, pp. 141–2, 211.

went into the Friary church and excommunicated all opponents of
the Provisions. That May, the bishops of Worcester, London and
Chichester marched with Simon's army to Lewes. The Song of
Lewes, which seems to represent the views of Bersted, Simon's
particular friend, and his Franciscan associates, confirms that the
king's assertion of his right to appoint aliens was the sticking-
point. The settlement after the battle provided that three electors,
Earl Simon, the earl of Gloucester and the bishop of Chichester,
should choose a council of nine. If there was disagreement between
the three or the nine (of whom Henry of Sandwich, the bishop of
London, stood first), a two-thirds vote should decide, provided
that there was a churchman in the majority in matters touching the
Church. The 'reformation of the state of the realm of England' and
the restoration of the English church to its 'proper state' were to
be undertaken together. Clerical discipline had broken down
during the fighting, and the rights of the Church, as ever, needed
defending, especially those of an archbishop of Canterbury in
voluntary exile. As to 'the rule of the kingdom', the peace agreed
in the summer of 1264 by the captive king and his son, the prelates
and great men, 'and the community of the whole realm of
England', concentrated on the workings of the royal court (the
regimen curie). The justiciar, chancellor and treasurer, 'and other
officials, great and small', should be chosen by the advice of the
council of nine, and always be 'native men': though aliens – both
merchants and clerics – might come and go peacefully, provided it
was not 'in suspiciously large companies'. Most strikingly, the
new regime was to hold into the reign of Edward; the form of
government should outlast the person of the king.[38]

A proclamation to the counties in March 1265 suggests the
enormous strains such a 'form of peace' was bound to be under.
Henry announced that he had sworn on the Holy Gospels not to
undermine the peace; if he or the Lord Edward should ever do so
('which Heaven forbid'), everyone must work to do them harm,
and persons convicted by the judgement of the council and the
magnates of assisting them should be perpetually disinherited. No
one was bound to obey any official till he had taken an oath to
observe the charters and the peace agreement, which were to be
read aloud in full county court at least once a year. Pointedly, the
proclamation ended with the statement that the king had submitted

---

[38] Above, p. 178; *Documents of the Baronial Movement*, ed. Treharne and Sanders,
no. 40.

his sworn undertakings to the jurisdiction of the bishops, and renounced 'in these matters all our privileges obtained or to be obtained, [or] granted or in future to be granted to us by the lord pope on his own initiative'. The conflict was narrowed to a struggle within England, in which the support of the knights of the shires and the townsmen assumed still greater importance. Immediately after the battle of Lewes a keeper of the peace ('Simon de Monfort's commissar') had been appointed to police each county and to see to the election of four knights to attend a parliament in London in eighteen days time. In December another parliament was summoned for late January 1265 to try to arrange for the release of the Lord Edward from captivity 'and finally complete the full security of tranquillity and peace': this was the parliament celebrated by seventeenth-century antiquaries because for the first time two burgesses were to be sent from each borough along with the two knights from the shire.[39]

Rifts began to appear in the ranks of Simon's young followers. The trouble seems to have arisen from the disputes over the ransoming of the people captured at Lewes and rivalries fomented by de Montfort's sons. Simon's occupation of Edward's boroughs of Bristol and Chester also aroused disquiet. The divisions became serious with the defection of the twenty-year-old Gilbert de Clare, one of the few representatives of the baronial families of 1258 who had been left with de Montfort at Lewes. The ageing bishop of Worcester was fading from the scene (after Lewes it is his nephew Thomas de Cantilupe, archdeacon of Stafford and chancellor, who appears in the council), and not able to work to keep the richest commoner in the land true to the cause as he had Gilbert's father in 1259. The earl of Gloucester withdrew to his lands and friends in the marches; the earl of Leicester moved towards them with King Henry and the Lord Edward still in tow. On 28 May 1265, by which time Earl Simon and the court were at Hereford, Gilbert de Clare and Roger Mortimer of Wigmore engineered the escape of the Lord Edward, their fellow marcher, as he rode out for exercise. Cut off in the west by hostile forces, Simon de Montfort spent the next two months concluding a peace with Llywelyn of Wales and attempting to shore up a crumbling administration. On 8 June the bishops of the province of Canterbury were called upon in the king's name to excommunicate the Lord Edward and his adherents. The keepers of the peace were also alerted. The last writ

[39] *Ibid.*, nos. 39–42; above, pp. 29–30, 211–12.

on the Close Rolls was issued from the chancery at Hereford on 1 July ordering the sheriff of Hereford to summon fifty named gentry to come 'with all haste' to defend the town, on pain of disinheritance. Trying to cross the Severn and join with his supporters in the east, Earl Simon was caught by Edward, Gloucester and Mortimer at Evesham on 4 August. The savage treatment of Simon's body and his popular canonization are both reminders of the passions the baronial movement had aroused.[40]

KINGSHIP TRIUMPHANT, 1265-90

Within three days of the battle King Henry, restored to 'full and royal power', was annulling the acts of Simon's government. The political maturing of the previous seven years could not be reversed, however, and set the pattern for the rest of the century. The enhanced role of the knights was shown by a general re-appointment of keepers of the peace, sometimes from the same families which had provided the baronial keepers. A key figure in the military pacification was Roger Leyburn, though he was hardly typical of the knights, with his multiple keeperships in the southeast and his command of paid troops. First he subdued the Weald of Kent, where he left behind 200 archers to clear the woods of robbers. In January 1266 he led a column of men with 106 packhorses to the capture of Sandwich, and then besieged Winchelsea, a more formidable proposition which involved summoning a fleet from East Anglian ports. With the Cinque Ports subdued, and while Henry summoned feudal service for an attack on the rebel garrison still holding out at the Montforts' stronghold of Kenilworth, Roger next led his hired force of knights and Welsh archers in a four-week campaign against rebels in Essex who were posing a threat to London. In 1267 he was back in the still restless Weald and at Winchelsea, and crossed to France to obtain troops Henry needed to help dislodge the earl of Gloucester from London.[41]

The royal government which appreciated the uses of the knights was not easily reconciled to the political assertiveness of the townsmen, who were subjected to large fines. The Lord Edward

---

[40] Powicke, *HLE*, pp. 494–502; *Documents of the Baronial Movement*, ed. Treharne Sanders, no. 43; *Close Rolls, 1264–8*, pp. 116–27; above, pp. 11–14.

[41] Rymer, *Feodera*, I (i), p. 458; A. Harding, 'The Origins and Early History of the Keeper of the Peace', *TRHS*, 5th ser., 10 (1960), p. 95; A. Lewis, 'Roger Leyburn and the Pacification of England, 1265–7', *EHR*, 54 (1939).

was given all the goods, both in England and in Flanders, of Londoners who had been against the king. The still crucial role of London was demonstrated by Gloucester's occupation of the city for two months in the spring of 1267 and revival of its commune, as a way of forcing the king to reach a settlement with the barons disinherited for their Montfortian connections. The Clare family continued to stand for old-fashioned baronial liberties. (Robert of Gloucester reports that when Earl Gilbert engineered Edward's escape from de Montfort's custody, he impressed on the prince that he must observe the good old laws and see that aliens were excluded from the king's counsels.) But the reform movement had placed baronial interests within a wider 'state of the kingdom', the fostering of which a victorious king would now claim as his particular responsibility. The papacy once more threw its weight behind the return of government (*gubernaculum*) to the proper hands from which de Montfort had allegedly schemed to seize it. Lagging some way behind events, Pope Clement wrote to Edward urging him to work for his father's freedom, and to 'reintegrate the state of the realm' with special care for the 'prosperous state of the clergy'; to assist in which task he was sending Ottobuono, cardinal deacon of St Adrian, to England. One of Ottobuono's first acts was to call a council to deal with the Monfortian bishops. Walter de Cantilupe died in February 1266 before his fate could be decided; of four others sent to Rome for correction, Gervais of Winchester died at Viterbo, and the remaining three were pardoned, Bersted of Chichester last of all in December 1272, in the new reign.[42]

The legate's next task was the more difficult one of promoting a settlement of 'the matter and the estate (*status*) of the disinherited by occasion of the late war in England, saving the estate of the king and his dignity'. The siege of Kenilworth was still dragging on when a commission of reliable prelates and barons was appointed on 31 August to draw up terms for the approval of the king, the legate and Henry of Almain. Its award, published in the castle at Kenilworth on 31 October, 'in the name of the Holy and Undivided Trinity', to the honour of Church and pope and for the 'good, prosperous and peacable state of King Henry', declared first that the king should have full and free exercise of his dominion, and that everyone should seek justice by the king's writs 'as was

---

[42] Above, p. 142; Rymer, *Feodera*, I (i), pp. 458–60, 462–4, 467–8; Powicke, *HLE*, p. 498.

the custom before the time of disorder'. The legate was asked to forbid anyone to make out Simon, earl of Leicester, to have been 'holy and just' or to relate 'vain and fatuous miracles of him'; and also to announce the absolution of the lord king and all men great and small who had fallen under general excommunication for not observing the Charters. Henry was nevertheless urged to recommit himself to the Charters, and to provide, by his council, for the immediate 'reform of the city [of London] in the matter of lands, rents, powers, and liberties'. The case of Simon's family was placed in the hands of King Louis, and the rebel earl of Derby, Robert de Ferrers, was effectively disinherited by the punitive terms singled out for him, but for the majority of the barons and knights who took part in the Montfortian cause there was to be not disinheritance, but rather the ransoming of their lands in proportion to their participation. The most active were to pay five times the annual value of their lands; those who roused men to support Earl Simon by spreading lies, twice the annual value; and weaklings who had been terrorized into sending their military tenants against the king, one year's value. Powerless people found to have done no harm at all were to recover their lands and damages in the king's court, and their accusers were not to be believed in the future. The king was invited to provide from the ransoms for the needs of his own landless supporters, lest their discontent became 'the material for a new war'.[43]

The Dictum of Kenilworth took its place in the succession of 'statutes of the realm', immediately before the 'provisions, ordinances and statutes' made at Marlborough in the presence of the king, his brother Richard, the Lord Edward and the legate Ottobuono late in 1267, when the disinherited and their champion, the earl of Gloucester, had at last been reconciled. Giving 'thought to the betterment of his realm of England' and (as 'the exercise of his kingly office' required) to 'the better administration of justice', in a gathering at Marlborough 'of the more discerning men, of high and low estate', King Henry largely re-enacted the Provisions made at Westminster eight years before. It must have been the baronage who continued to be distinguished as men 'of high and low estate' in several of the twenty-nine provisions of 1267, since there were no more general summonses of representatives of the knights and

---

[43] Powicke, *HLE*, pp. 529ff; *Calendar of Patent Rolls, 1258–66* (London: HMSO, 1910), pp. 671–2; *Documents of the Barnonial Movement*, ed. Treharne and Sanders, no. 44; above pp. 190, 257.

burgesses in Henry's reign after the parliament of January 1265, though there were consultations with particular estates. Before he left the country in 1268, Ottobuono issued constitutions for the English Church in a council at St Paul's, and at Northampton saw the king's sons Edward and Edmund, Henry of Almain, Earl Gilbert, Roger Leyburn and others take the cross. The projected crusade aggravated the need for money. The previous year Henry had been forced to pawn jewels from Westminster Abbey for his and the realm's 'necessities', and only in 1272 would he at last redeem 'a great and precious gold crown' and other regalia pawned through the agency of the queen of France at the Paris Temple in 1261. Aid had to be sought from the laity, after thirty years during which the clergy had borne the brunt of taxation. To the legatine council at St Paul's, the mayors and leading men of twenty-seven cities and towns were summoned to discuss a tallage with the king. Later in the year an aid was obtained from the barons which was to be administered by royalist lords elected in groups of counties. The bishop and other prelates and magnates were also called to Westminister in May 1270 to assent to the king's departure on crusade and provide for the state and rule (*de statu et regimine*) of the kingdom in his absence.[44]

In the event Henry did not go with Edward, because of his ill health and the dangers in their both leaving the realm together. Nor did Gloucester, who was apparently dissatisfied with the financial terms for the expedition, and fearful for his position in the marches if he went away; even King Louis failed to move him, though Richard of Cornwall obtained a pledge that he would go later. Edward arrived at Carthage in Tunisia in November 1270 to find that King Louis had died of the plague there two months earlier, and sailed on to Acre, the capital of the crusader kingdom, where he survived an attack by the Shiite sect of Assassins which was much embroidered in western chronicles. With an enhanced reputation, though little actually achieved, he was back in Sicily in December 1272 to receive the news of his father's death on 16 November. Richard of Cornwall had died in the previous April, a year after the murder of his son, Henry of Almain, by Guy de Montfort. The earl of Gloucester was the greatest of those sum-

[44] *Annales monastici*, ed. H. R. Luard, 5 vols. (Rolls Series, London, 1864–9), III.246–7 (Dunstable), IV. 217–18 (Wykes); *Select Cases in the Court of King's Bench*, ed. G. O. Sayles, 7 vols. (Selden Society, London, 1936–71), I, no. 20; *EHD*, III, no. 44; Rymer, *Feodera*, I (i), pp. 472, 483, 487; *Close Rolls, 1264–8* (London: HMSO, 1937), pp. 558–9.

moned to Henry's death-bed to swear to keep the kingdom for Edward.[45]

The new reign was dated from 20 November, the day of Henry's burial, though Edward was unaware of his own accession and would not be crowned for almost two years. Letters were immediately sent to the sheriffs proclaiming the *gubernaculum* of the kingdom to have devolved upon him by hereditary right. The government was now made to survive the king's person, as the baronial leaders of 1264 had envisaged. For the purposes of government Edward had long been assembling his own clerks, councillors and ambassadors. Well before he reached the Channel on his way home, his court was swelled by people coming to meet him with his kingdom's problems. The weight of royal administration during Robert Burnell's chancellorship, from the promotion of this most experienced of Edward's servants in September 1274 to his death in 1292, is palpable in the chronicles. Thomas Wykes and the Bury chronicler know nothing of ideological struggles between Church and State which boiled up in these years, or of the growing dominance of the king's wardrobe which Tout believed was what set 'the estate of the king' over against 'the estate of the kingdom', the latter represented by the 'traditional' offices of exchequer and chancery. What concerns the chroniclers are the repeated taxes: the tenth of clerical property granted by the pope to Edward as he travelled home in 1273; the scutages raised for the first Welsh war; the fifteenth demanded from the clergy in the parliament of 1280; the thirtieth granted by 'the whole commonalty of England' in 1283 as an aid for the second Welsh war; and the fifteenth of 1290. The control of weights and measures, the punishment of Jews and others for coin-clipping and the arrangements for exchanging the bad coin for new pennies and halfpennies are of equal interest, particularly to the Bury monks, who possessed a mint. The visit of John Kirkby, archdeacon of Coventry, to Bury St Edmunds in 1282, on his tour to extort 'loans' for the king, is indignantly recorded.[46]

The intent and authority of the state were expressed in extraordinary taxation and in the exploitation of the resources of towns,

[45] *Annales Monastici*, ed. Luard, IV.228ff; Powicke, *HLE*, pp. 589, 606; R. R. Davies, *Conquest, Coexistence and Change: Wales 1063–1415* (Oxford: Clarendon Press and University of Wales Press, 1987), pp. 282, 322.

[46] Rymer, *Feodera*, I (i), p. 497; above, pp. 8–9, 23, 292; *Annales Monastici*, ed. Luard, IV.254, 274, 278–80, 282, 302, 326; *Chronicle of Bury St Edmunds*, ed. and tr. Antonia Gransden (London: Nelson, 1964), pp. 66–9, 70–2, 74, 77, 83–4, 86.

but still also in the rigorous administration of justice. The eyres of the king's justices, which were carefully directed from the centre by the chancellor and duly recorded by the local chroniclers, provided the model for a series of inquiries into the whole government of the counties. Burnell had been chancellor for just three weeks when the writs went out to the commissioners who would conduct the inquests of 1275 recorded in the 'Hundred Rolls'. Twenty or thirty men working in eleven circuits – experienced sheriffs, constables of castles and occasionally justices in eyre and of the forest – were

to inquire by the oaths of good and lawful men of the counties . . . concerning certain rights, liberties, and other matters affecting us and our state and the state of the community of the said counties, and moreover concerning the deeds and the behaviour of all sheriffs and bailiffs of the said counties, as is more fully contained in the articles on the subject which we have sent you.

These articles ranged over the alienations of manors held of the Crown; the farming of the king's hundreds, wapentakes, ridings, cities and boroughs; the withdrawing of suit from the king's courts in the counties; the obstruction of the king's orders by private lords and their bailiffs, and even by the king's own officials, 'since the time when the constitutions were made at Marlborough'; the multifarious abuses of sheriffs and coroners and those who handled the king's money right back to the battle of Evesham, and similar misdeeds by the 'lords and bailiffs of all liberties whatsoever'; the behaviour of ecclesiastical judges; and the activities of forgers and clippers of coin.[47]

Article 10 'concerning liberties which obstruct common justice and overturn the king's power' looked forward to the Statute of Gloucester of August 1278, which began by lamenting the 'innumerable disinheritances . . . caused to the people of the kingdom' by default of law in cases 'of liberties as of other things', and went on to subject pleas of *quo warranto* to a new and peremptory procedure. Instead of the individual writs to franchise holders which had been used since Henry III's time, there was, under the statute, to be a general summons, announced by the sheriffs, of all claimants of 'liberties by charters of the king's predecessors . . . or in another way' to appear before the next session of the justices in eyre in their counties and 'show what sort

[47] Above, p. 168; *EHD*, iii.45, 52, 61; H. M. Cam, *The Hundred and the Hundred Rolls* (London: Methuen, 1930), pp. 39–40, 258.

of liberties they claim to have and by what warrant'. Again in 1279 three commissioners were appointed for each of twenty-six shires or pairs of shires to conduct an inquest which 'had its returns survived in full, would have been [in Miss Cam's judgement] a second and more detailed Domesday Book, giving an account of all England village by village and tenant by tenant as it was in the seventh year of Edward I'. And six years later there was 'Kirkby's quest', a more practical inquiry undertaken by the new treasurer into knights' fees held of the Crown and the behaviour of local officials answerable to the exchequer.[48]

On this occasion the complaints of individuals, which must very often have lain behind jury presentments to such inquiries, were invited directly; and in 1289 Wykes tells us that

the king ordered it to be proclaimed publicly throughout his realm that all and everyone wishing to complain of injuries and wrongs unjustly inflicted upon them by his justices, sheriffs or any of his ministers or bailiffs while he was absent from the country should attend the parliament already fixed, in order to submit their complaints (*querimonias*) and receive full justice.

This time special *auditores querelarum* were appointed, whom one litigant favoured by them claimed to 'have higher rank in their judgements and their records than any other justice, wherefore it seems . . . that none other than the lord king in his parliament ought to have cognisance of the judgements of the auditors'.[49]

Parliamentary petitions or 'bills' originated as just the highest variety of the bills which were being presented to royal justices at all levels – the bills that would animate new courts, from the sessions of the justices of the peace to the court of chancery and Parliament itself (Fleta's king's 'court in his council in his parliaments'). Edward's government encouraged the submission of complaints against officials like those which had been collected in 1258: the new development was that these began to be written down – naturally very often in French, the vernacular of the aristocratic complainants, not the Latin of chancery writs. Bills presented to the justices in eyre survive from 1286 onwards, and

[48] *Calendar of Patent Rolls, 1272–81* (London: HMSO, 1901), pp. 342–3.
[49] *Annales Monastici*, ed. Luard, IV.319; for the auditors of 1289 in action, see *Cases in King's Bench*, ed. Sayles, II.cxxxviii, 17–18, 86–7, 95, 111; *idem, The Functions of the Medieval Parliament of England* (London: Hambledon, 1988), pp. 196–8; above, pp. 157, 285; Harding, 'Plaints and Bills', pp. 68, 75–6, 80; *idem*, The Law Courts of Medieval England, (London: Allen and Unwin, 1973), pp. 81ff, 152–4, 168; *RP*, I.1–14 (e.g. nos. 22, 23, 26, 38, 43, 44, 57), 15–45.

are found to correspond to entries in the special *rotuli de querelis* which had appeared in eyre rolls from 1261. From 1278 we have seventeenth-century copies of sixty-five petitions presented to the king and his council in Parliament, many of which could well have gone to the justices in eyre: indeed 'parliamentary' petitions would regularly be referred to the ordinary courts, or to the chancellor for the issuing of writs. The Rolls of Parliament themselves begin with 'pleas' heard by the king and council at the Hilary assembly of 1290. To go by the rolls, the essential business of Parliament was the answering of petitions for the expediting of justice. But these bills – little strips of parchment about five inches long – set up a flow of messages from the shires to the king: going in the opposite direction to chancery writs, they represented an enormously important new form of political communication. Yet by 1280 Edward was showing impatience at 'the delays and disturbance' caused to those coming to parliaments 'by the multitude of petitions' brought before him, most of which could be disposed of by the normal procedures of the common law. It was provided, therefore, that petitions should go straight to the chancery, the exchequer or the justices, and only if the business was 'so important or a matter of grace' should they be brought by the chancellor and other principal ministers to the king and his council – who would otherwise be free to 'attend to the great business of his kingdom and of his foreign lands'. The matters which still came to Parliament itself were the pleas of magnates; petitions from communities of shires, townships and monasteries; and the complaints from across the whole community of England against the king's ministers which developed into the process of impeachment. Of the other 'great business of the kingdom' which may have been transacted in Parliament without petition we have too little record.[50]

While it remained the supreme organ of royal justice, Parliament developed in a way that recognised a need for the constant legislative reform of 'the state of the realm'. The chroniclers saw a new era of conscious state-making begin with the '*establissemenz* which the King Edward son of the King Henry made at his first

[50] Maitland, introduction to *Memoranda de Parliamento*, ed. F. W. Maitland (Rolls Series, London, 1893), reprinted in *Historical Studies of the English Parliament*, ed. Fryde and Miller, i.110–13; Sayles, *Functions*, pp. 164, 167, 170–3, 183; *Cases in King's Bench*, ed. Sayles, ii, pp. cxli, cxliii, 17–18; J. G. Edwards, ' "Justice" in Early English Parliaments', in *Historical Studies* of the English Parliament, ed. Fryde and Miller, i.

general parliament after his coronation on the morrow of the close
of Easter in the third year of his reign [1275], by the counsel and
assent of Archbishops, Bishops, Abbots, Priors, Counts, Barons,
and the commonalty of the land summoned there'. Edward is
represented as deciding on this occasion to reactivate and recall to
their proper state the laws which had long been dormant through
the impotence of his predecessors, or had languished because of
the tumult in the kingdom and the abuses of litigants. With the
advice of loyal counsellors and legal experts, he therefore drew up
new statutes that were consonant with the law and most necessary
for the country, and published them abroad in order that posterity
might observe them. At about this time the chancery clerks began
to keep a Statute Roll, which now starts with the 'supplementations
to the law' made at the Gloucester parliament of 1278, not the
statutes of 1275 – but it is likely that the first membranes of the
roll have been lost. In early April 1285 and again at Westminster,
we are told that the king began another debate *de statu regni* which
was so wide-ranging that parliament had to be prolonged to late
June. The succession of statutes was a narrower form of law-
making than treatises like Glanvill's or Bracton's, but it was a
more dynamic form which gave the state continuity of purpose.
Westminster II (c. 46) explicitly extended the clause of the fifty-
year old 'statute' of Merton concerning a lord's right to enclose
common land. The first demand of Wat Tyler in the Peasants'
Revolt of 1381 was for return to 'the Law of Winchester': that is,
peace-keeping by the local community as it had been laid down by
the Statute of Winchester of 1285. When it was proposed in 1824
to exempt combinations of workmen from the law of conspiracy,
thirty-three English, Irish and Scottish acts had to be repealed,
beginning with the original definition of conspiracy in a parliament
of 1305. No wonder collections of statutes quickly superseded legal
treatises as the essential equipment of lawyers.[51]

The statutes made at Westminster in 1275 and 1285, each with

---

[51] Above, pp. 15–16, 241; *EHD*, III, nos. 47, 52, 47; H. G. Richardson and G. O.
Sayles, 'The Early Statutes', *Law Quarterly Review*, 198 and 200 (1934),
pp. 201–3; V. H. Galbraith, 'Statutes of Edward I: Huntington Library', in *Essays
in Medieval History Presented to Bertie Wilkinson*, ed. T. A. Sandquist and M. R.
Powicke (Toronto: University of Toronto Press, 1969), pp. 177–8, 182, 184;
Annales Monastici, ed. Luard, IV.263, 304; A. Harding, 'The Revolt against the
Justices', in *The English Rising of 1381*, ed. R. H. Hilton and T. H. Aston
(Cambridge: CUP, 1984), pp. 165–7; *idem*, 'The Origins of the Crime of
Conspiracy', *TRHS*, 5th ser., 33 (1983), p. 103, J.–Ph. Genet, 'Droit, et histoire
en Angleterre', *Annales de Bretagne et des Pays de l'Ouest*, 87 (1980).

their fifty-odd clauses, dealt with the rights of landlords and tenants, wards, dowagers and merchants; and with the whole system of justice as it had developed since the reign of Henry II in the courts of king's bench and common pleas, eyre and shire, but also in seignorial courts, fair courts and borough courts. At the heart of the formation of the state was the great widening of the class of injuries for which people could seek public redress. The confirmation of legal rights and status was the main object of petitioning. Complaints laid before the Hundred Rolls inquiry were answered in the Statutes of Westminster I (1275) and Gloucester (1278). The Statute of Mortmain (1279) and Quia Emptores (1290) curtailed the alienation of land by feudal sub-tenants, whether to churches or lay purchasers, which had long been the subject of complaint from overlords whose rights to services were threatened. Sometime in Edward's reign the 'community of Chester' (Edward's own lordship, soon to be recognized as a 'palatinate' separate in government from the rest of the realm) petitioned for a new register of writs for use in its courts – a register applying the new statutes to Cheshire 'for the amendment of that country'.[52]

Judicial arrangements, as opposed to statements of law, would usually be made by administrative fiat, but the Statute of Gloucester (c. 8) was used to order that minor complaints of trespass continue to be pleaded before sheriffs, and that no one should have a writ of trespass before the king's justices unless damage of more than 40s. could be shown. The *quo warranto* provisions of the Statute of Gloucester reaffirmed that the lords ruled the countryside only as the king's representatives: the Statute of Winchester seven years later recognised that responsibility for the maintenance of the peace must still rest with the local communities and their lords. Two constables appointed in each hundred were to present defaults in watch-keeping to the justices who came round on circuit to take assizes – a method of supervising local government which would last for many centuries. But within two years the immediate enforcement of the Statute of Winchester was given to local keepers of the peace, because the justices of assize did not 'go every year as often as was ordained'. The statutory extension of the criminal

---

[52] Above pp. 202–4, 213, 258–9; *EHD*, III. 405 (30), 415, and nos. 53, 59, 64; T. F. T. Plucknett, The *Legislation of Edward I* (Oxford: Clarendon Press, 1949), pp. 94–109; Sandra Raban, *Mortmain Legislation and the English Church, 1279–1500* (Cambridge: CUP, 1982); *Cases in King's Bench*, ed. Sayles, II.cxlvi; *Early Registers of Writs*, ed. E. de Haas and G. D. G. Hall, (Selden Society, vol. 87, London, 1970), p. xciii; Sayles, *Functions*, pp. 157, 159, 164 etc.

jurisdiction of the keepers of the peace, and the granting to local gentry of commissions 'to hear and determine' complaints of civil trespass became chief interests of the knights of the shire in parliament.[53]

The emergence of legislation for 'the state of the realm' as the prime activity of the ruler made the exact process of law-making – whether with the advice of councillors and the assent of the community or by the king's unfettered power – a determinant of the character of a state. For Aquinas, writing in Paris around the year 1270 the 100,000-word treatise on law which is embedded in his *summa* of theology, it was the way the essential legislative function was exercised which distinguished a monarchy, with its 'constitutions of princes', from an aristocracy, in which law was made by the expertise of jurists and the decrees of a senate, and from a democracy, which legislated by plebiscite. By these criteria, England must have had a mixed constitution. Edward conformed well enough to Aquinas's model of the ruler, whose sovereignty consists in his power to dispense law and even more to dispense in an emergency with the laws he has made: in the Statute of Gloucester he claimed the sole right of a king to give swift justice to the people, Irish as well as English, 'governed under his rule' (*sub suo regimine gubernatus*), and to make the statutes most necess-ary and useful for them. But for England at least the second function involved consulting the community from time to time through representatives of the local communities. For his first general parliament of 1275, at the beginning of his reign and legislative work, Edward followed Simon de Montfort's prece-dent, though in more peaceful circumstances, and summoned representatives of the shires, boroughs and (uniquely) also 'mer-chant towns'.[54]

Though the presence of knights and burgesses would not be invariable at parliaments until the end of Edward's II's reign, and the framing of petitions by the Commons themselves is a four-teenth-century development, Edward I must be credited with establishing direct communication between the king and the com-munity at large. In the process, the lordship was superseded by the shire as the basic political institution. Stubbs described the county court as the first 'really exhaustive assembly' of the different orders

[53] Harding, 'The Revolt against the Justices', p. 168.
[54] Harding, 'Aquinas and the Legislators'; above, p. 115; Jenkinson, 'The First Parliament of Edward I', *EHR*, 35 (1910).

of society and the English equivalent of the provincial estates of France. In the shire, moreover, the third estate was defined in its peculiarly English form, as a combination of the knights and burgesses whose representatives were elected by identical procedures. The commons of England no longer received their political liberties from their lords but from the king in Parliament, through representatives who stood alongside the peers and prelates summoned by individual writs. Liberties were reduced to personal rights. Meaningful lordship was power to be exercised, but actions of trespass against infringements of liberties to hold markets or hang thieves, and of *quo warranto* requiring the justification of the liberties' very existence, were reducing even lordships to bundles of rights to be claimed in the king's court.[55]

To measure the extent of the ability of the new state to overwhelm traditional lordships it is necessary to go beyond Edward's dealings with English magnates to his treatment of the Welsh, Irish and Scots. The king's passionate concern for his rights, backed by the forces of English law, administration and Parliament, intensified his claims to overlorship of other peoples to the point of actual conquest. The growing administrative power of the Crown lay behind what for the chroniclers was the real story of the first half of Edward's reign: the crushing of the Welsh. After the death of the great Llywelyn ab Iorwerth, lord of Snowdon, 1240, King Henry had taken over the offensive of the marcher lords in Wales – with success until the arrival of the young Edward, newly granted the lordship of Chester and the king's Welsh lands, provoked in 1256 a general revolt led by the first Llywelyn's grandson, Llywelyn ap Gruffudd. From his base in Gwynedd, Llywelyn had by 1258 reversed Henry's territorial gains and brought such an unaccustomed unity to the Welsh that he could be called 'prince of Wales' at a meeting of Welsh lords with their Scottish allies. The troubles in England allowed him to establish himself so firmly that by the Treaty of Montgomery in 1267, Henry saw fit to confirm the title of *princeps Wallie* to him and his heirs, and (for a substantial payment) to accept his territorial gains. Llywelyn's acknowledgement of his obligation to do homage for the principality to the king of England must have seemed a small price to pay for the king's recognition that the fealty and homage of the whole Welsh baronage was owed to the

---

[55] Stubbs, *CH*, ii.166–7; above, pp. 39–40, 258–9; Harding, 'Political Liberty', p. 436.

prince. It was essentially his force of personality, however, and his demands, backed by the taking of hostages, for unity in war and peace, which held together often unwilling vassals. In 1274 his own brother Dafydd and Gruffudd ap Gwenwynwyn of Powys plotted against his life, and when they were discovered, fled from his anger to Edward's court. The struggles with the marchers went on, particularly around the earl of Gloucester's great new castle of Caerphilly. Llywelyn increasingly resented the non-compliance of the marcher lords with the treaty of 1267, which he suspected was with Edward's blessing.[56]

It would have required a different sort of Welsh prince to prevent a rift with the new king. Llywelyn had got from the pope the concession that he and his men should not be cited in England in ecclesiastical disputes; but Edward regarded him simply as 'one of the greater' among the magnates of his kingdom and bound 'to do and receive right in the court of the kings of England'. Llywelyn told Edward: 'the rights of our principality are entirely separate from the rights of your kingdom, although we hold our principality under your royal power'; stayed away from Edward's coronation; made a provocative marriage with the daughter of Simon de Montfort; and failed six times to appear to do homage to the king, even when, as Edward complained to the pope, 'we had so demeaned our royal dignity as to go to the confines of his land [at Chester]'. In November 1276 King Edward declared the prince of Wales a disturber of the peace, and after just a year of co-ordinated campaigning, of which a crucial episode was the seizure of Anglesey by a fleet from the Cinque Ports, Llywelyn had imposed on him the humiliating Treaty of Aberconway.[57]

Companies of diggers were set to cut military roads through the Welsh forests and work began on the great arc of Edwardian castles from Flint around the north-west coast of Wales to Cardigan. More formidable still was the administrative subjection. Before Llywelyn's defeat, his brothers Dafydd and Owain and their heirs had been commanded to attend parliaments in England like Edward's other earls and barons, if they wished to keep their lands. To the king were now transferred the homages of all but five lesser Welsh lords, these left with Llywelyn (but for his life

---

[56] Above, pp. 278–9; Davies, *Conquest, Coexistence and Change*, pp. 236, 307ff; idem, *The British Isles, 1100–1500: Comparisons, Contrasts and Connections*, ed. R. R. Davies (Edinburgh: John Donald, 1988), pp. 12, 16, 22.

[57] Davies, *Conquest, Coexistence and Change*, pp. 322–35 ; above, p. 191; *Annales Monastici*, ed. Luard, III.275–6.

only) as a mere token of his princely status. The final move was the appointment in 1278 of parties of English justices to conduct eyres in the marches and in Wales, and 'hear and determine all suits and pleas both of lands and of trespasses'. Llywelyn himself was compelled to appear before Walter de Hopton and his fellow justices to pursue his suit against Gruffudd ap Gwenwynwyn for the lands of Arwystli. Gruffudd claimed that as a baron of the march he should be heard in the king's court by the common law. On the other side Llywelyn made the famous statement that

each province constituted under the empire of the lord king has its own laws and customs, according to the mode and use of those parts where it is situated, such as the Gascons in Gascony, the Scots in Scotland, the Irish in Ireland, the English in England, which is more to the increase of the crown of the lord king rather than to the diminution of the same.

In 1277 Edward had in fact declared Irish law detestable and no law at all, but in the end he left the prelates, barons, 'and all other English of the land of Ireland' to decide whether the common law should be extended to the native Irish. The threat to Welsh custom, which was being written down in a great series of law-books, came from the king's cynical use of English law as an adjunct of conquest. The Arwystli case was spun out for four years in front of the justices, the king and Parliament, while inquiries were made into Welsh legal procedures. It was made clear that Edward would decide how justice was given to the Welsh.[58]

In March 1282, the treatment of their native laws provoked the Welsh into a revolt which began with an attack by Llywelyn's once disloyal brother Dafydd on Hawarden. Archbishop Pecham's attempts to mediate could do little to mitigate the outraged king's response. In December, as the noose tightened, Llywelyn was killed in a skirmish. Edmund Mortimer sent his head to Edward and Welsh poets bemoaned his death as the end of their world. Dafydd, who carried on the war till he was captured 'hiding on a mountain' in June 1283, was disposed of with the aid of a parliament of barons, knights and burgesses called to Shrewsbury for that express purpose. The peers of the realm having declared his treason, Edward decreed punishments which had none of the

[58] Davies, *Conquest, Coexistence and Change*, pp. 335–46; *The Welsh Assize Roll, 1277–1284*, ed. J. Conway Davies (Cardiff: University of Wales Press, 1940), p. 266; J. Lydon, 'Lordship and Crown: Llywelyn of Wales and O'Connor of Connacht', in *The British Isles, 1100–1500* ed. Davies; above, p. 179; Sayles, *Functions*, pp. 170–1.

mercy his father had shown the Montfortians. As a traitor to the lord king who had made him a knight, Dafydd was dragged to execution at the tails of horses; as the slayer of English lords he was hanged; because he killed at Easter time he was disembowelled and his entrails burned; and because he conspired the king's death in different places, he was dismembered and his parts distributed for display where they would be a terror to other malignants. The condemnation of Prince Dafydd was the beginning of a tradition of special and terrible punishments for those condemned of treason against the royal state.[59]

By the Statute of Wales of 1284, 'the first colonial constitution', the land of Snowdon and other lands previously subject to the king 'by feudal right' were converted into a 'dominion' of the king. A state was created somewhat on the model of England but separated from it by the marcher lordships, which would not be 'shired' till the sixteenth century. Sheriffs were appointed for Anglesey, Caernarvon, Merioneth, Flint, Carmarthen and Cardigan, the first three subject to a justiciar of Snowdon, Flint to the justiciar of Chester, the western counties to a justiciar of West Wales. Sheriffs' tourns, coroners, much of the English criminal law and procedure by writ were introduced, though the Welsh custom of partible inheritance was to be allowed. At Caernarvon well-developed executive and judicial machinery would develop, but not a legislature. Wales sent no representatives to the English parliament until the Act of Union of 1536. Welsh petitions were dealt with by the king, or by his eldest son as prince of Wales in his council at Kennington near London (after Edward of Caernarvon, the future King Edward II, was given the Welsh lands in 1301). With their native lordship destroyed, individual Welshmen, even bond men, would look to the English Crown for their 'common right', and for protection against the 'wilful lordship' of a marcher such as Hugh Despenser in Glamorgan, who threatened to destroy the customs of the community, 'used from all time in antiquity'.[60]

There were to be further Welsh rebellions, infuriating to Edward because they distracted him from his other tasks, but in 1286 he was able to leave for France to do homage to the new King Philip

[59] *Annales Monastici*, ed. Luard, III,291–4, IV. 290–1; J. G. Bellamy, *The Law of Treason in England in the Later Middle Ages* (Cambridge: CUP, 1970), pp. 24–30.

[60] Above, p. 179; *EHD*, III, no. 55; Davies, *Conquest, Coexistence and Change*, cap. 14; Harding, 'Political Liberty', pp. 440–1; J. Given, *State and Society in Medieval Europe: Gwynedd and Languedoc under Outside Rule* (Ithaca: Cornell UP, 1990), pp. 189–90.

IV and spend three years mediating in the struggle over Sicily between the Aragonese and the French dynasty in Naples. By 1289, at some cost to English taxpayers and Gascon hostages, he had succeeded 'in effecting the liberation of Charles, king of Sicily, his kinsman, whereby the state of the Holy Land and of the Church was improved and peace secured', and could return to call his justices and ministers to account for their actions in his absence.[61]

THE FIRST CRISIS OF THE ENGLISH STATE, 1290–1307

The political troubles which beset Edward in the second half of his reign were not caused by the old-fashioned resentments of alienated vassals. They were rather the troubles of a state under strain.

The chief of the strains was the protracted Scottish war. Edward's dealings with the Scots followed the same pattern as with the Welsh: the exercise of a presumed overlordship changed to conquest when Edward saw his feudal claims contested. Many Anglo-Norman lords held lands in Scotland as well as in England, and the kings of England habitually knighted Scottish kings. Alexander III went to the Michaelmas parliament at Westminster in 1278 to perform liege-homage for the lands of Tynedale, Penrith and Huntingdon given or confirmed to the king of Scots by the Treaty of York of 1237 in return for the recognition that Cumberland and Northumberland were English shires; he found himself, in that year when Edward was increasing his pressure on the Welsh and the native Irish, having to resist the suggestion that he held Scotland itself from the king of England. Scotland was in truth a kingdom within a community of North Sea kingdoms, its standing implicitly recognized by the treaty of 1237 and by the marriages of the king's children into other royal families. It possessed a system of law and administration, employing writs and working through sheriffdoms, which was similar to England's, though it had not developed such a powerful central bureaucracy or apparatus of records. The king's council and the magnates met together in parliaments to make laws and deliver judgements. University-trained clergy, hostile to southern claims to ecclesiastical superiority, argued at the papal court for the annointing of Scottish kings which would confirm the land's independent status. The relationship of the king of Scots to his powerful neighbour was not like that of the native prince of Wales: it was closer to the king of

[61] Powicke, *The Thirteenth Century*, pp. 251–61.

England's own feudal relationship to the king of France. Only at the end of John's reign had French overlordship in respect of continental lands been taken to justify an attempt to conquer England; that failed disastrously, and even the confiscation of the Plantagenet lands in France entailed decades of war. When the nobility of Scotland, native and Anglo-French, came to see that the best guarantee of their liberties was the king of their own in Edinburgh, Edward's costly enterprise was bound to run into the sand.[62]

Yet he came close to success. The accidental death of King Alexander in 1286, two years after the death of his son and heir-apparent and before his second marriage could produce another, seemed to offer Edward the opportunity to supervise Scottish affairs in the way his father had done in mid-century. The successor to the Scottish crown was Margaret, the three-year-old daughter of the king of Norway, whose mother, Alexander's eldest child, had died giving her birth. Robert Bruce, lord of Annandale began to make threatening moves in the south-west of Scotland. One of those lords with great estates on both sides of the border, Bruce had led his Scottish tenants to fight for King Henry at the battle of Lewes and later briefly held the chief justiceship of king's bench. More to the point now, if the absent Queen Margaret should be set aside he had a claim to the Scottish crown as the grandson of Earl David of Huntingdon, the brother of King William the Lion, by his second daughter – but Bruce's neighbour, John Balliol, lord of Galloway, was a great-grandson of Earl David by his *eldest* daughter. In 1286, 'the community of the realm of Scotland' proved strong enough to control the situation: two bishops, two earls and two barons were appointed as Guardians of the kingdom, kept the peace and in 1290 negotiated a treaty of marriage between Queen Margaret and the king of England's son Edward of Caernarvon, which contained guarantees of Scottish independence. According to this Treaty of Birgham, the kingdom of Scotland was to remain separate from England and 'be free in itself and

---

[62] A. A. M. Duncan, *Scotland: The Making of the Kingdom* (Edinburgh: Oliver and Boyd, 1975), 589–615; *Anglo-Scottish Relations 1174–1328*, ed. and tr. Stones, p. 41 and no. 12; R. R. Davies, *Domination and Conquest: The Experience of Ireland, Scotland and Wales, 1100–1300* (Cambridge: CUP, 1990), pp. 13ff, 51, 84–5; *The British Isles, 1100–1500*, ed. Davies, for W. D. H. Sellar on Scots law and R. Frame on cross-border landholding; G. W. S. Barrow, *Kingship and Unity: Scotland, 1000–1306* (London: Arnold, 1981), pp. 123–58; and in his *Kingdom of the Scots* (London: Arnold 1973), on 'The Clergy in the War of Independence'.

without subjection'; no parliament touching Scottish affairs should be assembled, and no Scots, clerical or lay, held to answer 'outwith that kingdom'.[63]

Nonetheless, Edward sent Anthony Bek, bishop of Durham, across the border to 'reform the state of the country', even before the death of 'the Maid of Norway' on the way to her realm in that same year of 1290 laid Scotland at the king of England's feet. The Scots now wanted an arbiter between the numerous competitors for the crown: Edward appeared as a judge who would decide the issue 'by virtue of the superior lordship which belonged to him'. He had taken the cross once more, but Scotland now became his obsession, and in May 1291, the very month in which Acre was lost to the Muslims, he convened a joint parliament of English and Scottish barons (and representatives, at least, of Oxford and Cambridge Universities) at Norham on the English side of the Tweed. The first part of the Great Cause was a pressing of Edward's rights. First Justice Brabazon in Norham parish church, then Chancellor Burnell at Holywell Haugh across the river and finally Edward in person addressed the Scots and required them to recognize his overlordship of Scotland before the case was heard. The chronicle of Bury St Edmunds gives colour to the notarial record, telling how the king had summoned monks from English churches to come with chronicles which would prove his rights; when the Scots could say nothing in reply, it was the competitors themselves who, beginning with old Robert Bruce, came forward one by one to swear fealty to Edward, and agree to the handing over to him of the kingdom and its castles, without which he would 'have no power of execution' of his judgement. Within two months of a decision 'all the royal power, dignity, privileges, laws, customs, possessions and everything belonging to the kingdom' were to be returned 'in the same condition as they were when seisin was entrusted to him . . . saving the right of the king of England to the homage of him who will be king'. But meanwhile Edward 'distributed the responsibility for the castles among his liege men as suited him. He also appointed keepers of the peace and of good order and others to carry out the king's business, to act on both sides of the Scottish sea'.[64]

[63] Above, pp. 32, 35, 278; G. W. S. Barrow, *Robert Bruce and the Community of the Realm of Scotland* (London: Eyre and Spottiswoode, 1965), caps, 1 and 2; *idem, Kingship and Unity*, pp. 125, 128, 151, 158–9; *EHD*, III, no. 65.

[64] Barrow, *Kingship and Unity*, pp. 159–62; *Edward I and the Throne of Scotland, 1290–1296: An Edition of the Record Sources for the Great Cause* ed. E. L. G. Stones

Edward's declaration of concern for 'the desolate state of the Scottish realm' may have been hypocritical, but it was not without meaning, given his legislation for the state of his own realm, and the first of the two crucial decisions made by the court which proceeded to meet under his presidency in Berwick-upon-Tweed, Scotland's largest town. (This special court comprised twenty-four members of the king's council and eighty Scots assessors chosen equally by Bruce and Balliol, and its proceedings were recorded by notaries public). After long adjournments and the consultation of doctors of canon and civil law from Paris and other universities, since Roman law was 'the law by which kings rule', it was decided in the autumn of 1292 that Scotland could not be partitioned between the claimants by descent from Earl David's daughters like a mere barony, as Bruce was reduced to arguing: 'of its nature' the land was impartible, like other kingdoms. The second decision gave the land to Balliol as the descendant of the eldest daughter. Three weeks before final judgement was given on 17 November 1292, the death occurred of Chancellor Robert Burnell, and there was a four-day adjournment until his body was escorted from Berwick on its way to his cathedral at Wells.[65]

Scotland was conferred on Balliol as an integral state, but the safeguards of Scottish independence in the Treaty of Birgham were repudiated, and appeals from John's court entertained by Edward as the king of Scots' 'superior Lord'. A similar course was followed as in Wales in 1278. In the course of the appeal of Macduff of Fife from a judgement of the Scottish parliament at Scone in February 1293, it was laid down in the English parliament that the king of Scots must answer in the court of king's bench to any appeal or complaint against him; if he failed to do so he would lose all jurisdiction in the matter, which would be settled according to English custom by a jury empanelled in either realm by an English official such as the sheriff of Northumberland. If John was found guilty of the disseisin of Macduff or of any other complainant, Edward would restore seisin, and the complainants would thenceforth be his vassals. At the Westminister parliament after Michael-

and G. G. Simpson, 2 vols. (Oxford: OUP for the University of Glasgow, 1978), I.137–62, II.5, 6, 14, 17, 19, 26, 33, 38–43, 52, 56, 58, 60, 66, 74; *Anglo-Scottish Relations 1174–1328*, ed. Stones, nos. 14–17; *Chronicle of Bury St Edmunds*, ed. and tr. Gransden, pp. 98–103.

[65] *Edward I and the Throne of Scotland*, ed. Stones and Simpson, I.106–7, 183–5, II.166–8, 170–2, 202, 205, 213, 214, 216, 228, 243, 246, 358–65; *Anglo-Scottish Relations 1174–1328*, ed. and tr. Stones, no. 19.

mas 1293 King John begged for an adjournment of Macduff's suit, since this matter touched the people of his realm as well as himself and he must consult them.[66]

The case was still dragging on when other events brought relations between England and Scotland to breaking point. The king of France had been the first to learn how to use claims of feudal overlordship in the interests of his state. In May 1293 a fleet from the Cinque Ports defeated a Norman fleet and sacked La Rochelle. Gascons were also involved, and Philip IV took action as Edward's overlord for Gascony. The king of England was ordered to appear in the *parlement* of Paris in January 1294, just a few weeks after the king of Scots was compelled to plead his case at a Westminster parliament. Edward thought he had made peace without the need to humble himself, but in May he was judged in default and the duchy of Gascony was declared confiscated. The English government's feverish mobilization of its resources in this crisis included a summons to King John to come with the steward of Scotland, eight earls and a dozen barons to join Edward's army in London by 1 September 1294. Then a Welsh rebellion halted the plans for a French expedition, and before they could be resumed the government of Scotland was taken out of Balliol's hands by his own people and the first treaty of the 'Auld Alliance' sealed between the Scots and King Philip. In March 1296 war began in the north. Edward descended upon Scotland 'with a vast concourse of soldiers' intent, so wrote King John in a letter renouncing his homage, on 'disinheriting us and the inhabitants of our realm', and inflicting 'acts of slaughter and burning . . . injuries and grievous wrongs . . . which we cannot any longer endure'.[67]

The Scottish wars were to be conducted with little regard to the laws of war, since to Edward they were against rebels, while to the Scots the best weapon was the raiding which ravaged the land and changed the society of the border areas. In the long run this only served to unite the Scottish nation in defence of the Scottish state. Immediately, however, Edward was able to sack Berwick, crush the Scottish army at Dunbar, deploy his siege-engines to capture the seemingly impregnable fortress 'called Maidens' Castle, otherwise Edinburgh' and march on to Perth to arrest the king of Scots. Just as the Welsh had seen their holiest relic paraded in

[66] *Anglo-Scottish Relations 1174–1328*, ed. and tr. Stones, nos. 20–1; *Acts of the Parliaments of Scotland*, vol. 1 (1844), p. 145; *RP*, I. 110–13.
[67] Powicke, *The Thirteenth Century*, pp. 612, 644–54; *Anglo-Scottish Relations 1174–1328*, ed. and tr. Stones, no. 23.

triumph through London, so the Scots saw their Holy Rood and the Stone of Destiny on which kings of Scotland were inaugurated carried off to London with their king. The records kept in Edinburgh Castle were also taken away, and two English justices, Hugh Cressingham and William Ormsby, were diverted from their normal business to administer Scotland. The Bury chronicler exulted that the king of England had thus obtained 'absolute power over England, Scotland and Wales, the former kingdom of Britain long torn and divided'. The Scottish nobility were compelled to give sealed undertakings of loyal service to King Edward. But soon his attempt to extend to Scotland the military recruitment and requisitioning measures used in England provoked a rising under William Wallace of 'the community of the land' – seemingly the lesser knights and rich peasants, the nobles remaining prudently inactive. In September 1297 Wallace defeated the English at Stirling Bridge, killed Cressingham and spread a warfare of atrocities into northern England. A greater effort still was required of Edward in order to win the battle of Falkirk in 1298, and even then Scotland beyond the Forth and Clyde and much of the south-west remained under the jurisdiction of Scots acting in the name of King John.[68]

In the summer of 1300 Edward was at Sweetheart Abbey near Dumfries when Archbishop Winchelsey brought him an order from Pope Boniface to stop hostilities in a country which was protected by the Holy See. The king's reply was an uncompromising: 'By God's blood, "For Zion's sake I will not be silent, and for Jerusalem's sake I will not be at rest", but with all my strength I will defend my right that is known to all the world.' Sometime after Falkirk, Wallace had retired to France, and the leadership of the community was now in the hands of William Lamberton, Wallace's nominee to the bishopric of St Andrew's, and a group of nobles including Robert Bruce, earl of Carrick, grandson of the competitor, and John Comyn of Badenoch. Pope Boniface's letter and the reply from Edward and his barons show that the Scots now concentrated on the presentation at the papal court of their account of the past relations of Scotland and England, and were already bolstering their claims to liberty and independence with the myths of the historical origins of the Scottish nation which would receive their most resounding expression in 1320 in the

---

[68] *Anglo-Scottish Relations 1174–1328*, ed. and tr. Stones, no. 25; *Chronicle of Bury St Edmunds*, ed. and tr. Gransden, pp. 132–3, 141–2, 147, 150, 154; A. A. M. Duncan, *The Nation of the Scots and the Declaration of Arbroath* (Historical Association pamphlet, London, 1970), pp. 12–17; above, p. 191.

Declaration of Arbroath. But Edward tightened his grip once again, having made a peace with France from which the Scots were excluded. Bruce, who was concerned chiefly with his own claim to the throne, submitted to Edward in 1302. When Stirling Castle was at last forced to surrender in 1304, Comyn and the other supporters of King John (who showed no wish to return) submitted also for the sake of their lands. Edward's great year was 1305. Wallace, who had returned to fight but would have submitted too, was specifically excluded from the peace-making, betrayed by the Scottish magnates and taken to London; there he was tried in Westminster Hall under a commission of gaol delivery, condemned on the king's testimony that he was an outlawed traitor (though he protested that he had never been in Edward's allegiance) and sentenced to the same penalties as David of Wales. Other Scots now looked to the king of England for their rights as the Welsh had been compelled to do. In the parliament at Westminster at Lent 1305, 136 petitions were submitted from Scotland, from abbeys asking for the confirmation of the feoffments and liberties they had been granted by the kings of Scots, and from burgesses seeking to be preserved in the liberties and land which they had used in the time of King David I: the personal liberties of the second type were the ones Edward was willing to admit.[69]

Finally, Edward proposed to legislate 'for the stability of the land of Scotland', as he had done for conquered Wales, but this time following traditions of community assent to statute-making which were Scottish as well as English. At his orders, 'the community of the realm of Scotland', nobles and freeholders, were assembled at Perth to elect ten representatives to a parliament which met at Westminster in mid-September 1305. The Scottish delegates there agreed with a party of twenty English prelates, barons and justices to arrangements for the government of Scotland. John of Brittany, the king's lieutenant in Scotland, and the three Englishmen appointed to the offices of chancellor, chamberlain and controller were to act with a council comprised of Scots as well as English; an Englishman and a Scot were paired in each of four judicial commissions; and most local officials were to be Scots. 'As for the laws and customs to be used in the government of the land of Scotland', the old 'custom of the Scots and the Brets'

---

[69] Powicke, *The Thirteenth Century*, pp. 227–30; *Anglo-Scottish Relations 1174–1328*, ed. and tr. Stones, nos. 28–32; Duncan, *The Nation of the Scots*; Bellamy, *The Law of Treason*, pp. 32–9; Harding, 'Political Liberty', p. 440.

was banned, but the laws made by King David and additions by later kings were to be read over in an assembly of the good people of the land, so that the king's lieutenant and council could 'reform and amend' those which were 'clearly displeasing to God and to reason', as well as they could in a short time and without the king. The great matters were to be referred to Edward in the Easter parliament of 1306, to which the Scots should send representatives 'with full power' to consent to what was decided, so that a revision might be agreed 'by which the realm of Scotland may best be guided and governed, henceforth and always'. But by then Robert Bruce had killed John Comyn and made his bid for the throne. Edward I ended his days in 1307 still campaigning against the Scots. Robert I was the king who would crown years of struggle and the defeat of Edward II's army at Bannockburn with the first wide-ranging statutes for 'the common utility and security of the realm' of Scotland, made at a parliament at Scone in 1318.[70]

The wars that proved the Scottish state were also the testing time for England. The Edwardian state was given a hard edge by its brutal violence towards other peoples, and by the weight of its administration on the king's own people. The military effort required in the 1290s brought pressure on magnates, knights and towns alike. Edward did not talk of a royal state to be reformed in parliament along with the state of the realm: rather he emphasized the king's 'urgent necessities' in acting for 'the common utility'. A French lawyer, Philippe de Beaumanoir, writing *c.* 1283, had given the classic expression of the powers of a king in an emergency: in time of war or expectation of war, necessity 'which knows no law' permitted the ruler to make decrees which would wrong his subjects if issued in peace-time, such as that gentlemen become knights, rich and poor supply themselves with arms according to their estate and towns strengthen their defences. But when King Edward ordered £20 landowners, whether knighted or not, to muster in London in 1297 for the Flanders expedition, the marshal and the constable refused to enrol them and led their men to the exchequer for a demonstration against the king's seizure of the wool crop and against the levying of a tax of an eighth which had not been granted by the commonalty of the realm. After heated debate in the Michaelmas parliament of 1297, Edward was per-

---

[70] *Anglo-Scottish Relations 1174–1328*, ed. and tr. Stones, nos. 33–5; *Acts of the Parliaments of Scotland*, I.105–14, 119–23; Duncan, *The Nation of the Scots*, p. 18; A. Harding, 'Regiam Majestatem amongst Medieval Law-Books', *Juridical Review* (1984), pp. 109–11.

suaded to issue from Ghent a confirmation of the Charters with additional clauses. One of these (c. 7) abolished the maltolt of 40s. on a sack of wool; another (c. 6) conceded 'that for no need will we take such manner of aids, mises or prises from our realm henceforth except with the common assent of all the realm and for the common profit of the same realm, saving the ancient prises due and accustomed'.[71]

Churchmen were required to pray for the success of Edward's campaigns against the seditious Scots and the deceitful French, and representatives of the diocesan clergy as well as knights and burgesses were summoned to parliaments in 1295 and 1296 to grant the king subsidies. The arrival of the papal bull *clericis laicos* in the latter year probably ended the possibility of the full integration of the clergy into parliament, but as barons the bishops would remain there. The *Monstraunces* in baronial French against the king's demands for aids and the maltolt, and against his insistence on military service overseas when the pressing threats were from the Scots and the Welsh, were presented in the name of the 'archbishops, bishops, earls, barons and all the community of the land'; and the Latin *Confirmatio cartarum* provided for the Charters to be sent to cathedral churches to be read to the people twice a year, and for bishops to pronounce greater excommunication against anyone who infringed them, incurring reprimand themselves from the archbishops if they failed in this. Whether they wished to or not, churchmen found themselves giving a lead in the ordering of the English state in this political crisis as they had in the two earlier crises of the century. It was canon law which declared that necessity could be invoked only for communal benefit, not for the advantage of individuals. In this bull *Etsi de statu* of July 1297 Boniface made a particular concession to the king of France, 'although the state' of every kingdom was the pope's concern: Philip and his successors might judge when the defence of the realm was threatened by a 'perilous necessity' justifying a call on the clergy's resources. In England, however, Winchelsey continued to decide when the 'common defence' or 'necessary defence' of the land against the Scots required clerical aid. As Professor Denton writes: 'To compare "Etsi de statu" with "Confirmatio Cartarum" is to reveal a striking contrast between the

[71] Above, pp. 147, 191–4, 260; Philippe de Beaumanoir, *Coutumes de Beauvaisis*, ed. A. Salmon, 2 vols. (Paris: A. et J. Picard, 1970), II.261–2; cf. *EHD*, III. 895, and nos. 73–8.

control which the king of France had over taxation and the constitutionally limited rights of the king of England.'[72]

Edward I would never have surrendered 'full power of ordering the state of our household and of our forementioned realm' as his son would surrender it to the Lords Ordainers in 1311; but he would have seen the point of the Statute of York of 1322, which repealed the Ordinances and asserted that things which were 'to be established for the estate of our lord the king or of his heirs and for the estate of the realm and of the people' should be established 'as formerly' in parliaments and by the assent of the whole community (i.e. not by a clique of magnates). The strength of the English state lay in the king's law-making and administration of justice in parliament under the eyes of the community. Similarly, the crisis of the state appears most clearly in the improvisation of judicial commissions to deal with the social disruption caused by the Scottish wars – a disruption which affected the courts themselves. The petitioning of the Crown for justice continued to grow and new provisions were made from time to time for the reception of petitions in parliament, or in the king's council when, as in 1303–4, no parliaments could be held because of campaigning. (At the time of Edward's death petitions were accumulating against his last chief minister, the treasurer Bishop Walter Langton.) Exchequer and the common bench could be moved to York to be nearer the war, and parliaments be held at Lincoln and Carlisle; but the eyres to which complaints were submitted in the shires were hamstrung when judges were diverted to such tasks as the administration of Scotland. In 1296, the people of Lancashire petitioned for 'special justices' because the eyre came so rarely. By this they meant parties of justices with limited commissions to hear assizes or try the criminals in the gaols, which could be sent more frequently. But the flood of *querelae* had to be dealt with by emergency commissions such as that Edward issued in 1298 to a lawyer and a local knight on each of a number of circuits 'to hear and determine all

[72] Above pp. 218, 224, 247; D. W. Burton, 'Requests for Prayers and Royal Propaganda under Edward I', in *Thirteenth-Century England,*, vol. III, ed. P. R. Coss and S. D. Lloyd (Woodbridge: Boydell, 1989); A. Harding, 'Legal Growth in St Thomas's Writings', in *Aquinas and Problems of his Time*, ed. G. Verbeke and D. Verhelst (Leuven: Leuven UP, 1976), pp. 33–4; J. H. Denton, *Robert Winchelsey and the Crown, 1294–1313* (Cambridge: CUP, 1980), pp. 172–3; *Registrum Roberti Winchelsey*, ed. R. Graham, 2 vols. (Oxford: OUP for Canterbury and York Society, 1952–6), I.178, 200, 212–14, 229, 232.

manner of grievances done to his people in his name' on account of the war.[73]

In 1300, 'because many more evildoers are in the land than ever there were', the king had to go further and allow three justices elected locally to hear and determine complaints of infringements of the Charters and of the Statute of Winchester. But prosecution by bill of complaint was too fruitful a medium for the 'conspiracies' and 'confederacies' by which the very gentry from whom these justices were drawn sought to confound their enemies. In 1293 a parliamentary ordinance had provided a specific writ of 'conspiracy and trespass' returnable in king's bench for anyone who wished to complain of 'conspirators, inventors and maintainers of false *querelae*'. At a higher level Edward clearly saw Keighley's organization of the first commons petition as a conspiracy against him. The onset of the pressures of war-time, the encroachments on the lands of tenants who were away on campaign, the resistance in markets and fairs to the purveyors of supplies for the army, the protection rackets which the violence bred and the concerted intimidation of jurors if cases were brought to court: all this called in 1305 for the drastic remedy of the commission of trailbaston. The chronicler Peter Langtoft, always ready to abuse 'the stinking Scot', seems to regard the capture 'of William Wallace, the master of thieves' as an achievement of this commission; while the author of 'the trailbaston song', who has served 'the king in peace and in war, in Flanders, Scotland, in Gascony his own land', laments that if he just cuffs his boy he will now find himself in prison, and invites those who are accused to join him in 'the green forest of Belregard . . . for the common law is too uncertain'. In fact, the justices of trailbaston reported, all 'great matters' were being concealed from them 'by the procurement and alliances of the people of the country', so that an Ordinance of Conspirators had to be issued in the same parliament which produced the Ordinance of Trailbaston, defining conspiracy as agreements amongst the powerful in the shires 'falsely and maliciously to indict or acquit men', and the retaining with liveries and fees of those who would 'maintain their malicious enterprises'.[74]

[73.] *EHD*, III.527, 544; Sayles, *Functions*, pp. 195, 209, 233, 242, 244, 252, 259, 261–2, 264, 279–80; Harding, *Law Courts*, p. 88.

[74] Above, pp. 213, 217; Harding, 'Origins of the Crime of Conspiracy', pp. 95–97; *idem*, 'Early Trailbaston Proceedings from the Lincoln Roll of 1305', in *Medieval*

More clearly than the hideous condemnations for treason, this first statutory definition of a crime marked out an offence against the state as an institution. *Conspiracy* was the corruption for private ends of the system of justice and rule in the shires which was the great creation of thirteenth-century kings. The last years of Edward I were a watershed. The king still fought to vindicate his rights as lord paramount, but after the Statute of Quo Warranto in 1290 baronial liberties could no longer be seen as a threat to royal power. Even the Welsh marchers were tamed, after the imprisonment for a time in 1292 of the earls of Gloucester and Hereford for waging a private war against each other from their lordships of Glamorgan and Brecon. The demonstration of Bigod and Bohun and their retainers at the exchequer in 1297 was a new kind of politics which challenged not harsh lordship but oppressive government.[75]

Records Edited in Memory of C. A. F. Meekings, ed. R. F. Hunnisett and J. B. Post (London: HMSO, 1978), pp. 144–51; *EHD*, III.258, 919–21.

[75] Above, pp. 258–63; Davies, *Conquest, Coexistence and Change*, pp. 377–9; *RP*, I.70–7.

CONCLUSION:
THE MAKING OF A STATE

How can the stories of the peasantry, the townsmen, the professional people and their lords be combined with a narrative of political events to produce a single story of 'what happened in thirteenth-century England'? Tout's struggle between the barons and administrators and Hilton's 'feudal crisis' are possible frameworks for such a history, but they have no basis in contemporary ideas and cover only parts of the century's experience. Powicke's formation of a 'community of the realm' out of the communities of manors, gilds and shires does have a contemporary resonance, but leaves out too much of the spite and conflict. A concept which is both adequate to the thirteenth-century experience and based in contemporary ideas is 'the making of a state'. The notion of the state takes its force from its ambivalence: it means at the same time the ordered community which is to be cherished *and* the coercive regime which enforces the order and easily comes to be feared and hated. Significantly, when the term comes into fairly regular use in the thirteenth century it is most often in the dual form: 'the state of the king and the kingdom' (*status regis et regni*). Social and governmental developments, and relations with other states can all be brought under the concept.[1]

At all levels feudal relationships were giving way to legal status.

---

[1] A. Harding, 'Aquinas and the Legislators' in *Theologie et droit dans la science politique de l'Etat moderne* (Rome: Ecole Française de Rome, 1991); *Documents of the Baronial Movement of Reform and Rebellion, 1258–1267*, selected by R. E. Treharne and I. J. Sanders (Oxford: Clarendon Press, 1973), pp. 72–5, 295–7, 308–9.

At the end of the century, the kings of England, France and Scotland faced one another as heads of nation-states, though they still argued in feudal terms when it suited them. But the transformation of royal lordship into state power is seen most closely in the internal relations of the government with the communities of the land, which were creative of new institutions just when they were most exploitative. What transformed 'the state of the king' between 1200 and 1300 was the growth of the towns and of a class of professional administrators based within them who gathered the resources for the king's projects. The little group of judges who handed on Henry II's legal system did not expand: the growth was in the body of clerks who supported them at Westminster and staffed the chancery, the exchequer and the powerful new office of the wardrobe. The advent of this aggressive and self-seeking bureaucracy gave Henry III's rule its nervousness, and made 'the government of the court' (*regimen curie*) the focus of baronial suspicion.[2]

Yet royal government was also the catalyst of the state in the sense of 'ordered community'. The various social orders or 'estates' described in chapters 2 to 6 were defined by royal justice and legislation. The growing body of townsmen was just one factor which caused the ancient model of a society divided into those who prayed, those who fought and those who worked the land to be reshaped. Statutes were required to compel the repayment of debts and set out the particular rights and liabilities of merchants in a state which needed their expertise. The place of the clergy and their courts also received definition by such royal edicts as *circumspecte agatis*. The service of a knight in war and in the local courts was redefined as an obligation to the Crown, not to the immediate lord; and even the peasantry followed the villeins on royal manors in seeking a status under a common law. English society was an amalgam of local communities as various as the types of soil from which they extracted a living, which were incorporated into a single national history only by the process of legal definition. From this viewpoint the most important events in the thirteenth-century making of an English state were 'Bracton's' compilation of *The Laws and Customs of England* and the continuation of the work of the law-book writers in semi-official registers of writs and collections of statutes.[3]

---

[2] *Documents of the Baronial Movement*, ed. Treharne and Sanders, p. 296.
[3] G. Duby, *The Three Orders: Feudal Society Imagined* (Chicago: Chicago UP, 1980).

In the end it was the process, not the content, of legislation which joined the states of the king and the kingdom in an English state. Thinking in Aristotelian terms appropriate to a classical or a medieval Italian city-state, where a democratic regime might suddenly change into an oligarchy, Thomas Aquinas formulated the proposition that a people's laws must change with 'the state of the regime' (*status regiminis*). In England the need was rather to find ways of adapting the laws of a monarchy which no one conceived of overthrowing to social change in a territorially extensive kingdom. Modern administrative and legal historians have worked out in detail the development of procedures for seeking royal justice by petition and bill. But to grasp the importance of the thirteenth century in English history we still need the insights of Stubbs, Hume and Dugdale, who looked for the origins of England's parliamentary regime in the transformation of feudal society, and in the replacement of the lordship by the shire court as the essential local institution. By 1300 'a body politic of England' was already visible in a parliament generally comprised of lords spiritual, lords temporal and an 'estate of the commonalty' chosen in the shire court, with the king as its head.[4]

[4] Harding, 'Aquinas and the Legislators', p. 59; above, pp. 28–9, 33, 38–9, 299–301; the description of the body politic given by the Chancellor, Bishop Russell, in 1483 (*English Historical Documents*, vol. IV, ed. A. R. Myers (London: Eyre and Spottiswoode, 1969), p. 420) became valid 200 years earlier.

GUIDE TO FURTHER READING

This is a guide to the most recent works: the classic books of thirteenth-century historiography are discussed in the Introduction.

SOURCES
General

A Bibliography of English History to 1485, ed. Edgar B. Graves (Oxford: Clarendon Press, 1975), is the starting point for any exploration. The two Oxford histories, A. L. Poole's *From Domesday Book to Magna Carta* (Oxford: Clarendon Press, 1951, 2nd edn, 1955), and F. M. Powicke's *The Thirteenth Century: 1216–1307* (Oxford: Clarendon Press, 1953, 2nd edn, 1961; issued in paperback, 1991), provide full narratives and bibliographies; *English Historical Documents*, vol III: *1189–1327*, ed. Harry Rothwell (London: Eyre and Spottiswoode, 1975), contains a wide selection of translated chronicle and record evidence, with bibliographical introductions.

Chronicles

Antonia Gransden, *Historical Writing in England* vol. I: *c. 550–c. 1307*, and *Historical Writing in England*, vol. II: *c. 1307 to the Early Sixteenth Century* (London: Routledge and Kegan Paul, 1974, 1982), are comprehensive guides; see also her edition and translation of *The Chronicle of Bury St Edmunds, 1212–1301* (London:

Nelson, 1964); Richard Vaughan, *Matthew Paris* (Cambridge: CUP, 1958; reissued with supplementary bibliography, 1979), and the same scholar's translated selections from the *Chronicles of Matthew Paris* (Gloucester: Alan Sutton, 1986), are a good introduction to the major figure.

Records

Guide to the Contents of the Public Record Office, vol. 1 (London: HMSO, 1963), describes the records of the king's government in the middle ages; see also V. H. Galbraith, *An Introduction to the Use of the Public Records*, corrected reprint of the 1934 edition (Oxford: OUP, 1963), and D. Crook's PRO Handbook, *Records of the General Eyre* (London: HMSO, 1982). *British National Archives*, Government Publications Sectional List, No. 24 (London: HMSO, regularly updated), lists the public records in print. The great wealth of material in the publications of national and local record societies is surveyed by E. L. C. Mullins in *Texts and Calendars*, vol. 1: *–1956*, and vol. 11: *1957–1982* (Royal Historical Society Guides and Handbooks, no. 7, London, 1958, and no. 12, London, 1983). See also D. M. Owen, *The Records of the Established Church in England*, and P. D. A. Harvey, *Manorial Records* (British Records Association, Archives and the User, no. 1, London, 1970, and no. 5, London, 1984).

ECONOMIC AND SOCIAL HISTORY

A. L. Poole, *Obligations of Society in the Twelfth and Thirteenth Centuries* (Oxford: Clarendon Press, 1946), and D. M. Stenton, *English Society in the Early Middle Ages (1066–1307)*, 4th edn (Harmondsworth: Penguin Books, 1965), are pioneering attempts to describe the whole of society; as in a slighter way is R. F. Treharne, *Essays on Thirteenth Century England* (Historical Association, London 1971). M. M. Postan's *The Medieval Economy and Society* (London: Penguin Books, 1972) distils some of the work by Postan and others in the *Cambridge Economic History of Europe*, vols. 1–111 (see below); R. H. Hilton's *A Medieval Society: The West Midlands at the End of the Thirteenth Century* (London: Weidenfeld and Nicolson 1966), and C. Dyer, *Standards of Living in the Later Middle Ages: Social Change in England c. 1200–1520* (Cambridge: CUP, 1989), are informative and stimulating analyses.

On **rural society**, see *Cambridge Economic History of Europe*, vol. I: *Agrarian life of the Middle Ages*, 2nd edn, ed. M. M. Postan (Cambridge: CUP, 1971); *Agrarian History of England and Wales*, vol. II: *1042–1350*, ed. H. E. Hallam (Cambridge: CUP, 1988); R. H. Hilton, *The English Peasantry in the Later Middle Ages* (Oxford: Clarendon Press, 1975), though it is mostly concerned with the period after 1300; and E. Miller and J. Hatcher, *Medieval England – Rural Society and Economic Change 1086–1348* (London: Longmans, 1978). To **towns** Susan Reynolds's *An Introduction to the History of English Medieval Towns* (Oxford: Clarendon Press, 1977) is an excellent guide with a full bibliography, and *The Medieval Town: A Reader in English Urban History 1200–1540*, ed. R. Holt and G. Rosser (London: Longmans, 1990), is a useful collection of articles with suggestions for further reading. See also the *Cambridge Economic History of Europe*, II: *Trade and Industry in the Middle Ages*, ed. M. M. Postan and E. E. Rich (Cambridge: CUP, 1952), and vol. III: *Economic Organisation and Policies in the Middle Ages*, ed. M. M. Postan, E. E. Rich and E. Miller (Cambridge: CUP, 1963). The only recent books entirely devoted to **aristocratic society** are S. L. Waugh, *The Lordship of England: Royal Wardship and Marriages in English Society and Politics, 1217–1327* (Princeton: Princeton UP, 1988), and P. R. Coss, *Lordship, Knighthood and Locality: A Study in English Society c. 1180–c. 1280* (Cambridge: CUP, 1991). See also K. B. MacFarlane, *The Nobility of Later Medieval England* (Oxford: Clarendon Press 1973). On the **clergy** there is nothing for the thirteenth century to put beside A. Hamilton Thompson's *The English Clergy and their Organization in the Later Middle Ages* (Oxford: Clarendon Press 1947).

LEGAL AND ADMINISTRATIVE HISTORY

A *Centenary Guide to the Publications of the Selden Society* (London, 1987) is the entry into the mass of material on the law in the introductions as well as the texts of the Society's volumes. S. F. C. Milsom, *Historical Foundations of the Common Law*, 2nd edn (London: Butterworth, 1981), J. H. Baker, *An Introduction to English Legal History*, 3rd edn (London: Butterworth, 1990), and A. Harding, *The Law Courts of Medieval England* (London: Allen and Unwin , 1973), cover the century. See also D. M. Stenton's *English Justice between the Norman Conquest and the Great Charter* (London: Allen and Unwin, 1965); and the important book by Paul Brand, *The Origins of the English Legal Profession* (Oxford: Blackwell, 1992), which appeared too late to be used here.

S. B. Chrimes, *An Introduction to the Administrative History of Mediaeval England*, 3rd edn (Oxford: Blackwell, 1966), and H. M. Jewell, *English Local Administration in the Middle Ages* (Newton Abbot: David and Charles, 1972), are good starting-points for the study of administrative history. *Handbook of British Chronology*, 3rd edn, ed. E. B. Fryde, D. E. Greenway, S. Porter and I. Roy (Royal Historical Society, London 1986), gives lists and dates of kings, officers of state, bishops, aristocracy and parliaments. The material on **financial administration** in Pipe Roll Society volumes can be tracked down, like much else, in Mullins's *Texts and Calendars*. P. Chaplais's *English Royal Documents: King John–Henry VI, 1199–1461* (Oxford: Clarendon Press, 1971) is an authoritative description of the royal **secretariat**, which M. T. Clanchy's stimulating *From Memory to Written Record, England 1066–1307* (London: Arnold, 1979) places in a wider context. **Ecclesiastical administration** is to be seen first and foremost in bishops' registers, for which see David M. Smith, *Guide to Bishops' Registers of England and Wales* (London, Royal Historical Society, 1981), and D. M. Owen, *Medieval Records in Print: Bishops' Registers* (Historical Association Helps for Students of History, no. 89, (London, 1982)). Useful for reference are D. Knowles and R. N. Hadcock, *Medieval Religious Houses, England and Wales* (Harlow: Longmans, Green, 1971), and *A Map of Monastic Britain* (Chessington: Ordnance Survey, 1950).

POLITICS
General

M. C. Prestwich, *English Politics in the Thirteenth Century* (London: Macmillan, 1990).

Reigns

W. L. Warren, *King John*, 2nd edn (London: Eyre and Spottiswoode, 1978); J. C. Holt, *Magna Carta* (Cambridge: CUP, 1965); M. T. Clanchy, *England and its Rulers, 1066–1272*, (Fontana History of England, 1983); D. A. Carpenter, *The Minority of Henry III* (London: Methuen, 1990); R. C. Stacey, *Politics, Policy, and Finance under Henry III, 1216–1245* (Oxford: Clarendon Press, 1987); F. M. Powicke, *King Henry III and the Lord Edward* (Oxford: Clarendon Press, 1947); M. C. Prestwich, *Edward I (London: Methuen, 1988)*.

Wars and relations with the other peoples of Britain

G. W. S. Barrow, *Feudal Britain* (London: Arnold, 1956); *idem, Kingship and Unity: Scotland, 1000–1306* (London: Arnold, 1981); R. R. Davies, *Conquest, Coexistence and Change: Wales 1063–1415* (Oxford: Clarendon Press and University of Wales Press, 1987); *idem, Domination and Conquest: The Experience of Ireland, Scotland and Wales 1100–1300* (Cambridge: CUP, 1990); *The British Isles 1100–1500: Comparisons, Contrasts and Connections*, ed. R. R. Davies (Edinburgh: John Donald, 1988); M. C. Prestwich, *War, Politics and Finance under Edward I* (London: Faber, 1972); *idem, The Three Edwards, War and State in England 1272–1377* (London: Methuen 1980).

Parliaments

Historical Studies of the English Parliament, ed. E. B. Fryde and E. Miller, 2 vols. (Cambridge: CUP, 1970); *The English Parliament in the Middle Ages*, ed. R. G. Davies and J. H. Denton (Manchester: Manchester UP, 1981); G. O. Sayles, *The King's Parliament of England* (London: Arnold, 1975); *idem, The Functions of the Medieval Parliament of England* (London, 1988).

INDEX

329

LIVERPOOL
UNIVERSITY
LIBRARY

FIAT LVX